In the Balance

The Case for a Universal Basic Income in South Africa and Beyond

HEIN MARAIS

WITS UNIVERSITY PRESS

Published in South Africa by:
Wits University Press
1 Jan Smuts Avenue
Johannesburg 2001

www.witspress.co.za

First published 2022

http://dx.doi.org.10.18772/12022077724

978-1-77614-772-4 (Paperback)
978-1-77614-693-2 (Hardback)
978-1-77614-773-1 (Web PDF)
978-1-77614-774-8 (EPUB)
978-1-77614-714-4 (Open Access PDF)

This publication is peer reviewed following international best practice standards for academic and scholarly books.

The financial assistance of the National Institute for the Humanities and Social Sciences (NIHSS) towards this publication is hereby acknowledged. Opinions expressed and those arrived at are those of the author and should not necessarily be attributed to the NIHSS.

NATIONAL INSTITUTE
FOR THE HUMANITIES
AND SOCIAL SCIENCES

Project manager: Alison Paulin
Copyeditors: Inga Norenius and Lee Smith
Proofreader: Alison Paulin
Indexer: Marlene Burger
Cover design: Adam Bohannon
Typeset in 11 point Minion Pro

CONTENTS

LIST OF FIGURES AND TABLES

ACKNOWLEDGEMENTS

Grateful thanks go to Michelle Williams, for her wise guidance and unstinting encouragement; Vishwas Satgar for the opportunities to test, debate and clarify my thinking in various forums; Emancipatory Futures Studies for generously supporting some of the research; Neil Coleman, the Institute for Economic Justice and Asghar Adelzadeh for sharing research material; Seeraj Mohamed for his important analyses of financialisation in South Africa; Franco Barchiesi for his foundational writing on waged work and social citizenship in South Africa; the National Institute for the Humanities and Social Sciences for supporting the open access version of the book; the Wits University Press team for their careful stewardship; and Susan O'Leary for her bountiful patience and support.

The book is dedicated to Sandile Dikeni.

We have come to believe that working for a wage or salary is our passport to a life free of want and full of good prospects. And we are routinely told that a simple formula underpins this state of affairs: the right policies lead to economic growth which then generates jobs, while in the background, regulation ensures that the jobs are relatively safe and well-paid.

But what happens when the formula does not work? When the jobs do not materialise, or are only sporadically available, or pay poverty wages? This is the lived reality for hundreds of millions of people across the world, and their ranks are growing. Economic growth is not creating jobs of the kind or on the scale needed to shield people against poverty and distress.

Paid work[1] that provides a livable income on reasonably secure terms is rare in 'developing' economies and is becoming increasingly scarce in 'developed' economies.[2] The intensity of this change differs between regions and countries, but the secular trend in the most populous regions has been stagnant or downward.[3] The world employment rate has been declining for three decades and stood at about 57.4% in 2019, down from 63% in 1991.[4]

In developed countries, low official unemployment rates hide a reshaped 'geography of livelihoods' in which unsteady and atypical work – separated from welfare systems, labour market regulation and unionised protection – proliferates, along with growing informal economies.[5] In many of those countries, real wage increases have stalled or reversed in recent decades, especially for low-skilled workers.[6] Job and income insecurity, poor working conditions and low wages have long typified employment in developing economies. In many of them, self-employment and family-based work still eclipse formalised waged work as the main money-based foundation for livelihoods. But even when considering only formal sector employment, real wage growth in the past decade has been flat (in the Arab States and in Latin America and the Caribbean, for example) or negative (as in Africa). In Asia and the Pacific, considered the most economically dynamic region in the world, real wage growth has averaged at about 1.7% since the turn of the century, if China is excluded.[7]

These trends have worsened dramatically during the COVID-19 crisis. According to the International Labour Organization (ILO), approximately 144 million jobs were lost in 2020 as the pandemic forced countries into shutdowns.[8] People reliant on insecure forms of employment and income generation bore the brunt of the impact, with women and migrant workers especially affected.[9] Within a few weeks, the pandemic pushed 88–93 million people globally into extreme poverty, an unprecedented increase, according to the World Bank.[10]

Globally in 2020, about 1.4 billion workers were in vulnerable employment – either self-employed or working in family businesses – and they accounted for well over 40% of total employment.[11] Their incomes are typically low and highly variable. In 2020, at least 730 million workers in employment in developing countries were surviving on less than US$3.20 per day (in purchasing parity terms), that is, they were living in what the World Bank considers to be 'moderate' or 'extreme' poverty.[12]

The crisis of paid work – with respect to its availability, rewards, terms and conditions – is disturbingly obvious in a country such as South Africa, which is stricken with extraordinarily high levels of unemployment and inequality. In addition to having one of the world's highest unemployment rates – over 34% in mid-2021, when conservatively measured[13] – close to one-third of employed individuals in South Africa do not earn enough to afford basic food and non-food items.[14] When polled in mid-2021, almost half (46%) of respondents said they or someone else in their household went without cash income at least 'several times' in the previous year, and about one-third (32%) said they had repeatedly gone without enough food.[15]

For many decades, economic growth in South Africa has occurred amid rising numbers of unemployed people, many of whom are more or less permanently surplus to the labour market.[16] The country sharply illustrates David Harvey's remark that 'labour is becoming less and less significant to how the economic engine of capitalism functions'.[17] Yet the country's economy continues to generate vast – but maldistributed – wealth. In this respect, South Africa is no outlier.

Global economic growth has slowed and the income generated by that growth is funnelled increasingly towards the wealthiest percentiles.[18] The share of income going to the richest 1% of the global population increased in 46 out of 57 countries reporting those data during the period 1990–2015. The poorest 40% earned less than one-quarter of national income in all 92 countries reporting those data.[19] Wealth inequality follows a similar trend: across China, Europe and the United States, the share of wealth claimed by the top 1% increased from 28% to 33% between 1980 and 2018 – very likely an underestimate given how difficult it can be to measure wealth at the top.[20]

Understood as a system encompassing not only the economic, but also the ecological, social and political domains, capitalism over the past four decades has become increasingly crisis-prone, with corrective actions at best stalling, but not resolving the underlying problems.[21] These travails are embedded in the propulsive logic of the capitalist system. Its ceaseless pursuit of profits inclines it towards over-reach (evident in excess capacity and overproduction) and exposes it to destabilising dynamics that steadily erode the very conditions that enable it to thrive (Chapter 2). In Nancy Fraser's analysis, the instabilities can be traced to an entanglement of 'crisis tendencies'.[22] Those tendencies take hold when the pursuit of capitalism's economic imperatives (maximising and safeguarding profits) generates internal contradictions and degrades the non-economic conditions that enable that quest. Those conditions include non-human nature (from which raw materials and energy are extracted, and into which waste is dumped), the unwaged work of social reproduction (performed mainly by women and girls, and which produces and sustains potential workers), the state (which manages the legal, regulatory and coercive arrangements and provides the public goods necessary for capitalism's functioning), and the cultivation of general consent (our basic trust in state institutions and the system they serve).

The resultant instabilities are abundantly evident: frequent financial crises; vast human 'surplus populations'; political and social disorder linked to the hollowing out of democratic institutions; ecological devastation and associated public health disasters (such as zoonotic pandemics like COVID-19) are a few examples. Consequently, far-reaching imbalances now disturb political legitimacy, social consent, economic performance, geopolitical relations, and international finance and trade, for example. The costs of the turmoil are growing, but are being distributed evermore unequally.

With capital 'trapped in a seemingly endless cycle of stagnation and financial explosion',[23] the scope and intensity of the instabilities will, in all likelihood, increase. The dividend-boosting pressures of financialised capitalism will propel that trend, as will the rationing of decent paid work, as smart machines are deployed more widely to bypass human labour. These multiplying upheavals will sabotage the prospects of stable 'normality'.

A DOUBLE FICTION

In these conditions, a double fiction catches the eye: the idea that paid work is available to those who seek it and that the work bestows security and comfort. In reality, many hundreds of millions of people across the globe are unable to build steady, viable livelihoods by working for a wage.

The pursuit of more jobs – and more decent jobs – is vital, but it cannot substitute for more far-reaching efforts to address these crises: by shifting to sustainable and just developmental paths, and by realising core social and economic rights that can assure everyone their social citizenship.[24]

It is neither sufficient nor realistic to focus our solutions on reconstituting past arrangements or recovering missed opportunities, or to proceed as if current trends are mere aberrations.[25] A retooling and drastic expansion of social policy is necessary. It is in this context that the concept of a universal basic income (UBI)[26] has been making headlines and attracting supporters – and critics – from across the political spectrum[27] (Chapter 1).

UBI proponents claim that such an intervention would afford people vital means for survival, reduce poverty and inequality, and broaden their life choices. They expect it to bolster the bargaining leverage of low-wage earners, spur a rethink of the role and status of waged work in society, support transitions towards ecologically sustainable economic models, and reinvigorate democracy, among other benefits (Chapter 3). Critics argue that a UBI would encourage work-shy idleness, and offend the principle that we should 'earn' our entitlements by working for a wage or salary. Besides being fiscally unaffordable, they also argue, a UBI would open the door for removing existing social protection and for reinforcing the rule of the market (Chapter 4).

These debates occur in and focus largely on developed countries. Although relevant and instructive, they do not seamlessly transfer to developing-country settings, where social policy arrangements are very different, as are the nature, extent and historical trends of paid work.[28] Thoroughly assessing the desirability and viability of a UBI requires a sound understanding of the economy, the distributive order and the normative presumptions that govern access to the means for life (Chapters 5 and 6). Those factors differ from place to place.

In many developing countries, South Africa included, social protection mechanisms are proliferating and expanding,[29] and there is strong evidence that these schemes contribute to a range of desirable outcomes.[30] As a highly unequal upper-middle-income country with an embattled, semi-industrialised economy, South Africa also has a relatively uncomplicated but unusually extensive social protection system. This potentially offers both political and policy momentum for seriously considering more radical, forward-looking forms of provisioning, such as a UBI.

* * *

This book tries to move the UBI debate beyond the fenced-in camps of support or opposition, by examining the option against a backdrop of key concerns. First and most obvious are the ongoing failures to devise exits from social crises that are fundamentally tied to the chronic absence or inadequacy of income-earning opportunities for very large proportions of the adult population. In this respect, South Africa resembles a real-world precursor to the dystopian forecasts in which paid work becomes a scarce, unpredictable and insufficient basis for a dignified life for ever-growing numbers of people.

Analysis and policymaking continue to assume the feasibility of both full employment and a regulatory environment that can guarantee decent work. Yet decades of evidence show that policies that peg entitlement and well-being chiefly to paid work are highly incomplete. In places like South Africa, they are glaringly inadequate and very probably inappropriate.

These are not passing trends. The changing nature, functions and availability of paid work require that we understand the underlying dynamics and consider the alternatives along longer trajectories than is usually the case. And the far-reaching implications of a UBI require that the debate range across the boundaries that usually separate economics, political-economy, labour studies, sociology, anthropology, social policy, gender studies and more.

A UBI is also a slippery concept, attracting advocates and critics of all stripes. This has allowed a potentially disruptive intervention to become a mainstream topic. But rather than nourish productive debate, this pliancy tends to channel discussions towards brusque verdicts about the desirability and feasibility of such an intervention. A UBI implicitly challenges key assumptions about prevailing economic and social orders, policies and distributive systems that tether people's prospects of a dignified life to the sale of their labour, the role and duties of the state, and the claims citizens can rightfully make on one another and the state. It also challenges the mistaken equation of economic growth with societal well-being and social justice. Productive debate about a UBI has to delve into these issues.

The common tendency is to think of a UBI as a technocratic tool that can be used to advance measurable objectives, such as fewer people living in poverty or narrowing the poverty gap. But the stakes and benefits – and risks – are much greater than that. Approaching a UBI as a standalone cure-all that can be dislodged from movement politics, from striving for broad social and economic transformation, and from sage macroeconomic choices and political strategies seems foolhardy.

A wiser approach would be to try to establish whether and how a UBI might advance or hinder a push towards egalitarian change. And that requires us to also consider the political-economic, social and normative questions and dilemmas that are posed by a UBI. We need to examine the underlying assumptions about a UBI, explore how people think about the concept, weigh its social and political implications, and test its financial feasibility. Only then can we arrive at a clear sense of whether a UBI is desirable and viable in extreme settings like South Africa.

1

Behind the Idea of a Universal Basic Income

A decade or so ago, UBI proposals were being met with a roll of the eyes and brisk dismissals for being utopian and unrealistic. Today, these demands and debates routinely make headlines. Political parties and national and city governments with diverse ideological leanings are exploring such a mechanism for distributing income support, many to the point of launching pilot projects.

Switzerland staged a national referendum on the issue in 2016: 23% of voters (and up to 35% in some cantons) supported the proposal to pay every Swiss national a monthly guaranteed universal income of CHF 2 500.[1] The European Citizen's Initiative is campaigning for the introduction of unconditional basic incomes throughout the European Union. Basic income pilot schemes or studies have been launched in cities and countries in Africa,[2] Asia,[3] Europe[4] and North America.[5] Some trade unions support the concept, as do some Silicon Valley billionaires, many grassroots activists and utopian socialists, not to mention sworn enemies of the welfare state. In South Africa, a growing coalition of civil society groups is demanding the introduction of a guaranteed monthly income for all adults.

How can the same basic idea attract support from such disparate quarters? Part of the answer is that UBI means different things to different sets of interests. It is a highly contested concept, with supporters spread enigmatically across the political spectrum – from the post-capitalist Left[6] to the progressive reformist Left,[7] from mainstream liberals[8] to right-wing libertarians.[9] Before considering the merits of a UBI, we need to be clear about the concept itself.

ORIGINS

The basic idea of a guaranteed income is centuries old. It made an appearance in English social philosopher Thomas More's 1516 novel *Utopia* and in Juan Luis Vives' *On Assistance to the Poor* a decade later, and it resembles the concept of 'ground rent', which the American philosopher and activist Thomas Paine described in his 1796 pamphlet *Agrarian Justice*.[10] Paine regarded agricultural land as 'natural property' to which every citizen had a claim. However, he also saw an 'efficiency case' for private ownership of the land. The compromise was to tax private ownership of agricultural land (the 'ground rent') and to distribute that revenue equally to all adults in society – not as charity, but as a right, since all citizens had an original claim to privately owned land.

Drawing on the thinking of the French socialist Charles Fourier (set out in his 1836 text *La Fausse Industrie*),[11] the philosopher John Stuart Mill also argued for a form of guaranteed income in the 1848 edition of his textbook, *Principles of Political Economy*.[12] It would require, he wrote, that 'a certain minimum is first assigned for the subsistence of every member of the community, whether capable or not of labour'.[13] The concept then languished, eclipsed by the rapid expansion of both industrial capitalism and the ranks of waged workers – and with that, the rise of radical political programmes that centred on transforming relations and conditions of production. As the power and influence of workers' organisations grew, proposals for basic income-type arrangements tended to recede.[14]

At the end of World War I, the mathematician and philosopher Bertrand Russell called for an income for all.[15] The concept also featured in a pamphlet that circulated prominently in the British Labour Party, claiming that a basic income would boost economic production. In response to the Great Depression during the early 1930s, US senator Huey Long championed an annual 'homestead allowance' of US$5 000 for families.[16]

It was after World War II that Britain, and several western European and Scandinavian countries, introduced variants of a guaranteed minimum income as part of their social welfare systems. These schemes were targeted and/or highly conditional – thus not universal. They included, for example, payments to families with children (often irrespective of income levels) and old-age pensions. Universal provisioning tended to focus on essential services and other public goods, such as education, healthcare, sanitation, emergency services, maternity leave, childcare and so on.

Social policy proposals resembling a basic income entered mainstream policy debate in the United States in the 1960s, as economic planners struggled to deal with the re-emergence of structural unemployment: the economy was growing, but job creation lagged. President JF Kennedy's economic advisers floated the idea of a guaranteed income in the form of a negative income tax. Popularised by Chicago School economist Milton Friedman in his 1962 book, *Capitalism and Freedom*,[17] a negative income tax entailed an income transfer to people earning below a specified income, with the amount varying according to a person's level of income (see below). The proposed mechanism was basically a means-tested income transfer to low-income earners.[18] Friedman and other advocates promoted it as a replacement for what they regarded to be a complex, intrusive and costly mosaic of welfare entitlements. One of the motives was to remove the alleged disincentive effect of conditional welfare programmes on labour market participation.

In 1969, President Richard Nixon proposed a Family Assistance Plan, which resembled the mechanism outlined by Friedman. The intervention would have amounted to an annual payment of US$1 600 for low-income households on condition that they sought employment.[19] The idea gained attention amid concerns about persistent poverty and findings from social science research suggesting that cash assistance would most rapidly reduce poverty.[20] Criticised from both the political Right and Left, however, that proposal languished. It was then revived during the run-up to the 1972 US presidential election, as more than 1 000 economists called on the federal government to introduce some kind of income guarantee to reduce poverty.[21] The Family Assistance Plan eventually made it to the floor in the US Congress, where it failed to pass. The biggest concern seemed to be not the affordability of the scheme, but that it might discourage people from seeking waged work.

In western Europe, an activist network with a footing in academia began promoting a UBI in the 1980s. The Basic Income Earth Network (formerly the Basic Income European Network), set up in 1986, became an important institutional base for research and advocacy. It was a paper by Philippe van Parijs,[22] in which he made a liberal-egalitarian case for a universal basic income, that seemed to spark wider interest in the concept.

In the early 2000s, a campaign for a small basic income grant (BIG) in South Africa, led initially by trade unions allied with the ruling African National Congress (ANC), attracted enough attention to prompt the government to appoint a committee of inquiry to examine the option. The Committee of Inquiry into a Comprehensive System of Social Security for South Africa (known as the Taylor Committee) recommended that a small basic income be phased in nationally. There was support for the proposal inside the government, with then Minister of Social Development, Zola Skweyiya, noting that a 'basic income grant system is one of the excellent ideas we might consider introducing'.[23] Both the National Treasury and the Presidency, however, opposed the scheme, deeming it unaffordable – and the proposal was rejected (see Chapter 5).

Internationally, awareness about a UBI dimmed during the first decade of the new millennium, but the idea then burst into prominence in the

2010s, as societies reeled from the impact of the 2008 global financial crisis. By mid-decade, the concept had become a staple of media coverage and public debate. Popular support has grown and some mainstream political parties are even adding basic income proposals to their election platforms.

THE CONCEPT

Broadly defined, a UBI is a universal and regular (monthly) cash payment to individuals, without conditionalities (such as work requirements or enrolling children in school), means-testing or targeting.

But proponents differ on the details. Mainstream supporters focus on the more prosaic potential of a UBI to provide an indiscriminate safety net that can eliminate precarity, reduce inequality and perhaps even increase aggregate economic demand. Those on the libertarian and neo-liberal Right are attracted to a UBI as a mechanism to purge existing systems of welfare protection and further limit the state's obligations to citizens. Recipients would use the basic income payment (and any other income or credit they have) to purchase all goods and services as commodities from private providers. In the United States, Charles Murray, for example, touted a guaranteed income as the next best option to obliterating state-managed redistribution;[24] the scheme would be financed by eliminating almost all existing state-funded support for individuals. Some technology-sector proponents of a UBI seem to lean towards a similar approach, seeing a basic income as 'the ultimate hack to get around the complexities of creating equitable social welfare policies', as Eileen Guo has put it.[25]

Progressive proponents support a UBI that functions as an important element of far-reaching social and economic change, emphasising its role in reducing constraints and inequalities that are outside individual control. Proponents in the 'futurist' or 'accelerationist' camp[26] see it as an important feature of a 'post-work' society[27] in which widespread automation and other advances render waged work increasingly superfluous to the production and distribution of goods and services.[28] Other supporters on the Left[29] see a UBI operating as part of a system of distribution that protects everyone against deprivation and grants them the freedom to choose whether and when to perform waged work. For them, the intervention would supplement – not replace – other forms of social provisioning and it would function against a backdrop of regulation, standard-setting and subsidy, and of macroeconomic, industrial and labour market policies that are designed to increase access to decent waged work. Such a UBI would force the principle of social justice into the heart of economic and social policymaking. For proponents such as Erik Olin Wright, a generous-enough UBI also harbours the potential to reshape power relations, including class relations.[30]

The payment would be 'universal' not because it replaces other entitlements, but because it is available to everyone.[31] Martin Ravallion, for example, has proposed positioning a UBI as an element or aspect of a 'full income', with income defined expansively.[32] A full income would resemble a social wage (or the public provision of essential amenities) and would – in addition to a UBI – encapsulate essential non-cash provisioning (such as housing, education and healthcare) by or via the state, as well as subsidies favouring low-income households (for example food, energy, fuel and water subsidies). In this book, we examine the potential merits and pitfalls of a UBI that is defined in these expansive terms.

A UBI is sometimes confused with a negative income tax (of the kind proposed in the United States in the 1960s and early 1970s). Such a tax provides supplemental income to low-income families, with a portion (scaled according to income) 'clawed back' through taxation. The actual net income transfer therefore varies, depending on the recipient's income level. An obvious hitch is that all adults need to file tax returns (including zero and very low-income earners) if this type of income guarantee is to reach the people who need it the most. Substantial variation in people's monthly earnings (an increasingly common phenomenon) also makes a negative income tax a less attractive and an administratively challenging intervention. In addition, it lacks the stability and predictability of a UBI: people with fluctuating monthly incomes are likely to receive income support that reflects their earnings several months earlier. In rough outline, a negative income tax corresponds with a libertarian understanding of distributive justice, while a UBI supports egalitarian principles,[33] making them very different kinds of distributive devices.

Beyond the issue of definition lies the thorny matter of eligibility. In principle, and for proponents such as Van Parijs and Kathi Weeks,[34] every member of society – child or adult – should be eligible for a UBI. Other conceptions would limit the payment to individuals 16 or 18 years and older. Views also differ on whether a UBI would be paid to national citizens only, or also to legal residents, or to everyone who has resided in a given country for a specified period of time (whether legally or not). The definition of 'universal' (or 'everyone') has both fiscal and political implications and requires clear delineation.[35] At stake here is the nature of an ostensibly inclusive society, the criteria that are used to determine inclusion, and the principles that are used to select those criteria. These are weighty matters that tend to be settled on seemingly pragmatic (often fiscal) grounds rather than by considering the implications for the goals of social justice, inclusion and egalitarianism.

Also controversial is the monetary value or amount of a UBI payment. A basic income should, by definition, be sufficient for a basic livelihood: a 'foundation … for dignified living',[36] it should be sufficient to cover basic needs beyond a set of basic, free or subsidised public services, thereby enabling a person to participate more fully in social life.[37] However, income supplements that are too small to constitute such a guarantee are typically also presented as 'basic incomes'. Even fixing a UBI at the level of a livable income leaves unsettled how such an amount would be determined in a given context. An amount close or equal to the poverty line is one option (it guided the amount proposed in the 2016 Swiss referendum, for example),[38] though the manner in which poverty is defined and the calculation of poverty lines are controversial. Statistics South Africa, for example, calculates and updates three poverty lines: an upper-bound poverty line, a lower-bound poverty line and a food poverty line.[39]

Many of the desired effects of a UBI could conceivably be achieved with a payment that significantly contributes to, but does not in itself constitute, a livable income. The amount of an efficacious UBI would be context-specific, as would the political and fiscal factors that shape its size, and the macroeconomic strategies that accompany it. For now, it bears emphasising that, depending on the design and scope, a basic income can perform radically different functions and serve very different sets of interests.

EXPLAINING THE NEW-FOUND APPEAL

While the slipperiness of the concept partly explains the growing attraction of the UBI idea, we should ask: why now in particular? There are several possible explanations, some self-evident, others less obvious.

The 2008 global financial crisis and subsequent flurries of progressive activism (notably the Occupy Movement) led to greater acknowledgement of widening income, wealth and social inequalities, of a decades-long trend of stagnant or falling real wages (especially for low- and middle-income workers) and of the extraordinary accumulation of income and wealth by the top 1% of earners (forensically analysed in French economist Thomas Piketty's 2013 book, *Capital in the Twenty-First Century*).[40]

The governance response to the financial crisis in industrialised countries came in the shape of substantial infusions of liquidity, much of it channelled into financial markets rather than towards recuperation in the real economy and/or direct income support to households. Massive layoffs and wage depression were followed by a slow, skewed recovery, as relatively secure employment was increasingly displaced by insecure, piecemeal jobs and shift work, stripped of regulatory protection and often remunerated well below the living wage. Austerity policies decimated social programmes. In the United States, the Occupy Movement rallied against increasing economic inequality and social vulnerability.[41] Elsewhere, the Arab Spring uprisings in North Africa and the Middle East, which erupted in the context of harsh domestic austerity programmes, highlighted the potential for sudden, radical contestation even in places that had seemed solidly barricaded against popular discontent. As countries doubled down on austerity-based 'recovery' programmes, the restiveness fed anxieties about the prospects of chronic social and political unrest. The rise of right-wing populist political formations underscored the concerns.

These events coincided with an upsurge of both optimism and alarm about the potential impact of innovations in artificial intelligence and other forms of digital automation. Some on the post-capitalist Left predicted that those changes would steadily transform utopian visions of work and society into tangible prospects. If new technologies massively boosted productivity, output could be maintained or increased using less labour input – and, in theory, work time could be reduced and shared without cutting into wages and salaries.[42] But the technological changes also evoked dystopian scenarios in which dozens of job categories would disappear,[43] leading to massive increases in unemployment and poverty. Sluggish economic recovery and further restructuring of labour markets (mostly at the expense of low-skilled and low-wage workers) also encouraged a rethink of social protection (and social policy in general).[44] A UBI began to seem like a reasonable, even advisable option. But this seeming respectability of a UBI emerged also in a broader context: penetrated and reshaped by forty years of neoliberal capitalism, social policy had shifted profoundly.

Neoliberalism is often portrayed as an assault on the state. In fact, it involves a radical recasting of the ways in which state power and resources are deployed in society. Under neoliberal capitalism the priorities for state action shifted more emphatically towards expanding and sustaining conditions for profit-taking. This included drastic steps to extend and safeguard private property rights (including intellectual property rights), remove barriers to the circulation of capital, and privatise commons and other collective assets. The neoliberal state is an interventionist state.

It has redesigned tax and labour regimes, removed regulatory constraints and adopted monetary policies that unabashedly privilege corporate capital, and it has intervened to displace economic risk onto society at large through corporate subsidies and bailouts. Having introduced that template, the state has then allowed market forces to determine the allocation of capital and the production, circulation and use of products and services.[45]

These changes included several shifts in social policy, which reflected a repositioning of the state in relation to the market and society. The state was recast as 'facilitator' rather than 'provider', and the principle of social solidarity was replaced with an ideology of individual responsibility and risk-taking. Being poor was presented as an individual character flaw, a moral defect. The state's obligations towards citizens swung towards providing 'public support for private responsibility'.[46] Erstwhile welfare states retreated from their social responsibilities, ceding public assets and provisioning roles to profit-seeking enterprises (typically via privatisation and outsourcing).

Facilitating and incentivising opportunity and enterprise – rather than guaranteeing access to the basic means for dignified life – became the state's central duty towards citizens. In social policy, the principle of universalism was displaced by the increased use of individualised, targeted and conditional forms of provisioning, often in a coercive administrative context. The centrality of waged work was reinforced, with access to social support tied more firmly to having had a paid job (in the recent past) or actively seeking one. Social policy was remodelled to herd individuals into the labour market on the terms and rates offered. This 'coercive use of social provisions'[47] came loaded with a moralising discourse that condemned individuals' or families' dependency on public spending. Subsidies and tax breaks lavished on businesses were spared such disapproval.

These changes also saw social policy increasingly penetrated and appropriated by private enterprise (through, for example, the privatisation and subcontracting of public services). One effect was the detachment of social policy from overarching economic and development strategies, with discrete instruments (such as cash transfers or the discredited micro-credit fad of the 1990s) paraded as catalysts for 'pro-poor' development.[48]

It is in this context that cash transfers were elevated as multipurpose social policy instruments.[49] From the 1990s onward, cash transfer pro-grammes proliferated, initially in Latin America and parts of Asia, and then in Africa, where donors became ardent enthusiasts.[50] By the late 2000s, almost every Latin American country was operating some form of cash transfer programme, with Brazil's *Bolsa Família* and Mexico's *Progresa/Oportunidades* programmes among the best-known examples.[51] Within a few years, numerous African countries were doing the same, albeit on smaller scales. Cash transfers were celebrated for being much less expensive and more cost-efficient than universal welfare provision, and for being effective at reducing poverty and income inequality, and at improving health and other social outcomes.

Usually targeted and conditional (on, for example, school attendance or health-seeking behaviours), these transfers contrast with the universalist principles that had earlier characterised much progressive social policy. In Andrew Fischer's analysis, conditional or not, cash transfers mark an abandonment of the egalitarian and equalising ambitions of twentieth-century social policy, and instead legitimise segregation and inequality.[52] There remains an emphasis on universal *access* to certain services or entitle-ments (for example, all children should be able to attend school), but there is less concern about the overall levels of investment in those services, their quality, the terms of access and whether the services are provided through the private or public sector. This has profound implications.

Rather than form part of an overarching redistributive strategy (which would encompass macroeconomic policy, labour policy, industrial strategy, social protection and other forms of social provisioning), cash transfers typically serve as piecemeal proxies. In many instances, they are deployed in the context of dismantled public provisioning and faltering development strategies,[53] with the financial sector expanding down the 'income ladder' in a process of 'financial inclusion' – 'commodification all the way down', in Nancy Fraser's words.[54] One aspect of this, highlighted by Lena Lavinas,[55] is the proliferation of credit markets and the incorporation of cash (or credit) transfers into new strategies to extract debt and rent from low-income earners. Facilitating these predatory incursions is the bundling together of cash transfer programmes and 'financial inclusion' in global development discourse.[56] Access to financial services has been elevated into a developmental principle. The World Bank[57] regards it as a core factor for development and it features prominently in the United Nations 2020 Sustainable Development Goals.[58] Financial corporations are adeptly exploiting this tenet by teaming up with technology firms to secure contracts for managing electronic disbursement systems for cash transfers, thereby gaining direct access to many millions of grant recipients and their income streams. Those strategems were plainly evident in the 2015–2017 social grants crisis in South Africa, when transnational corporations successfully used the grant disbursement system as part of wider financial predation strategies among low-income earners.[59] Social grants were turned into collateral for credit in ways that made the cash transfers 'a site of nearly risk-free profit' for the companies.[60]

Viewed in this light, the mainstream appeal of a potentially transformative intervention such as a UBI is less perplexing. The mechanism seems compatible with the prevailing policy and ideological environment, as critics on the Left have charged.[61] It also reflects an awareness that many traditional sources of material security and well-being are becoming increasingly fragile and inaccessible, and it speaks to anxieties about the social and political implications of those changes. Indeed, some supporters seem attracted to the idea of a UBI precisely because they see it as a discrete, technical mechanism that can be deployed to improve specific socioeconomic metrics (such as poverty gaps and rates) irrespective of the surrounding dynamics that generate precarity and inequality.

Yet progressive proponents also invest a UBI with a liberating potential that exceeds such a narrow, instrumentalised function. For them, a UBI potentially subverts orthodoxy in multiple, profound ways. It could even help unlock a new social order in which the prospect of a fulfilling life is no longer dependent solely on the ritualised sale of one's labour. They see it contributing to the conditions for radically new, egalitarian societies in which labour and production are harnessed to serve social life, rather than the inverse. The concept of a UBI therefore is too rich with possibilities, too problematic, too pliable, and too subversive to settle unambivalently in 'pro' or 'con' camps.

THE IDEA GOES MAINSTREAM

Basic income pilot schemes or studies have been launched in numerous places, including Finland,[62] Germany,[63] the city of Utrecht in the Netherlands,[64] the Canadian province of Ontario,[65] India,[66] Namibia[67] and Uganda.[68] Some of those projects were halted prematurely after new governments took office: the Ontario trial, which involved paying up to Can$17 000 per year to 4 000 individuals across the province, was discontinued after a conservative government assumed power in the province. Pilot projects were also under way in the United States, including the Stockton California SEED demonstration.[69] California has allocated US$35 million to fund basic income pilot projects that favour youth and pregnant mothers.[70] At the time of writing, a large-scale, 12-year study of a basic income was being conducted among 21 000 adults in Bomet County on the shores of Lake Victoria in western Kenya.[71]

These initiatives encompass different types of income guarantee. Most of them retain elements of conditionality and/or are targeted at low-income earners – making them less-than-universal income transfers. During the early months of the COVID-19 pandemic in 2020, for example, Spain's governing coalition of the Socialist Party and the left-wing Podemos movement pledged to introduce an income transfer scheme that would target families with no or low income. Recipients who found jobs would keep receiving the payment for the first few months of employment, after which the payment would end.[72] The Utrecht pilot involved paying six different groups of participants different stipends, each with slightly different conditions attached,[73] while the Finnish pilot was designed to pay 2 000 unemployed people aged 25–58 years €560 a month for two years (making it a targeted payment).[74] In contrast, a controlled trial planned in Germany envisaged paying about 120 participants €1 200 (US$1 350) a month for three years regardless of their employment status.[75]

As the COVID-19 pandemic took hold, support for UBI-like interventions grew markedly. Survey results showed that 71% of Europeans favoured the introduction of a UBI, according to an Oxford University study from March 2020, with support spread evenly across age groups.[76] In a large 2019 survey across 14 European Union countries,[77] 46% of respondents supported paying a guaranteed income to each citizen, whether working or not. Twenty-nine percent were opposed (the remainder took no position). Support was strongest in Germany (62%) and it exceeded 50% in Belgium, Hungary and Sweden.[78] An earlier survey in Germany reported a 45–52% approval rate for an unconditional basic income.[79] Even in the United States, with its ingrained culture of self-reliance, 45% of people polled by the Pew Research Center in 2020 supported a guaranteed income of US$1 000 per month for all adult citizens,[80] while a 2019 poll found 37% supported a UBI and 40% opposed it.[81]

By May 2020, according to the Swiss bank UBS, almost 39 million people who had lost their jobs or working hours in France, Germany, Italy, Spain and the United Kingdom were receiving stipends from governments.[82] Even the United States offered temporary income support in the shape of cash transfers. The pandemic both heightened and highlighted acute vulnerability, which was no longer limited to the proverbial 'poor'. Across the planet, middle-class households discovered that the barriers separating relatively comfortable lives and secure livelihoods from precarity were much flimsier than previously thought. At the same time, social unrest and the rise of right-wing populism on every continent has focused the minds of political elites. The upshot is a broadening recognition that current distributional systems require a rethink.

A UNIVERSAL BASIC INCOME IN THE 'REAL WORLD'

Among the best-known examples of a basic income is the so-called Mincome Programme, which ran from 1974 to 1979 in Canada and became part of social policy folklore subsequently. The scheme entailed paying a supplemental income worth CAN$19 500 per year per four-person family to about 1 000 low-income families in Dauphin, a small town in Manitoba province. The guaranteed income was reduced by 50 cents for each dollar a family earned above that amount, in effect directing the income support to low-income families.[83]

After the Conservative Party won the Canadian federal election in 1979, the new government scrapped the experiment without analysing the results. Many years passed before an economist examined the data and found that numerous health and other indicators had improved among recipients of the income payment. A larger proportion of children in recipient families had completed Grade 12 when compared with those living in similar towns in the province. Hospital visits and admissions had declined, especially for mental health diagnoses, accidents and injuries, and reports of domestic violence had decreased. Employment rates had stayed steady throughout the five-year trial, except among new mothers (who were able to spend more time with their children) and teenagers (who were able to give up part-time jobs and focus on schoolwork). All those effects disappeared when the experiment ended.[84]

More closely resembling a universal income is an instrument that the US state of Alaska introduced in 1999. The Alaska Permanent Fund Dividend annually pays each resident an equal share of the returns from investments in the specially created Alaska Permanent Fund, which is financed from a portion of the state's oil revenue.[85] Studies have found that income distribution and poverty alleviation improved significantly after the dividend was introduced, though it has been difficult to determine to what extent the scheme has been responsible for those outcomes.[86] Analysis of the macroeconomic effects suggests that the payment does not discourage recipients from taking jobs and may increase uptake of part-time work.[87] Matt Bruenig has gone as far as calling the Alaska Permanent Fund 'a kind of market socialism … a way to socialize the ownership of capital resources without centrally planning anything or otherwise disrupting normal market operations'.[88]

An 'accidental' basic income pilot in North Carolina also offers instructive insights. It occurred in the 1990s when the construction of a casino on Cherokee land coincided with a longitudinal comparative study of mental health among Cherokee American Indian children aged 9–16 years. As part of the casino deal, all Cherokee Indian adults received about US$4 000 per year. Children in families receiving the payments performed better in school (with test scores 22 points higher, on average, than children in the control group), and displayed significantly better mental and behavioural health than their peers from non-tribal families (who did not receive the payments). Self-reported consumption of alcohol and drugs among adults also decreased.[89]

On a smaller scale, a basic income grant was introduced as a pilot project in 2008 and 2009 in the Namibian town of Otjivero-Omitara, near the capital, Windhoek. The payment of 100 Namibian dollars per month was unconditional and went to everyone younger than sixty years. Data were skewed by an influx of family members from elsewhere, which is why per capita income seemed to fall during the project. But substantial social benefits were recorded. The percentage of residents living in poverty fell from 76% to 37%, and among those who did not take in migrating family members, it fell to 17%. School drop-out rates fell sharply, with 90% of school fees paid in full, while cases of child malnutrition declined by more than half (from 42% to 17%). Recipients also became more active in income-generating activities.[90]

Several analogous pilot projects have been conducted in India, three of them by the Self-Employed Women's Association, in which thousands of men, women and children received a small, monthly, unconditional income.[91] The recipients' experiences were compared with those of a control group of thousands of people who did not receive the payments. In the first pilot, implemented in Delhi in 2009, food rations were provided to low-income families along with cash transfers that were paid into the bank accounts of the eldest women in households. Both the diets and nutrition levels of recipient families improved. In another pilot, in rural Madhya Pradesh, 5 500 women and men received a cash payment directly into their bank accounts, while an equal number of people (not receiving payments) served as control group. Nutrition levels and school attendance for children were markedly higher in the recipient households, especially for girls. Women's participation in the labour market was not affected, though the kinds of work they performed did change (more women worked for themselves, fewer women worked for wages), which tended to lift household incomes. Debts were also reduced. There was no observed increase in alcohol or tobacco consumption during the 18-month pilot.[92] Five years after the experiment ended, a few families had reverted to their previous conditions, mostly due to health crises, but many of the positive outcomes endured due to sustained growth of income. Encouraged in part by these findings, the India Economic Survey in 2017 recommended that a UBI be made available to all women in India.[93]

Of the dozens of basic income pilots or trials under way or planned across the world, however, very few involve paying *universal* incomes. Many are cash transfer pilots or demonstration projects that are targeted at unemployed and/or low-income individuals. Some are also conditional. These pilots usually involve small numbers of people and last a few years only, which limits their power and what they can reveal about the societal effects of such support. The ongoing 12-year study in Kenya promises to be an important exception.[94]

Nonetheless, pilot studies thus far provide encouraging data and insights regarding the short-run positive effects of basic income transfers, and they show little sign of the predicted negative effects. The available evidence indicates that a basic income reduces poverty and hospital admissions; improves diets and nutrition, schooling performance, mental health and psychological well-being; enhances independence and confidence (especially among women); and supports other income-generating activities and community-focused work. None of the studies supports concerns about recipients retreating from the labour market, or spending the income on 'temptation goods'.

But the evidence also indicates that a basic income guarantee is not a silver bullet or panacea. Unless set at a relatively high amount, the intervention will not do away with income poverty, though it can substantially reduce poverty gaps and rates (even if set at a modest amount). Neither will it – on its own – dislodge the dynamics that reproduce poverty and inequality. Its full effect depends on whether and how it functions as part of a broader set of changes (including changes to social, macroeconomic and industrial policies). Proponents on the Left believe that a UBI, if deployed as part of a larger transformative project, can have a resoundingly positive impact. The past 150 years have demonstrated that when all people have the security of a reliable income (whatever the sources) and can access other basic support and services, societies thrive as a whole.

At the moment, though, working for a wage or salary continues to be seen as the central and sufficient basis for meeting basic needs, avoiding poverty and 'earning' a rightful place in society.[95] The overriding challenge is therefore seen as the need to pursue economic growth in order to generate more jobs. That view is out of sync with today's realities.

2

The Crisis of Waged Work

'Unemployment and underemployment rates that stay stubbornly high.[1] New jobs that are mostly irregular, poorly paid and lacking in benefits and security. Real wages that are stagnant or falling for a majority of workers. Social protection systems that are shrunken, miserly and humiliatingly rationed and policed. Widening income and other inequalities.' These descriptions used to apply almost exclusively to countries on the margins of the global economy; today they are generic, including in industrialised economies. In Jan Breman's summary:

> With every recession since the 1970s, prolonged episodes of high unemployment, privatisations and public-sector cutbacks have served to weaken the position of labour in North America, Europe and Japan; trade-union movements were hollowed out by the shrinkage of the industrial workforce, through factory re-location or robotisation, and the growth of the non-unionised service and

retail sectors; the rise of China, the entry of hundreds of millions of low-paid workers into the world workforce and the globalisation of trade helped to depress wages and working conditions further. Part-time and short-contract work has been on the rise, along with that ambiguous category, self-employment.[2]

The intensity, pace and scale of these changes differ across countries, but the overall trend is relatively homogenous, with employment not expanding rapidly enough to absorb the growing labour force. Thus, the world employment rate continues to fall (Figure 2.1).[3]

Conservative calculations put the global unemployment rate[4] in 2019, before the COVID-19 pandemic, at 5.4% (about 188 million people).[5] The absolute number of unemployed people has risen in East and South Asia, Latin America, the Caribbean and Africa, and this is likely to continue as the demographic 'youth bulge' matures. In developed countries, unemployment rates have risen considerably since the 30 years known as the 'golden age' immediately after World War II. That trend accelerated after the 2008 global financial crisis, especially in southern and eastern Europe. Declining official unemployment rates often hide large shares of discouraged workers and a growing prevalence of involuntary underemployment.[6] The COVID-19 pandemic has worsened matters considerably. According to the ILO, workers lost US$3.7 trillion in earnings during the first nine months of the epidemic, with almost 9% of global working hours lost (the equivalent of 255 million full-time jobs).[7] Women and younger workers bore the brunt of income losses and reductions in work hours.

The strength of workers' organisations in developed economies varies considerably (compare the United States with France, for example), but their influence overall has weakened significantly over the past thirty years.[8] The global rate of trade union membership declined from about 25% in 2000 to 17% in 2017.[9] Growth in the industrial and service sectors has seen workers' organisations proliferate in some developing economies.[10] Their impact, though growing, remains limited. Job and income insecurity

Rate %, Employment, Multiple locations

75
70
65
60
55
50
45

1991 1992 1993 1994 1995 1996 1997 1998 1999 2000 2001 2002 2003 2004 2005 2006 2007 2008 2009 2010 2011 2012 2013 2014 2015 2016 2017 2018 2019 2020 2021 2022 2023

Eastern Asia

Northern, Southern and Western Europe

Sub-Saharan Africa

Latin America and the Caribbean

South-Eastern Asia and the Pacific

World

Northern America

Southern Asia

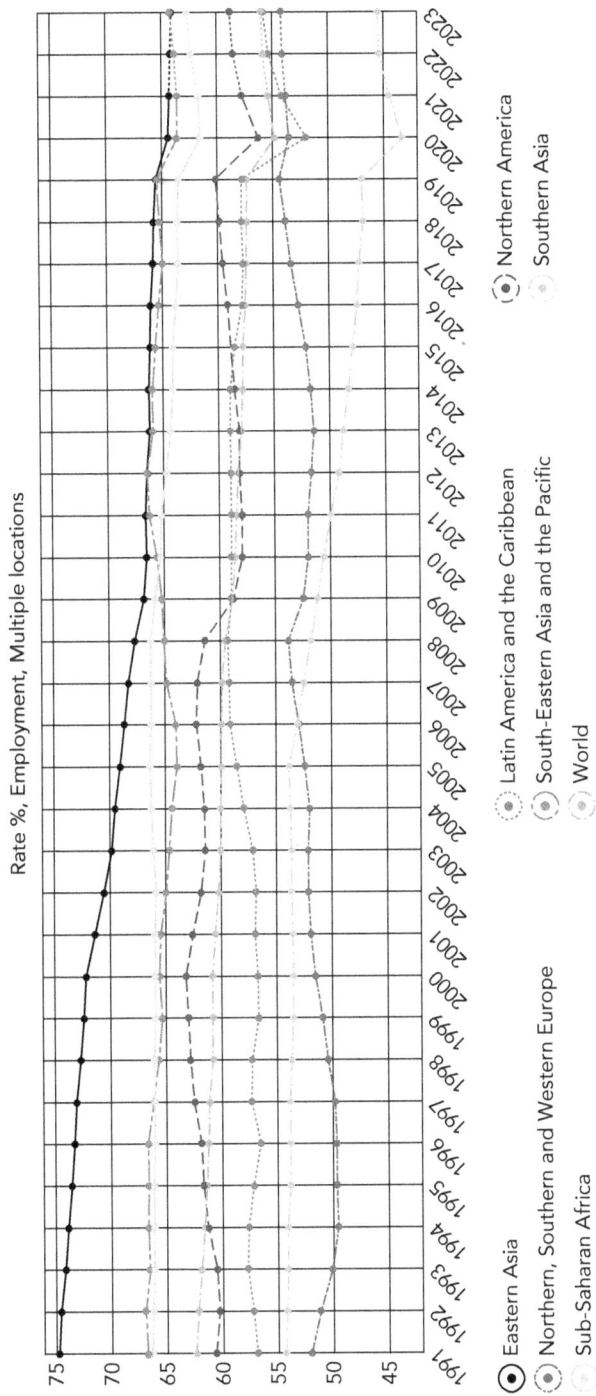

Figure 2.1: World and regional employment rates (%), 1991–2021

Source: ILO. *World Employment and Social Outlook: Trends 2022*. Geneva: © International Labour Organization, 2022.

Note: The employment rate is defined liberally to include all persons of working age (15+ years) who, during a short reference period, were engaged in any activity to produce goods or provide services for pay or profit. The data points for 2022 and 2023 are modeled projections.

and poor working conditions therefore continue to typify employment in developing economies. In most of them, self-employment and family-based work – along with remittances and sharing of incomes across households and families – are the main means for survival.[11] Large proportions of workers in developing countries are less likely to

> be covered by social protection such as pensions and healthcare or have regular earnings. They tend to be trapped in a vicious circle of low-productivity occupations, poor remuneration and limited ability to invest in their families' health and education.[12]

This insecurity occurs on a massive scale. Three decades ago, the World Bank was touting the 'informal' sector as an incubator for entrepreneurial activity, economic growth and formal job creation. It was wrong. Informality remains pervasive and continues to be associated with low economic growth, low productivity and poverty.[13] In South Asia and Africa in 2019, more than three-quarters of employed workers were in what the ILO considers to be vulnerable employment (they were self- or family-employed). Globally, about two billion workers, over 60% of the total employed workforce, were in informal employment in 2019. They earned a fraction of the income of their regularly waged and salaried counterparts and were much more likely to be living in poverty.[14]

Calculations done by the ILO showed that one-fifth of the estimated 3.3 billion employed workers worldwide in 2019 (or 630 million people) were living in 'extreme or moderate poverty' (that is, they were living on less than US$3.20 per day in purchasing power parity terms).[15] The COVID-19 pandemic consigned an additional 108 million workers to 'extreme or moderate poverty' in 2020.[16] Due in part to limited access to vaccines, the pandemic's effects will be prolonged in low- and middle-income countries. Past experience also shows that economic crises allow companies to restructure their use of labour by replacing jobs or parcelling them into irregular, piecemeal employment. The ILO expects that many of the newly created jobs will pay low wages, and be poor in quality and low in productivity.[17]

In developed countries, decently paid, secure work is increasingly atypical, with those jobs created since 2008/2009 disproportionately of the low-skills, low-pay and low- or no-security variety. But the association of work and precariousness remains strongest in developing countries: only about 4% of people in vulnerable employment reside in the developed countries, according to the ILO.[18]

The predicament of workers is reflected also in the declining share of income that reaches them. Globally, the percentage of gross domestic product (GDP) paid out in wages (the global labour share) has been falling for at least two decades; it declined from 54% in 2004 to 51% in 2017.[19] Figure 2.2 shows the trend in four major economies.

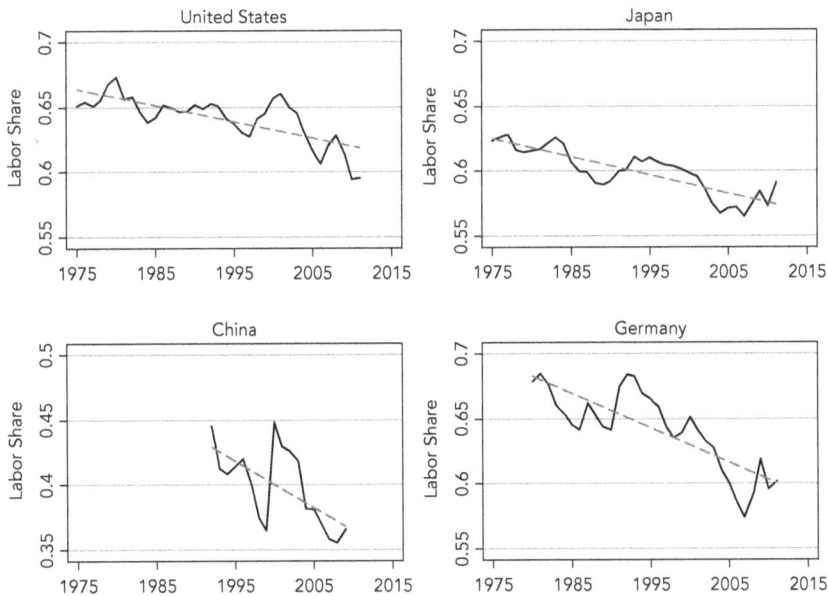

Figure 2.2: Labour share of national income in China, Germany, Japan and the United States, 1975–2013

Source: Karabarbounis, L. and B. Neiman. *The Global Decline of the Labor Share*. National Bureau of Economic Research Working Paper 19136. Washington, DC: National Bureau of Economic Research, 2013.

One might expect that the labour share in developing countries would have risen in recent decades, as their economies became more integrated internationally. Yet labour's relative income in those countries also declined, despite rises in overall productivity.[20] In the decades preceding the 1970s, labour's share of national income fluctuated slightly from year to year, but stayed within a stable range overall. Then the trend changed – across dozens of countries with very different policies and economic institutions, and across industries. Of the 59 countries with at least 15 years of data between 1975 and 2012, 42 countries showed downward trends in their labour shares – including China, India and Mexico. The fact that the labour share has been shrinking also in major locations of outsourced production (in Asia especially) indicates that the trend cannot be attributed strictly to offshore production or international trade patterns.[21] In developing countries, this downward trend has accelerated since the early 1990s, with the labour share dropping most sharply in low-income countries (Figure 2.3).[22]

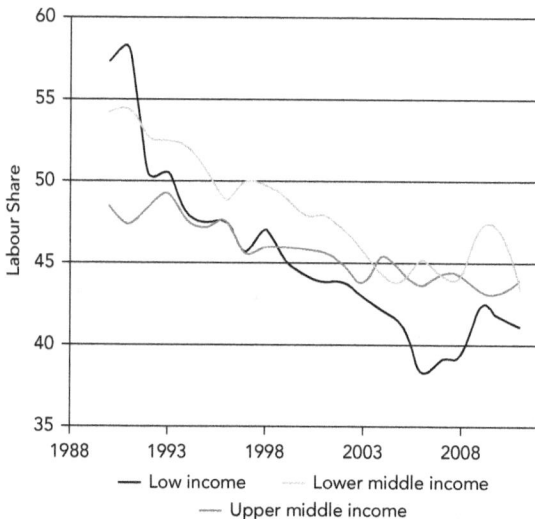

Figure 2.3:   Labour share (%) by country income classification, 1990–2011

Source: Trapp, K. *Measuring the Labour Income Share of Developing Countries: Learning from Social Accounting Matrices*. WIDER Working Paper 2015/041. Helsinki: World Institute for Development Economics Research, 2015.

Not only has the labour share of income declined, the distribution of that income among paid workers has skewed further. According to the ILO, almost half (49%) of total global pay in 2017 went to just 10% of workers; the poorest 20% of workers (around 650 million people) earned less than 1% of global labour income.[23] Workers in the top income decile earned on average US\$7 475 a month, compared with the average US\$198 earned by workers in the bottom 50%, and the US\$22 earned by those in the bottom decile.[24]

Powerful structural changes are driving these trends. Among them is the incorporation, from the 1970s onward, of tens of millions of peasants around the world into the labour reserve, mostly in Asia. This coincided with the entry of vast numbers of women into labour markets. The resulting glut of labour supply dramatically depressed the 'reservation wage' – the lowest wage that workers are willing to accept for any given job. It also removed the constraint of labour scarcity, a factor that tends to boost the bargaining power of workers. Along with sustained attacks on workers' organisations over the past forty years, those developments have pushed and held workers on the defensive.[25]

Shifting production to zones with attractively low labour costs, allied with adequate transport and other infrastructure, has been another key strategy used by capital to reduce aggregate labour costs and increase profitability. From the 1980s onward, China in particular successfully positioned itself to take advantage. However, its low-wage attractions have faded, with labour costs rising at a much faster rate than the average for G20 developing countries.[26] Since 2009, real wages in China have more than doubled. The latest available data show that real wages in Asia and the Pacific grew faster than in any other region over the 2006–2019 period.[27] Other countries, mostly in South and South-East Asia, have tried to capitalise on the proliferation of global value chains, but with limited success due to scattered geography and transport systems (across archipelagos, for instance), small labour markets and comparatively poor infrastructure. At a global level, therefore, the options for cutting labour costs by reallocating production to new zones have diminished. Africa may beckon with low wages, but volatile currencies, poor infrastructure and unreliable transport and communications systems dim its attractions for substantial industrial production beyond extractive activities.

A GLOBAL CRISIS WITH DEEP ROOTS

Thomas Piketty's analysis suggests that the global growth rates and the income distribution patterns associated with the 'golden age' of industrial capitalism in developed economies after World War II were exceptional and are unlikely to be repeated, at least in the foreseeable future.[28] That period, which ended in the early 1970s, boasted accelerated growth in productivity, output and profitability, along with rising real wages and a rich array of work-related entitlements. Much of the impetus for those improvements came from workers' movements that were powerful enough to act as sturdy stakeholders in corporatist arrangements. This occurred against the geopolitical background of the Cold War, with capitalist governments anxious to prevent worker and other social movements from radicalising to the point where they might challenge the system on fundamental terms.

The grand compromise broke down in the early 1970s, inaugurating the current phase of capitalism. As the economic historian Robert Brenner has shown, the recuperation of the Japanese and western European economies (Germany, especially), and the rise of the first generation of 'Asian tiger' economies (Hong Kong, Singapore, South Korea and Taiwan), drove fierce competition between producers.[29] That led to excess industrial capacity and overproduction in the advanced capitalist countries, which depressed economic growth and profitability. In the Group of Seven (G7) countries, the rate of profit in the manufacturing sector was 40% lower between 1970 and the early 1990s than between 1950 and 1970. Across the advanced economies, average rates of growth of output, investment, labour productivity and real wages for the years 1973 to the late 1990s were one-third to one-half of those for the years 1950 to 1973, while the average unemployment rate was more than double. The result was what Brenner termed a 'long downturn'.[30]

This was no aberration. It stemmed from 'the unplanned, uncoordinated and competitive nature of capitalist production', and from investors' 'inability to take account of the effects of their own profit-seeking on the profitability of other producers and of the economy as a whole'.[31] This feature is built into the logic of the system, which demands a relentless pursuit of growth. Failure to do so spells disaster for enterprises, while success paradoxically undermines the system as a whole and generates periodic 'long downturns'.

Many corporations responded by shifting production to low-wage zones with minimal labour protection (as discussed earlier), and by adopting just-in-time production regimes. This drove the cost of labour inputs lower and reduced the profit-sapping down-time when workers, machines and other capital inputs are idle. The world's biggest economy, the United States, was kick-started by busting unions and through harsh wage repression and dollar devaluation; real wages there reverted to 1960s levels and the number of workers trapped in poverty rose, as did income inequality.

Another outcome was a growing reluctance to invest surplus capital in the 'real economy', routing it instead towards financial speculation that promised higher returns. Under these conditions, and facilitated by deregulations driven by the United States and Britain, the financial sector grew rapidly and became domineering.[32] As the financial sector expanded, so did its need for new avenues and circuits of accumulation – and its political and economic leverage. The prerogatives, markets and institutions of finance capital became increasingly dominant in investment decisions, economic and social policymaking, and regulatory framing.

Finance capital used to function largely in service of industrial growth, by promoting industrial development through the merger of industrial and financial capital.[33] That bond has been cut. Focused on extracting maximum returns in minimum time, finance capital now typically bypasses the 'real economy' or even dismantles industrial capacity, and gravitates towards mergers, acquisitions and rentier opportunities.[34] Even ostensibly non-financial corporations now derive large proportions of profits from financial operations.[35] Corporations have aligned their priorities with those shifts; shareholder value (or financial worth) drives decisions that override longer-term economic calculations, not to mention social and ecological considerations:

> Institutional investors [demand] that nonfinancial corporations produce rapid earnings growth so they could satisfy their clients, while top nonfinancial corporate managers [need] to generate rapidly rising stock prices or their stock options would be worthless.[36]

These motive forces have kept wages and working conditions in the firing line. As noted, worker organisations were kept under sustained attack and production chains were extended to low-wage, union-free zones.[37] The 'fixes' both prolonged and compounded the underlying problems. Productivity and output recovered somewhat, but in the developed economies, wages remained under attack (except for top earners), which depressed aggregate demand. In countries undergoing rapid industrialisation (and those in the former Soviet bloc), real wages rose and the ranks of wage earners grew, but this was not enough to generate sufficient final demand to absorb the excess capacity at the global level. Intense competition continued and held the prices of consumer staples in check. That compensated somewhat for the effect of falling real wages, but it also maintained the pressure to prevent those wages from rising (which would eat into profits or push prices up). Easy credit became an attractive stopgap – allowing people to keep spending by borrowing against income they do not have (and may never have) or assets (homes especially) they do not fully own. Equity and real estate bubbles keep these improvisations aloft for a while, but they eventually crash and generate the regional and global financial crises that have become increasingly frequent since the 1970s.[38] The upshot is constant volatility.

Bewildering paradoxes catch the eye. In mid-2020, as the COVID-19 pandemic brought economies to a near-halt and forced tens of millions of people out of work, stock prices kept rising, as if oblivious to underlying realities. Wall Street profits in the first six months of 2020 were over 80% higher than the year before.[39] At first glance baffling, this was due largely to central banks flooding markets with vast amounts of liquidity (and signalling their determination to keep doing so). A regular recourse since the 2008 global financial crisis, these infusions of capital are underwriting the delinking of financialised capital from the rest of the economy, with the 'mundane' processes of production and consumption in the 'real economy' receding in importance, at least from the vantage point of finance capital.[40] Increasingly powerful sectors of the economy – particularly those centred on financialised activities – are able to flourish while productive activities crumble and poverty increases.

A dim outlook

There are indications that capitalism's resilience – its ability to renew itself through crisis – is waning. With the system steadily eviscerating the economic, social, political and ecological conditions needed for its continued growth, it may be entering a phase of prolonged instability and gradual breakdown.[41] Global warming is a dramatic aspect of this trajectory.[42] The increasing frequency, intensity and disruptive impact of climate change shocks will increase economic, social and political instability.[43] So too will zoonotic pandemic threats such as COVID-19, SARS and MERS,[44] which will continue to emerge. These upheavals will arrive unpredictably, reducing the effect of purely reactive policies (like emergency relief). The repercussions will hit the lives and communities of the poor the hardest.[45] Over the medium term, rates of global economic growth – already in secular decline – can be expected to stagnate or continue declining. This will further destabilise income distribution systems that treat waged work as the prerequisite for economic well-being. Left unchecked, these dynamics will deepen precarity, spark social and political tumult, and choke the prospects of sustained and smooth economic recovery. Protracted instability is a very realistic prospect.[46]

In this scenario, and with technological 'fixes' (such as large-scale automation) likely to be deployed at the expense of workers,[47] waged work would become an increasingly inaccessible and insufficient basis for dignified life.[48]

Compounding the impact is the diminishing access to livelihood options outside the wage economy. In recent decades, subsistence agricultural and other activities have become less viable for many of millions of people as the encroachment of industrial farming and the impact of climate change upends agrarian livelihoods. The blurring of informal and formal economies makes it much more difficult for families to diversify and juggle sources of income and subsistence, and thereby avoid complete dependence on waged work.[49] Their supplementary options for assembling viable livelihoods are being eroded rapidly. But as their reliance on regular waged work increases, access to that work narrows.

A 'fourth industrial revolution'?

There is growing alarm also about an impending mass erasure of jobs as new artificial intelligence technologies are developed and deployed more extensively. A 2013 study by Oxford University's Martin School, for example, caused consternation when it estimated that close to half of existing jobs in the United States were at high risk of being replaced by artificial intelligence and robots within the next few decades.[50] Neoclassical economics tends to dismiss the threat of automation to jobs. Rather than destroy jobs, automation is said to displace them while stimulating the creation of new, different jobs. The argument is that digitisation and automation boost productivity while lowering costs, a benefit that is partially passed on to consumers in the shape of lower prices, which in turn fuels demand, thus generating more jobs. But other outlooks are less cheerful and foresee drastic, technology-driven disruptions of labour markets and massive job losses.[51]

Sceptics remind us that similar, gloomy forecasts in the 1990s failed to materialise. Robert Solow's famous 1987 aphorism that 'you can see the computer age everywhere but in the productivity statistics' may still be appropriate despite the growing use of robots and artificial intelligence in developed economies.[52] In United States manufacturing, for example, there has been a steep increase in the use of robots since 2010, yet labour productivity growth has stayed sluggish – as it has across developed economies generally.[53]

It may be too early to detect the impact of smart machines, or measurements of output may be too imprecise in some industrial sectors to capture the impact, or the effects may be exaggerated or misunderstood. This is an interesting debate, but it is also somewhat misleading.

New productive technologies are not used simply because they exist. Their function is to increase profit by reducing input costs (over time they become cheaper than the labour inputs they replace) and/or boosting output (they produce more in less time). If a surplus of suitable labour exists and wages can be depressed – and policy environments promise to sustain those conditions – the temptation to automate jobs (at great initial expense) diminishes. Enough 'surplus value' can still be extracted from the labour of workers to generate profit and avoid costly capital expenditures. These are the conditions that currently pertain across much of the world. Conversely, if workers successfully organise and campaign for higher wages and improved working conditions and terms of employment, labour input costs will increase – and so might the attraction of labour-substituting technologies. These are not monolithic trends: they play out unevenly across industries, economies and time.

No doubt, jobs are being lost to automation and artificial intelligence (think, for instance, of bank tellers, assembly-line welders or farm workers). But that trend is occurring against a wider backdrop: the replacement of better-paid jobs (especially in the manufacturing sector) with low-productivity, low-wage work (mostly in the service sector), which adds to the pool of cheap, exploitable labour.[54] Those changes are not merely or even principally the doing of smart machines: they are driven by structural pressures in capitalist economies. Rather than consigning large proportions of workers to wageless life, an outcome some 'accelerationist' theorists predict for industrialised countries, automation at the moment is accompanying the spread of unpredictable low-grade jobs that pay poverty wages.[55] Immiserating work, rather than outright joblessness, seems to be the overriding effect.

These dynamics are cornering vast numbers of workers between the prospect of having no paid work or accepting offers on going terms, with draconian work regimes rapidly cycling workers in and out of paid employment. That maintains a constant labour surplus that is big enough to keep wages depressed for low-skilled workers, many of whom work in conditions that make it very difficult to stake and defend their rights as workers. In such a scenario, low unemployment rates need not reflect actual labour scarcity, which usually strengthens workers' bargaining power. If workers successfully press for higher wages and improved working conditions, more extensive use of labour-replacing technologies would become more attractive for companies. We can then expect the stuttering succession of precarious employment and piecemeal work to blur steadily into lengthening periods of no work for certain sectors of workers.

More jobs – particularly more decent jobs – will remain a crucial basis for livelihoods. But given current trends and outlooks, it is highly questionable that work-centric income systems can substitute for a more encompassing strategy that recasts the distribution of income and other basic means for life.[56]

SOUTH AFRICA: THE FUTURE NOW

South Africa presents a grim example of the trends described thus far, with a very large proportion of the working-age population surplus to the labour needs of the economy, high levels of poverty (including among people working for a wage) and severe inequality. The country is caught in a crisis of waged work that dates back decades, spanning periods of modest economic growth and several national development strategies and labour market reforms.[57]

South Africa's employment-to-population ratio (the proportion of the population aged 15 years and older that is in employment) has been exceptionally low for decades. It stood at an estimated 40% in 2019; the average for middle-income countries was 57%.[58]

The (narrow) unemployment rate has not fallen below 20% since the mid-1990s: in mid-2021, as the COVID-19 pandemic continued, it topped 34%. If people who had stopped looking for work were included in the calculations, 44.4% of working-age South Africans were unemployed.[59] By way of comparison, the government's 2012 National Development Plan aimed for an unemployment rate of 14% for 2020, and 6% for 2030.[60] Many of the jobless are unlikely ever to have regular employment.[61] Analysis of data for 2019 revealed that 71% of unemployed persons were 'long-term unemployed' – that is, they had been trying to find work for a period of one year or longer – and 34% had been unemployed for at least five years.[62]

The COVID-19 pandemic has brought further aggravation, reducing the employment-to-population ratio in South Africa to 36.7%.[63] Approximately 2.2 million people lost their jobs during the first three months of the first 2020 lockdown, with low-skilled workers and women worst-affected.[64] Two-thirds of job losses in the first month of that lockdown were among women.[65] Almost all workers who had lost their jobs in those early months of the pandemic were still unemployed three to four months later, after the initial lockdown had been lifted.[66]

This attrition occurred against the backdrop of chronic job scarcity and insecurity. A very large percentage of working-age adults in South Africa is superfluous to the labour needs of capital. The third-largest economy in Africa[67] operates with the paid labour of about 40% of the working-age population and by paying a substantial proportion of workers' wages so low that their survival requires subsidies from family members and the state.[68]

For a majority of low- and semi-skilled workers, working life comprises short periods of employment bracketed by unpredictable durations of unemployment (with little access to unemployment insurance). They and their jobless counterparts assemble livelihoods by juggling makeshift economic activities, qualifying for or sharing social grant payments, and servicing reciprocal arrangements.[69] The trend is long-standing and there is no indication of significant change.

Patterns of poverty and inequality

South Africa's very high unemployment rates and low wages are reflected in rising poverty levels and in widening income inequality.[70] Small sections of society monopolise the rewards of economic growth, while punishing costs are imposed on the poor.[71]

Exceptionally high unemployment, stagnant incomes for a majority of wage earners, rising energy and food prices, and great household dependency on unsustainable debt continue to pull households and individuals into poverty. More than half of South Africans – 30.4 million people – were living in poverty in 2015, the most recent year for which comprehensive national poverty data are available. Of them, almost 14 million were classified as extremely poor, meaning they could not regularly buy essential food items. Patterns of poverty continue to be skewed glaringly by race and gender. Women are more likely to be living in poverty than men, and black and coloured South Africans are much more likely to be living in poverty than other population groups.[72]

The government's 2012 National Development Plan called for reducing the percentage of South Africans living below the lower-bound poverty line from 39% in 2009 to zero in 2030.[73] The most recent national poverty data from Statistics South Africa show that 34% of South Africans were living below that level and 49% were living at or below the upper-bound poverty line in 2015.[74] The poverty gap had widened. People living in poverty in 2015 tended to be in deeper poverty than in 2006 or 2011.[75]

Regular, nutritious meals are beyond the means of a large proportion of South African households. In 2021, it cost approximately R2 945 per month to provide a family of four with a basic 'thrifty' but nutritious food basket, according to the Bureau for Food and Agricultural Policy.[76] That amount exceeded the *total* monthly expenditure of about one-quarter of households in major urban centres.[77] Conditions worsened during the COVID-19 pandemic: the percentage of South Africans who reported experiencing hunger rose from 4.3% to 7.0% during the first lockdown in 2020.[78] This was probably an underestimate: the 2018 General Household Survey had found that 11.1% of South Africans were experiencing hunger and almost 18% of households had limited access to food in 2018.[79]

Yet, even when performing listlessly, the South African economy generates great wealth – hence it being classified as an upper-middle-income country. But the distribution of that wealth is inordinately unequal. The country's highly unequal social structure continues to be reproduced along many of the same racial and spatial patterns as under apartheid.

Income and wealth inequality are among the worst in the world. The top 20% of income earners pocketed 68% of national income in 2017 (the median is 47% for similar emerging economies).[80] The poorest 40% received a little over 7% of national income, a share that has changed little for almost three decades and which is among the smallest in the world (Angola, Bolivia, Colombia, Haiti and Namibia are among the few other countries that rival South Africa's income inequality).[81]

The distribution of wealth is equally distressing. The poorest 50% of South Africans have negative net worth: in other words, their debts exceed whatever assets they own.[82] Tax and survey data show that the top 10% of income earners in South Africa own 55% of all forms of assets and 99% of all bonds and stocks held in the economy.[83] Of the estimated 38 000 'dollar millionaires' in South Africa in 2019, the vast majority were white men.[84] But inequality within population groups has also worsened dramatically, and the contribution of black South Africans to overall inequality has increased since the mid-2000s.[85]

South Africa's severe income inequalities are mirrored in access to healthcare and to quality education. In the past 25 years, state investment in the social wage has reduced inequality in access to sanitation, potable water, electricity and refuse removal. Generally, though, the affordability of those services remains a major barrier for many black South African households, especially those in rural areas.[86]

Links between waged work, poverty and inequality

Not having paid employment is an obvious and major cause of poverty. But the inverse is not necessarily true: having a job is not a sure defence against poverty. In South Africa, unemployment is estimated to be the main cause of about half of poverty. Low earnings are a major cause for the other half. From 2004 to 2012, the working poor became a significantly bigger segment of the country's large population of working-age poor. By 2012, the majority of poor South Africans in 2012 (58%, using the upper-bound poverty line) lived in a household with at least one employed person.[87]

The introduction of a national minimum wage has been a positive development, though the amount is very low, and stood at a maximum R3 320 per month in January 2021. If spread across a family of four, that is equivalent to R830 per person, less than the lower-bound poverty line (R890) and much lower than the upper-bound poverty line (R1 335).[88]

Working poverty has persisted across periods of moderate or low economic growth, persistently high levels of unemployment, a stuttering recovery from a major financial crisis and the introduction of protective labour market legislation.[89] Extremely high unemployment has kept the reservation wage very low,[90] and there has been a sustained shift towards the use of casual and subcontracted labour in ways that evade many regulatory protections. These patterns reflect companies' attempts to extract maximum profits by imposing new paradigms of work. They increasingly rely on a small core of skilled, full-time workers and a larger stock of less skilled, casual and outsourced labour that is deprived of the wages, benefits and rights enjoyed (for now) by their better-off peers.[91]

Inequality in earnings among employees has also increased in the post-apartheid period. Higher-income earners pocket a bigger share of the total wage bill than they did in 1994, while the bottom 50% of wage earners have lost ground.[92] In other words, the average real wage is propped up by the improved fortunes of small numbers of high-skilled, high-wage workers. Wage differentials, not unemployment, are the largest source of income inequality in South Africa, responsible for about 56% of inequality. Unemployment is responsible for approximately 35%, while investment income makes up the remainder.[93]

Understanding these realities

Economic growth in South Africa has been comparatively listless for decades. GDP growth averaged at 3.3% per annum in the two decades after 1994, but slumped below 2.0% during the 2008 global financial crisis. After a brief recovery, annual GDP growth has stayed below 2.0% since 2014, consistently running 2%–4% lower than the average for other middle-income countries.[94]

Mainstream economists typically attribute South Africa's low levels of investment and high unemployment primarily to microeconomic factors, such as an allegedly rigid labour market, shortages of skilled workers, low labour productivity, infrastructure constraints and bureaucratic hindrances. Those factors are not irrelevant to the predicament, but they provide a highly incomplete and misleading explanation.

The country's comparatively low rate of economic growth is due largely to the skewed structure of its economy, the unfavourable terms on which it is integrated into the global economy,[95] and, recently, the rapid growth of a voracious financial sector. The outsized influence of the latter results in extensive misallocation of capital, while also blocking structural economic change (see Chapter 6).[96] Economic policy choices since the early 1990s, some of which built on incipient policy moves of the apartheid regime in the 1980s, accelerated processes of financialisation and corporate restructuring, while inhibiting the state's capacity to manage and respond to those processes.[97]

In the analysis of Ben Fine and Zavareh Rustomjee, capital accumulation in South Africa was primarily based on extractive mining and the energy sector, and a core set of other evolving industrial sectors.[98] The latter were closely interlinked but branched weakly to other sectors of the economy, which distorted the allocation of capital and the development of industrial activities. This held back sustained industrialisation, leaving the economy with an uneven and stunted manufacturing sector. It also encouraged investment in capital-intensive industries with very limited capacity to absorb the large and growing population of low-skilled workers.[99] Economic policy choices made in the past thirty years have failed to alter these fundamental features.

Macroeconomic policy in the 1990s was focused on appeasing the concerns of corporations through a series of adjustments. They included allowing South African corporations to diversify abroad, relaxing capital controls and introducing investment incentives that enabled corporations to circumvent tax obligations and spirit profits into off-shore havens. Unlike the Asian developmental states of yesteryear, the South African state largely relinquished its sway over the banking and financial sector, including by ceding vital leverage to an independent Reserve Bank.[100] Credit, savings and investment have been channelled into capital-intensive ventures and sectors that favour the extraction of economic rents.[101] The macroeconomic policies pursued since the 1990s have thus facilitated both massive capital flight and misallocation of capital inside South Africa.

Today the South African economy rests on a stagnating industrial base, characterised by highly concentrated ownership, excessive dependency on the extractive sector (for export earnings) and other sources of rents, and heavy reliance on portfolio capital inflows to stabilise the balance of payments. A powerful financial sector has arisen, facilitated by the economic policies of both the late-apartheid and post-apartheid eras.[102]

Since 2000, the financial sector has grown almost twice as fast as GDP and it now contributes a larger share of GDP than any other sector of the economy.[103] Despite the turbo-charged growth, the sector produces little of tangible value, least of all jobs – it accounts for only about 2% of employment. Meanwhile, potentially productive sectors of the economy have shrunk,[104] with the manufacturing sector, including labour-intensive production, atrophying rather than expanding and diversifying. The textbook narrative of economic modernisation seems to be running in reverse in South Africa. It is effectively an arrested semi-industrial economy with no use for about 40% of its labour force, yet capable of generating vast wealth.[105] In these conditions it does not make sense to tie the prospect of a dignified life to waged work.

South Africa's post-apartheid labour regime was designed to promote and protect decent work. But liberalised economic policies increased both the perceived need and opportunities for companies to sidestep the provisions of the new labour regime. Labour-saving technologies were introduced where feasible, though a volatile currency made this option unpredictably expensive. As noted earlier, it was more common for companies to turn to casualised and subcontracted labour, which allowed them to squeeze workers' wages and the terms and conditions of work. Companies opted for 'restructuring production, establishing new patterns of work organisation and/or relocating production units'.[106] Those shifts had begun in the 1980s already and gathered momentum subsequently.[107]

The labour movement has struggled hard to make decent work a reality. It remains committed to centralised bargaining, and some of its affiliates have mounted successful campaigns in defence of sector-wide bargaining.[108] But powerful pressures are pushing in the opposite direction and union membership is shrinking in important sectors.[109] Despite protective labour laws, there is considerable flexibility in a labour market that is highly segmented and characterised by 'shell' wage agreements in which trade unions win high standards on paper but the protections apply to fewer and fewer workers in reality.[110] The sectors with the strongest labour market protections (manufacturing and mining) have also been the targets of deep and sustained job cuts. The situation in the public sector is somewhat anomalous, though outsourcing and subcontracting is common. Compounding matters is the labour movement's failure to organise the 'new working poor' in meaningful numbers. Organising these workers is notoriously difficult; so, too, is convincing them that the potential benefits of formalised solidarity outweigh the immediate risks of harassment and lay-offs. In addition, their work status is highly unstable as they shuttle between employment, self-employment and unemployment.[111]

Economic, labour and social policies have to respond to these realities. Economic (particularly macroeconomic and industrial) strategies and labour market policies that can both increase access to decent paid work and transition the economy onto an ecologically sustainable path are vital.

But recent decades do not offer evidence for assuming that, for a large proportion of South Africans, waged work can function as a sufficient and viable basis for avoiding poverty. The National Treasury believes that a structural reform programme can add one million jobs in a decade – but, at 100 000 jobs a year, that would be far fewer than the number of people entering the labour market each year in search of employment. The gap between people entering the workforce and the economy's capacity to provide jobs for them has widened in the past decade, and stood at nearly 20% in mid-2021. Job losses during the early months of the COVID-19 pandemic in 2020 alone approached three million.[112]

Social grants in South Africa

In the absence of significant job creation and improvements in real wages, social policy has become a vital stopgap against even greater precariousness,[113] with the expanded provision of social transfers especially important.[114]

In twentieth-century welfare states, social policy (particularly social protection) became seen as a powerful instrument for transformation. It was assigned at least five complementary functions: it had to enhance protection, redistribution, production, reproduction and freedom.[115] An important component was the redistribution of income for greater equity, which, as Thandika Mkandawire noted, also carried social, political and economic relevance:

> Redistributive social expenditures can contribute to political stability by enhancing the legitimacy of the state. Social policy, as an instrument for ensuring a sense of citizenship, is thus an important instrument of conflict management, which is in turn a prerequisite for sustained economic development.[116]

Social policy in South Africa has been less ambitious and more ambivalent than the model described by Mkandawire. In the post-apartheid era, it has been touted as a constitutive part of the country's development strategy, though the reality is more mundane.[117] To be sure, the social wage has been broadened substantially since the early 1990s and is a central component of social policy.[118] It includes the subsidised provision of certain basic services for low-income earners (including basic healthcare, school feeding programmes, sanitation, potable water, electricity, refuse removal, and primary and secondary education), as well as various forms of cash or in-kind assistance. However, cost-recovery interventions at local government level have reduced the actual benefits of some of those services. The social grant system has become an important source of livelihood support, serving as a thin but vital safety net for many millions of people.[119] The system centres on six major grants: the old-age pension, disability grant, child support grant, foster care grant, grant in aid, and the care dependency grant. All the grants are targeted, some are means-tested, but none is conditional.

The old-age pension is available to individuals aged sixty and older. It amounted to R1 890 per month in 2021.[120] In the 1990s already, pensions eclipsed migrant remittances both in terms of size and reliability as a source of economic support for poor rural households.[121]

The child support grant was worth R460 per month per child in 2021,[122] as was the 'grant in aid' – 25% less than the official food poverty line of R624[123] and almost 40% less than the average monthly cost of feeding a child a nutritious diet (R720).[124] Approximately 13 million primary child caregivers received a child support grant in 2020,[125] equal to about 30% of households. The child support grant was temporarily increased to R740 per child during the early months of the COVID-19 pandemic in 2020, before being reduced again to the previous amount. In 2020, the foster care grant was worth R1 050 – almost 2.5 times more than the child support grant,[126] while the care dependency grant amounted to R1 860.

A separate government agency, the South African Social Security Agency, administers the grants. A biometric system of identification is used and payments are made via cash advances that can be collected at automatic bank teller machines. The grants appear to be relatively well targeted towards eligible poor households, with estimates suggesting that, by the early 2010s, about 76% of grant payments were going to the poorest 40% of the population.[127] However, the system does not directly provide income support to able-bodied adults (18–59 years) who are unemployed. Paid labour continues to be regarded as the core foundation of the social order, with income support available to people who are too young, old or infirm to work (via social grants) or who are recently unemployed (via unemployment insurance).

Even the child support grant slots into this labour-centric framework. Introduced by the South African government in 1997, the grant was championed as a form of 'developmental social welfare' that would support personal and community development. As a subsidy to the basic living expenses of children, the grant is tied to the raising, educating and acculturating of future participants in the labour market.[128] It fits squarely within a paradigm that makes livelihood security dependent on the (eventual) ability to trade one's labour for a wage or salary.[129]

In 2021, approximately 11.5 million South Africans were receiving at least one social grant (mostly in the form of an old-age pension or a child support grant),[130] up from about three million in 1994.[131] These payments have become a vital source of livelihood for close to half of all households in South Africa,[132] including a large number of households with wage earners.[133] In 2018, 44% of households received at least one social grant, and 20% of households depended on these grants as their main source of income.[134] In the poorest provinces, such as Eastern Cape and Limpopo, grant payments were the main source of income for at least 30% of households.[135] Female-headed households are especially reliant on the grants.[136]

During the first year of the COVID-19 pandemic, a special Social Relief of Distress grant ('COVID-19 grant') worth R350 per month was made available to individuals not covered by the existing grants or the Unemployment Insurance Fund. In addition, the other main social grants were increased by R250 per month for six months in 2020. A caregiver's allowance worth R500 per month was also introduced for each caregiver, supplementing the child support grant. These emergency payments were extended in October 2020 and again in February 2021. Although meagre, the additional grants helped curb worsening food insecurity. But an estimated eight million people in low-income households still received no form of direct income support, a reminder of how 'leaky' and inefficient targeted systems of income transfer can be.[137]

The heavy reliance on existing social grants underscores the fact that, for a majority of working-age adults in South Africa, waged work is either unavailable or a highly unreliable basis for livelihood security and social citizenship. Social policy, however, remains grounded in the expectation that waged work is an available and sufficient source of income. Thus, the income support provided by the state goes to people who, due to age or infirmity, are not expected to sell their labour in the market. The support misses the large numbers of people for whom waged work is either unavailable, too infrequent or too poorly paid to shield them against poverty.

* * *

The conditions and trends described in this chapter are neither incidental nor fleeting. The trajectory of neoliberal capitalism, particularly in its current financialised phase, inclines towards decreasing employment rates, depressed real wages, and unstable and insecure work regimes. In these conditions, development strategies that hinge on waged work as the means to realise social and economic rights and achieve social inclusion are inappropriate.

Sheer necessity will see workers evolve new ways of organising to challenge these realities. But the instabilities and dilemmas besetting capitalism do not favour the generalised win-win compromises that gave rise to the post-World War II 'golden age' in developed economies. The past forty years provide very little basis for sunnier prospects; conditions are likely to become increasingly hostile to the productivist, work-centric models of social transformation that defined the industrial era.

Looking ahead, the likelihood of ongoing global economic instability, accumulating climate change upheavals and public health crises reinforces that scepticism.

The resultant job crisis – which encompasses joblessness, underemployment, poverty wages and inadequate social security – is a calamity. It is also an opportunity to consider additional kinds of distributive processes that are more suited to current and unfolding realities, particularly ones that are not anchored in access to waged work.

3

The Attractions of a Universal Basic Income

Everyone deserves the means for building a dignified life. For supporters, the attraction of a UBI lies in the payment's potential to indiscriminately trigger elemental but vital improvements in people's lives. These include lower poverty levels and income inequality, improved diets and health, and better education attainment for children. As a dependable source of income, it is claimed, a UBI would also reduce the stress, anxiety and vulnerability associated with irregular and low-income waged work.

A UBI would provide income-less people with a regular, dependable source of income. It would replace or supplement poverty wages and provide an income cushion for people who shuttle between insecure, low-wage jobs and stints of unemployment. Supporters argue that the payment would be more effective than most current forms of social protection at reaching people with no or very low incomes and therefore would be better at reducing severe income poverty. Since a UBI would be less intrusive than most conventional welfare instruments, it also would spare recipients the stigma and humiliation associated with targeted and means-tested support.

The payment would, in effect, also remunerate and value unpaid care and volunteer work, supporters claim, and it would subsidise participation in community activities, social networks and income-generating ventures. It would benefit workers in the labour market (affecting both the supply and demand sides), and act as a fillip to local economies (by strengthening aggregate demand). The latter effect could help shift the composition of spending towards local production and labour-intensive sectors.

Some advocates see a UBI as much more than a social policy intervention to alleviate poverty and strengthen the social safety net; they assign it transformative power. If pursued as part of a broader push for social and economic change, these proponents argue, a UBI could help rebalance power relations in the labour market, shift gender relations by strengthening women's financial independence and remunerating their domestic and care work, and support a transition away from fossil fuel-based economic models. It would alter the relationship between the state and citizens. Instead of acting as a paternalistic dispenser of assistance to 'deserving' beneficiaries, the state would serve as an indiscriminate source of support to all who need it. In this view, a UBI implies a different kind of state – one that socialises the means to dignified life. Such a transformative UBI could serve as a springboard towards a social order that no longer condemns parts of society to misery and humiliation, holding them hostage to the edict that, 'no matter how it dulls the senses and breaks the spirit, one must work'.[1]

These are rousing claims. Do they hold up?

REDUCING INCOME POVERTY

All else staying equal, a basic income payment can be expected to reduce income poverty and narrow the poverty gap, irrespective of the amount. Supporting that expectation is the documented evidence of the effects of basic income-type programmes discussed in Chapter 1. It is also backed by evidence from current cash-transfer and other income-support schemes.[2] The World Bank, which has enthusiastically promoted the expansion of cash transfers in low- and middle-income countries in recent decades, claims that cash transfers and other social safety net programmes reduced the number of people living in absolute poverty by 36% between 2008 and 2016.[3]

In South Africa, expanded eligibility and greater take-up of social grants (especially the child support grant) was singled out as an important cause of declining poverty levels in the early 2000s already.[4] Subsequent research confirmed those findings. Analysis of data from the 2010/11 Income and Expenditure Survey data showed that receipt of social grants significantly reduced poverty levels in areas with high poverty rates among the African population, in female-headed households and in rural areas.[5] Although the child support grant was worth only R260 per month in 2011, it reduced poverty levels in the Eastern Cape and Limpopo provinces by 11% and 10%, respectively.[6] According to a more recent estimate, levels of persistent poverty in South Africa would have been 8% higher in 2014/15 in the absence of social grants.[7] Gaining access directly or indirectly to state cash transfers is, according to Andries du Toit and David Neves, probably the single most important component of what they termed the 'arts of survival' for people living at the margins of the formal economy in South Africa.[8]

During 2020, the first year of the COVID-19 pandemic, the South African government introduced a monthly R350 social relief of distress grant and a monthly R500 caregivers' allowance grant. Although the eligibility criteria were restrictive, the emergency grants reduced the number of people living below the food poverty line (R585 in 2020) by more than half within less than a year, from an estimated 9.8 million to 4.1 million.[9]

While cautioning against over-attributing direct and linear effects to social grants and emphasising that they 'cannot single-handedly move people out of poverty', Stefan Granlund and Tessa Hochfeld have concluded that

> the grants have opened up new possibilities, primarily for women and pensioners, to increase their status and position in households and communities in South Africa. Social grants are indeed key to survival in impoverished rural communities in South Africa and to those who traditionally had less economic power.[10]

There is controversy elsewhere, however, about the impact of cash transfers on poverty reduction, with some studies in Latin America attributing a much larger impact to job creation and wage increases. Lena Lavinas found that 'it is primarily rising labour earnings that have accounted for the decline in poverty in Brazil, as was the case elsewhere in Latin America'.[11] Other analysis of Brazil's *Bolsa Familia* between 1999 and 2009 also indicates that minimum wage legislation (and possibly also a tightened labour market in the context of a commodity export boom) contributed considerably more to inequality reduction than did cash payments.[12]

That is not surprising, given that labour income accounted for about 70% of total income in Brazil at the time and the unemployment rate was falling: it was 10% in 1999 and it decreased over the next decade.[13] But the broader point stands: increased job creation and higher real wages, particularly at the lower end of the wage spectrum, can have a substantial income-raising effect across society. For that to happen, though, large proportions of adults must have access to wage employment, and job creation has to benefit low-skilled workers. Unfortunately, such an achievement has proved elusive in South Africa, where more than 40% of the working-age population is unemployed.[14]

South Africa's social grants system has also been credited with slowing the pace at which income inequality has widened. In one estimate, income inequality, measured by the Gini coefficient, would have been 0.74 without the payments in the early 2010s, instead of 0.69.[15] Ultimately, the redistributive effect of a UBI would depend on how it is financed, a matter discussed in more detail in Chapter 6. If financed by taxing the income and wealth of recipients above specific income thresholds, a UBI would reduce income inequality (all else being equal). But if financed by replacing current social wage provisioning that favours the poorest deciles (the scenario favoured by UBI supporters on the Right), the intervention would redistribute income upward, with a catastrophic effect on the poor.[16]

Inequality, of course, also manifests beyond the domains of income and expenditure. It operates along the axes of subordination and domination, and the uneven liberty available to people for safeguarding their interests, improving their prospects and pursuing their goals. It plays out in the respect and trust people are afforded, and it is palpable in the assigning of rank, status and entitlement. In all these respects, a UBI can contribute to narrowing inequalities.

ADVANTAGES OVER TARGETED AND CONDITIONAL SUPPORT

Crucially, the kind of UBI considered in this book reaffirms the principle of universalism and thereby satisfies the criterion of fairness. Everyone gets a UBI, a payment for which they do not have to work. Anyone who chooses to work can seek and accept work offers – and still receive the payment. Since a UBI is neither targeted nor means-tested, it sidesteps many flaws and undesirable consequences associated with conventional forms of welfare support. It does not rely on divisive and moralistic assumptions about entitlement and deservingness, and it does not propagate imageries of citizens as untrustworthy and lacking responsibility. It reduces the intrusive and overbearing features of conventional welfare support and it spares recipients the humiliation of 'proving' their impoverishment and needs to state officials. Such a UBI would also be easier to administrate. With no need to judge, ration or police income support, the state's role would shift towards indiscriminately supporting people's livelihoods and well-being.

A UBI would also be more effective than targeted and means-tested methods for distributing income to poor households. Means-tested and targeted programmes require detailed information about the intended recipients, which can pose administrative nightmares. It is often very difficult to identify people with very low or no income, since they tend not to be reflected in tax and other databases; their lives intersect minimally with the statistical and administrative arms of the state. Social or household registries would help, but they are difficult and costly to compile and almost impossible to keep up to date. Using proxy data sources (for example, unemployment insurance or tax data) to determine people's eligibility does not solve those challenges. This was evident with South Africa's COVID-19 social relief of distress grant. In the grant's initial cycle, in 2020, only 6.4 million applicants were approved, even though the eligible population was estimated at 10–12 million people.[17]

Burdensome, inaccurate and prone to error and delay, targeted programmes tend to miss substantial proportions of intended beneficiaries, and therefore are not very effective for drastically reducing income poverty, as Thandika Mkandawire has shown.[18] High exclusion rates have bedevilled targeted cash transfer programmes in Latin America and elsewhere: those rates reached up to 46% in Brazil's flagship *Bolsa Familia* programme (despite the country's relatively strong administrative capacity) and were even higher in Mexico's *Oportunidades* programme.[19] None of the 42 targeted social protection schemes investigated by Stephen Kidd and Diloa Athias[20] had exclusion errors of less than 44%; 12 of them had exclusion errors of over 70%.[21]

Yet some forms of targeting do seem valid, even necessary, for achieving a generalised desirable outcome. For instance, if the purpose of a subsidised public housing programme is to help ensure universal access to affordable housing, it makes sense to target the programme at specific eligible beneficiaries, rather than across the board. But targeting remains a highly incomplete method for pursuing a 'universalist' objective. Context matters. In a market-driven context, unless the public housing programme operates as part of an overarching housing strategy that includes financing systems, pricing restrictions, zoning regulations and so on, and that advances universalist principles, it will reproduce underlying inequalities. In and of itself, targeting does not promote universalism: it asserts differences and endorses segmentation. It is also insensitive to the small changes in people's circumstances that can shift them in and out of eligibility, making it difficult to reliably identify who should receive support at a given point, and causing interruptions and delays in the despatch and receipt of support.

Means-testing and targeting also carry the risk of establishing capricious differences between those who are deemed eligible for income and those who are not, based on ephemeral and very slight differences in income or other circumstances. In societies with pervasive and deep poverty, targeted income support ends up pivoting on a cruel, bureaucratic arbitrariness – by administratively separating and then allocating or denying support to individuals and households who, in terms of income and life circumstances, are almost indistinguishable.[22] Analysing income distribution data from Ethiopia, Malawi and Zambia, Frank Ellis found that very small differences in personal and family circumstances separated people in the bottom 50%–60% of per capita consumption.[23] When eligibility is structured around 'tiny variations in circumstance [which] ordinary people do not perceive as real differences', it feeds a sense of unfairness, resentment and social tension, Ellis concluded.[24] More generally, targeted support tends to fuel social stigma against beneficiaries and feed self-stigma among those beneficiaries.[25]

For such reasons, Thandika Mkandawire argued that, in places where very large proportions of the population are poor, targeted cash transfers defy common sense, especially if transfers to the 'non-poor' can be taxed back.[26] Similarly, Martin Ravallion has suggested that a UBI is preferable to targeted income support and 'may well make sense – possibly more sense – in places with poor information, weak capabilities for targeting, and a high poverty rate'.[27]

The pitfalls and perverse effects of targeting and means-testing are not limited to contexts of pervasive poverty. Ostensibly reflecting a compassionate concern for the poor, this 'focused' support aligns with the narrowed understandings of the state's obligations towards society during the neoliberal era. Instead of consistently enhancing people's capabilities and supporting their well-being, the state is expected merely to intervene *in extremis* to manage indigence – which emphasises difference and division. By undermining cross-class solidarities, targeted and means-tested programmes tend to reduce broad-based support for universal public provisioning and antipoverty interventions,[28] and can lead to reduced investment in and deteriorating quality of public services. Celia Kerstenetzky presciently highlighted that risk in the

Brazilian context,[29] where political and fiscal attacks (with mobilised support from the middle and upper classes) ultimately dismembered the *Bolsa Família* income transfer programme.[30] Evidence from Europe also suggests that redistribution tends to be weak in welfare systems that rely on targeted assistance to the poor, and stronger where universal provision occurs.[31]

A UBI avoids the segmentation and implicit judgements about deservedness that are associated with conditional forms of social assistance. Internationally, many cash transfer schemes are tied to certain conditions, often involving school enrolment for children and/or health-seeking behaviours. Brazil's *Bolsa Família* and Mexico's *Oportunidades* scheme are among the best-known examples, though dozens of other countries have introduced similar programmes.

Conditionalities are loaded with paternalism and distrust. They express a working assumption that many recipients will fail to use the public assistance to the benefit of their households unless forced to do so. A particular idea of the state – as a dominant though beneficent authority – is built into conditional social support. Yet there are compelling grounds for questioning a causal relationship between the conditionalities that are attached to cash transfers and the reported positive outcomes.[32] And there is scant, if any, evidence that unconditional transfers are associated with increased expenditures on so-called 'temptation goods' (such as alcohol and cigarettes): a metareview of thirty studies on cash transfers from Africa, Asia and Latin America found the evidence pointed firmly in the opposite direction.[33]

Lessons from the COVID-19 pandemic

Income support provided during the first wave of the COVID-19 pandemic in 2020 provided similar insights into the deficiencies of conditional, targeted or means-tested social protection. The emergency cash transfers provided in South Africa brought vital relief to millions of people, but were marred by serious inefficiencies and coverage gaps. Almost half of eligible individuals who were not receiving the social relief of distress grant by mid-2020 were in the poorest third of households.[34]

In the United States, as well, pandemic relief underscored the many limitations of that country's social security architecture. As analysts pointed out, work-seeking conditionalities made no sense during 'stay-home' lockdowns; the usual six-month eligibility limit for assistance was unrealistic, and the exclusion of contract and self-employed workers from support was unjust. An eventual US$600 per week unemployment insurance payment involved additional unfairness: people deemed to be 'essential workers', many of them working for very low wages, received no supplemental benefits even though they were risking their health and that of their families. In Almaz Zelleke's opinion,

> had lawmakers approved a universal US$600 weekly supplement for all, regardless of work status, essential workers would have received a well-deserved bonus while the unemployed would have received a financial cushion and the prospect of financial gain, not loss, from returning to work.[35]

The scale and nature of need that erupted during the COVID-19 pandemic also highlighted how out of date and inappropriate current forms of income support are. Due to its universality, a UBI would avoid the paternalism, arbitrariness, lack of fairness, stigmatisation, inefficiencies and burdensome administrative aspects of conditional, means-tested and/or targeted support.

PROMOTING HEALTH, EDUCATION AND WELL-BEING

That is not to dismiss entirely the potential positive effects of rationed cash transfers and other targeted forms of income support. A large amount of international evidence on the effects of both conditional and unconditional cash transfers points to the kinds of benefits that a UBI can trigger. They include improvements in maternal and child health, and children's nutritional and education status,[36] reduced psychological distress,[37] as well as enhanced dignity of the elderly and of young mothers.[38] Cash transfer programmes are associated with improvements in health outcomes, nutritional status and school attendance, and increased use of healthcare services, according to Cochrane reviews, the gold standard of study-based evidence.[39]

Significantly, a 2009 Cochrane review also highlighted the importance of wider, contextual factors for those outcomes.[40] Although plausibly the result of cash transfer programmes, the reported improvements in health outcomes also depended on access to quality primary healthcare services, for example. This is a reminder that the effects of cash-based forms of income support are shaped profoundly by the contexts in which they are deployed. They seem most effective when used as components of (rather than substitutes for) broader strategies for more egalitarian provisioning and development.

Unfortunately, cash transfers currently tend to be detached from or poorly coordinated with broader systems of social provisioning. In some cases, they are being introduced while other forms of social provisioning or support (such as education, food or fuel subsidies) are restructured or reduced.[41] Alert to these patterns of provisioning, Andrew Fischer has argued that the key consideration is not whether a cash transfer nudges people above a designated poverty line, but whether such marginal improvements occur in ways that counter or reinforce wider stratifying and segregating dynamics across society.[42] This again draws attention to the overarching importance of the roles and obligations the state assumes towards society, and the priorities it pursues.

Implied in such a perspective is the vital importance of how we discern and measure impact. When assessing cash transfers, for example, the emphasis tends to be on whether income or access to certain services and entitlements have increased. That focus is much too narrow. When gauging the impact on, for example, people's health or education, it is not enough to measure changes in health-seeking behaviour or in school attendance and attainment. We have to consider the overall availability, terms of access to, and quality of basic health and education services – not just the coverage or access of a specific section of society.

In many countries, South Africa included, health and education systems are deeply segmented and unequal, with investment and resources inordinately concentrated in private facilities that a small minority of the population can use. Overburdened and under-resourced, the public health system struggles to provide quality healthcare services, forcing households (even those with modest incomes) to spend large portions of income on private health insurance and healthcare.[43] Education and health outcomes are correspondingly unequal. A cash payment (or other intervention, such as the removal of healthcare user fees) may increase the uptake of poorly resourced and overburdened services, while leaving wider health and other inequalities untouched. In the absence of sufficient investment in public education or health infrastructure and other resources, cash transfers are unlikely to significantly improve education or health outcomes overall – which should be the objective. Thus, the *Progresa/Oportunidades* programmes in Mexico were credited with increasing food consumption levels, school attendance and certain health outcomes at relatively low cost, but actually appeared to have a negligible impact on academic performance and employment prospects.[44] Other large reviews of cash transfers have noted similar shortcomings,[45] as did Diego Sánchez-Ancochea and Lauro Mattei in their study of Brazil's *Bolsa Família*:

> Most of the evidence points to Bolsa Família's positive contribution to the reduction of poverty and inequality in the short run … Bolsa Família cannot, however, deliver a sustained improvement in health and education outcomes and a reduction of poverty and inequality in the long run. These goals will only be met through an expansion in health and education services and, especially, an improvement in their quality.[46]

The lesson is that the scale and endurance of socioeconomic benefits attributed to cash transfers and predicted for a UBI depend on their being embedded in wider strategies to uphold universalist principles, pursue egalitarian goals and create inclusive societies.[47]

BOOSTING ECONOMIES

A UBI can also affect how economies operate, including by stabilising aggregate demand. The expectation is that the payment would increase purchasing power and demand among low-income consumers, whose expenditures tend to focus on basic, locally produced and labour-intensive commodities and services. In a semi-industrialised setting such as South Africa, which does not import many basic commodities, this could further stimulate local production and job creation in some sectors.

Modelling of UBI scenarios in the United States suggests that, irrespective of the financing method (whether through increased debt or raising income taxes), basic income payments would grow the economy.[48] The larger the payment, the larger the growth effect (more than 12% growth in GDP over eight years for an annual UBI payment of US$1 000 for all adults). In addition to increases in output, the model also predicts rises in employment, labour force participation and wages.[49] Mark Blyth and Eric Lonergan argue that infusions of cash directly to households via such income transfers could also reduce dependence on the banking system for growth.[50]

On a more immediate and localised level, a UBI would support small-scale, community-based economic activities, including food production,[51] repair work and other services, as well as support community economies of care.[52] Studies of cash transfer programmes show that the payments are often used for local income-generating or bartering activities, including purchasing agricultural inputs, and for supporting community-focused initiatives such as food projects, cooperatives and cultural production.[53] This is not to romanticise the impact: in an impoverished rural area such as Keiskammahoek, in South Africa's Eastern Cape province, for example, social grants are a vital source of income, but are too small to release recipients from survivalist livelihoods. Nonetheless, the transfers provide reliable and regular means for organising and participating in community economies which otherwise would be inaccessible.[54] It is at local levels that a UBI can also provide vital support as communities struggle with the impact of climate change and the restructuring of industries and jobs as economies shift away from hydrocarbon-based activities.

SUPPORTING A JUST TRANSITION

South Africa, like every other country on the planet, is in the path of coinciding and escalating crises: the multiple upheavals associated with global warming, including floods and prolonged droughts; zoonotic disease epidemics that emerge from the destabilisation of ecologies by unchecked extractive activities; successive financial crises; increasing social precarity; and the faltering legitimacy of political systems.

In every foreseeable outlook, economies will have to shift progressively away from fossil-fuel dependency and greenhouse gas-intensive modes of extraction, production and mobility. This will require well-targeted investments and policies for economic diversification and rapid development of new or nascent sectors. Since these changes will especially affect workers and communities whose livelihoods currently depend on the fossil fuel-based activities, it is vital, as noted in the Paris Agreement, to also prepare a 'just transition of the workforce'.[55] In addition to its many other benefits, a UBI can be an important supplement to that process and to the wider project of a just transition.

As with a UBI, there are competing understandings of a just transition and of a 'green economy'.[56] While some conceptions are compatible with 'green growth' economic models that 'perpetuate or exacerbate current patterns of inequity',[57] others focus on achieving wide-ranging social and environmental justice. It is important to note, as Dimitris Stevis and Romain Felli do,[58] that these different conceptions imply different degrees of concern about social inequality and particularly about the fact that environmental harm – and the responsibility for that harm – is distributed unequally between and across societies.

In more conversative understandings of a just transition, the scale and scope of interventions tend to be narrow. There is a focus, for example, on incentivising renewables and 'green jobs', promoting 'green consumerism', pursuing carbon trading and 'green techno-fixes' such as carbon sequestration, while leaving untouched the political economies that drive ecological crisis and generate social injustice. Somehow, in the face of ecological collapse, there survives a compulsion to turn a 'system-threatening prospect into a short-term source of commodification, speculation and profit'.[59]

A deep just transition

In this book we favour a concept of 'just transition' that emphasises the links between ecological catastrophe, economic exploitation and social injustice – sometimes referred to as a deep just transition. It recognises the need for structural changes that drastically reduce the harm done to both people and the environment, and that promote a fair distribution of resources and the means for dignified life.[60] It rejects the idea 'that industrial societies can be made sustainable with modest adjustments and corrections'[61] or, to use the cliché favoured by policymakers during the COVID-19 pandemic, by merely 'building back better'.

The principle of equity is central. A deep just transition involves actions and seeks outcomes that are indiscriminately good for both humans and the ecologies that sustain us[62] and that can overcome long-standing inequities and inequalities.[63] It therefore slots into a broader emancipatory project. At a minimum, it has to prevent the impact of environmentally destructive human activities, of global warming, and of mitigating actions from being deflected onto disadvantaged communities.[64] And it has to confront the fact that, even though low-income communities are least responsible for the ecological crisis, they are most affected by it. This is clear in South Africa, where racism, economic exploitation and expropriation, and environmental destruction overlap horrendously.

A deep just transition requires pursuing – in a unified way – both environmental and social justice; it therefore cannot be entrusted to market forces that are nudged along by state incentives and regulation.[65] It demands an active and accountable state that can manage phased, long-term strategies and establish the necessary conditions and supportive institutional arrangements. Central elements of a deep just transition include ending investments and subsidies in extractive and carbon-intensive industries; shifting to renewable energy sources and low-carbon modes of production, distribution and transport; repairing environmental damage; and supporting workers and communities affected by the restructuring. While the state is responsible for stewarding these changes, the transition will have to be driven also from the community level upwards – and it will have to align with the understandings, support and actions of communities and the workers among them.

The environmental justice movement routinely encounters 'job blackmail' tactics, with companies claiming that tighter environmental regulation or restructuring will destroy jobs and livelihoods. Existing environmental protections in industrialised settings have tended to have minimal negative effects on employment,[66] and there is evidence that innovative transitions to environmentally sustainable economic activities can lead to increases in employment.[67] But expectations of a frictionless transition to an environmentally sustainable and just economic model do seem unrealistic: workers and communities who depend on mining and other extractive industries, and on fossil fuel-based energy and energy-intensive production, will be affected, as the United Nations Framework Convention on Climate Change recognises.[68]

It is therefore vital that public policy minimises the disruptive impact of the transition to a low-carbon economy and supports affected workers and their communities.[69] Active labour market policies (including education, retraining and subsidised employment) are among the interventions needed to protect affected workers and communities.[70] However, as Dimitris Stevis and Romain Felli have warned:

> compensation or retraining may alleviate the distress of laid-off workers but they often do not extend to the community in which these workers are embedded ... just transitions have to take into account all the affected parties, as well as the unequal power relations amongst them.[71]

By providing predictable income support across entire communities, a UBI can be an important element of a phased, equitable transition. In doing so, it can also help create space for labour environmentalism to go beyond defending jobs in a 'green economy' and to pursue broader economic and social emancipation.

Linking a universal basic income to a just transition in South Africa

The South African government's approach to climate change policy to date has lacked ambition, even though it is the 13th-largest emitter of carbon dioxide in the world.[72] The emphasis has been on 'bringing the efficiency of the market to bear on nature and its reproduction',[73] with both policy and practice reflecting the continued power of corporations active in the extractive and energy sectors. Its renewable energy policy, for example, relies chiefly on competitive, private sector provision, encouraged by subsidies and other incentives. The Integrated Resource Plan 2010–2030 sets out an unaspiring route that combines decommissioning coal-fired power stations and increasing the uptake of renewable energy with adding new coal-fired power. This hesitant approach reflects, at root, political-economic challenges – including an apparent inability of the state to subject powerful corporate actors[74] to a state-led restructuring process, and the timid commitment of important trade unions to support such a transition.

The mining and utilities sectors in South Africa are prime targets for shifting away from a carbon-intensive model, with coal mining and electricity generation particular priorities. The country's abundant coal reserves – it is the world's seventh-largest coal producer – favoured the development of a carbon-intensive economy that relies heavily on cheap coal, in particular coal-based electricity generation.[75] 'Mining grew through its reliance on coal energy and the coal industry grew through mining's ever-growing demands for more energy', as Michelle Williams has pointed out.[76]

South Africa relies on coal for 90% of its electricity and 25% of its liquid fuel production.[77] However, it is technically feasible to decarbonise the power sector and transition to a renewable energy system. The falling prices of renewables add to the appeal and viability of such a strategy, as do the job-creating prospects.[78] But those changes will affect the livelihoods of many thousands of workers and their families and communities, at least in the short term.

The coal mining industry employed about 94 000 workers in 2017, mostly in Mpumalanga,[79] while Eskom (the national electricity supplier) employed about 47 000 workers[80] and Sasol (the state-owned petroleum-from-coal enterprise) about 28 000 workers.[81] A shift to renewables that gradually shutters the coal mining industry and coal-fired electricity would seem to be dauntingly costly in terms of jobs (and wages) lost. A UBI would compensate only very partially for the lost incomes.[82] A specific transition strategy for the affected industries is needed. It will have to be state-brokered and driven by trade union organising if workers are to be properly protected (including via severance packages) and have viable post-restructuring livelihoods.[83] Such a strategy is both feasible and affordable.

Calculations done by Michelle Cruywagen and colleagues[84] suggest that if coal mining in South Africa were to be entirely phased out over twenty years alongside 'natural' attrition via retirement in the workforce, an average 2 700 workers per year would need to be shifted into other employment and/or receive livelihood support until they can do so.[85] If the transition away from coal halves the labour force over the next two decades, it will entail 600 younger workers annually requiring new employment. The scale of this challenge seems manageable.[86]

In Cruywagen's estimates, it would cost about R16 billion over twenty years to shrink the coal mining workforce by 75%.[87] By way of comparison, according to estimates done by the International Institute for Sustainable Development, coal-based fuels produced by Sasol's Secunda plant received more than R8 billion in total government support during 2019 alone.[88] The direct, worker-related transition in this sector therefore seems manageable.[89]

But beyond this lies the wider challenge of supporting the communities in which those industries operate. Some of this community-level support can be built into sector transition strategies (for example, via the 'rehabilitation' component in the estimates of Cruywagen and her colleagues). And some of it would come via a UBI, functioning in the background as a support system to ease the 'collateral' costs of restructuring and bring income support to workers and communities who indirectly depend on income and other resources linked to the phased-out industries.

A UBI therefore would address the need for interventions that go beyond job substitution, worker retraining and severance packages. By providing tangible recompense, it would also respond to the historical practices of dumping onto disadvantaged communities many of the hidden costs associated with industrial growth and restructuring. By extending predictable, regular income support to the households and wider communities of vulnerable workers, it can help soften potential resistance to restructuring and help counter the job blackmail tactics that are customarily used against the environmental justice movement.[90]

A UBI can also support activities that drive social reproduction and improve well-being and livelihood security in communities, such as local food production, mutual aid networks, repair work and local services, and artisanal and cultural production. Neighbourhood-level food production and urban agriculture will become increasingly important as climate change disruptions accumulate. In South Africa, food security is predicted to deteriorate due to rising food prices (as input costs rise, extreme weather phenomena cause crop damage or failure, and arable land is diverted from food production to biofuels).[91] Regulatory and other state interventions will be crucial to counter food price inflation, as will be systematic support for greater food self-sufficiency at community level, which a UBI can help underwrite. In these varied ways, a UBI that supports community livelihoods and sustainability can be a powerful component of a just transition.

PROTECTING AND SUPPORTING WORKERS

Some supporters of a UBI claim that such a scheme is needed to protect workers against an anticipated erasure of jobs, as smart machines displace work which humans used to perform.[92] As discussed in Chapter 2, predictions about the impact of a 'fourth industrial revolution' are vulnerable to charges of exaggeration[93] or of misreading the evidence.[94] They also tend to rely on blunt understandings of why new technologies are deployed in capitalist economies.[95] New technologies are not used simply because they are available. Companies tend to try to operate in a 'goldilocks zone', where they can employ enough automation to hoist profits and depress labour costs, while avoiding the major capital expenditures of full-scale conversion. This is evident also in a country such as South Africa, which has to finance technology imports and maintenance with a volatile currency and in a vulnerable balance of payments context. Artificial intelligence and other automating technologies are highly attractive in some service sectors – for example, banking, communications and media. However, the incentive to automate low-wage, low-skill work tends to be offset by the abundance of cheap, quickly replaceable labour. In the South African setting, the case for a UBI draws its strength perhaps less from the prospect of a 'fourth industrial revolution' than from the other, less literal effects of such a payment.

THE TRANSFORMATIVE POTENTIAL OF A UNIVERSAL BASIC INCOME

For supporters on the Left, the appeal of a UBI goes beyond the upliftment and well-being of individuals. They see it as a forward-looking intervention which, if used as part of wider strategies for social and economic change, has a strong transformative potential.[96] A UBI would be attuned to unfolding realities in which precarity and distress is not an aberration, but a chronic phenomenon that threatens ever-larger parts of society, including people in paid employment.[97] As the link between waged work and secure livelihoods continues to fray, systems providing temporary, conditional redress and support are no longer suitable. In settings where that link has been effectively severed – such as South Africa – those systems are plainly deficient. A UBI recognises that in these conditions, social citizenship and societal well-being cannot hinge strictly on paid work.

A liberating effect

Part of a UBI's radical promise lies in its potential to relieve the fundamental unfreedom which workers, employed or not, are subjected to in capitalist society: the compulsion to work for a living. A UBI could weaken the most powerful sanction capital commands, which is the threat of hunger and deprivation. Social policy typically reinforces that power by affording assistance only to those who are too young, old or frail to do waged work, or to those who can demonstrate a consistent willingness to sell their labour. A UBI can destabilise that coercive principle. In theory, the right to turn down offers of employment is essential for a well-functioning labour market; after all, a free contract requires that both parties have the ability to decline an offer. But in the absence of other sources of livelihood, labour markets are intrinsically coercive – all the more so when jobs are scarce. Capitalist economies drastically skew power relations between employers and workers, and the imbalance is reinforced institutionally, including through labour market regulation and social policy design.

If large enough, a dependable source of income that is independent of waged work would reduce that power imbalance, by providing workers with the means to hold out for improved offers – in line with Michal Kalecki's argument that employers' power would diminish if people could make a living without having to accept whatever job was on offer.[98] Erik Olin Wright saw even greater potential and argued that a generous UBI that releases people from the duress of selling their labour at the going rate and on prevailing terms could destabilise capitalist class relations:

> A generous, unconditional basic income which would allow employees a meaningful exit option from the employment relation that directly transforms the character of power within the class relations of capitalist society.[99]

That expectation might seem overambitious. A more literal positive effect – on wage levels – seems more plausible. A UBI that enables sufficient numbers of workers to refuse demeaning, undesirable work should tighten the labour supply, leading to upward pressure on the reservation wage (the lowest wage at which workers are likely to perform a given task). This could have a kick-on effect across other wage bands (in the manner of a minimum wage). By endowing 'the weakest with bargaining power',[100] a UBI would function like a 'permanent strike fund',[101] and offer a basis for altering the balance of power between workers and employers:

> Where workers individually have easier exit options, employers may have greater incentives to agree to new forms of collective cooperation with organizations of workers.[102]

Similarly, Yanis Varoufakis sees a UBI not as a mere safety net, but as a foundation for free, enabled action.[103] To the extent that the payment enables people to turn down or leave jobs without risking penury, it would introduce countervailing power, he believes. It would grant people the freedom not to sell their labour and to withdraw, at least temporarily, from a 'race to the bottom' that pits low-skilled workers against one another. If the bare necessities of life can be secured elsewhere, exploitative or demeaning wage labour is no longer the only option on the table.

These expectations remain untested in practice. Even if realised, the extent of such empowering and liberating effects would depend on the size of the UBI: the larger the amount, the stronger the effect. A small UBI, which finances only short breaks between jobs, may subsidise the search for (better-paying) employment without releasing people from the compulsion of waged labour. This could add upward pressure to wages and increase people's scope for choice, but it would lack broader liberating power.

Critics, meanwhile, dispute the likelihood of positive work-related outcomes. They argue that if a basic income is too small, people would still be compelled to accept low-wage jobs in order to survive. This would subsidise low-wage employers, undermine wage demands, weaken worker organisations and boost the coercive power of employers and the market.[104] Those are important concerns. In Canada, the United Kingdom and the United States, for example, businesses are adept at using welfare benefits to suppress wages. But those concerns seem less applicable in a setting such as South Africa, where the alternative for exceptionally large proportions of workers is not between 'bad' jobs and 'better' jobs, but between any jobs and no jobs. For many millions of people, not having paid work is not a worst-case alternative; it is the default reality. A UBI that augments their ability to survive in that reality is likely also to boost their ability to say 'no' to demeaning offers of work.

Critics also warn of other possible perverse outcomes. If the ability to refuse degrading, low-wage jobs pushes wages higher, could it lead to the gradual replacement of those jobs with new technologies, again tilting the job supply/demand balance against low-skilled workers? Their jobs are preponderantly in the service sector, and some are indeed eminently replaceable (for example, store check-outs, customer services, product packaging and shipping). However, especially in the care sector (where women predominate), many of these jobs involve tasks and capacities which machines cannot provide, and which will continue to require human labour. We can expect the demand for care work and other forms of social reproductive labour to remain high.

Empowering women and shifting gender relations

Social reproductive labour refers to activities that nurture future workers and sustain current ones, and that transfer social knowledge and skills across generations. They are 'the set of tasks that together maintain and reproduce life, both daily and generationally'.[105] This labour includes domestic work, child-rearing, care for sick and infirm family members, and building and maintaining social bonds – making it 'an indispensable condition for the possibility of capitalist production'.[106] The work of social reproduction and the resources needed for it are taken for granted, as a sort of 'gift'; capital treats it as a free and infinitely available resource, much as it treats non-human nature.[107] The work is seldom acknowledged and rarely remunerated, even though societies and economies cannot function without it.

Historically, the responsibility for social reproduction has been laid at the feet of women and girls, a gender division that was intensified under capitalism, with men assigned the role of wage-earning 'breadwinners'. Broadly speaking, economic production was 'masculinised' and separated from 'feminised' social reproduction. Economic production was rewarded with wages, while social reproduction was deemed the 'natural destiny' of women – with entire societies and economies relying on the routine exploitation of women's and girls' labour, time, energy and life prospects. This process also plays out along class and racial lines – glaringly so in places like South Africa, where, as Jacklyn Cock reminds us,

> the work of social reproduction is mostly performed by black, working-class women, either in their own homes or in a commodified form in the households of the dominant classes as domestic workers.[108]

The gendered character of social reproductive labour also highlights the deficiency of the wage system as the core mechanism for distributing income across society: it is both highly incomplete and iniquitous. The family, and its reliance on gendered exploitation, also does not currently function as a fair and sound basis for social reproduction.

A 'crisis of care' has arisen. From the mid-twentieth century onward, welfare states in wealthy countries increased state support for social reproduction through, for example, tax credits, subsidised child and frail care, and other subsidies – moves that also enabled larger numbers of women to enter the labour market. Those shifts were largely in tune with demands of the feminist movement. After the 1970s, as neoliberal restructuring intensified, state support for social reproduction was cut back, while women came under greater pressure to work for a wage or salary, as falling real wages and social cuts made it increasingly difficult to sustain families on a single wage. This intensified the exploitation of women's labour, both in the domestic domain and in waged work (where women are channelled disproportionately into energy-sapping, low-wage jobs). The hours of paid work needed to sustain a family have risen, as have the hours needed for social reproductive labour, creating a crisis of care.[109]

This crisis does not play out uniformly; it is experienced differently, depending on class and location. In most of the global South, the severe double burden of wage and social reproductive labour associated with neoliberal capitalism has been the norm for many decades, with women simultaneously performing care work and poorly paid or unpaid piecemeal labour.

Some feminist theorists therefore see in a UBI a potential to present 'a more rational and equitable way to sustain the conditions that allow the economy – narrowly conceived as the waged sector – to exist'.[110] Although it would not directly remunerate women's domestic and other care work, it would implicitly recognise the value of that unpaid work (and the fact that men, employed or not, enjoy a free ride on women's unpaid labour).[111] By undermining 'the primacy of waged labor as the most legitimate form of human behavior',[112] a UBI might subvert those gendered roles and it could help blur the normative distinctions between people with paid work and those who perform unpaid work. If a UBI enables people to perform care and social reproductive work with greater economic security, it might contribute to a fairer distribution of that work across society.[113] Such an effect becomes even more important in the context of the climate crisis and especially in settings like South Africa, where the impact of that crisis is channelled inordinately into the lives of black working-class women.[114]

A UBI could then contribute to women's economic independence, which many feminists have seen as a prerequisite for women to achieve autonomy, realise their rights and social citizenship, and improve their general well-being.[115] Financial insecurity, for example, compels many women to enter into or remain in relationships and households that are abusive and dangerous. A UBI will not eliminate those realities, but it could introduce additional options for women. Unlike many current forms of welfare support, where eligibility is determined at household level, a UBI would be paid to individuals, which could increase women's autonomy and life options, including by enabling them to leave abusive relationships.[116] It is possible that a UBI, if designed and deployed appropriately, could also make waged work, care work, marriage contracts and child-rearing more of a choice than they currently are for women.[117]

Feminists differ, however, on the desirability of a mechanism such as a UBI. Many place high value on waged work as a source of autonomy for women, boosting their self-esteem and connecting them to the 'sociality' of work and collegial networks. They warn that a UBI would entrench the sexual division of labour by encouraging and enabling women to keep working in the domestic sphere.[118] The preference is to enable women to be equal wage-earners with men. In the context of supportive changes, including subsidised childcare, economic policies that stimulate large numbers of new jobs, social insurance reforms, and wage and work-place reforms, this would have more durable and far-reaching effects than a UBI, it is argued. The Scandinavian countries opted for such an approach, which still emphasises the employment ethic.[119]

At root, that stance seems similar to the concern that a UBI would be a disincentive for waged work – though it seems odd to disapprove of an inter-vention that increases rather than narrows women's choices. The payment would increase women's options to decide and act autonomously, even if the choice is to not perform waged labour. In addition, opting out of the formal labour market need not be a bad thing, in Kathi Weeks' view, par-ticularly for the many women who toil simultaneously in paid employment and unpaid work at home: '[S]lavery to an assembly line is not a liberation from slavery to a kitchen sink.'[120]

This is not to overstate the transformative power of an intervention that boosts the choices of individuals. Receipt of the child support grant in South Africa, for example, empowers women to control how the money is spent and can contribute to their financial autonomy.[121] Stefan Granlund and Tessa Hochfeld have noted the effects at community level, especially, where the grant enables many women to maintain reciprocal relations and foster solidarity in their communities (for example, by participating in rotating savings schemes and other social networks).[122] But there is scant evidence that the grant changes social relations or reshapes gender inequalities.[123] It seems unrealistic to expect that cash payments on their own would affect the gendered division of social reproductive labour. Women's choices are shaped by social relations and structures that are too well-entrenched to be dislodged by meagre cash transfers. But, if large enough, a UBI could help destabilise those power relations if it operates alongside other liberating interventions.

Struggles for a UBI, a shorter work week, livable wages, public childcare services and other social wage provisions can potentially combine into reorganising social reproductive work along fairer lines. This echoes the radical vision of the Wages for Housework movement of the 1970s, which was aimed in part at fusing feminist demands with working-class consciousness.[124] Recognising this, Lindsey Macdonald has sought to position the UBI demand within the history of women's struggles over reproductive work – an important move that underlines the different (in this case, gendered) ways in which exploitation occurs and surplus value is extracted under capitalism.[125] She argues that a UBI that challenges capital's ability to freeload on unpaid social reproductive work 'poses a similar set of provocations as Wages for Housework.'[126]

Indeed, the burden of unpaid care work tends to be in inverse relation to the provision and quality of essential services through public institutions such as schools, hospitals, day care, hospices and so on. This has been glaringly obvious during the AIDS pandemic in hard-hit societies like

South Africa. Home- and community-based care, performed mainly by women, has been celebrated as an example of resilience and solidarity (which it is), but too often without acknowledging the underlying deflection of obligations (and costs) from the public sector to communities, households and the women in them.[127]

The critiques also assume that paid employment is a realistic option for significant proportions of women – which is patently not the case for black African women in South Africa, for example. In such contexts, a UBI that is paid alongside other social provisioning will likely be of greater benefit for women than the faint prospect of waged work. Moreover, entry into the labour market is not necessarily liberating for all women. Class and race heavily influence those outcomes; some women find themselves exchanging the proverbial 'chains of the kitchen sink' for the chains of the call-centre or sweat shop.

The image of isolated women, trapped in nuclear family structures and lives of 'mandatory domesticity',[128] also seems somewhat parochial. It may fit the suburbs of wealthy countries, but it seems less appropriate in many other settings, where domestic and other care work often occurs in lively social contexts and is shared across households as one of many webs of reciprocal exchange. Large proportions of ostensibly 'home-making' women also participate in communal activities, work in informal economies to supplement incomes, and volunteer their labour.[129] In addition, many of the non-material benefits ascribed to waged work are also attainable through unpaid work, including voluntary work.[130]

A UBI potentially supports women's capabilities to engage in those and other forms of (re)productive work, including neighbourhood-level food production, participation in community organisations, volunteer work and income-generating activities.[131] But those effects and their extent will depend on the UBI amount and on the availability of essential infrastructure and supportive social provisioning, a concern Shireen Hassim has raised more generally in relation to the impact of social welfare on women.[132] The empowering effect of a UBI will be greatly reduced in settings that lack access to basic social and other services.

Untethering life from wage labour

A central tenet of industrial capitalism is the idea that human beings realise themselves as social beings through their labour, for which they are remunerated. That claim is broadcast across the political spectrum – from Karl Marx and Friedrich Engels positing the 'equal liability of all to work' as one of the ten distinguishing features of a communist society,[133] to former US president Richard Nixon's insistence that 'labour is good in itself; that a man or woman becomes a better person by virtue of the act of working'.[134] It is an outlook that supports the neoliberal insistence that 'full citizenship revolves around individual responsibility, labour market activation, and the avoidance of dependence on public spending'.[135]

In American writer Kurt Vonnegut's first novel, *Player Piano*, machines have taken over all menial work and people's basic needs are met – but Vonnegut pictures a world of unhappiness, as people struggle to cope without the anchoring and dignity they used to derive from waged work.[136] He was channelling the received wisdom that not working for a living is demoralising, isolating and unhealthy – for reasons beyond sheer material need. A great deal of evidence supports that position.

Lacking access to the social intercourse which many jobs facilitate, unemployed individuals tend to have significantly worse health and well-being than people in paid work,[137] and involuntary unemployment is strongly associated with depression and feelings of diminished self-worth.[138] Marie Jahoda's research attributed such negative outcomes to unemployed people's lack of access to the positive features of waged work, such as shared experiences, collective purpose and teamwork, structured time, affirmed status and identity, and regular activity.[139] There is evidence that some recipients of unemployment benefits opt to work in 'hidden' economies not only to earn extra money but also to restore a sense of pride, status and respect.[140] When these positive aspects of waged work are unavailable to people, their health tends to suffer.

Andrew Clark and Andrew Oswald's research found high levels of stress, unhappiness and loss of self-esteem among unemployed people.[141] Any combination of those effects can encourage behaviours that undermine physical and mental health, such as self-isolation, poor diet, lack of exercise, excessive smoking, and alcohol or narcotic abuse. Unemployment and job insecurity are also linked to a higher risk of suicide, according to analysis of data collected from 63 countries between 2000 and 2011,[142] although the association between unemployment and suicide appears to be strongest in high-income countries.[143] Suicide is an extreme reaction, but it seems clear that the general life satisfaction of unemployed individuals diminishes significantly and is not fully restored even after having been unemployed for a long time. By contrast, people who return to work after unemployment appear to have better health than those who remain unemployed.[144] For such reasons, Cynthia Estlund, for example, insists that 'work should remain a central organising feature of people's economic and social lives, and should be one goal of public policy even in a future in which there is less work to go around'.[145]

Yet the effects attributed to being unemployed are not necessarily inherent in the fact of joblessness.[146] They are magnified by the knowledge (and reality) that not having paid work can render one indigent, and they seem to diminish when unemployment is widespread.[147] Generous unemployment benefits have been found to offset the impact of unemployment on suicide rates, for example.[148] Other research indicates that life satisfaction among the long-term unemployed increases significantly when they officially retire from the labour market and the social expectation of wage labour is lifted.[149] This suggests that much of the psychological damage associated with unemployment is tied to the social and self-stigma that clings to joblessness. Daniel Sage's analysis of the large European Values Study supports that view.[150] He found that people who are less aligned with prevailing employment norms tend to have better well-being than those who subscribe to strong work ethics. Other analysis of the same datasets has also concluded that the well-being of unemployed men tends to be lower in countries that are marked by a strong social norm to work for wages.[151] One way to reduce the harmful effects of unemployment would be to challenge the centrality of paid work in our lives.

Context matters in other ways as well. Jobless women in societies with high rates of female participation in the labour market appear to have more adverse experiences of unemployment than jobless women elsewhere.[152] That hints at another, overlooked aspect: the stigma attached to unemployment is laden with patriarchal notions of what constitutes work and what kinds of work are valued. In South Africa, for example, where waged work is intimately bound up with conservative gender roles and theatrical norms of masculinity, unemployment is closely associated with feelings of emasculation, self-disdain, anxiety and anger among men.[153] But it is highly unusual to attribute low self-esteem and depression to interventions that relieve women of some of the work burdens of child- and homecare (for example, through the introduction of piped water or washing machines or hired care). Instead, those changes are typically seen as liberating. Our standard ideas about the innate value and worthiness of paid work have been refracted through these skewed gender roles and our distorted assumptions about what counts as work.

There is good reason to question assumptions that equate paid employment with a normal, healthy state of being and that ascribe automatic moral value to paid work. The association of waged work with happiness and well-being derives as much from subjective experience as from social norms that valorise that work and stigmatise unemployment. A UBI that delinks subsistence from the wage invites us to think beyond the standard notions of what constitutes work and the hierarchies of value and reward that are embedded in those assumptions.[154] It can help destabilise the moralising binary that establishes waged work as a prerequisite for recognition, dignity and entitlement, while denigrating unemployment as a symptom of shiftlessness, sloth and defective character.

One may also ask: if not having paid work is unhealthy, does the inverse hold: does paid employment make or keep one healthy? For very many workers, such a claim is untrue and indefensible, as the prevalence of workplace-related physical injuries and mental health complaints attest. According to the ILO, approximately 2.8 million workers died due to occupational accidents in 2017 and there were more than 374 million non-fatal work-related injuries (that led to at least four days' absence from work).[155] The latter estimate rises considerably once people struggling with work-related illnesses (such as respiratory and cardiovascular diseases) and complaints (such as chronic back pain) are added.[156] There is good evidence that low-paying, stressful jobs are at least as harmful to people's health as unemployment.[157] Not only does the valorisation of waged work seem entangled in the coerced reliance on wages for survival, for very many workers it does not correlate with their lived experiences of work – as Studs Terkel reminded readers in the opening passages to his book *Working*, which,

> being about work, is by its very nature about violence – to the spirit as well as to the body. It is about ulcers as well as accidents, about shouting matches as well as fistfights, about nervous breakdowns as well as kicking the dog around. It is, above all (or beneath all), about daily humiliations. To survive the day is triumph enough for the walking wounded among the great many of us.[158]

Nonetheless, productivist ideology and the celebration of waged work remain dominant – despite the scarcity of paid work in many settings and the fact that much of the work on offer is demeaning, exploitative and life-sapping. A long-standing reality outside industrialised economies, and particularly in the informal sector, the divide between private and work life is becoming increasingly porous also in developed economies as 24/7, on-call labour becomes pervasive and salaries are delinked from working hours.[159] These experiences have intensified during the COVID-19 lockdowns and are likely to become even more generalised in the future. The effects are especially egregious for waged workers. Employers are stripping waged work of security while commanding control over ever-growing parts of workers' lives. That includes the aggressive and 'pervasive process of enclosure',[160] in which people are required not only to sell their time, skills and labour, but their civility, emotions and dignity. Increasingly, it is life itself that is put to work.[161] The challenge is not simply to find work that can finance the means to life, but to reclaim life from the insatiable demands of the work that is on offer.

A UBI that enables people to meet their basic needs without routinely having to sell their labour would delink subsistence from waged work. At a minimum, such a UBI would have to be universal and unconditional, provide enough income to subsist on, and supplement rather than replace other forms of social support. A UBI of that sort would open the possibility to think beyond the hierarchies of entitlement and worth that are baked into current definitions of work, making it more than a means for individual enablement. By detaching social citizenship from waged work, a UBI could become a liberating intervention that helps unsettle power relations across society.[162]

Some proponents see that liberating potential evolving into an eventual repudiation of waged work as the organising framework for much of human life. This would go beyond the ability to reject specific job offers: it would facilitate a rebellion against the entire system of coerced 'economic cooperation' on which capital accumulation rests. The refusal would not be an individual stance, but an aspect of collective political action, the goal of which 'is to transform the institutions and ideologies that tether us to the existing world of work, waged and unwaged', as Kathi Weeks put it.[163]

Such a transgressive potential has drawn 'futurist' or 'accelerationist' theorists (such as Aaron Bastani,[164] Nick Srnicek and Alex Williams,[165] and Paul Mason[166]) to a UBI as an important element for transitioning to a post-work (and possibly post-capitalist) society. They picture scenarios in which labour-replacing smart machines become ubiquitous, generating wealth and prosperity while rendering paid employment increasingly superfluous. Instead of leading to grim dystopias, technology could be used to create economies that abolish scarcity and share prosperity. This would make it possible to redistribute paid working hours more equitably across populations, with a UBI redistributing income.

The post-work vision has a rich intellectual pedigree that encompasses thinkers like Paul Lafargue[167] in the nineteenth century to Bertrand Russell and André Gorz in the twentieth century,[168] and Aaron Bastani in the twenty-first.[169] At risk of oversimplification, they have all visualised scenarios in which wage relations steadily lose their pre-eminence in securing the means for life, in organising societies and fuelling economies, and in conferring fulfilment and worth. Post-work, though, does not mean 'no work'. An idealised post-work scenario would restructure the (im)balance between waged work and human life. Waged work would not disappear entirely, but it would shed its economic, social and moral authority as the central axis for structuring human life and society. People would be able to reclaim their time and liberty, as well as opportunities for socially and personally productive activities, and for reorganising society.[170] 'Accelerationists' like Paul Mason anticipate a chain reaction of effects that incline towards utopian outcomes. As the hours of human labour required to produce what humanity needs decrease to a minimum, wages themselves would eventually transform into collectively provided services or disappear, as would a basic income, since it would no longer be needed.[171]

Such outlooks titillate, but they seem overcooked. More likely are more prosaic effects where a basic income, instead of replacing the wage system, loosens the grip of that system by providing a reliable alternative or supplementary income. It would help people meet basic needs and make it easier for them to reject exploitative employment and, at least temporarily, to devote their energies and time to other activities, should they wish to do so. That liberating effect is key.

But it is also possible that a UBI could be appropriated as temporary support for a capitalist wage system and family model that is 'inadequate to the task of distributing income and organising productive cooperation', thereby materially and ideologically helping prop up that system, as Kathi Weeks has warned.[172] While the benefits of a UBI are not insubstantial, she cautions, 'they do not add up to some revolutionary post-capitalist vision'.[173] On its own, a UBI is unlikely to contain the propulsive, radical powers some champions on the Left assign to it. The transformative potential will depend on whether and how a UBI is linked with other interventions that expand or wither the substance of citizenship.[174] That proviso is crucial. In André Gorz's view, the reduction of obligatory waged work could open opportunities for what he termed 'socially determined' work: activities that generally contribute to people's usefulness to society and enable them to exist as fully social individuals.[175] But he saw risks as well:

> The guarantee of an income independent of a job will be emancipatory or repressive, from the Left or the Right, according to whether it opens up new spaces for individual and social activity or whether, on the contrary, it is only the social wage for compulsory passivity.[176]

Gorz's concern was that a universal income could also be used to ensure social control and passivity by paying very low 'placating' amounts to people who have effectively been reduced to supernumeraries within the capitalist order.[177]

The available evidence indicates that a UBI can have a wide range of desirable effects, including reductions in the depth and extent of poverty, and improvements in people's physical and mental health and their educational status. The extent of those effects would depend on the size of the basic income payment and how a UBI synchronises with other forms of state provisioning. Those same factors would also shape the likelihood of the emancipatory effects which proponents of a UBI predict, including shifting social power relations, supporting a just transition, and recasting the terms on which social citizenship and entitlement are decided. Crucially, a UBI would reflect an understanding that dynamics beyond individual control determine the unjust distribution of means and opportunities and that this calls for systematic redistributive actions. But a UBI's transformative effects are by no means automatic: its functions and impact will depend on the social, economic and political processes it operates in.

4

Testing the Arguments Against

G iven the potential advantages of a UBI – and the obvious need for reliable income support that is not inflexibly tied to selling one's labour – one may ask why a UBI does not yet exist on a large scale. The unsuccessful campaign to introduce a basic income grant (BIG) in South Africa in the early 2000s offers some important insights.

WHY THE BIG CAMPAIGN IN SOUTH AFRICA FAILED

South African trade unions, religious organisations and non-governmental organisations (and, intermittently, the former social development minister)[1] began championing a BIG in the late 1990s. The grant was formally proposed during bilateral discussions between government and trade unions ahead of the 1998 Presidential Jobs Summit. The envisaged amount was very small – R100 (about US$12.50 at the time) per month – an amount that proponents believed was politically 'winnable'.

The government convened the Committee of Inquiry into Comprehensive Social Security (the Taylor Committee) in 2000 to investigate a proposed BIG in the context of the country's overall social security system. Three years later, the Taylor Committee recommended that an income grant worth R100, payable to all South Africans without a means test, be introduced. The payment would form part of a comprehensive social protection package, including increased support for health, education and housing, and for strengthening various forms of social capital. The Committee accepted that a BIG could not be implemented immediately due to administrative and fiscal considerations. It therefore proposed that the basic income be phased in over time until, by 2015, it would include all adults up to retirement age.[2]

The anticipated socioeconomic benefits were plentiful. Financial simulations suggested that a payment of R100 per month for all South Africans could close the poverty gap by 74%,[3] and lift about six million people above a poverty line of R400 (US$50 at the time) per month.[4] The grant would be spread thinner than existing social transfers, but the benefits were expected to ripple further.

Some proponents saw the BIG as a means to address both poverty and labour market failures. Especially significant was the recognition in the report of the Taylor Committee that 'the wage-income relationship' was 'breaking down':

> A key underlying principle of the old [apartheid] system remains in place, i.e. the assumption that those in the labour force can support themselves through work, and that unemployment is a temporary condition. In reality, those who cannot find work ... fall through a vast hole in the safety net.[5]

The Congress of South African Trade Unions (Cosatu) saw the BIG as a way to reduce poverty and lay 'the foundation for more productive and skilled communities'.[6] It would form part of a broader strategy to build livelihood security that could help people cope with labour market failures and personal catastrophes such as illness or sudden loss of income. Concerns in labour circles about 'welfare dependence' saw the BIG positioned as part of an active labour market policy, rather than as an alternative to low-wage work.

Supporters also saw the BIG as a way to help people seek additional sources of income, as an 'investment' in 'human capital' and as a 'springboard' for mini-entrepreneurs.[7] The concept therefore also found support in some conservative quarters, where it was seen as a limited cash transfer that would alleviate poverty and subsidise 'self-help' activities, while ultimately leaving recipients reliant on and available for low-wage jobs. As James Ferguson noted, proponents tended to blend social-welfarist and neoliberal reasoning.[8]

Sympathetic critics favoured low-wage job programmes as an alternative. But most opponents objected that a BIG would be unaffordable, too small to have significant positive effects, and that it would distort labour supplies, depress wages and foster dependence. South African president Thabo Mbeki reportedly dismissed the BIG proposal with the claim: 'If you give everybody R100 a month, it will not make a difference … To introduce a system which indiscriminately gives R100 to a millionaire and a pensioner does not work.'[9] The academic Charles Meth responded that no one

> who has observed the efforts of the poor to scratch a living out of some enterprise that requires endless hours of toil will believe that R100 per month will put an end to the aspirations of most of them for self-improvement. What cannot be called into question is the welfare improvement in, for example, workerless households, among whom the slightest risk (e.g. borrowing or spending money for a job search) threatens an already precarious existence. Their menu of choices could be considerably expanded by the existence of a secure income source, be it ever so small.[10]

If set at R100 (US$12.50) per month per person, the BIG would have cost approximately R54 billion (US$6.8 billion) per year, according to Pieter le

Roux's calculations.[11] That estimate assumed, though, that current recipients of social grants would receive downward-adjusted BIG payments (i.e. the BIG would 'top up' existing cash transfers). Servaas van der Berg and Haroon Bhorat calculated the overall cost at about R60 billion (US$7.5 billion) per year – equivalent to about 4% of GDP at the time, or roughly equal to the national education budget.[12] Around the same time, Anna McCord calculated that a public works programme providing 3.2 million jobs, or 845 million workdays, at R35 (US$4.40) per day, would have cost between R37 billion and R61 billion (US$4.6 billion and US$7.6 billion) per year, depending on administrative and other costs.[13] Such a scheme would have absorbed about 40% of the potential workdays of the unemployed in South Africa.

Various financing options for the BIG were put forward. Le Roux proposed a value-added tax (VAT) increase of 7.3% (in addition to the 14% rate at the time) and a 50% increase in excise and fuel taxes.[14] He claimed this would have entailed a significant increase in taxes for higher-spending individuals, while being much less burdensome for low-income individuals, who spend little. However, using VAT increases to finance the BIG would have reduced the net payment to individuals far below the face-value R100 amount – by up to one-third for low-income, non-taxpaying recipients. Other financing options included increases in the marginal income tax rate, which would have increased the net benefit to low-income earners.

The debate was heavily influenced by the neoliberal macroeconomic framework (Growth, Employment and Redistribution plan, or GEAR) adopted in 1996 and staunchly defended by the finance ministry.[15] The ruling African National Congress (ANC) showed little appetite for the BIG recommendation and the government stood implacably opposed. Shunted into various policy summits, discussion of a BIG steadily faded from view.[16] The preferred route was to pursue livelihood protection through job-creating economic growth and by reforming the current social assistance system. Operating in the background was the evergreen assumption that a combination of waged work and entrepreneurial zest eventually would do away with a need for social transfers to manage indigence. Thus, the finance minister, in his 2004 budget speech, stated that the government's approach was

> to extend social security and income support through targeted measures, and to contribute also to creating work opportunities and investing further in education, training and health services. This is the more balanced strategy for social progress and sustainable development.[17]

The core objection to a BIG, former trade and industry minister Alec Erwin later remarked, appeared to be 'not the money but the idea'.[18] Speaking in 2002, land affairs minister Thoko Didiza, who headed the ANC's Department of Social Transformation, had highlighted the ruling party's concerns 'about the values underpinning such a grant'.[19] Government spokesperson, Joel Netshitenzhe, called for interventions that would enable South Africans to 'enjoy the opportunity, the dignity and the rewards of work',[20] while President Mbeki urged his government colleagues to 'reduce the number of people dependent on social welfare [and increase] the numbers that rely for their livelihood on normal participation in the economy'.[21] The ANC clung to the view that 'grants must not create dependency and thus must be linked to economic activity'.[22] Yet the government continued to expand the social grant system, prompting David Everatt to remark that

> the dominant voice within the ANC after Mandela was one that chided the poor for remaining poor, rejected [a basic income grant] but was unable to resist pressure for major cash transfers to the poor in the form of social grants.[23]

The South African government seemed to recognise both the felt need for social grants and their political value for shoring up popular consent. Yet it would remain resistant to the principle of state-provided income support as an entitlement or right for poor households. Although defeated, the

BIG campaign did make an impression. Prior to the general election in 2008, media reports claimed that the ANC had been costing various configurations of expanded social assistance, among them a BIG, though the results were not made public.[24] In 2010, the Congress of South African Trade Unions again called for a BIG, along with other social and economic reforms, though to no avail.[25] Less than a decade later, a large and growing coalition would again emerge around a demand for a UBI (see Chapter 6).

ECONOMIC AND LABOUR MARKET DISTORTIONS

Condensed in the reactions to the BIG campaign in South Africa were many of the themes that typify current scepticism or outright opposition to a UBI. Central among these objections are claims that a UBI is too costly and that it will distort the labour market and wider macroeconomy.

Unaffordability

Most common is the complaint that a UBI is unaffordable and would expose governments to populist demands for increasing the payment amount. This would cause costs to spin out of control, creating what economists call 'open-ended fiscal exposure'. Critics also claim that financing a UBI through taxation in developing countries is unrealistic, since relatively small proportions of adults pay income taxes and value-added tax already disproportionately burdens low-income households.[26] A relatively generous UBI payment – for example, an amount that corresponds to the poverty line – would seem highly unfeasible in such circumstances if financed from personal income taxes, they charge.

The affordability of a UBI has to be determined on a case-by-case basis, taking account of the proposed amount, eligibility decisions, feasible financing options, fiscal circumstances, and how the scheme aligns with social wage and other pro-poor interventions. Blanket verdicts about affordability are unsound and misleading (as discussed in detail in Chapter 5).

Economic disruption and inefficiency

Economic disruption and inefficiency are other common concerns cited by UBI critics. They warn that the mechanism would distort the labour market, inhibit labour supply and productivity (due to a putative loss of work incentives), encourage fiscal profligacy, reduce competitiveness (due to higher taxation) and lead to price inflation.

The 'inefficiency' argument may seem persuasive theoretically, but it weakens in real-world settings. Chronic un- and underemployment, and depressed real wages sap aggregate demand, which further dampens employment and adds macroeconomic inefficiencies. By contrast, 'paying cash benefits will enhance macroeconomic efficiency if it upholds aggregate demand and raises employment', as William Jackson has noted.[27] A universal payment would also avoid standard economic inefficiencies associated with current targeted and/or conditional transfers, including distorted resource allocation, high administrative costs and incomplete coverage.

The alleged inflationary effect is tied to an assumption, rooted in neoclassical economics, that distributing large amounts of 'free money' to non-working people would boost demand without generating corresponding increases in output or productivity.[28] The resultant relative scarcity would cause prices to rise. The objection suffers several flaws. The inflation fear assumes that human labour is the only source of large-scale increases in output and productivity, ignoring the potential contributions of automation, restructured value chains and more. The trepidation also overlooks the persistence of excess capacity in the global economy, which tends to absorb the inflationary effect of increased demand. And it is undermined by the fact that massive infusions of liquidity since the 2008 global financial crisis have not sparked untrammelled inflation. After the US Federal Reserve's quantitative easing programme pumped over US$4 trillion into the money supply after the 2008 crisis, there was no indication of rising inflation. In fact, the Federal Reserve's concern was the opposite: there was not enough inflation.[29]

Moreoever, there is persuasive evidence from developing countries that cash transfers do not have an inflationary impact. A review of programmes in Lesotho, Malawi and Zambia found no evidence of price inflation or distortion attributable to the transfers.[30] In Kenya, a large study across 653 rural villages found minimal price inflation associated with one-time cash transfers of US$1 000 to poor households, while documenting major positive effects on household consumption and assets.[31] Careful analysis of Mexico's *Programa de Apoyo Alimentario* (or Food Aid Programme) also concluded that inflation concerns about distributing 'free money' to poor households were misplaced.[32] That food programme was preceded by a randomised experiment in 200 rural villages. In some, villagers got US$20 per month cash grants, while food parcels worth the same amount were distributed in others. A third set of villages served as a control group. In villages receiving the cash transfer, food prices barely changed (they rose by 0.2%), suggesting that even in a contained setting a UBI need not spur inflation.

A disincentive for work

Basic income proposals routinely spark dismay about their anticipated effect on people's desire to seek and perform waged work. For critics of unconditional income support it is almost axiomatic that the intervention will distort labour markets. That stance has been highly influential in the restructuring of welfare systems in developed countries over the past three decades, most obviously in the promotion of 'workfare' (or employment-oriented welfare),[33] which places great emphasis on linking income support to constant job searching.

Those contentions bristle with moral censure. Paid work is venerated as the desired norm, and it is assumed to be attainable despite the abundant contrary evidence. As South African parliamentarian Michael Masutha put it in 2000, when commenting on calls for a small basic income: 'If you have all these nice social benefits, where is the incentive to want to go back to work?'[34] At the time, about 35% of

South Africa's adult population had no reasonable prospect of finding decent paid work in the near future.

There is very little empirical evidence to support the 'work disincentive' objection. Neither basic income-type projects,[35] nor cash transfer programmes (including South Africa's social grant system), indicate that income transfers discourage people from working.[36] An analysis of 16 historical UBI trials found no significant impact on the likelihood of participants performing paid work.[37] Studies of cash transfers in impoverished settings have found no significant effect on labour supply either, including in Asia and Latin America[38] and in Africa.[39]

Damon Jones and Ioana Marinescu's analysis of study evidence from the United States (including the Alaska Permanent Fund) found a tiny, close-to-zero effect on labour supply.[40] Many of the reviewed studies had reported no impact on labour supply, and where an impact was detected, it was small. Among the latter studies, a 10% increase in income from unconditional cash transfers resulted in an average 1% drop in labour supply.[41]

Abhijit Banerjee and colleagues re-analysed the results of seven randomised controlled trials of government-run cash transfer programmes from six countries[42] and also found no systematic evidence that the programmes discouraged work for either women or men.[43] Similarly, Emmanuel Skoufias and Vincenzo di Maro's analysis of Mexico's *Progresa* programme revealed no significant effect on adult labour force participation.[44] Similar findings have been made in Argentina, Chile, Ecuador and Uruguay,[45] Bangladesh and Ethiopia[46] and Cambodia.[47]

There is, however, evidence of a contrary effect – of *increased* employment. Miguel Foguel and Ricardo de Barros found that conditional cash transfer programmes in Brazil increased male labour participation,[48] while Diego Vera-Cossio's research in Bolivia made a similar finding (including in family businesses).[49] Some studies of the impact of cash transfers on farm labour in Africa have found decreased participation in casual waged labour,[50] accompanied by increases in own-account farming:

> The results do not indicate a reduction in work effort – rather, they show that beneficiary households have increased their autonomy over productive activities and have more flexibility in how they allocate their time – often choosing to work on their own farms instead of agricultural wage labor.[51]

More generally, cross-country evidence points in a similar direction: increased social policy expenditure and levels of public investment improve people's labour market prospects, as Elissa Braunstein and Stephanie Seguino discovered when they reviewed data from 18 Latin American countries for the period 1990–2010.[52]

The claim that a cash transfer would undermine work incentives seems grotesquely misplaced in a society like South Africa, where the social grants target people who, due to age, frailty or disability, are not expected to fend for themselves by selling their labour. Strictly speaking, those payments cannot discourage beneficiaries from employment. However, since the money is frequently also distributed among other household and/or family members, might the grants discourage job-seeking among those secondary beneficiaries?

When Statistics South Africa analysed data from the 2003–2007 General Household Surveys, it concluded that low-income households receiving grants were not less economically active than non-recipient households.[53] In a review of other South African and international evidence, the effect appeared to be ambiguous and depended on the context. In some cases, grant payments increased labour market participation by covering costs or credit associated with working (for example, for women in the case of child support grants).[54] That aligns with earlier findings by Deborah Posel and her co-authors, who reported that rural South African women living in households where someone was receiving the state old-age pension were more likely to be working than their peers in non-recipient households.[55] In other instances, the grants may temporarily relax the pressures for seeking waged work (a reasonable reaction in the context of hyper-unemployment).[56] In the background is the fact that the bulk of social grant recipients in South Africa are adults (mostly black African women) who are raising or fostering children, or tending the frail: they *are* working, but are not being remunerated for their labour.

Overall, the evidence supports an expectation that even with a subsistence-level cash payment, at least some people with marketable skills can be expected to seek paid work, take up self-employment, or strive to improve their skills or education in search of better, more decent work. "'I get $10 000 a year; that's enough for me" – said nobody, ever', as Max Sawicky quipped in response to the claim that a UBI in the United States would encourage sloth.[57]

ETHICAL OBJECTIONS: 'SOMETHING FOR NOTHING'

A range of ethical objections are levelled at UBI proposals. Critics find the lack of targeting and conditionality to be particularly disturbing. Some object, for example, that it is ethically problematic to apply a universalist principle in a 'literal' or 'mechanistic' way by providing income support to everybody, including people who do not need the support. A targeted approach that focuses support on the least privileged sections of society is seen as a preferable way to ensure that no one goes lacking. However, many current proposals for a UBI rely on complementary arrangements to offset at least part of the cost through progressive changes to the tax system, such that only low-income earners would receive a net income gain from a UBI. This particular ethical objection seems addressed in such arrangements.

There is also a claim that a UBI would be divisive, by separating society into 'productive' and 'non-productive' sections (rather than regarding every adult as a current or potential worker). The concern is strange, given the prevailing normative and administrative separation between adults with and without employment, and the stigmatising and coercive discourse associated with that framework. An income which *everyone* receives cannot easily be construed as divisive.

A UBI destabilises deeply held ideas about the role and status of paid work as a basis for having legitimate claims on one another and on the state. As seen during South Africa's BIG debate in the early 2000s, waged work is laden with notions of deservedness, merit, earned social membership and the promise of recognition. Waged work, no matter what the actual job, is seen to bestow value and worthiness. A UBI distorts those social-moral landscapes and unbalances the ways in which social obligations and entitlements are assessed and assigned. Thus, universalist welfare is frequently opposed for rewarding passivity and encouraging idle entitlement. 'Where is the fairness, we ask, for the shift-worker, leaving home in the dark hours of the morning, who looks up at the closed blinds of their next-door neighbour sleeping off a life on benefits?' is how former United Kingdom Chancellor George Osborne reportedly put it to the 2012 Conservative Party congress.[58] The moralising contrast of hardworking citizen and idling freeloader remains a staple of fiscal sermonising.

Work seems to occupy an 'unassailable position in politics, policy and popular discourse'.[59] When a claim to an entitlement is not in some way attached to paid work, it is commonly treated as a moral offence: a basic principle, that of social reciprocity, seems violated. This feeds a deeply and widely felt affront, even when the reaction seems irrational – for example when waged work is unavailable to large proportions of working-age people. There is a prevailing insistence that it is chiefly through waged work that we contribute to society and 'earn' our claims to social citizenship.[60] Social policy in South Africa typifies such perspectives (see Chapter 2). The social grant system targets recipients as individuals, with little regard for the interdependencies – the social and other obligations and claims – that shape their lives. And it does so in an ideological environment that denounces dependence, disparages social assistance as 'handouts', and exults waged work as the prime source of worth and recognition.

Rewarding the 'undeserving'

The logic of means-testing, targeting and conditionality feeds the evergreen notions of the 'deserving' and 'undeserving' poor, a framework that divides society into 'saints' and 'sinners'.[61] At least for the past 150 years, that line has been drawn on the basis of a person's capacity to work for a wage:

> Traditional 20th century conceptions of social welfare took for granted an economic world within which waged labour was socially generalised, and the domain we have come to know as 'the social' was constructed on the foundation of the able-bodied male worker. Indeed, the list of those requiring 'social' interventions (the elderly, the infirm, the child, the disabled, the dependent reproductive woman) traces a kind of photographic negative of the figure of the wage-earning man.[62]

In this kind of framework, the state (or another designated entity) dispenses support to people who have 'earned' it by way of paid work, or it gives 'charitably' (it 'grants' assistance) to those who are not reasonably required to work for a wage. A principle of reciprocity may seem to be the hinge in this relationship between citizen and state, but the act of 'charity' is laden with power and authority, and functions as a disciplinary tool that ultimately services the interests of employers.

The deserving/undeserving yardstick for social assistance retains powerful traction. Both the framing of social assistance and the attitudes of potential recipients are weighted with moral judgement. Data from a 2009 survey among 3 000 young people in Cape Town prompted Jeremy Seekings to conclude that the respondents 'tend to favour both public and private support for deserving people and to oppose both for undeserving people'.[63] Their responses indicated little support for automatic claims or universal provision, whether public or private. The preference was for training, job creation and free tertiary education – even though their own lived experiences showed that neither education nor training qualifications guaranteed jobs, let alone 'decent' jobs. The elderly and the disabled were generally seen to be most deserving of state support, with young able-bodied adults the least deserving.[64]

Hannah Dawson and Liz Fouksman have made similar observations, noting that even individuals who are effectively excluded from the labour market insist on a link between labour and income.[65] Their research among unemployed young people in Zandspruit, north of Johannesburg, encountered heartfelt opposition to the idea of extending eligibility for the child support grant to 23 years (from the current 18 years). There is ample other evidence that the provision of welfare benefits tends to elicit stigma and disapproving tropes, often politically inflamed, about the recipients – with women, especially single mothers, especially attractive targets.[66] Other criteria for 'deservingness' are also invoked. Depending on the assistance and circumstances, a claim for support might be regarded as stronger for kin than non-kin, or for people who are in dire straits compared with those having potential access to other means of support. In the Cape Town survey, though, need was not the only criterion for determining 'deservingness'; the social conduct of individuals also featured:

> Deservingness with respect to both public and private support is affected dramatically by the attitude and reciprocity of the claimant, with the important exceptions of mothers who should be supported unconditionally.[67]

Similarly, Dawson and Fouksman's research revealed disagreement not only about the state's role in providing income support, but about who deserves the support.[68] Respondents were concerned that 'lazy people' would abuse the system, that recipients would choose not to work, or that they would squander the money. It may be that the laziness trope is a substitute for an adequate explanation for the (more complex) causes of unemployment and poverty, as Christine Jeske has suggested.[69] But the value attached to waged work is also bound up with gender relations, including the authority men derive from the role of 'breadwinner'.

Dawson and Fouksman have noted that resentment was especially strong among male respondents (South Africa's child support grant is paid to caregivers, who are almost exclusively female).[70] These kinds of findings are in tune with the dominant tenor of social policy during the neoliberal era, which assigns to

> wage labour powerful disciplinary and pedagogical meanings, educating the poorest sections of the population to the idea that full citizenship revolves around individual responsibility, labour market activation, and the avoidance of 'dependency' on public spending. Conversely, the government regards with suspicion policies of generalised access to social provisions funded via redistributive transfers.[71]

In post-apartheid South Africa, as David Everatt has suggested, an element of shame possibly helps to explain the ongoing attachment to such cleaving, moralising assumptions.[72] Even though none of the participants in Dawson and Fouksman's study counted themselves among 'the lazy', the implied self-loathing was striking, not least in its mirroring of racist stereotypes and the image of the 'feckless native'.[73] This may also explain the aversion among many politicians and state officials towards unconditional, universal assistance:

> The combination of the scars of apartheid experience, and [people's] own success in surmounting the monumental obstacles that characterized this system of oppression, has caused them to elevate 'self-reliance' and an abhorrence of 'dependence' to mythical status.[74]

Recipients of child support grants in South Africa seemed to view the assistance with gratitude rather than a sense of 'just deserts', according to Tessa Hochfeld and Sophie Plagerson's research in Soweto.[75] The payment was not seen as fulfilling a right, but as meeting a necessity – not so much 'deserved' as needed. Prominent in South Africa and many other countries are paradoxical ethical stances that combine norms of communal solidarity with assertions of individual responsibility, and qualified claims on state support. But, rather than expressing steadfast principles, the attitudes encountered by Seekings and Matisonn and by Dawson and Fouksman may be more circumstantial than they seem – as the groundswell of popular support for a UBI during the COVID-19 pandemic suggests (see Chapter 6).[76]

Encouraging dependence

Even as the South African government expanded its social grant system in the 2000s, officials continued to moralise about the cash transfers, fretting that 'hand-outs' would encourage dependency. Former president Jacob Zuma, for example, called for linking 'the social grants to jobs or economic activity in order to encourage self-reliance among the able-bodied',[77] and highlighted as a priority the need to change the 'culture' of 'laziness', especially among youth.[78] Those were not new sentiments. Zuma's predecessor, Thabo Mbeki, had sermonised on the need

> to cultivate that sentiment among our people to say, 'I too have a responsibility to do something about my own development' ... so that people don't think it is sufficient merely to hold out their hands and receive a handout, but to understand that all of us, as South Africans, have a shared responsibility to attend to the development of the country.[79]

The South African government was so sunk in this view that, in 2005, the Presidency tasked the Department of Social Development to work with the finance ministry to address 'issues of dependency, perverse incentives and sustainability of the social grant system' and to ensure that the grants were linked to 'reducing poverty and unemployment'. The process included a survey of 14 000 households aimed at assessing 'potential perverse incentives and dependency'.[80] Even the Reconstruction and

Development Programme, the development strategy crafted by the ANC and its allies in the early 1990s, had emphasised that

> although a much stronger welfare system is needed to support all the vulnerable, the old, the disabled and the sick who currently live in poverty, a system of 'handouts' for the unemployed should be avoided. All South Africans should have the opportunity to participate in the economic life of the country.[81]

This conflation of waged work with sovereignty and independence misrepresents people's lived experiences – starting with their obvious *dependence* on waged work itself and extending to the intricate webs of dependencies that constitute social life and enable economic survival. Dependence is an empirical fact of life. And people actively establish, manage and manipulate these dependencies. It is what we do when we organise as workers, or participate in networks of social reciprocity, or borrow money from a friend.

Income (waged or not) and other forms of support constantly circulate informally across kin and other social networks. In southern Africa, as elsewhere in the developing world, a powerful interdependence exists between wage earners and their dependents (and individuals constantly shift between those two roles). People establish and maintain claims on support in a variety of ways, ranging from reciprocity and indebtedness to supplication or dominance. The currency of these interdependencies is not limited to money but extends to various forms of labour (childcare work, nursing or handiwork, for instance) and bartering. Rather than view dependence as a lack of freedom, James Ferguson sees it as a basis for making distributional claims, with social dependence in particular serving 'as the very foundation of polities and persons alike'.[82] Dependence is a social tool that can be used to position oneself for participation in distributive systems.

The authority of waged work in the public imagination of South Africans is closely tied to the country's history of capitalism, its dismantling of agrarian livelihoods, and the corralling of African men into wage labour in mining and other industries and on white-owned farms.[83] For men in particular, personhood, social status and 'manhood' became increasingly – though not entirely – tied to waged work, all the more so in settings where bridewealth-based marriage required wage-earning capacity.[84] But this did not entirely displace the importance of other relations of (inter)dependence, given the unstable nature of waged employment. South African capitalism, as Ferguson has reminded us, 'did not do away with personalistic and dependent relations between employer and employee'.[85] To a large extent, those relationships of dependence have been woven into networks that are served by reciprocity and recompense. Social reality does not support the image of dependence as passive entitlement (though outright claims-staking, especially by men on women, does occur).

As rising unemployment accompanies listless economic growth, many of the jobless are pushed aside more or less permanently. In that context, new relations of dependence have emerged, increasingly revolving around social assistance (in the shape of social grants and other cash transfers), much of it paid to women. Another fascinating finding in Hochfeld and Plagerson's research in Soweto was the importance many recipients attached to their ability to control the payments.[86] The grants were seen not as a form of dependence, but as a means for broadening women's opportunities to participate in social life. As the researchers noted, this echoes Amartya Sen's emphasis on choice and control as an essential 'capability'.[87] The cash transfers, in Ferguson's view,

> enable less malevolent sorts of dependence to take root and a circuit of reciprocities to unfold within which one-sided relations of dependence can become more egalitarian forms of interdependence.[88]

This also points to a more accurate understanding of the so-called informal economy, which seems less entrepreneurial (in the sense of being budding 'start-ups') and more a means for servicing participation in networks of (inter)dependence – or 'distributive labour', as Ferguson puts it.[89] Andries du Toit and David Neves have shown how people weave social grants and informal enterprise activities into the give-and-take that nourishes social networks.[90] Ferguson is correct to observe that 'it is really only via relations of "dependence" that most of the population survives at all'.[91]

These can be messy, disruptive processes. Structures of households and kin relations evolve: in South Africa they have changed significantly in recent decades, with both marriage rates and the prevalence of male-headed households declining markedly.[92] By the early 2000s already, women headed almost as many households in South Africa as did men,[93] and a majority of adult women had never been married.[94] In the context of hyper-unemployment and widespread poverty, men find themselves dislodged from traditional roles, lacking the means to fulfil their perceived duties as 'breadwinners', and with their sense of self and their place in society destabilised. At least some of the violence men inflict on women and children in South Africa can be traced to this mismatch between the idea of what 'makes a man' and the limited available means for living up to those norms of masculinity.[95]

As access to wage incomes narrows, distributive claims on kin are focused more tightly on smaller groups of relatives – increasingly women, who receive child support or foster care grants, and the elderly, who receive pensions. The 'non-productive' are themselves becoming key sources of income. Consequently, the current social grants system in South Africa also fuels tension, resentment and division within households and kinship circles,[96] and it is loaded with opportunities for moralising judgement. Grant recipients become the sources of income for others, acquiring a redistributive role that can expose them to harassment and danger, while affording them a degree of social power. This, too, upends a simplistic understanding of dependence. Rather than referring to a relationship of passivity – a sort of social stasis – dependence is a dynamic process, a form of actual or pending exchange which implies reciprocity (now or deferred into the future). 'For poor South Africans,' Ferguson notes, 'it is not dependence but its absence that is really terrifying – the severing of the thread, and the fall into the social void.'[97]

The real challenge is not so much to erase dependence 'but to construct desirable forms of it'.[98] Wage labour offers a suggestive analogy. In capitalist society, it very clearly constitutes a form of dependence, egregiously so in the context of high unemployment and weak social protection. But it also provides a basis for staking claims to entitlements, for contesting access to resources, even for altering social relations. The imbalances built into the relationship between workers and employers generate reactions that constantly threaten to also destabilise the relationship; the dependence is never passive.

Legitimising passive citizenship

The sense that it is unfair for an able-bodied person to live off the labour of others resonates deeply. The perceived lack of reciprocity is an intuitively powerful concern, including among proponents of a UBI. Philippe van Parijs has referred to this as the 'Malibu surfer' conundrum: should taxpaying workers subsidise the lifestyle of a person who chooses an 'unproductive' life – such as a 'surfer bum'?[99]

It is widely felt that any such obligation is unfair, and that facilitating a lifestyle of apparent idleness is socially undesirable. Thus, the American philosopher John Rawls claimed that someone who wished to surf all day can do so using her own income, but cannot expect society to develop institutions and mechanisms to subsidise her life.[100] In the Rawlsian liberal tradition, a UBI is deemed unjustified since it violates the principle of reciprocity. A person is justified in receiving income support that is financed through a tax on the income of working people only if she is unable to work for a living or shows a willingness to work (in line with the standard framing of income support).

Van Parijs has argued, somewhat intricately, that an obligation to subsidise idleness need not be unfair.[101] Even in a well-functioning modern economy, some unemployment continues to exist. This is partly because some workers choose to quit or refuse jobs in search of higher wages than those on offer, which (by increasing demand) adds upward pressure to wage levels. Workers who do have employment benefit from that buoyant effect on wages – which makes it ethically justifiable, according to Van Parijs, to tax part of that 'surplus income' and distribute it to people who are not employed. This counter-argument seems strained.

The Rawlsian position suffers a less technical and more profound weakness, in that it equates (social) worthiness with paid work and risks neglecting other forms of socially valuable and/or personally enriching work. The tendency to associate worth with waged work troubled Hannah Arendt, for example, who preferred to draw distinctions between labour, work and action.[102] Feminist historians and theorists have critiqued the Rawlsian position along similar lines – for imagining the rights-bearing adult fundamentally as male and as an autonomous individual who is neither dependent on the work of others nor responsible for dependents. On what grounds, they have asked, should money not be paid to female adults, who preponderantly perform essential but unpaid care and reproductive work?[103] In Juliana Bidadanure's view, it 'seems difficult to claim that any formal job is a more adequate form of reciprocation than activities outside the labor market that are sometimes more useful or productive.'[104]

André Gorz approached the issue of reciprocity from a similar angle. He shared the concern about income support that is detached from any reciprocal obligation – but for social rather than moralistic reasons:

> Excusing people from working by securing them an income anyway is not a way of giving them full membership of their society. You cannot become a member of any community if you have no obligation whatsoever to it … There can be no inclusion without reciprocal obligations.[105]

Gorz worried that a guaranteed minimum income might compensate people for their economic exclusion while leaving untouched the reality of an unequal and exclusionary society. Crucially, he released the concept of reciprocity from the fiction that it can only be expressed through the mechanism of waged work. But a guaranteed income would have to facilitate arrangements that promote full participation in society and that involve some form of positive obligation that would expand

> those activities which create nothing that can be bought, sold, exchanged – and hence nothing that has value (in the economic sense) – but [add] only non-marketable wealth with an intrinsic value of its own.[106]

In addition to enabling individuals, a UBI must have a social function: it has to facilitate socially engaged citizenship. For Gorz, as for Arendt, the chief concern was not only material security, but a person's ability to live a socially rooted and socially meaningful life. A UBI therefore needs to do more than release people from poverty and the compulsion of waged work; it also has to open opportunities for activities that allow one to exist in a socially useful manner.[107] Not merely a source for financing the basic necessities of life (through consumption), a UBI should also provide a basis for engaging in forms of socially productive activity (other than wage labour), for enriching social life and for political engagement – all of which, in Arendt's view, nourishes societies and helps build and deepen democracy beyond the routine of voting.[108] Ideally, a UBI would nurture all three aspects of what Arendt termed the 'vita activa': labour, work and action.[109]

Proceeding along similar lines, Anthony Atkinson has sought to reframe a basic income as a 'participation income' and to build the principle of social reciprocity or productivity into the concept.[110] There is a conundrum, though, in whether and how to structure such expectations in a UBI. Various forms of 'participation' (such as reproductive and other unpaid care work) could constitute a basis for entitlement. This, the argument goes, would remove the 'surfer problem' and shield the mechanism against the 'free-rider' objection.

Framing a basic income as a 'participation income' transforms it into a transaction and turns reciprocity into something of a contractual relationship, in which a person receives a monetary reward in return for performing some action or role. This is quite different from the idea of a basic income as an entitlement or a just dividend. But Pateman seems correct to insist that a preoccupation with specific kinds of 'free-riding' should make way for 'an examination of how to reinforce reciprocity in the sense of mutual aid across the social order'.[111] In the absence of large-scale, real-world evidence, it is not year clear how a UBI would underpin or support such extensive reciprocity. But it is clear that the 'something-for-nothing' objection is widespread. The sense that a UBI offends, even violates a basic 'moral bargain' carries considerable reflexive power and should not be underestimated. A viable case for a UBI has to address this objection (a matter we return to in Chapters 5 and 6).

UNDERMINING WORKERS' STRUGGLES

Another perceived threat troubles progressive critics of a UBI, especially those linked to the labour movement. They fear that a UBI might undermine collective bargaining rights, partly because the UBI demand would absorb attention, resources and organising energies at the expense of workplace and other struggles for workers' rights. In this critique, a UBI at best functions as a minor palliative that offers some individuals an opportunity to temporarily opt out of wage labour, while subsidising low-end wages and leaving labour relations structurally intact.

Critics like Alex Gourevitch and Lucas Stanczyk go further and dismiss the emancipatory potential of a UBI as an illusion.[112] The power relations that are needed to achieve an adequate UBI, they argue, are not achievable under capitalism: those relations 'presuppose an organized working class that already has effective control over the shape and the direction of the economy'.[113] And that, clearly, is not the case. It is much more sensible, they insist, to mobilise the social and political power of poor and working people through labour organising than to focus it on a fantastical intervention like a UBI.

They may be correct in contending that an effective movement for progressive change cannot be built around a social policy demand. But that criticism also hitches the cart before the horse. A UBI would acquire much of its transformative power from the extent to which it links with and boosts *other* projects of progressive change. Set against current economic and social realities, Gourevitch and Stanczyk's binary seems anachronistic and misplaced. The ongoing importance of labour organising is indisputable, but it has long ceased to be the sole or most decisive platform for mobilising and organising movements for progressive change.

By definition, trade unions are organisations of people who exchange their labour for wages and benefits. To the extent that a UBI destabilises the relationship between paid work and society, it fits awkwardly with the logic and rationale of trade unionism. Trade unions everywhere have struggled to adjust to the radical restructuring of work in capitalist economies over the past forty years.[114] The support for a UBI among some trade unions in South Africa, for example, partly reflects this ongoing search for tangibly relevant ways to link employed workers' struggles with those of unemployed people.

One can argue the converse to Gourevitch and Stanczyk's claim: that better jobs are possible only if jobs are freely chosen, rather than being compelled by the demands of life in a capitalist economy.[115] As discussed in Chapter 3, a UBI that enables unemployed low-wage workers to hold out for improved job offers can strengthen their bargaining power and that of their employed counterparts. To the extent that a UBI strengthens people's ability to refuse unfair or exploitative wages and terms of employment, it boosts the collective power of workers.

SURRENDERING LIFE TO THE MARKET

Since a UBI involves the receipt of money that is then exchanged for goods and services in the market, charge critics on the Left, it would further commodify human life. It would reinforce, as Ana Cecilia Dinerstein puts it, both the myth of the 'free citizen' and the social power of money, making it what she terms a 'bad utopia'.[116] The complaint carries intuitive force, yet it hinges on an oddly romanticised picture of current reality.

Almost the entirety of society, including impoverished people, engage in capitalist market relations as consumers, commonly by taking on and recycling debt.[117] Cash money – or the lack of it – is central to the lives of low-income households, especially so when the option of subsistence agriculture is unavailable or unviable. In South Africa, low-income households spend about 35% of monthly income on food, according to the Pietermaritzburg Economic Justice and Dignity Group.[118] The rest of their spending prioritises transport, electricity and energy, and education, as well as burial insurance, repayment of debts, and telecommunications (a 'typical' low-income household spends about R300 (or US$20) per month on mobile phone airtime).[119] While some of those expenditures are subsidised and some could be communally produced (food, for example, and renewable electricity and energy), all currently involve some engagement in market relations and require payment in money. It is worth recalling, too, that waged work (the preferred alternative for UBI critics across the ideological spectrum) is profoundly commodified. While some labour contracts may include free or subsidised access to healthcare or transport or other benefits, one does not often hear the demand that wages should *not* be paid in money because this would unduly commodify workers' lives.

However, concerns about the commodifying effect of a UBI are highly relevant for versions of a UBI that convert other forms of social provisioning into a single cash payment. This conception of a UBI is favoured on the Right and among some mainstream advocates. In the United States, for example, Andrew Yang (contender for the Democratic Party presidential nomination in 2020) proposed a 'Freedom Dividend' of US$1 000 per month, to be financed by consolidating some welfare programmes and implementing a 10% value-added tax.[120] In that formulation, current welfare and social programme beneficiaries would have a choice between their current benefits or the basic income payment.

Similarly, Andy Stern, former head of the US Service Employees International Union, proposed funding a UBI by cashing out several major welfare programmes (food stamps, housing assistance, the earned income tax credit and more) and imposing a value-added tax on consumer goods.[121] Such a UBI would lay even greater emphasis on individual risk and responsibility, a central tenet of neoliberal dogma. It would not only commodify the lives of impoverished people more thoroughly, but leave them more exposed to the vagaries of the market and deepen their insecurity. The UBI considered in this book *complements* rather than replaces free or subsidised healthcare and education and other provisioning of public goods.

The commodification complaint matters in another respect, too: when financial corporations are able to exploit cash transfer disbursement systems as entry points for profit-taking strategies. Even though large proportions of adults in South Africa are surplus to the labour needs of capital, they continue to be subjected to 'secondary exploitation' which typically is achieved through debts and rents.[122] Under the mantle of 'financial inclusion', financial corporations use cash transfer systems to draw low-income beneficiaries into credit markets. Shifts to electronic payments of cash transfers have provided finance and technology firms with new opportunities to lock welfare recipients into predatory credit relationships.[123]

This happened in South Africa in 2015–2017, in a telling example of financial capitalism's pursuit of 'commodification all the way down'.[124] The contract for disbursing social grants nationally was held by Cash Paymaster Services, a subsidiary of the transnational corporation Net1. The latter partnered with another transnational corporation, Grindrod Bank (owned by the Remgro multinational), to administer the bank accounts of beneficiaries. Many of the bank accounts in which beneficiaries received their social grants were linked to payment channels for pre-paid electricity, water and mobile phone credit. Recipients were also targeted with offers of loans and advances against their cash transfers. The linkages made it possible to directly debit beneficiaries' accounts to settle debts, some of which were owed to subsidiaries of Net1. From the companies' point of view, the arrangement seemed near-perfect: recipients had 'no ability to default, as Net1 exerted near total control over [their access to] social grant payments', as Erin Torkelson noted.[125] The corporation also used its access to the millions of grant beneficiaries as a marketing and advertising resource.[126]

Such predatory strategies can be avoided or undone, at least partially. In the South African case, community activists joined with the Black Sash, a campaigning non-governmental organisation, to launch successful lawsuits against Net1. That led to the company losing its disbursement contract, and distribution of cash transfers was brought back under public control via the national Post Office. However, by creating a new financial services platform for low-income earners, Net1 went on to capitalise on its access to grant recipients and was able, in Samantha Ashman's description, to 'build a customer base which is now independent of the state contract for social grants ... and [to turn] social grants into collateral to receive loans and to acquire debt'.[127] Nonetheless, more than 70% of grant recipients now receive their payments in ways that do not allow for automatic deductions.[128]

Ferguson questions another assumption implicit in the 'commodification' objection, specifically the notion that money contaminates a 'money-less solidarity' which is said to typify relations in poor communities.[129] In reality – and this is evident in South Africa and elsewhere – that solidarity takes diverse forms, including cash-based distributional networks (such as 'stokvels', or informal loan schemes, and burial societies) that help sustain livelihoods and prop up social personhood. This is borne out also in Michelle Williams' research among social grant recipients in the Eastern Cape province, which found that the cash payments circulate promiscuously within local communities.[130]

Thus the allegedly commodifying effect of a UBI can operate in another direction if the payment enables people to engage in activities that are decommodified – volunteering, care work, studies, hobbies, food cultivation, home repairs and improvement, artisanal production, recycling and energy generation are a few examples. There is a potential, rich interplay between a UBI and the community economy strategies promoted by JK Gibson-Graham and others.[131] Highlighting the affinities between a UBI and community economies, Mary Lawhon and Tyler McCreary suggest that

> the economic security provided by a UBI enables experimentation with alternative economies and an income that might supplement the higher production costs of some locally produced goods.[132]

This is especially relevant in the context of climate change shocks, economic instability and social crisis. A UBI, even though paid in the form of money, has the potential to serve as more than sheer 'income'. It can offer a platform for creating and participating in socially relevant work and productive activities, including cooperative production, and it can serve campaigns and actions in pursuit of local social and economic change. Those potentials should not be exaggerated, especially if the payment amount is small. But even a modest UBI could provide a basis for local and democratised production and exchange alongside the dominant circuitries of the capitalist economy, and for anchoring and broadening people's repertoire of social, economic and other activities.

IS A JOB GUARANTEE PREFERABLE?

The option of a job guarantee is frequently presented as a more desirable alternative to a basic income, not least because it aligns with prevailing waged work-centred frameworks.[133] A job guarantee scheme is a direct public employment policy, managed by the state, which offers a guaranteed job to all people who are willing and able to work. It maintains the link between employment and income, with the state acting as 'employer of last resort' by creating a buffer stock of jobs that fluctuate in line with private sector employment trends.[134]

Proponents claim a job guarantee would be at least as effective for achieving many of the stated objectives of a UBI, while being more affordable, productive, socially desirable and morally supportable. They predict a slew of advantages. In Pavlina Tcherneva's view,

> a well-structured guaranteed employment that offers opportunities for meaningful work at a living wage, counters the precariousness of the labour market by eliminating unemployment, drastically reducing poverty and enhancing the individual freedom to say 'no' to bad jobs.[135]

According to the US Center on Budget and Policy Priorities, a national job guarantee would eliminate working poverty, revive the tax base, support the provision of socially desirable goods and services, and have a stabilising macroeconomic effect (since it would expand and contract in inverse relation to the private sector labour market).[136] Even though a job guarantee may be administratively costly,[137] it would be considerably cheaper than a UBI.[138] Supporters also claim it would be 'self-targeting'. Since well-off individuals are unlikely to take up job guarantee employment, the scheme would reach and benefit very poor people, who would 'self-select' as job guarantee beneficiaries. In satisfying the demand for a 'right to work', a job guarantee would combine the material benefits of cash income with the intangible, affective rewards of enhanced self-worth, social status and inclusion.[139] By substituting wages for welfare, it would neutralise the 'something-for-nothing' objection that is levelled against UBI proposals.

A job guarantee is also expected to push up the minimum wage. In a competitive labour market, a job guarantee that assures any eligible person a job with a prescribed wage and benefit package would establish the floor for wages and benefits in the private sector. Since workers would be able to reject work offers at lower wages, private employers would have to raise their employment offers accordingly.[140] Advocates believe these schemes could help stabilise the economy by guaranteeing incomes during downturns, and they could bring supply-side benefits by maintaining skills levels and keeping unemployed workers connected to the labour market. In more visionary scenarios, a job guarantee and/or a job-share programme could be linked with a shorter work week, so everyone who wants to work can do so.[141] In this manner, a job guarantee could invert the conventional approach to job creation in capitalist economies: instead of hinging access to work on a market-driven demand for labour, it would manipulate the demand for labour to the needs of workers.[142]

A job guarantee programme could also be synchronised with forward-looking development strategies – for example, with a low-carbon industrial strategy, environmental protection programmes, and with more equitable labour market inclusion (favouring women and excluded minorities). Whereas the 'greening' impact of a UBI is unlikely to be direct and would depend more on tax and other financing mechanisms such as a carbon tax, a job guarantee could achieve a more direct impact if the jobs were designed explicitly to advance environmental objectives. Antoine Godin modelled a 'green' job guarantee in the United States (including retrofitting insulation in public buildings and other 'eco-friendly' work) and found it to be cost-effective for the public purse.[143]

An important criticism is that the jobs on offer are likely to be makeshift and 'artificial', though that risk can be reduced if the scheme is embedded in democratic decision-making in communities. This would hold especially for 'green' jobs. A job guarantee can service and democratise local development if it is aligned with democratic local institutions and processes that decide development strategies at local levels. A job guarantee would not introduce those conditions, but it could support and deepen their impact.

Critiques of a job guarantee

A job guarantee conforms with the view of waged work as a central basis for social merit and belonging, and with the view that paid work is a morally necessary condition for cash transfers to poor people (which also underpins the concept of workfare). Bill Mitchell and Thomas Fazi, for example, prefer a job guarantee to a UBI on the basis that it offers 'dignity' in addition to cash and is not vulnerable to objections about 'free-riding',[144] while Tcherneva has argued that a job guarantee would offer empowerment and validation which welfare programmes lack.[145] Embedded in such claims is the assumption that the act of working itself fulfils basic rights (rather than potentially enabling one to realise those rights).

Although a job guarantee is sometimes characterised as a 'right to work', advocates prefer framing in terms of a 'duty to work' – a duty which, they argue, carries potential social and economic benefits, and promotes social solidarity. Nonetheless, given that job guarantee schemes are likely to involve low-productivity and low-wage state-sponsored jobs, it is not clear how they will, in essence, differ from workfare (where people are required to work for welfare benefits). Matt Bruenig has warned that a job guarantee would, by design, function like a workfare programme.[146] He argues that the kinds of jobs appropriate for a programme that serves as an 'employer of last resort' are not likely to be 'good' or desirable ones, and will be suitable only for low-skilled workers. It is likely that business employers would prefer to limit the remit of a job guarantee scheme to only those jobs which the private sector cannot or will not provide. They would also prefer that wages are set at levels that do not generate competition with low-wage private sector jobs. Schemes of that sort are unlikely to yield the potential benefits that attract supporters to the concept. Martin Ravallion's review of existing schemes lends weight to those concerns, prompting his observation that

> having a good and worthwhile job no doubt adds to one's satisfaction with life, but that is not as a rule the type of work provided in workfare schemes in poor countries. That work is typically, and deliberately, unpleasant.[147]

In Bruenig's view, the job guarantee is essentially a revival of the ideal of full-time, full employment – an elusive goal which was at the centre of the New Deal in Depression-era United States, and which shaped labour market policies in many other countries in subsequent decades.[148] It gained renewed attention in 2020 when it was included as a plank in the presidential candidacy of Bernie Sanders.[149] These kinds of proposals are grounded in the assumption that people 'deserve' a livable income insofar as they are willing to perform waged work. That value claim is built into a job guarantee, even versions that focus on care work, community-building and 'green' jobs. It ties subsistence to wage labour and deepens the stigmatising gap between 'productive' and 'unproductive' individuals. Unlike a UBI which, as Gillian Hart has noted, 'lacks points of leverage for instilling in its recipients the "correct" attitudes and aspirations', a job guarantee is invested with strong disciplinary overtones.[150] Referring to public works programmes in South Africa, Shireen Hassim has highlighted

> an in-built normative choice in the emphasis on public works programmes as opposed to expansion of the scale of welfare benefits that sets up a two-tier system of benefits, with people on work-related programmes treated as 'deserving poor' and those on welfare (and particularly mothers drawing the child support grant) as either passive dependent subjects or cunning exploiters of the system.[151]

A job guarantee poses significant practical questions and concerns, too. Experience shows that the programmes are administratively burden-some, unexpectedly expensive, frequently wasteful and difficult to target accurately at households that are most in need. They are also prone to capture by local elites and potentially can be reconfigured in ways that depart from the original visions of their proponents. A job guarantee can also be used to tie access to social provisioning to work requirements. In addition, if private sector companies (including companies contracted by the state) are able to draw on job guarantee-funded labour, the scheme could function as a disguised state subsidy to capital – though Tcherneva believes this can be avoided by targeting job guarantee activities at social provisioning ('production for use' rather than 'production for profit').[152]

What happens in the 'real world'?

Real-world examples of job guarantee programmes have received uneven reviews. Argentina's Plan Jefes, for example, has been evaluated favourably, while India's National Rural Employment Guarantee Act has earned less glowing assessments. Introduced in 2002 in response to a severe economic crisis, the Argentinian scheme was aimed at heads of households, offering them four hours of work per day. It employed about 13% of the country's labour force (approximately two million workers) and was rolled back as the national economy improved. Remuneration was set a little below the minimum wage for unskilled workers. Evaluations have shown that the programme helped beneficiaries (most of whom worked in community projects) avoid or escape indigence and that its positive impact extended beyond increased incomes. People were able to identify unmet needs in their communities and help develop suitable jobs, including in day care, public libraries, after-school activities, artisanal production, and environmental clean-up and recycling.[153]

India has undertaken similar interventions, in the shape of employment guarantee schemes, the first of which began in Maharashtra state in 1973. That scheme was scaled up nationally in 2005, via the National Rural Employment Guarantee Act, which (in theory) guarantees at least 100 days of waged work to each household per year and enshrines the right to work in law. The work is typically unskilled manual labour that is performed in labour-intensive public works projects.[154]

According to Tcherneva, the Indian programme has reduced the pay gap between men and women among the poor and has helped raise wages for low-income private sector workers.[155] However, Ravallion noted the high administrative and management costs associated with the programme, its capture by local leaders (who rationed and used access to jobs for political and personal gain), as well as other forms of corruption.[156] The overall impact on poverty appeared to be small when set against the administrative and other costs (which tend to be very high in decentralised programmes). In Bihar state, the Indian programme reduced rural poverty by about 1%,[157] much lower than the predicted 14% reduction.[158] In addition, the programme failed to provide work to everyone who needed it, failed to pay them on time, and was costly to implement. There is some evidence that the scheme has worked better in other states (including

Andhra Pradesh), where it has been associated with some wage gains.[159] Overall, according to Ravallion, the evidence suggests that India's

> Employment Guarantee Schemes have been less cost effective in reducing current poverty through the earnings gains to workers than one would expect from even untargeted transfers, as in a UBI. This calculation could switch in favor of workfare schemes if they can produce assets of value (directly or indirectly) to poor people, though the evidence is mixed on this aspect of the schemes so far in India.[160]

In South Africa, a job guarantee programme has not yet been attempted, though a national public works programme has evolved through several iterations. Anna McCord's research findings caution against exaggerated expectations.[161] She has noted that South African and international evidence suggests that public works programmes tend to provide respite from poverty for participants and reduce the depth of poverty *during* employment, but that the effect soon wanes and that very few participants transition to full-time jobs. Complementary social development interventions are needed to achieve a lasting impact.

Analysing recent data from the Expanded Public Works Programme (EPWP) in South Africa, Christi van der Westhuizen has highlighted the small proportion of unemployed South Africans who have benefitted, and the evidence that the EPWP may be undermining the provision of decent jobs, replacing them with precarious, underpaid employment.[162] Other researchers have concluded that South Africa's wage-subsidy and public work programmes have failed to make an impact on either unemployment rates or inequality.[163] Those findings match earlier concerns about the South African state's capacity to effectively target the public works programmes towards the poorest sections of society and to efficiently administer them on the scale needed. After reviewing the early phases of the EPWP, Charles Meth described as 'hollow' the claim that the EPWP was functioning as an 'employer of last resort'.[164]

Combining a job guarantee and basic income

The respective attractions and drawbacks of a job guarantee and a UBI tempt the question whether the two schemes can be combined. Cynthia Estlund believes they are difficult to reconcile due to excessive cost and because they advance conflicting norms: the non-stigmatising right not to work versus the conditionality of paid work.[165] The normative objection seems weak, though. The value-laden authority assigned to waged work will not disappear overnight, even when paid work is scarce – as is evident in South Africa. Those two norms will unavoidably coexist for some time. And they may be more compatible than is commonly assumed. For example, the demand for radically reduced but well-remunerated working hours simultaneously expresses both the right not to work and the right to work, by challenging the subjugation of human life to waged work.

Tcherneva also argues that the two mechanisms could be combined, and looks to the Jefes programme in Argentina for clues on how to do so.[166] That programme started as a quasi basic income scheme. Once registered, unemployed heads of household immediately began receiving income payments (until the jobs programme was up and running, at which point they took up their public sector jobs). In combination with a range of other income guarantees (child grants, old-age pensions, disability allowances and so on), the job guarantee programme would guarantee an income to all, but require able-bodied persons to perform community work.

An approach proposed for South Africa goes much further.[167] Its social policy elements hinge on an interplay between a series of guaranteed income payments (the existing social grants plus a new caregiver grant and an unemployment grant) and continued expansion of the extended public works programme until the latter becomes an employer of last resort by 2030. The difference between the unemployment grant (about R1 000 or US$70 per month initially) and the public works wage (about R3 500 or US$235 per month) would counter any disincentivising effect the grant might have on job seeking. Crucially, the interventions would occur alongside an ambitious set of macroeconomic, trade and industrial policy changes, as well as a major public–private investment initiative targeting selected, mainly manufacturing, sectors. The modelled outcome for this scenario foresees uptake of the unemployment grant steadily declining as job creation increases. The combination seems promising as a way to reduce poverty, though it would be an administratively complex and expensive undertaking. Moreover, it is anchored in a waged work framework, which deprives it of the liberating potential of a UBI.

A more innovative way of blending the two options would be a participation-based income guarantee, which Tony Atkinson has proposed.[168] Eligibility for the basic income would be based not on citizenship or residence, but on 'participation' – a conditional basic income, in other words. 'Participation' would be defined liberally as a verifiable commitment – a 'contribution contract' with the local community, for instance – to support and contribute to one's community through, for example, care work, teaching, mentoring and so on, or to perform other socially useful activities such as studying or undergoing training.[169] This has the advantage of being decentred and of linking a basic income to local community dynamics and needs, and to a sense of localised belonging and mutual obligation. The approach would be compatible with collaborative and participatory 'civic economy' approaches where people together identify local needs and conceive and implement socially useful projects.[170] As such, according to Carolyn Kagan, it would challenge 'conventional thinking about work, social protection and participation'.[171]

Those kinds of outcomes are highly desirable, though the approach invites a temptation to monitor and enforce participation, thus retaining the coercive characteristics of workfare and conventional welfare programmes (at considerable administrative cost). Even if the supervision is ceded to local community organisations, a coercive potential and opportunities for corruption remain. Democratised and vibrant civic life and governance could avert or resist capture by local economic and political elites, though this can be difficult to achieve in settings of extreme inequality and dire need. It would be less risky to part with the participation requirement – which effectively would convert the scheme to a UBI.

5

Financing a Universal Basic Income

For many people, it goes without saying that a UBI scheme would be unaffordable. But such blanket verdicts are misguided. Before pronouncing on the cost of a UBI scheme we have to be clear about its design. And before declaring it unaffordable, we have to consider the financing options.

The cost will depend on many variables, including the payment amount, decisions about who is eligible, whether and how the payment is gradually phased in, whether it is indexed to inflation or another indicator, whether it is paid instead of or in addition to other social provisioning, the administrative burden it entails, and more. In addition, the context in which a UBI operates is decisively important. That context is shaped by fiscal considerations, macroeconomic choices and political calculations – and they differ from country to country.

WHAT A BASIC INCOME WOULD COST

An abundance of UBI costing calculations has been done in recent years, mostly in industrialised countries and often arriving at exceedingly expensive estimates. Widely varied assumptions are built into these costings, and they should be assessed carefully.

In the context of the United States, for example, Robert Greenstein of the Center on Budget and Policy Priorities calculated that paying a UBI of US$10 000 per year to each of the over 300 million Americans would have cost US$3.3 trillion in 2016.[1] That amounted to approximately three-quarters of the entire federal budget and almost equalled the total annual federal tax revenue. Making the UBI taxable would reduce the annual cost by roughly one-third, to about US$2.4 trillion. Halving it (to US$5 000 per year) would reduce the cost further, but would put the payment well below the poverty line for individuals (US$12 700 in 2016).[2] Paying the income only to adults would reduce costs even further, while also reducing its impact. Other, less eye-watering estimates have also appeared. A household-based negative income tax that is set at the poverty line in the United States (to lift all families' incomes above that line) would cost about US$219 billion per year, according to calculations done by Jessica Wiederspan and her colleagues.[3] A negative income tax is not an ideal way to achieve a basic income, but the broader point remains: the claim that a UBI is unaffordable is not axiomatic.[4]

In Canada, the UBI Works campaign has proposed a combination of a Can$500 per month non-taxable payment to every adult (effectively a basic income) and a variable guaranteed income to ensure that each adult has a minimum income of Can$2 000 per month. It calculated the total cost at Can$199 billion per year,[5] a little more than the Can$180 billion in federal bonds which the Bank of Canada purchased in 2020 as part of its Quantitative Easing programme.[6] Groups in the United Kingdom have campaigned for a similar UBI, which would phase into a permanent UBI. One such proposal, from the social advocacy network Compass, is to use a UBI to introduce a solid income floor for everyone.[7] The design is complex and includes topping up an existing child benefit – in effect a basic income for children.

The basic income would then be pared back to a smaller but permanent basic income, to provide a floor beneath the current social security system (while additional unemployment, housing and disability benefits are maintained). Compass claims the scheme would be highly affordable.

In one Compass proposal, an eventual UBI would be small, totalling about £10 400 per year for a family of four, but eminently affordable at £20 billion (equal to about half of the aggregate cuts made to benefits in the United Kingdom since 2010, and equal to the cost of the government's 2020 wage subsidy scheme over three months). Larger payments would, of course, involve higher net cost. To finance the intervention, Compass proposes a small rise in tax rates and adjustments to some personal income tax allowances that are of no benefit to low-income earners and people who are out of work.[8]

Variables affecting the cost in South Africa

South Africa has a much less complicated and less extensive welfare system than most developed countries, which simplifies the ways in which a UBI would interact with other forms of social assistance. Many of the remaining considerations, though, resemble those shaping the examples cited above: who is eligible, what payment amount is chosen, whether or not the UBI is phased in, at what rate the amount changes, whether the UBI is paid in addition to (which) existing forms of social support or as a supplement, and more. The first two variables have the biggest effect on the cost of a UBI scheme.

Consider, for example, setting a monthly UBI payment at an amount equivalent to the food poverty line (R585 per month in 2020), or the lower-bound poverty line (R840 in 2020) or the upper-bound poverty line (R1 268 in 2020),[9] and paying it to adults aged 18–59 years (older people would receive the old-age pension, worth R1 860 per month). In 2020, there were approximately 34.1 million South African citizens and residents in that age group, so a UBI equivalent to the food poverty line would have cost approximately R239 billion (or US$15.9 billion at an exchange rate of 15:1). The corresponding annual amounts for a UBI pegged to the lower-bound poverty line and the upper-bound poverty line would have been R343 billion and R519 billion, respectively. By way of comparison, current social grants were expected to cost approximately R188 billion in 2020/21.[10]

The cost would also be influenced by how a UBI links with existing forms of income support. It could represent the floor or basis for certain other cash transfers. For example, a UBI of R840 per month that is paid to adults aged 18–59 years could constitute the first R840 of the disability grant (worth R1 860 in 2020) or of the foster care grant (R1 040 in 2020) paid to people eligible for those grants. Or it could be paid in addition to those grants. The choice skews the total costs significantly.

Similarly, the UBI could subsume the child support grant (R440 in 2020), or be paid in addition to it (since, strictly speaking, that grant is intended for children younger than 18 years even though the money is transferred to an adult caregiver). A truly universal UBI would be paid to both adults and children, which is especially important in societies with high rates of child poverty and where single parenthood is common. If children are eligible, it requires deciding whether they receive the same amount as adults or a smaller amount. If children are not deemed eligible, the cut-off age (15 years or 18 years, for example) becomes relevant and has cost implications: in South Africa, about 29% of the population is younger than 15 years of age and 34% is younger than 18 years.[11] Whether a UBI is paid only to citizens or to all documented residents or to all residents also has cost (and other) implications. There is a strong moral case to include documented residents, including asylum seekers.[12]

The criteria need not remain fixed and can evolve over time, allowing a UBI to be phased in even though its initial versions are not, strictly speaking, *universal*. So, a UBI can be phased in by restricting access initially to certain categories of beneficiaries (starting with out-of-work adults, or with adults earning less than a specified amount, for instance), then steadily relaxing access; and by progressively increasing the amount (starting with a small amount that increases along a schedule or as specified criteria are met).

Ideally, a UBI payment would have to be indexed, to prevent it from being devalued by inflation over time. A UBI therefore can be configured along different lines, each of which leads to different cost estimates.

Ultimately, the goal of universality has to define the process, even if the steps towards achieving a UBI are incremental.[13] What must be clear is that the mechanism is not simply an elaboration of safety-net social policy, with the basic income functioning as a supplementary 'grant' to support 'those left behind' during times of crisis. As Scott Santens puts it:

> The basic income should be designed with flexibility and long-term viability in mind. It should operate as a platform we construct above the poverty line, that we can continue ratcheting up year after year ever further above the poverty line, but at any point adjust and optimize through ongoing funding method decisions.[14]

Some costing estimates for South Africa

The debate around a basic income in South Africa revived in the late 2010s, but it was the COVID-19 crisis that sparked fresh recognition of the need for new forms of social provisioning.

In mid-2021, a coalition of forty civil society organisations,[15] along with prominent religious figures, academics and human rights lawyers, called for the introduction of a monthly payment of R1 268 (equal to the upper-bound poverty line) to all adults. In-principle support for a basic income has been voiced in other quarters, too, including the Congress of South African Trade Unions, the South African Federation of Trade Unions, the ANC and the national Department of Social Development. In mid-2021, President Cyril Ramaphosa said that a BIG for unemployed people was being considered.[16] But very different arrangements were being mooted.

Whereas the activist-driven #UBIGNOW campaign campaigned for immediately introducing a basic income worth R1 268 per month, other proposals were much less ambitious. For example, in August 2020, the ANC's Social Transformation Committee proposed a phased approach, starting with a R500 per month payment for unemployed (but economically active) adults from 2024 and then gradually expanding. The proposed initial amount was lower than the minimum a person needed to meet basic daily nutrition needs and it would be paid on highly exclusive terms, only to adults (aged 19–59 years) who do not receive any other cash transfers.[17] Operating alongside the payment would be job programmes to train and channel young people into employment. The payments would be funded through the tax contributions of employed individuals and other tax mechanisms. Estimates indicated that paying such a basic income to about 33 million eligible recipients would cost R198 billion annually.[18]

In 2020, the Department of Social Development proposed offering a basic income payment to age groups it considers to be at greatest risk (18–24 or 18–35 year olds and the 50–59-year age group) and then gradually broadening coverage over three to five years. It emphasised combining a basic income payment with job training and other support to ease people's entry into the labour market.[19] As the COVID-19 pandemic raged on, the department went further. In August 2021, it released a Green Paper (or draft policy document) which signalled emphatic support for converting the COVID-19 social relief of distress grant into a UBI, as part of a broader reform of social security.[20] The preference was for an income payment for people aged 18–59 years, which would be 'unconditional, individually targeted and at a level that will at least lift the individual out of poverty'.[21] It would be paid in addition to the existing social grants for children, the elderly and people with disabilities. The Green Paper highlighted the simplicity, efficiency and social inclusiveness of a UBI:

> The key benefit of universal benefits is that it promotes social solidarity and buy-in to the system; and it is administratively much simpler to administer with fewer exclusion challenges. It reduces stigma of the poor and discontent amongst the wealthy who feel that they are the ones funding the system. It also reduces fragmentation of systems as we see in South Africa where we have tax thresholds and grant thresholds set at very different levels. South Africa's tax authority is

also significantly more advanced than the Social Security Agency, hence relying on the Tax Agency ability to test income is likely to be a lot more effective than through Social Security Agency.[22]

Financing could occur at least partly by recouping the cost through technical adjustments to income tax brackets. If set at the food poverty line, the income support would cost approximately R200 billion, requiring a 10% increase in income tax, according to the Green Paper. At that amount, the main objective would be to reduce hunger, though the paper held out the prospect of a basic income graduating to higher, aspirational amounts.[23] Weeks later, following criticism from the National Treasury and business organisations about a proposal to use income tax increases to fund a state-controlled social security fund, the paper was withdrawn.[24]

The Department of Social Development's proposal closely resembled that of the Black Sash, which also recommended converting the COVID-19 social relief of distress grants into a 'basic income support' for unemployed people aged 18–59 years. In December 2021, an expert panel convened by the Department of Social Development and the International Labour Organization made a similar recommendation.[25] Pegged at first to the food poverty line, the payment would increase stepwise until it became a fully fledged UBI. It would augment, not replace, the wider social protection system.[26]

The most detailed costed options have come from the Institute for Economic Justice.[27] These also use a phased-in approach, with scaled-up versions of the COVID-19 emergency grants functioning as a bridge to an eventual comprehensive UBI.

Such an incremental approach is likely to be more palatable fiscally and more marketable politically, while providing some socioeconomic support. Despite its low amount of R350 per person per month, the COVID-19 social relief of distress grant reduced food poverty within the first few months of implementation (though hunger and food insecurity remained at distressingly high levels).[28] Even with incomplete uptake, the grant could prevent approximately 6.8 million people from going hungry if it were increased to R585 per month (equivalent to the food poverty line).[29]

The Institute for Economic Justice calculated cost scenarios for monthly payments pegged to the food poverty, lower-bound poverty and upper-bound poverty values, amounts it believes are affordable in the short term.[30] It also calculated the total cost of monthly R2 500 and R3 500 payments (both well under the national minimum wage of R4 045 in 2020). Recipients (people aged 18–59 years) were grouped into several eligibility categories (Table 5.1).

The targeted options shown in Table 5.1 reflect an awareness that, 'in the context of finite resources, there is a trade-off between increasing the pool of recipients and the amount which they receive'.[31] However, targeted and means-tested options are also administratively burdensome and costly, and can be highly inefficient for reaching the designated beneficiaries, as experiences with the COVID-19 social relief of distress grants showed (discussed in the final part of this section). They are prone to long delays and to missing individuals who churn in and out of piecework or informal employment. Some forms of targeting would be very difficult to administer fairly and efficiently – for example, if the basic income targets people who are unemployed or who work in the informal sector, as the income sources for impoverished people constantly shift.

Targeting obviously also renders the basic income less than universal. A UBI that is paid to everyone aged 18–59 years (with an old-age pension going to everyone aged 60 years and older) should be the goal – with a target date and schedule for reaching the goal. That would provide campaigning organisations with the leverage to hold the state accountable to its commitments.

A UBI paid to all residents aged 18–59 years (roughly 34.1 million people in 2020) is also more expensive (Table 5.1). Annually, it would cost:
- R239 billion for a UBI payment equal to the food poverty line;
- R343 billion for a payment equal to the lower-bound poverty line;
- R519 billion for a payment equal to the upper-bound poverty line; and
- R1 023 billion for a payment worth R2 500 per month.

Table 5.1: Total estimated annual cost of a basic income at different levels of eligibility, uptake and value (in rand) in South Africa, 2020

18–59 years	Number of recipients	R585 per month (food poverty line)	R840 per month (lower-bound poverty line)	R1 268 per month (upper-bound poverty line)	R2 500 per month	R3 500 per month
All	34.1 million	239 billion	343 billion	519 billion	1 023 billion	1 432 billion
All (80% uptake)	27.3 million	192 billion	275 billion	415 billion	818 billion	1 146 billion
All (60% uptake)	20.5 million	144 billion	206 billion	311 billion	614 billion	859 billion
Informal workers*	2.5 million	18 billion	25 billion	38 billion	76 billion	106 billion
Unemployed	11 million	78 billion	111 billion	168 billion	330 billion	462 billion
Not economically active	13.4 million	94 billion	135 billion	203 billion	401 billion	562 billion
Not formally employed	22.4 million	157 billion	226 billion	341 billion	672 billion	940 billion

Source: Institute for Economic Justice. *Financing Options for a Universal Basic Income in South Africa.* Social Protection Series Policy Brief No. 2. Johannesburg: Institute for Economic Justice, 2021. https://www.iej.org.za/wp-content/uploads/2021/08/IEJ-policy-brief-UBIG-july2021_3.pdf.

Note: Numbers of eligible recipients were calculated using Statistics South Africa data and have been rounded. Unless otherwise indicated, the costings assume 100% uptake in each of the categories.

* This refers to informal sector workers only (not domestic workers, precariously employed persons, etc.).

By way of comparison, South Africa's 2020/21 budget allocated R384.7 billion for education; R229.7 billion for health; R221.5 billion for social protection; R207.1 billion for police, courts, prisons, defence and state security; and R229.3 billion for debt service costs.[32] Table 5.2 places the annual cost of various UBI payments in a wider fiscal context.

The impact on poverty and inequality would be substantial. Modelling done by Applied Development Research Solutions indicates that, even if set at a low amount (equal to the food poverty line), a UBI that is paid to all adults aged 18–59 years would reduce the poverty gap in South Africa by more than half within five years (Table 5.3).[33] If raised to the level of the upper-bound poverty line, the payment would reduce the

Table 5.2: Estimated costs (in rand) of various UBI payments annually and as a percentage of education and health spending, projected tax revenue and projected GDP in South Africa, 2020/21 financial year

UBI amount paid to all 18–59 year olds per month (2020)	UBI cost per year (2020) (billions)	As % of 2020/21 budget allocation for education and health	As % of total projected tax revenue for 2020/21* (R1 425.4 billion)	As % of projected GDP for 2020/21* (R5 428.2 billion)
R585 – equal to food poverty line	R239	39%	17%	4.4%
R840 – equal to lower-bound poverty line	R343	56%	24%	6.3%
R1 268 – equal to upper-bound poverty line	R519	84%	36%	9.6%
R2 500	R1 023	167%	72%	19%

Source: Author's calculations based on data provided in National Treasury. *Budget Review 2020.* Pretoria: National Treasury, Republic of South Africa, 2020.

* Projections at February 2020. As in other countries, due to the COVID-19 pandemic, both actual GDP and tax revenue for 2020/21 decreased.

poverty gap by more than 80% over five years and by over 40% within the first year. A UBI paid to residents of all ages (adults and children) and pegged to the upper-bound poverty line would entirely eliminate the poverty gap within a year. Both an adult basic income and a UBI would reduce income inequality by 14–18% over five years.[34] In addition, the payment bias towards low-income households (which have a higher propensity to consume than high-income households) would generate a positive impact on economic growth and employment, especially in the UBI scenarios.[35]

Devil in the detail

Although fiscally more attractive and politically more 'winnable', an evolving UBI that is phased in poses important conceptual and practical issues. There is a very obvious, immediate need for additional

Table 5.3: Estimated annual cost (in rand) of different types of UBI at different amounts, and modelled impact on poverty in South Africa, 2020–2025

Payment type	Eligibility*	No. of recipients 2021 (rounded)	Monthly amount 2021	Monthly amount 2025****	Direct annual cost 2021	Poverty rate*** change 2020–2025	Poverty gap*** change 2020–2025
Unemployment grant**	Unemployed, 18–59 years, not receiving any other grants, not in school	8.9 million	R882 (L-BPL)	R1 072 (L-BPL)	R94.2 billion	38.8% to 27.6%	13.3% to 7.6%
Unemployment grant**	Unemployed, 18–59 years, not receiving any other grants, not in school	8.9 million	R1 331 (U-BPL)	R1 618 (U-BPL)	R145.6 billion	38.8% to 23.3%	13.3% to 6.5%
Adult basic income A**	Adults, 18–59 years	35.3 million	R614 (FPL)	R747 (FPL)	R259.9 billion	38.8% to 25.3%	13.3% to 7.6%
Adult basic income B**	Adults, 18–59 years	35.3 million	R1 331 (U-BPL)	R1 618 (U-BPL)	R563.4 billion	38.8% to 13.2%	13.3% to 2.0%
Universal basic income A**	All ages	59.5 million	R614 (FPL)	R747 (FPL)	R438.7 billion	38.8% to 13.9%	13.3% to 3.6%
Universal basic income B**	All ages	59.5 million	R1 331 (U-BPL)	R1 618 (U-BPL)	R950.9 billion	38.8% to zero	13.3% to zero

L-BPL = lower-bound poverty line; U-BPL = upper-bound poverty line; FPL = food poverty line

Sources: Adapted from Adelzadeh, A. 'Preliminary Modelling Results of a Basic Income Grant in South Africa.' Presentation to #UBIG Workshop, 29 January 2021; Applied Development Research Solutions. 'Fiscally Neutral Basic Income Grant Scenarios: Economic and Development Impacts.' *The Bridge* no. 7 (May 2021).

* Unemployment defined according to Statistics South Africa's 'broadly unemployed' category.

** Current state grants such as the child support, care dependency, old-age pension and disability grants remain in place.

*** Both the poverty rate and poverty gap were calculated using the upper-bound poverty line (2021 value) and annually adjusted upward by 5%.

**** Payments adjust upward by 5% annually.

support and protection in the face of chronic lack, insecurity, suffering and stress, not least during the COVID-19 pandemic. Hence the emphasis to be found in several UBI proposals in South Africa on prolonging the emergency relief grants that were introduced in 2020 and extended in 2021, and then transforming those grants into a basic income payment, with steadily widening eligibility. Such a phased, maturing strategy would respond to a pressing need for non-wage livelihood support.

But such a tactical compromise turns the putative *universal* basic income, even if only for the time being, into something qualitatively different: a means-tested and targeted income payment. The pitfalls of means-testing and targeting were on clear display with the COVID-19 social relief of distress grant. Research commissioned by the Black Sash found that the design of the application system effectively excluded large numbers of eligible beneficiaries, and that up to one-third of applications were rejected due to incorrect or out-of-date information on government databases. Successful applicants had to wait several months before receiving their first payment and were re-assessed on a monthly basis to ensure that they had no other income source. The amount the eventual beneficiaries received was enough to pay for about 60% of the minimum nutrition intake for an adult.[36]

In sum, the grant combined the worst of means-tested and targeted social support. Miserly and inefficient for reaching all eligible recipients, it was designed and implemented in ways that underscored the state's intrusive authority, distrust of citizens and unjustified faith in its own efficiency.[37] In every respect, that conflicts with the democratising and emancipatory appeal of a fully fledged UBI. There is also no guarantee that a phased-in intervention will steadily evolve towards a generous UBI without being arrested in stunted form. That will depend on the social and political forces driving the UBI demand, a matter considered more closely in the next chapter.

PAYING FOR A UNIVERSAL BASIC INCOME

For a middle-income country such as South Africa, a debt-financed UBI would be an unattractive route over the medium to long term. However, there may be scope in the short term for some debt-based financing of a UBI, while other financing options are introduced. (Some of the tax-related mechanisms, for example, could require several years of legislative and other preparation.) In some economies, a social dividend fund financed from the exploitation of natural resources (such as the Alaska Permanent Fund) has been proposed. However, relying on natural resource rents is not compatible with an ecologically responsible growth path, nor are options that require high rates of carbon-intensive economic growth to increase the tax base.

Income and other taxes

Most attractive to UBI proponents is a combination of existing tax instruments, such as increased VAT or general sales tax, excise tax (for example on luxury items and/or capital goods), personal income tax and wealth tax, as well as 'sin' taxes on tobacco and alcohol.

During the BIG campaign in South Africa, Pieter le Roux argued that the net impact of a VAT increase would be progressive and that the mechanism would distort the economy less than increases in income taxes or corporate taxes.[38] Similarly, Jeremy Seekings and Heidi Matisonn have claimed that VAT increases would 'spread the burden across a wider range of quintiles, although the top quintiles continue to pay the lion's share.'[39] While increased excise taxes (particularly on luxury goods) could be a redistributive source of financing, increasing VAT would be regressive (all else being equal), since VAT represents a much larger share of spending for low-income households than for those in higher-income brackets (the lower half of income earners spends approximately 80% of income on items or services that are subject to VAT). Relying on increased indirect taxes would significantly reduce the net gain to low-income recipients.

In the South African scenario, for example, Le Roux calculated that a 50% increase in indirect taxes would reduce a nominal R100 monthly UBI payment to between R59 and R90 per month for people in the bottom five income deciles.[40] A basic contention of the BIG Financing Reference Group remains valid:

> The structure of taxation must ultimately be overhauled, both to make the tax system more progressive (i.e., to shift a larger proportion of the total tax burden onto higher income earners) and to increase total revenue collection.[41]

Among the most detailed tax-based calculations currently available for South Africa are the estimates prepared by the Institute for Economic Justice.[42] Those calculations suggest that a combination of 18 financing sources (16 of them tax-related) could yield almost R260 billion in the 2022/23 financial year, rising to R335 billion in 2024/25.

The largest financing sources would be a social security tax (contributing about 25% of the total), a resource rent tax (15%), reducing or recovering a minor proportion of wasteful or irregular state expenditure (about 15%), eliminating retirement fund contributions and medical tax credits for high-income earners (about 11%), removing corporate tax breaks (about 7%), and introducing a 25% VAT on luxury items (also about 7%).[43]

The biggest single financing source in the Institute's scenarios is a social security tax on income, levied on a sliding scale on all taxable incomes. Starting at 1.5%, it would rise to 2% for annual incomes higher than R80 000, 2.5% for incomes between R350 000 and R1 million, and 3% for incomes higher than R1 million. It would be ring-fenced and dedicated to expanding social security. Having an earmarked funding source could help safeguard a UBI against cutbacks or removal;[44] the Alaska Permanent Fund, for example, is explicitly tied to Alaska's guaranteed income.[45]

Levying a social security tax on low-income taxpayers, however, would slash the net benefits they receive from a UBI. In addition, relying predominantly on a personal income tax, especially if levied against relatively modest incomes, may stoke resentment and undermine public support for a UBI, a concern which Yanis Varoufakis has highlighted.[46] Given that upward income redistribution towards the top 10% of earners in South Africa appears to occur also at the expense of earners in the middle-income deciles,[47] it may be advisable to consider targeting a social security tax at higher-income brackets (for example, R200 000 and up). Certainly, people earning less than the minimum wage equivalent (about R42 000 per year) should be exempted.

In greater detail, the other financing mechanisms proposed by the Institute are:

- a resource rent tax, levied on the economic rent of extractive industries;
- a luxury goods VAT of 25% and a temporary increase in excise duties;
- a wealth tax of 1% on the top 1% of taxpayers, rising to 3% on the top 0.1%;[48]
- abolishing medical tax credits and retirement fund contributions for high-income earners (above R1 million per year);
- increasing the dividends tax from 20% to 25%;
- increasing the estate duty tax, on a sliding scale, for large estates;
- a currency transaction tax of 0.005% on onshore currency transactions;[49]
- a financial transactions tax of 0.1%;
- cancelling the employment tax incentive;
- raising the carbon tax to one-quarter of the European Union standard;
- reducing irregular state expenditure (by 30%) and wasteful expenditure; and
- reducing profit-shifting by multinational corporations.

Several of these options are necessary sources of redistribution irrespective of whether or not a UBI is introduced. A wealth tax holds both fiscal and moral appeal, despite some concerns about its administrative complexity. It is estimated that the wealthiest 10% of South Africans own more than 90% of total private wealth.[50] Many of these high-income earners substantially reduce their tax liabilities by converting income into illiquid assets, such as real estate, stocks and other investments. A wealth tax would narrow that iniquitous option. Similarly, medical tax credits for high-income earners deepen inequality and function as mechanisms for transferring income upwards. The same can be said of the current lack of a progressive inheritance tax, which helps sustain economic inequality across generations. The surfeit of corporate subsidies and tax breaks or exemptions also requires rigorous review.[51]

The Institute for Economic Justice also sees VAT (currently at 15%) as a possible way to recoup part of the UBI cost.[52] As noted earlier, the net effect would be to 'tax back' a portion of UBI payments from the individuals who need them the most. To boost the impact of a UBI, it would be preferable to broaden current VAT exemptions to include more of the goods and services which low-income households are most likely to purchase regularly. As the Davis Tax Committee highlighted, the efficiency of VAT as a revenue source is undercut by unfairness in the absence of pro-poor exemptions and if significant revenue is not 'recycled' in the form of social grants.[53]

A corporate dividend

It is vital, of course, to find the money for a UBI, but it matters also *where* one finds the funds. Relying on personal income tax increases as a primary source of UBI financing raises more than fiscal concerns: it could have a corrosive effect of alienating low- and middle-income taxpayers, which could doom a UBI politically. It seems more advisable to fund a UBI from returns on capital. Notably, many of the UBI financing options circulating currently neglect or play down taxes on the business sector, and focus instead on individuals. This is not surprising. A tax on capital returns speaks implicitly to the ways in which wealth is produced and appropriated in capitalist societies. Such a tax would acknowledge the reality that wealth is created collectively, but is then 'privatised' and appropriated as the ostensible product of individual risk, enterprise and toil.[54]

Capital accumulation is underpinned by the extraction of value from human labour, soil, air and water, and it is bankrolled by public money and social labour: care and reproductive work, publicly funded education and healthcare, research and development, infrastructure, corporate subsidies, tax breaks and more. At this fundamental level, wealth is socially produced (by people's labour, paid or not, and by the state) and is reliant on commons (most obviously, non-human nature). The wealth is then privately appropriated. This reality is expunged from the standard narrative which claims that wealth is privately generated and then socially appropriated (through taxation).

Given the unacknowledged and largely unrecompensed collective contributions to corporate wealth, argues Varoufakis, 'the commons have a right to a share of the capital stock and associated dividends'.[55] That share can be used to finance a UBI and other public goods. Varoufakis proposes that a portion of the returns to capital be channelled into a social wealth fund from which everyone is paid a dividend. The Alaska Permanent Fund operates along similar lines; it is capitalised from oil revenues (by way of a resource rent tax; see below). An increasing number of social wealth funds have been established since 2000, though most are not deployed primarily or at all for social purposes.[56]

There are several ways to bring capital into such a fund. Legislation can be passed requiring, for example, that a percentage of capital stock (shares) from initial public offerings (an 'IPO tax') be channelled into the fund. Or it can be financed through a one-off tax on the market capitalisation of publicly traded companies or a lower ongoing tax (the total market capitalisation of the Johannesburg Stock Exchange, for example, was approximately US$1 trillion in 2020).[57] A mergers and acquisitions tax is an additional option. It can be set at 2%–3% of the transaction value (with a minimum threshold to exclude small businesses). A financial transactions tax (see below), a resource rent tax and a raised inheritance or estate tax are other options to bring capital into the fund.[58] If used to finance a UBI (or 'universal basic dividend', as Varoufakis prefers), such a corporate dividend would represent a small but significant step towards socialising the wealth countries produce and towards reducing inequality.

A resource rent tax

Contemporary capitalism is driven increasingly by the extraction of economic rents that do not require additional expenditure or effort from companies.[59] Platform capitalist giants like Facebook and Google, for example, extract digital rents by monetising data which users freely provide (and selling the resulting services to advertisers). It has become commonplace for companies, including non-financial ones, to drive up their stock prices by buying back their own shares (thus generating financial rents) rather than investing in productive activities. The capital gains of those rising stock prices add nothing of value to the real economy. Mining, oil, gas, lumber and other extractive companies are able to extract high economic rents when commodity booms increase prices well in excess of the levels needed to cover their inputs and reasonable profit margins.[60] That excess economic rent represents a profit glut that arises from factors that companies themselves are not influencing. A resource rent tax, as proposed by the Institute for Economic Justice,[61] would redistribute a portion of those excess profits, much of which would otherwise not enter the real economy. Several countries and territories already impose such a tax. China levies it on oil sales (once the oil price exceeds a designated level) and Alaska's Permanent Fund does the same. In East Timor and India, the tax is activated when rates of return for oil companies top a projected rate. The trickiest aspect of such a tax is to accurately determine the rent portion of targeted profits. Because the value of extractive commodities tends to fluctuate wildly, it is also difficult to reliably predict the amounts that can be raised with the tax.

Financial transactions tax

A tax on financial transactions (an FTT, sometimes called a 'Robin Hood tax' and occasionally also likened to the 'Tobin tax' which made headlines in the late 1990s) is frequently proposed as a financing option.[62] Such a tax would be levied on the transfer of ownership of designated financial assets (for example, stocks and equities, bonds, international currencies, and derivatives and securities such as futures, options and credit default swaps). In Joshen Bivens and Hunter Blair's view, FTTs are most effective when applied to a broad base rather than to particular classes of assets or financial marketplaces, an approach which reduces the space for tax avoidance and increases the efficiency of collection.[63]

The tax has two major potential benefits: it can discourage financial market speculation by raising the costs for speculators, and it can be a substantial source of additional government revenues. Proponents claim it would help reduce asset price volatility and bubbles, and encourage longer-term investment.[64] Hardly a novel tool, FTTs are being used effect-ively, though conservatively, in different market conditions. The United Kingdom, for example, raises about US$6.5 billion per year from a 0.5% tax on stock trading (via a stamp duty). At least 15 other countries operate some kind of FTT or have done so in the recent past.[65] Several European Union countries have adopted FTTs in some form, as have Brazil, Egypt, Hong Kong, India, Malaysia, Singapore and South Africa, among others. United States Democratic Party presidential candidate Bernie Sanders proposed an FTT in 2019, as part of his free college tuition plan.[66]

By way of example, the French FTT is set at 0.3% on French equity trades and 0.01% on high-frequency trading. Belgium imposes a sliding-scale stock exchange tax on transactions of stocks and bonds, while Switzerland taxes the transfer of equities and bonds at 0.15% for Swiss securities and 0.3% for foreign securities. Brazil's version targets a range of financial operations, including currency transactions and transfers of bonds and securities, while India imposes a securities transaction tax on share purchases and sales at designated stock exchanges. South Africa implemented a very limited FTT in 2008, in the shape of a securities transfer tax that levies a 0.25% tax on the purchase and transfer of securities. These arrangements commonly include numerous exemptions.[67]

Part of the attraction of such a tax is that the base is so large that a very low tax rate can yield impressive revenues: the 0.1% tax applied on stock trading in Hong Kong, for example, raised 1.3%–2.1% of GDP in 2008–2009.[68] It can also reduce incentives for rent-seeking and speculation. Varoufakis points out that a tax on financial capital can help stabilise financial markets and mitigate harmful macroeconomic effects.[69] This is particularly important in a period when financial capital is increasingly detached from the real economy,[70] while exerting great influence on the design of macroeconomic policy, the allocation of investment across economies, and the distribution of incomes across societies. The tax can be seen also as a form of partial reparations for the economic costs and damage associated with the activities of the financial sector in recent decades.

An FTT tends to draw two main criticisms: that it would encourage tax avoidance (through offshoring and other ruses) and that it would distort productive financial trading (which, by reducing liquidity, will raise the cost of capital and discourage investment). The potential for tax avoidance highlights the need for efficient regulatory institutions and the effective enforcement of those laws and regulations. South Africa, for example, possesses the regulatory and technical means for minimising such avoidance, but has chosen a macroeconomic strategy which relies heavily on large flows of portfolio capital;[71] the obstacles to prudent governance in this case are less technical than political. The second objection seems anachronistic, given the surfeit of liquidity since the 2008 global financial crisis, a glut which has been augmented again during the COVID-19 pandemic.

Leonard Burman and his colleagues have counselled caution with regard to the amounts of revenue an FTT can realistically raise.[72] They calculated that a putative FTT in the United States context would raise a maximum of 0.4% of GDP (equivalent to US$75 billion in 2017), with a base tax rate set at 0.34%. They also warned that higher rates would have a discouraging effect on all trading, not only speculative and rent-seeking activities, and could contribute to market volatility. In addition, they argue, as a tax on gross rather than net activity, a broad FTT would be poorly targeted at the most harmful financial sector activities. Another study arrived at a similar estimate for the United States and an estimate of €119 billion (0.69% of GDP) for the European Union as a whole.[73] Focusing on the United States economy, Robert Pollin and his collaborators have criticised Burman's estimates as overly conservative and for being inconsistent with empirical evidence from financial markets.[74] Bivens and Blair also regard those estimates as 'excessively pessimistic'.[75] Depending on how financial transaction volumes are affected by an FTT (their elasticity), they envisage potential gross revenues of US$110–403 billion annually, in line with several other estimates which predict a net revenue potential in the United States of about US$220 billion per year (equal to about 1.2% of GDP).[76]

Whereas wealth taxes are readily avoidable through tax avoidance manoeuvres, a wide-angled FTT would narrow such escape routes. The only way to avoid it would be to reduce trading, that is to say, lessen demand for goods and services in the financial sector. Pollin and his co-authors believe that if an FTT is designed to apply across stock, bond and derivative markets (and with minimal tax exemptions), it can be expected to lower trading elasticity, all else being equal.[77] Current evidence leaves it unclear whether such reductions would be mainly in unproductive trading or also in transactions that provide liquidity.[78] But the converse has not been true: as noted, increased financial transactions have not been associated with rising productive investment. Other empirical evidence suggests that a reduction in stock market trading need not have a significant negative effect on productive investments by non-financial corporations.[79]

Carbon tax

A carbon tax is an attractive financing source, as well as a potentially effective way to discourage and reduce greenhouse gas emissions.[80] An increasing number of countries are introducing such a tax. It can be levied in a number of ways, for example against carbon emissions as well as against the consumption of carbon-intensive goods and services. The tax can be calculated at a set rate, which can be increased annually to function as a steadily growing disincentive for carbon-emitting economic activities. The revenue can be fashioned into a 'climate dividend' to be paid to citizens as a UBI or in some other form. Canada, for example, is considering an option that would recycle about 90% of carbon tax revenue to citizens.[81] A carbon tax will not, in the long term, be a sustainable source of financing for a UBI if it successfully spurs shifts away from carbon-based economic activities. Over time, its contribution would need to be supplemented increasingly from other sources.[82]

South Africa introduced a carbon tax in 2019 on entities that operate emissions-generating facilities at a combined installed capacity equal to, or above, a specified carbon tax threshold.[83] In the first phase, a tax rate of R120 (approximately US$8.30) per tonne of CO_2 was imposed, with the rate increasing annually by inflation plus 2% until 2022, and then by inflation thereafter. This is an exceedingly light touch. Extensive tax-free emissions allowances have also been built into the policy (ranging from 60% to 95%). The actual carbon tax rate will be between R6 and R48 per tonne of CO_2, which is negligible and which hardly pays lip-service to the stated goal of prompting rapid reductions in carbon emissions. The rates amount to a mere 1%–8% of the US$40 cost per tonne, which the World Bank sees as the lowest level of carbon tax that would be compatible with the objectives of the Paris Agreement.[84] Eskom, the national energy supplier which produces about 90% of the country's electricity, will not have to pay the tax until 2023.[85] Clearly, there is considerable room and need to increase a carbon tax in South Africa.

The very low current carbon tax rate in South Africa reflects the National Treasury's concerns with minimising possible trade-offs between economic growth, job creation and reducing greenhouse gas emissions. Received wisdom holds that a carbon tax would reduce economic growth – by up to 5% in a country with South Africa's energy profile, according to some estimates.[86] But more detailed economic modelling in

South Africa has found that a carbon tax with broad sector coverage, if coupled with efficient recycling of the revenue, would have a marginally negative impact on GDP growth in the short term, while significantly contributing to greenhouse gas emission reductions. Over the long term, the tax would support a transition to a low-carbon economy.[87]

Land-value tax

This revenue option is oddly neglected. Not to be confused with a property tax (which taxes the value of the built structures on an area of land), a land-value tax would be applied against the value of real estate minus the structures built on it. Given the very high levels of wealth and asset inequality in many countries (South Africa being an especially egregious example), some of it tied to the skewed distribution of real estate ownership, a land-value tax would be highly progressive. Implicit in such a tax is the recognition that the value of individual assets derives from and is dependent on larger collectives; the value of a piece of land is fundamentally dependent on its surroundings.

A strong practical case also exists for a land-value tax. It is difficult to evade (since the tax base is literally immovable and can be verified relatively easily by assessors) and it is considered to be the least distortive of taxes.[88] Because the tax is levied irrespective of whether and how the land is used (i.e. whether or not 'economic rent' is extracted), it may promote more efficient use of land. It is also likely to discourage land price bubbles.[89]

Land-value taxes have the potential to become significant sources of government revenue. Research in New Zealand has indicated that a 1% per annum tax on all non-government-owned land would have raised the equivalent of 20% of all income tax revenue in 2010.[90] More recent research from Indonesia, Nicaragua, Peru and Rwanda suggests that taxing one-half of land rents could increase government budgets by up to 15%.[91]

In South Africa, a recurrent land-value tax could gradually replace the existing transfer duty.[92] To safeguard the redistributive effect of a land-value tax, it would be necessary to use a tax threshold that exempts subsistence farmers and low-income households from the tax. Other practical considerations include liquidity and the ability to pay the tax (for example, retired persons with limited income); such concerns can be addressed through careful exemptions.

There is a perception that implementing a land tax would be expensive and administratively challenging in developing countries. Like many other countries, however, South Africa has fairly robust municipal property registers (though the valuation methods vary across municipalities) and it commands the technical tools for assessing land values.[93] Until the early 2000s, the taxation of urban land values in fact was a significant source of revenue for many local governments in South Africa. However, legal changes then eliminated the option of a 'split-rate tax' in favour of a single property tax.[94]

* * *

Given the range of financing options that are available, there is no straightforward answer to whether a UBI is financially feasible or not. That will depend on the amount of the payment, how eligibility is determined, how those two variables change over time (by, for example, phasing in a UBI scheme), and which financing strategies are selected. On the latter front, the scope for action is much larger than is typically claimed by UBI sceptics. Viable scenarios exist for a country like South Africa, almost all of which can have a progressive redistributive impact, irrespective of whether they are used to finance a UBI.

6

The Politics and Economics of a Universal Basic Income

Debates about a UBI quickly circle to the issue of affordability and the default assumption that such a scheme would bankrupt countries. Yet the massive infusions of liquidity into financial markets and the charity given to corporations after the 2008 global financial crisis and again during the COVID-19 pandemic show that the limits of 'affordable' state spending are much more elastic than is commonly acknowledged. Often, those limits are political constructs. Moreover, as shown in the previous chapter, there are numerous feasible ways to finance a UBI.

The question of affordability, it seems, should be reshaped: is a UBI seen to be important and desirable enough to be made affordable? Are there strong enough social and political forces to drive those processes? And does the context favour such an undertaking? These are eminently political questions. Thandika Mkandawire's observation about social policy decision-making applies also to a UBI:

> No amount of evidence of the instrumental efficacy or of the intrinsic value of particular social policies will lead to their adoption if they are not deemed politically feasible.[1]

TIPPING THE SCALES

The mainstreaming of the UBI debate reflects growing unease about the failure of current economic and social policy models to shield societies against crisis. That trepidation was visible in the haste with which many states provided social support alongside the customary corporate welfare during the first year of the COVID-19 pandemic. Those kinds of social interventions had been uniformly absent in the aftermath of the 2008 global financial crisis. But the support offered this time around did not signal a change in direction: it was a pragmatic reaction to increased social distress and disaffection. Indeed, in these kinds of circumstances, a small targeted basic income that temporarily replaces at least some existing welfare entitlements – in effect disguising further rounds of social austerity – might well appeal to both the capitalist class and state managers. Such an outcome must be avoided in favour of a sizeable *universal* basic income that supplements other essential social provisioning. Achieving *that* will require overcoming formidable organised opposition.

The context

It is important to view the UBI debate in historical context. Daniel Zamora and Peter Sloman see the basic income demand following cyclical patterns over the past century and attracting support in periods of crisis, particularly when social gains attached to the world of work seem unlikely.[2]

During the golden age of social welfare expansion in high-income countries (from the 1930s to the late 1960s), programmes providing subsidised or free healthcare, education, housing and transport flourished alongside a push for full employment. Basic income demands surfaced, but usually as a secondary and limited facet of those larger, state-driven forms of social provisioning.[3]

A different outlook became dominant during the subsequent rise of neoliberal capitalism (see Chapter 1). Economic and social policies were remodelled to serve, above all else, the needs of capital. The distribution of goods and services to citizens was entrusted increasingly to the price system or market, with the state retreating into a facilitating role. The compromises that enabled the social welfare model to arise from the 1930s onward were erased, as the capitalist class sought to maximise opportunities for profit-taking and consolidate control over ever-larger portions of those profits. This occurred chiefly through corporate tax cuts and subsidies, the relaxation or removal of regulations, and attacks on workers' organisations (enabling real wages to be suppressed and job benefits and security to be rescinded).

Some critics on the Left argue that a basic income would entrench such a model.[4] In their view, the intervention would allow for some rationed redistribution towards the poorer sections of society, but this would be done in ways that make people more reliant on the market – for example, cutting back on the remnants of state-managed provisioning and replacing it with cash payments. But equating a UBI demand so neatly with neoliberal interests underestimates the instability of the current period.

Unlike twenty or thirty years ago, capitalist societies are today visibly beset with multiple crises that span the economic, ecological, social and political domains of life. The precarity and deep disquiet caused by the 2008 global financial crisis and the ongoing calamity of COVID-19 has aggravated this instability. Neoliberal capitalism has not been upended, but its ideological authority has faded. The intersecting crises of the current period require fresh innovations or new compromises.

In the 1930s and 1940s, the balance of forces in industrialised countries favoured compromises that led to the social welfare experiments that defined the post-World War II era. Currently, however, social formations (such as worker organisations) and allied political organisations seem less capable of forcing compromises that prioritise egalitarian goals. At the same time, faced with listless profit rates and operating under increasingly volatile conditions, neoliberal capitalism lacks a coherent route forward. Lavished with stimulus packages, bailouts and cheap credit, but bogged down in contradictions, it plods on in pursuit of growth and profit. It is as if the current phase of capitalism, assailed by crisis, has entered a kind of purgatory – unable to revisit its heydays but incapable of creating the conditions for a viable, forward-looking exit from this impasse.

Although the UBI demand has gained traction in this context of flux and foreboding, the current prospect of broad social gains seems dim, as UBI critics like Daniel Zamora and Anton Jäger have correctly noted.[5] In their view, the demand is a deficient and distracting stand-in for wider progressive restructuring. But this presumes that other routes for advance beckon and that the push for a progressive UBI is a mere tactical misjudgement fed by naive optimism. In reality, popular social and political forces are too weak currently to drive a profound restructuring of the economic and social order. The UBI demand draws its appeal at least partly from that fact. The search for a way forward continues; rather than being a digression, the struggle to define and achieve a generous and lasting UBI can contribute to that task. At stake in that struggle – and the countervailing push against it – is much more than the design of a social policy tool.

High stakes

Financing a UBI that is more than tokenistic and short-lived will require substantial changes in fiscal policy (most obviously in taxation) and in broader macroeconomic policy. Even a tax-neutral financing model that reallocates existing tax revenues and reduces wastage will require a profound shift in the politics of fiscal decision-making – in other words, which sets of interests are privileged. A sufficiently large UBI will require even more intrusive changes, in the shape of elevated – and new – taxes for companies and wealthy individuals.

A UBI therefore implies a struggle over access to fiscal bounty and, by implication, the surplus[6] generated through economic activities, the bulk of which is appropriated by capitalists. Their sway over the distribution of that surplus across society is threatened when large expansions of social provisioning occur.[7] For the past forty years, those arrangements were systematically overhauled to favour capital (in the shape of tax cuts and loopholes, state subsidies, corporate bailouts, deregulation, social austerity and more). Relaxing control over that surplus is no small matter in an era of sputtering growth and squeezed profit rates, when reliable and untrammelled access to large infusions of capital at low cost has become indispensable to the capitalist class. Sustained increases in social spending threaten that access.[8]

Expanded state provisioning in the shape of unconditional income support offends capitalist interests in other respects, as well. It potentially democratises the state by setting up a direct relationship between citizens and the state around material security, a relationship that exposes the state to politically charged popular demands. Such a democratising effect is to be celebrated. But, insofar as a UBI involves distributing a larger share of the surplus to citizens, expands the role of the state as a source of basic means and exposes it to popular pressure, it clashes with capitalist interests. Yet it is also obvious, in the midst of growing precarity and instability, that new forms of social support are needed – as is evidenced when even a former Goldman Sachs chief publicly speaks out in support of a basic income in South Africa, for example.[9] Instead of dogmatic opposition to the very idea of such an intervention, the battle lines are shifting toward defining the purpose, content, design and scale of a basic income.

As the evident need for additional income support grows, opponents are digging in mainly along two fronts. The one line of defence still stigmatises social support as a handout and insists that waged work is a viable and sufficient basis for social citizenship and inclusion. This view does not rule out a basic income as such, but it stops far short of a *universal* basic income. Here, the preferred format is a small, temporary payment that functions alongside overhauled job creation efforts (including public works schemes, skilling and retraining). The primary goal remains job-creating economic growth. The other core line of defence continues to be the matter of cost and affordability. Relying on the contention that a *universal* basic income is fiscally unrealistic and unsustainable, this position, too, is becoming flexible enough to allow for a minimal, 'emergency' basic income.

BUILDING POLITICAL SUPPORT

The World Bank and UBI sceptics such as Robert Greenstein have argued that achieving a UBI will require support that cuts across partisan lines.[10] Such broad-based support will entail compromises that shift the scheme in more conservative and potentially regressive directions, including perhaps turning it into a stalking horse to replace other forms of social provisioning. In settings with patchy forms of social welfare, as is the case in many developing countries, concern about dismantling existing social assistance seems less relevant than in developed countries with established, often complicated welfare systems. Yet even there, other forms of pro-poor support (such as education, health, fuel, food and transport subsidies) may be vulnerable if fiscal policy is tightened.

There is a possibility that, once in place, a UBI will become politically too costly to abandon, yet fiscally too expensive to sustain. In the absence of powerful progressive forces, states could react by cutting other social entitlements. This is a real risk. And it highlights the political dimensions of a UBI demand: which sets of interests are powerful enough to decide on the design, financing and implementation of a UBI, and to defend those arrangements.

Some lessons from South Africa

South Africa's massive inequalities arise from successive development strategies that have served the priorities of capital in fundamental ways but at calamitous social cost. Both the state and the capitalist class remain committed to the belief that market-friendly economic policies will generate new jobs and thereby reduce poverty to manageable levels. Historical experience in South Africa offers no grounds for this faith. The structure of the economy and the terms of its insertion into the global economy militate against a strategy that relies centrally on job-creating economic growth to solve the social crisis.[11] Yet political forces on the Left and allied social movements (chiefly trade union organisations) have been unable to divert the post-apartheid state from these policy paths onto a social-democratic route.[12] Two institutions, the National Treasury and the Reserve Bank, play decisive roles in resisting and diluting redistributive economic and social policies that threaten to compromise the interests of corporate capital.[13]

Circumstances occasionally disturb this status quo. In the early 2000s, for example, the government resisted demands for a national basic income (see Chapter 4), only to relent to a steady expansion of the social grant system.[14] In the same period, the National Treasury had resisted a free, national treatment programme for people living with HIV. That opposition buckled under pressure from a powerful social movement and was overridden politically.[15] Both 'retreats' reflected political calculations that were made in the context of strong domestic pressure and obliging international sentiments.

Concerned about the destabilising impact of neoliberal economic adjustments, the World Bank in the 1990s began to broadcast the advantages of social 'safety nets' in developing countries. By the 2000s, it and the United Kingdom's Department for International Development were enthusiastically promoting conditional cash transfer schemes.[16] The 2008 global financial crisis further concentrated minds around the need for mitigating interventions. Soon even the International

Monetary Fund was signalling support for expanded social protection as part of 'inclusive development', a prominent theme also in the United Nations Sustainable Development Agenda 2030.[17] Some observers saw the expansion of social protection programmes as evidence of a shift away from neoliberal orthodoxy, led by 'emergent' powers in the South (Brazil, India and South Africa were often cited as examples).[18] In reality, the enthusiasm for and design of cash transfer programmes – particularly in Africa – appears to be driven primarily by northern donors and multilateral organisations (notably the World Bank, United Nations funds and programmes, and the United States Agency for International Development).[19] It was in that endorsing context that the South African government decided to expand the social grant system in the 2000s, despite the fiscal implications.

The government's decision in 2004 to fund a free, national HIV treatment programme also ran against the grain of fiscal austerity. It, too, was in step with evolving international policy guidance and sentiment. A big difference, though, was the added impetus of a strong, sophisticated activist movement. While the international context favoured effective activism around the AIDS epidemic, the victory in South Africa was mainly the doing of the most powerful social movement of the post-apartheid era, the Treatment Action Campaign.[20] The Campaign combined charismatic leadership, dramatic social protest, legal challenges and extensive transnational networking to legitimise progressive demands that centred on the rights of people living with HIV to receive free, life-saving treatment.[21] South Africa today has the largest HIV treatment programme in the world, the bulk of it funded domestically (a rarity among low- and middle-income countries). Healthcare (and specifically the response to AIDS) became the only arena in which major policy choices of the South African state – and, even more impressively, the National Treasury's authority – have been successfully challenged since 1994.

The Treatment Action Campaign's success is shadowed, though, by a reminder that victory in one domain and in one set of conditions is not easily repeated in others. The campaign has struggled subsequently (to very modest effect) to refashion itself into a broader social justice movement, despite the validity of its demands. It may be that the ambient factors that enabled its success around HIV have been absent subsequently. Or it may be that the current demands are not as amenable to 'clear-cut' solutions as the demand for HIV treatment may have been.

Might it be more feasible to mobilise a politically influential force around a UBI demand? To date there is no example from a developing country to support such expectation. The BIG campaign in South Africa in the early 2000s gained traction in policy circles and the institutions of some social movements (trade unions, for example), but it was not driven by a groundswell of popular support. This holds lessons for UBI campaigns and for how they frame and position their demands.

MOBILISING POPULAR SUPPORT

Whereas the demand for free HIV treatment carried indisputable moral force, a UBI can be a jarring, disorientating concept. Referring to survey data from Cape Town, Jeremy Seekings and Heidi Matisson, for example, claimed that 'not even poor voters are unambiguously supportive of a BIG ... public opinion clearly favours the extension of social assistance, but not unconditionally'.[22]

Misgivings among the public about non-wage forms of income support may be fading, though, especially during the aggravated hardship of the COVID-19 pandemic. In the COVID-19 Democracy Survey (conducted by the Human Sciences Research Council and the University of Johannesburg in 2020), 62% of respondents favoured the introduction of a basic income during the pandemic crisis. Support was highest among lower-income respondents.[23] This was in line with findings from an earlier survey, in which 63% of respondents supported a basic income.[24] Those kinds of sentiments have fuelled organised mobilisation, with dozens of activist and other civil society organisations uniting around a demand to increase and then convert the COVID-19 grant into a basic income guarantee (see Chapter 5).

Earlier research unearthed more ambivalent attitudes towards state-sponsored income support. An Afrobarometer survey done in 2018 found that most South Africans (76%) wished to see the state supporting low-income households through cash transfers, and two-thirds (67%) believed the state had a duty to support poor households. But more than half of respondents (53%) also said that able-bodied adults should work for their social grants. A similar proportion of respondents (59%) agreed with the claim that recipients 'become lazy when they rely on' social grants.[25] There is no empirical evidence that grant recipients are work-shy,[26] but the fact that this notion endures is a reminder of the extent to which non-wage income for the poor remains stigmatised. Even people with no prospect of full-time work cling to the stubborn creed that one has to work a waged or salaried job in order to earn a rightful place in society. Steven Friedman sees in this attitude a perverse echo from the apartheid era when, indeed, every white adult who wanted a job was guaranteed one.[27] That assurance, of course, did not apply to the rest of society. But it reinforced the idea that waged work is the only 'real', productive form of work, dismissing the value and productivity of domestic and other care work, or subsistence agriculture, or barter work.

That notion continues to shape policymaking. As hardship induced by the COVID-19 pandemic increased, a coalition of activist and non-governmental organisations, trade unions and research entities called on the government to transform the temporary social relief of distress grant into a permanent payment. The finance ministry balked. 'The weakness I see in the debate is there is more focus on how you support the unemployed [and] little attention to the long-term issue of growth,' said newly appointed finance minister, Enoch Godongwana, in August 2021, as the official unemployment rate passed the 34% mark. Young people should not be 'placed into a cycle of dependence', he told journalists, adding that 'what we need to do is invest in skilling' young people.[28] The preference was for some combination of skills training, public works employment and rationed income support, while again trying to reboot economic growth. The income support would likely be in the form of a 'jobseeker grant' that would support young people to enter the labour market[29] – essentially a variant of workfare. While support for a UBI is growing, substantial proportions of 'ordinary' South Africans still lean towards Godongwana's thinking.

If a UBI demand is to succeed, it has to reshape the assumptions and 'common sense' we draw on when considering the claims and obligations that link us to one another, the state and the economy.[30] A UBI is laden with challenging propositions about the responsibilities and entitlements that connect people in society. It calls into question commonplace understandings of waged work, its authority in our social order, and the hierarchies of worth and value we attach to different kinds of work. The UBI demand will need to be framed in ways that make all this unexceptional, part of a new kind of 'common sense'. The struggle to achieve a UBI should

> open conversations about what counts as work, about the value of different kinds of work, and also about what else besides work we might want to do with our time, what other models of care, creativity and cooperation we might want to build.[31]

So, a UBI campaign also has to become a process, a vehicle for critique and revelation – not least about the injustice of using paid work as the principal basis for allocating and distributing income and wealth in society. This makes a UBI demand important also for building a broad-based movement that is capable of advancing social justice in the context of deepening crises. A UBI is not a cure-all. But it can function as a substantive and empowering component of a push towards egalitarian outcomes.

Framing the UBI demand

In a society like South Africa, the UBI demand evidently speaks to common need. But equally important is the normative basis for the demand. Is it an appeal for the state to 'grant' assistance in extreme circumstances? Or is it a demand rooted in the state's duty to 'guarantee all members of society the means of existence', in Maximilien Robespierre's words?[32] Or is it a claim arising from rights inscribed in a constitution? Or a claim for just dues, for a share of common wealth, which in capitalist society is privately appropriated?[33]

A radical perspective would frame a UBI as a dividend of the collectively produced wealth in society, recognising that the entirety of society is entitled to a rightful share of the total social product (see Chapter 5). A UBI then becomes an income that is paid to people as members of a society that collectively produces wealth – a proposition that is in tune with powerful political traditions in South Africa.[34] For Yanis Varoufakis, this framing steers the debate beyond the deserving/undeserving binary: 'Society stakes a claim to aggregate capital and that claim becomes a dividend, an income stream that goes to everyone.'[35] Instead of being an entreaty, an appeal to power, a UBI then constitutes a claim on the surplus generated in capitalist society. 'If payments can be conceived as rightful shares,' James Ferguson has noted, 'then there's no expectation of a return, no debt and no shame. No one is giving anyone anything. One is simply receiving one's own share of one's own property.'[36] A UBI then dismisses the fiction that personal responsibility decides social outcomes and it pushes the principle of social justice to the fore. Its starting point is an acknowledgement that factors beyond individual control decide the distribution of resources and capabilities – and that those means have to be distributed fairly.

Thinking of a UBI as a dividend also emphasises the collective character of a UBI, rather than seeing it merely as a multitude of separate payments to individuals. Picturing a UBI as a 'citizens' dividend' seems especially appealing in a country where the economy has been built on systemic expropriation and exploitation spanning the colonial and apartheid eras, and continuing subsequently.[37] Reinforcing that appeal is the fact that the bulk of the environmental costs of South Africa's development path has also been imposed on poor communities. Their environments and their health were degraded, while they benefited the least from developmental 'progress'.[38] Similarly, a UBI can be seen in part as a form of 'just dues' or remuneration for unpaid work performed by women.

Demanding a UBI as a dividend, or a form of 'just dues', profoundly changes its implications. Tax systems and fiscal policies are instances of a wider struggle to decide how to organise and distribute the collective surplus that is generated through economic activity. When presented as a dividend, a UBI becomes a demand to democratise that surplus – and that poses a political challenge to the capitalist class. Once a UBI shifts from being a 'grant' or a 'concession' handed out by the state, to being a dividend to which people are entitled, it implies a different relationship between the citizenry and the state. A UBI then involves a sustained act of demand-making, rather than concession-seeking. That harbours the potential to alter the power dynamics between citizens and the state – and, given the fiscal implications of a UBI, also between the state and capital. A UBI can then function as a wedge that helps to disrupt the hierarchy of claims among capital, the citizenry and the state.

If we understand neoliberalism as a fundamentally *political project* to radically reorganise the distribution of resources in favour of the capitalist class, then a substantive UBI implies a challenge to that arrangement. A generous UBI will not dislodge neoliberal capitalism, but it would be in harmony with broader efforts to do so.[39]

Framing a UBI as a dividend also highlights the dimension of justice and links to the socioeconomic rights enshrined in the Constitution of the Republic of South Africa which assigns to the South African state a constitutional obligation to progressively realise the right to social security and social assistance for all.[40] Section 27 of the Constitution stipulates that everyone has the right to social security, including appropriate social assistance for those who are unable to support themselves and their dependents. It also states that 'everyone has the right to have access to sufficient food' and that every child has the right to basic nutrition, basic healthcare services and social services. The state is obligated to take reasonable legislative and other measures, within its available resources, to achieve the progressive realisation of these rights.

Measures introduced to date do not fulfil those obligations, which are also underpinned by international law. When South Africa's progress towards fulfilment of its obligations within the International Covenant on Economic, Social and Cultural Rights was reviewed in 2018, it was found wanting. The South African Human Rights Commission concluded that the country 'has failed to discharge its international and national obligations regarding the provision of social assistance to those most in need'.[41] The limited scope of social security protection was among the weaknesses highlighted, along with the inadequate value of social grant payments and the fact that large numbers of people living in poverty were excluded from the current grant system.[42] It was against that background that the Human Rights Commission requested the National Treasury and the Department of Social Development to examine the viability of a basic income and to prepare a roadmap for a pilot study.[43]

WHAT KIND OF STATE WILL IT TAKE?

Ultimately, the design, size and financing of a UBI are highly charged questions that will be decided by the prevailing balance of power in society. Whether a UBI amounts to mere temporary relief – 'buying time' – or contributes to more substantive transformation will depend on the organised strength of popular movements, the state's exposure or responsiveness to citizens' demands, and the capacity of the capitalist class to ensure that state policies serve its core priorities.

The technical tasks of implementing an inclusive UBI – compiling and maintaining a register of, say, all citizens and legal residents aged 18–59 years and paying those individuals an income every month – lie within the capacity of the South African state. Though somewhat tarnished by scandal, the existing social grant system suggests that the technical expertise and infrastructure for such an undertaking is either available or can be introduced.

It is less clear that the South African state currently is capable of introducing and managing the kinds of macroeconomic policy changes and institutional arrangements that will be needed for a UBI to function as part of a broad strategy of transformation. Doing so will require an active state which, rather than mainly facilitating capital accumulation and mitigating the social costs, steers society along a much more egalitarian path. The ambition, commitment and capacities required for such a feat are often associated with 'developmental states'. In the post-apartheid era, the South African government has regularly claimed to be building such a state, though that claim has been convincingly disputed.[44]

In broad outline, the developmental state refers to a model of economic growth and social redistribution in which the state acts formatively to promote growth, determine the broad pattern of that growth and ensure social development. In Chalmers Johnson's account of the 'Japanese miracle' after World War II, the state stewarded economic development, leading long-term macroeconomic planning and industrial development, and channelling investment flows towards targeted sectors and regions, as well as subsidising labour costs.[45] Several other variants of the developmental state have been studied and described.[46] These states typically shared certain attributes, including dense ties between political and business elites, the ability to leverage sources of finance, and a robust state bureaucracy that was sufficiently insulated against the narrow, partisan interests of powerful economic and social forces and capable of functioning reliably, predictably and efficiently. 'Embedded autonomy' was seen as a particularly important attribute.[47] Partially embedded with key social classes, the developmental state acquired the mix of autonomy and connectedness it needed to foster alliances or accommodations that allowed it to deploy its resources in the service of ostensibly inclusive national interests and strategic development goals.[48]

The creation of a developmental state has been a consistent, stated ambition of the ANC government in South Africa.[49] While the government legitimately claims credit for expanding the social wage and introducing a wider (though thin) social protection system, it has left intact many of the underlying conditions and relations of power that reproduce inequality and generate impoverishment. Its economic policy choices have failed to mobilise productive investments and make inroads into one of the highest unemployment rates in the world.

Those choices have serviced the prerogatives of South African conglomerates, whose operations are now threaded into global networks of accumulation. The choices have also facilitated the emergence of a powerful financial sector, and have badly undercut the state's leverage with domestic capital. South Africa seems no different from the many other countries where

> deeply established reliance on local private economic elites, the growing centrality of transnational capital to local accumulation and the proliferation of alliances between local and transnational capital have transformed the political landscape.[50]

It is moot whether the current South African state is capable of emulating the developmental state experiences of the past. On current evidence it is even less clear that the South African state is capable of steering and managing a redistributive, democratic and ecologically sustainable development path. There is considerable evidence of dysfunction and widespread corruption at all levels of the state.[51] Great damage has been done to state institutions during the past 10 to 15 years, with even the revenue service and state statistical agency not escaping the harm. Large sections of the South African public service underperform, with the parlous state of the public health and education systems undercutting any developmentalist credentials.[52] But those institutions are reparable. In addition, key institutions and public assets remain, for now, under the (nominal) control of the state. They include the Industrial Development Corporation, the South African Development Bank, a great deal of the rail and harbour system and infrastructure, a large portfolio of TV and radio stations, and the sole electricity supplier, Eskom, mismanaged and indebted though it is. Though damaged, the revenue service remains relatively well-run, and a sophisticated and independent judicial system exists. Civil society organisations are numerous and diverse, and are capable of imposing a degree of accountability on the state.

It is also highly doubtful that the archetypal developmental states of the twentieth century are suitable blueprints for stewarding ecologically sustainable and viable societal progress in the twenty-first century.

Many of the geopolitical and political-economic factors that under-pinned the developmental state successes of the twentieth century no longer seem available. The emphasis on economic growth and the focus on industrial manufacturing as the wellspring of job creation and social development seem anachronistic. A manifest need remains for a state that is capable of acting in the national interest and that commands institutions that function professionally, predictably and reliably. But, as Peter Evans has emphasised, it also requires much greater focus on building and nurturing human capabilities, for example through ensuring reliable access to quality education, healthcare and livelihood support.[53] This perspective rearranges the building blocks of 'develop-ment' and the relationships between them. It differs from an approach that conflates development with economic output, and in which human and social development are treated as functions of economic growth, driven by industrial production. Instead, it reframes development as the equitable enhancement of human and social capabilities, with economic and social policies serving those objectives.[54] For Evans, 'policies that expand capabilities may look like "social policy" or "welfare policy" but they are essential to growth policy'.[55]

If development is understood as the expansion of capabilities, the state becomes even more important than in earlier conceptions of develop-mental states. The capabilities emphasised by Evans and Patrick Heller are not only relevant insofar as they serve enterprise-based output, nor are they important strictly 'in their own right'.[56] They are a means also for a decentred recuperation and flourishing of social and economic life at community level. The necessary capabilities are tied up with access to quality education and healthcare, transport, and telecommunications and information technologies. Similarly, if a UBI is to be more than a poverty-reducing tool – if it is to function as a liberating and trans-formative factor in people's lives – it has to operate in a context where capability-enhancing services and support are available. This requires an active, provisioning state that is capable of dependably providing the support, services and infrastructure that people need to build fulfilling lives. Providing those services in reliable and equitable ways requires complex state capacity and new kinds of 'embeddedness'.[57]

In earlier conceptions of the developmental state, this 'embeddedness' involved ties between various state apparatuses and particular elite formations (especially those involved in industrial activities). To meet contemporary challenges, however, state apparatuses have to command enough autonomy to proactively design and implement policies that serve collective needs and goals rather than reflexively align with the prerogatives of corporate capital. That flexible autonomy requires deepened democracy, especially at local levels, with citizens able to participate in meaningful processes of decision-making and accountability. This democratising aspect is important in other respects, too. Successful capability-building both requires and leads to the enhancement of freedom – and that tends to generate friction and resistance from elites, especially the political, religious and traditional elites who police social relations and norms, not least at local levels. Overcoming those kinds of obstacles requires 'interactive ties that connect the apparatus of the state administratively and politically to civil society'.[58]

It is also in such democratised and enabling contexts that a UBI is most likely to fulfil its potential to facilitate and underwrite the kinds of 'organic', local, social and economic activities that are essential amid upheaval and turmoil. This implies overhauling the state to some degree – in terms of its overall administrative capacity, its probity, the ways in which it relates to civil society and its relationship with capital.

WHAT KIND OF MACROECONOMIC STRATEGY IS NEEDED?

Economic policy in South Africa has failed to shape an economy that creates enough decent jobs, supports livelihoods and builds the capabilities of people and their communities. The manufacturing sector remains poorly diversified and weak, and there has been scant progress towards expanding labour-absorbing activities outside the service and construction sectors. The financial sector, which has grown to inordinate proportions, is neither geared for nor inclined towards a developmental role. The upshot is an economy

> characterised by low growth, rising unemployment and increasing inequality, which together with rampant corruption and govern-ance failures combine to threaten the very core of the country's stability and democracy.[59]

Still, vast wealth is generated, most of it siphoned towards a small minority. This entrenched state of affairs is morally untenable, and socially and politically unsustainable. The same can be said of the environmentally destructive ways in which the wealth is generated and consumed.

Drastic restructuring is needed. In addition to servicing the material needs of all, economic policies have to steer and enable decisive moves away from extractive, fossil fuel-based activities to 'green' and labour-intensive, value-adding activities. A 'green' industrial strategy that greatly reduces the ecological impact of economic activity and that prioritises the needs of ordinary people over the interests of conglomerate and financial capital is crucial. Increased and targeted public investment will be essen-tial, particularly to transition rapidly from a hydrocarbon-based economic model and to introduce and support social and productive infrastruc-ture in deprived communities.[60] A UBI would slot into such an overhaul. A supportive macroeconomic framework is essential to enable the neces-sary investments. Without such a framework 'other economic and social policy interventions for addressing growth, employment and inequality will likely fail to gain much traction for budgetary and related reasons'.[61]

Current macroeconomic policy in South Africa stands in the way of such drastic change. Neoliberal in orientation, it proceeds along a route that was initially plotted in the 1980s amid anti-apartheid uprisings and associated economic difficulties. In the mid-1990s, the restructuring efforts were resumed with greater resolve, overseen by the country's new democratic government. Marketed as a pathway towards economic stability and growth, the 1996 GEAR plan prioritised tight monetary policy (including high interest rates and inflation targeting) and fiscal restraint, along with the dismantling of tariff barriers and capital controls, while counselling increased privatisation.[62]

The GEAR plan enabled South Africa's largest corporations to restructure and overhaul their operations, and to re-engage with a rapidly financialising global capitalist economy. It facilitated profit-seeking strategies that would rely increasingly on rent-seeking and speculative ventures,[63] outward investment, offshoring and capital flight, while depriving the economy of private and, via tax revenue, public investment in productive sectors.[64]

The current ground rules

The ground rules embedded in the GEAR plan have proved very difficult to dislodge.[65] The country's macroeconomic policy continues to hinge on restrictive counter-cyclical fiscal policy (though it allows for some spending on economic infrastructure and for stimulating economic demand), monetary policy that focuses on inflation targeting, and the promotion of an open capital account.[66]

As in other middle-income countries like Argentina and Brazil, the deregulation of financial markets in South Africa (particularly the liberalisation of the capital account) fuelled destabilising processes of domestic financialisation. This is evident in the disproportionately large and powerful financial sector (see Chapter 2). Intensified financial integration is reflected also in the increased volume of capital flows in and out of the country, and in the international trading of South African assets. By 2015, South African assets held by non-residents amounted to 137% of GDP, compared with less than 40% in the late 1990s. Portfolio investments comprised the largest (and growing) share of those foreign liabilities – more than 40% in 2015.[67]

Financialisation tends to generate a structural pull away from productive investments and toward rent-seeking and speculative ventures that promise attractive short-term returns.[68] In South Africa's case, it has been marked by the massive misallocation of capital, shifting the allotment of 'capital, infrastructure and skills towards speculation, consumption and unproductive services [which] led to deindustrialisation'.[69] The manufacturing sector, especially labour-intensive firms, has atrophied, rather than growing and diversifying.[70] South Africa's non-financial corporations earn increasingly large shares of corporate revenues from financial activities that do not directly link to their core operations. Flow of funds data from the South African Reserve Bank show that forays into financial markets, and other financial investments, now outstrip these corporations' fixed investments.

Allied with a deformed industrial structure and an ongoing reliance on extractive industry exports, these processes deepen financial risk and instability. They also stoke balance of payments hazards. South Africa uses monetary policy to manage its balance of payments, including by keeping interest rates high enough and exit routes flexible enough to consistently attract portfolio capital investments. The main beneficiaries are local and international finance capital. Macroeconomic policy privileges 'the interests of international investors and (internationalised) domestic finance capital, chiefly by ensuring market liquidity and guaranteeing immediate rand–dollar convertibility and preserving ease of exit'.[71]

Bowing to the market

A major effect of four decades of neoliberalism globally has been the weakening of the national sovereignty that is needed for discretionary macroeconomic policy. This is especially apparent in economies, such as South Africa, that are both reliant on and exposed to the caprice of finance capital. By exposing the economy to transnational financial market reactions, the heavy reliance on short-term capital flows functions as a powerful 'disciplinary' device in relation to economic policymaking.[72]

The effect on the real, productive economy in South Africa is disheartening. As Gilad Isaacs and Annina Kaltenbrunner have shown, since the early 2000s shifts in capital flows in and out of South Africa have been largely disconnected from economic conditions, with the changes prompted mainly by international monetary and liquidity factors.[73] No matter the catastrophic social outcomes, policymakers' fear of unforgiving reactions from the markets functions as a powerful deterrent against necessary policy corrections. Consequently, the central macroeconomic policy choices have endured.[74] But attributing such 'path dependence' strictly to external factors seems incomplete; macroeconomic policy is also closely aligned with the interests of finance capital in South Africa.[75]

The continuing adherence to the macroeconomic policy choices of the 1990s can be traced to several overlapping factors. These include the ideological acceptance of key precepts of neoliberal economics among top policymakers in the Treasury and the Reserve Bank;[76] the growing size and influence of (nominally) domestic finance capital and its entanglement with global financial circuitries, which heightens the exposure of the economy to the 'discipline' of financial markets; and policymakers' keen awareness of the economy's vulnerability to capital flow volatility (especially for financing the balance of payments and sustaining public spending).

Additional factors are also at work. Macroeconomic policy – in particular the focus on attracting portfolio capital inflows – also facilitated the emergence of a black economic elite, which is submerged in alliance with incumbent capitalist elites, both in South Africa and abroad.[77] Bill Freund likened this new elite to Peter Evans' concept of 'an embedded elite, which transcends the private-public divide' and whose political-economic location enables it to pursue both personal financial enrichment and advance larger political projects. In Freund's view:

> For the political leadership of the ANC, relying on and integrating with such an elite is very preferable to the distanced if inevitable relationship the ANC enjoys with the previously existing white business elite.[78]

This has created a powerful political lobby inside and around the ANC against radical economic change. A 'convergence of interests' between these incumbent and emergent economic elites has been achieved.[79] In addition, the governing ANC has become increasingly intertwined with those economic networks – through the business operations and ties of individual party luminaries and via its business wing, the Progressive Business Forum, which connects business operations with the ANC in government.[80]

Thus, the macroeconomic framework chosen in the 1990s, and its underlying assumptions, remain bolted in place. This speaks also to the balance of forces within the South African state. For almost a quarter of a century, the Treasury, along with the Reserve Bank, have successfully resisted macroeconomic and other policy shifts that are needed for a redistributive development path. While the Trade and Industry and Economic Development departments intermittently have tried to promote an industrial strategy that has longer-term planning horizons, the Treasury and the Reserve Bank have insisted on policies that guarantee short-term access to liquidity, a stance that favours both economic and political elites.[81] These powerful state institutions have stayed firmly committed to a path of tight money, balanced budgets, low inflation and capital mobility, and they remain reflexively opposed to social expenditure decisions that require relaxing fiscal policies.[82]

A macroeconomic framework that serves society

The current macroeconomic framework is incompatible with a viable exit route from the social and ecological crises that grip South Africa. It has also failed demonstrably to achieve its own advertised objectives: stimulate sufficient job creation, redistribution and economic growth. A progressive macroeconomic framework is urgently needed. It will have to underpin and facilitate industrial, labour and social policies that service the enhancement of capabilities, an ecologically sustainable development path and a much more equitable distribution of incomes and wealth.

Public investments have to be channelled away from hydrocarbon- and capital-intensive ventures and towards sustainable, livelihood-supporting and employment-generating activities, including at community levels and scales. South Africa has mature development finance institutions that are capable of supporting such shifts.[83] But the changes pose, in addition, a significant political challenge for the state, which will have to shift from its current facilitating role in relation to capital and adopt a more directive role as 'a driver of growth, effective demand, employment and equality'.[84]

A macroeconomic framework along such lines was, in fact, on the table in the early 1990s, having been proposed by the ANC-convened Macro-Economic Research Group (MERG).[85] The MERG proposed a two-phase, 'crowding-in' approach for economic recovery and inclusive development. The MERG proposals were dismissed by the ANC leadership after cursory review.[86] But its overall approach and several of its proposals remain highly relevant.

In summary, the MERG envisaged a phased recovery, with an initial stage of strong public investment in social and physical infrastructure (prioritising housing, education, health and physical infrastructure). This would draw in greater volumes of private capital as economic growth accelerated – a 'crowding-in' effect. An active fiscal policy was proposed, along with financial regulation (to temper potentially destabilising capital in- and outflows) and trade protection (through a tariff structure that could nurture domestic industrial development). Rather than ritually enforcing macroeconomic targets throughout the cycle, the MERG favoured assessing, maintaining or restoring macroeconomic balances across set periods (a ten-year reconstruction cycle, for example) and against key social and economic indicators.[87] Many of those policy elements remain apposite.

Fiscal policy can be a powerful lever for economic and social change, which the state can deploy 'to shift the allocation of resources towards specific sectoral priorities'.[88] It can be used to reduce poverty, distribute income, wealth and power, and improve the welfare of the majority.

An activist fiscal policy is badly needed in South Africa to align (public) investment with societal priorities; it is also a prerequisite for interventions such as a UBI.

However, in South Africa, as in other economies that opted for neo-liberal policies, fiscal policy has been relegated to a minor, conservative role, with fiscal discipline an overriding norm and anxiety about public debt a key motivation. The preference is to use monetary and financial policies 'for the manipulation of interest rates, bank reserves and cap-ital flows to stabilise inflation, business expectations and asset prices.'[89] This approach typified the Washington Consensus, which was popularised in World Bank policy advice in the early 1990s.[90] It continued to shape macroeconomic policy in South Africa and elsewhere, long after the Consensus had been sidelined in Washington.[91]

The preference in South Africa is still to cede monetary policy to the Reserve Bank, insist on tight-fisted fiscal policy and stoke alarm about the public debt.[92] That approach is becoming outmoded, however. The 'new view' of fiscal policy recognises the effectiveness of discretionary fiscal stimulus, its usefulness for 'crowding in' private investment, and its potential to pay for itself by stimulating economic growth.[93] This per-spective is hardly heterodox. There is strong evidence, including from the International Monetary Fund and the US Congress, that the customary reflex of fiscal 'consolidation' tends to depress economic growth.[94] International Monetary Fund research shows that a sustained increase in government investment equal to 1% of GDP fuels economic growth through boosted investment and consumption, and widens future fiscal space through increased government revenue and by reducing the debt-to-GDP ratio.[95]

Declining tax revenues and rising state expenditures (particularly social grant payments, public sector wages and debt service obligations) are commonly used to justify calls for fiscal restraint.[96] The alternative, it is claimed, is to risk plunging off a 'fiscal cliff'.[97] While concerns about reckless spending are merited, South Africa's social grants payments cannot reasonably be seen as profligate. Nor does it seem fair-minded to single out the public service wage bill as culprit, without also taking account of the distribution of wage and salary expenses in the public sector – an approach that would reveal the extravagant salaries and perks paid to the upper tiers of the civil service, as Vishnu Padayachee has pointed out.[98]

Moral panics about rising public debt are a standard theme of the neoliberal era, with anxiety often directed at the impact of higher social spending on public debt levels. South Africa's debt-to-GDP ratio was modest until the 2008 global financial crisis, but rose steadily subsequently, reaching 62% in 2019 and exceeding 80% during the COVID-19 pandemic in 2020.[99] By way of comparison, the debt-to-GDP ratio in the United States was 79% at the end of fiscal year 2019 and was projected to rise to over 100% in 2021.[100] It remains controversial at what levels and in which conditions public debt constitutes a threat to economic stability and growth, though there is persuasive evidence that public debt-to-GDP ratios can safely range considerably higher than mainstream economists customarily proclaim.[101] In recent years, economists subscribing to modern monetary theory have counselled a much more tolerant approach to public debt.[102]

There are also practical ways to avoid profligacy while creating the space for a progressive fiscal policy that prioritises livelihoods, creates employment, builds social and capital infrastructure, and puts the economy on a more sustainable footing. Padayachee, for example, has proposed separating the budget into a 'current' and 'capital' budget, with the former balanced annually and the latter managed against a benchmark indicator over a longer period. The separation would allow 'growth-enhancing capital expenditure in areas such as infrastructure, and non-wage expenditure on education and health, among others, to grow even at the short-term risk of running deficits'.[103]

An array of fiscal tools is available for pursuing redistributive policies, yet many are either misused or shunned. South Africa has a modern, relatively sophisticated tax infrastructure, but there is substantial, unused scope for interventions to prevent offshoring of wealth and incomes, for the enforcement of stricter tax laws, and for reducing or eliminating the deductions, exemptions and loopholes that privilege large corporations and the wealthy. The redistributive impact of fiscal policy can be boosted through tax policies that help finance social policy interventions such as a UBI. As discussed in Chapter 5, this can be achieved with expanded and/or new taxes such as a wealth tax, taxes on unearned income, a land-value tax, a resource rent tax, a carbon tax and a financial transactions tax.

Fresh approaches are needed to deal with balance of payments constraints and to prevent and/or manage balance of payment volatility. On the current account (trade) side, industrial and other policies have to promote value-added exports with a bias towards 'greened' goods and services (which requires active state involvement in picking and supporting 'winners') and they have to reduce luxury imports.[104]

On the capital and financial account side, sage regulation can be introduced to temper volatile cross-border flows, and to route domestic capital towards local productive investment.[105] The changes need not be drastic, and the latitude for making them has grown considerably in the past two decades. According to Ilene Grabel,[106] for example, a 'productive incoherence' reigns currently in global financial governance and developmental finance, which creates space for financial policy and institutional experimenting.[107] Grabel argues that controls on capital in- and outflows have 'been normalized as a legitimate tool of prudential financial management, even within the corridors of the IMF'.[108]

Padayachee has argued that certain capital controls could be reintroduced in South Africa for a limited period (of five years, for example), with the Reserve Bank empowered and tasked to regulate capital flows more closely.[109] Disruptive inflows can be better managed also by imposing a nominal tax on short-term transactions or using non-interest-bearing 'quarantines' on investment flows, and by requiring investors to place a share of their capital in long-term holdings, for example.[110] Such controls would have to be applied in ways or in a context that can prevent unmanaged currency depreciation which, among other perils, would force even greater reliance on extractive commodity exports (sabotaging the economic restructuring that is needed for a just transition). The controls will be burdensome for South African monetary authorities, but they are unlikely to exceed their administrative capacity.

Additional changes would expedite and bolster these attempts to refashion macroeconomic policy so that it serves societal needs rather than bends to corporate prerogatives. There is a strong case for a Reserve Bank which, while operationally autonomous, is publicly accountable and which is tasked with a mandate that extends beyond price stability to include broader growth and development priorities.[111] Although the South African Reserve Bank, the prime monetary authority in the country, is wholly owned by private shareholders, it derives its mandate from the Constitution.[112] Nationalisation is therefore not required to improve accountability and broaden its mandate.[113]

Significant changes to the status and lines of accountability of the Reserve Bank are likely to provoke unhappy reactions from the financial markets, which will have to be managed politically. However, a loosening of the 'narrow inflation targeting mandate' of the Bank is both necessary and feasible, and it can be achieved in a democratically accountable and developmentally effective manner. For example, instead of the (current) inflation target, an investment target (with price stability constraints), or employment target, or poverty gap target would seem more appropriate in a country facing the predicaments that burden South Africa.[114] The Reserve Bank has to adopt a more imposing stance that shifts the private banking sector away from predominantly rent-seeking and speculative activities to raising and allocating capital that can support a sustainable development path.

The South African state will have to assume a much more directive role in designing and implementing macroeconomic, industrial, labour and social policies that service the redistribution of income and the enhancement of capabilities, and that are ecologically sustainable. To do so, it will have to distinguish and play off the divergent interests that exist within the South African corporate sector, while at the same time defusing resistance.

The corporate sector in South Africa is not monolithic and is not equally beholden to the country's current economic structure and path; sections stand to gain from a pro-renewables strategy, for example. The appetite for risk may still be limited, but for some corporations it is likely bigger than at any point since the end of the apartheid system. The havoc which the COVID-19 pandemic has added to already desperate social and economic conditions makes it increasingly difficult to promote confidence in business-as-usual approaches.

A more active and directive state also assumes that a bloc of support can be built within the ANC and the state for such a programme of restructuring. While not routine, assertions about the need for radical economic change are not uncommon in ANC discourse. However, in the past decade especially, these pronouncements have been deployed also – and perhaps increasingly – as rhetorical devices in political struggles inside the ruling party. In Mark Swilling's assessment, 'radical economic transformation is [being] used to give ideological legitimacy to what is essentially a political project to repurpose state institutions for the benefit of a power elite'.[115]

It is unclear which, if any, factions in a fractious ANC can reliably consolidate and act on a commitment to a pursue redistributive and just development path. In addition, and especially in the wake of the governance failures and corruption scandals that characterised the 2010s, corporations are likely to remain reluctant to invest greater regulatory and interventionist authority in the South African state. Much clearer is the fact that the status quo is both unconscionable and unsustainable.

E ven before the 2008 global financial crisis, it was becoming obvious that, for hundreds of millions of people, waged work is a scraggy and often unavailable basis for dignified life. The myriad of collapsed livelihoods left in the wake of that crisis drove home this realisation and revived a search for more appropriate, egalitarian and reliable sources of income support. The havoc of the COVID-19 pandemic has made that quest even more urgent.

Those kinds of upheavals are likely to recur. Scientists expect that, even when (or if) COVID-19 eventually recedes, similar zoonotic epidemics will follow in the near-future.[1] In addition to public health crises, both developed and developing countries across the world are contending with overlapping turmoil: economic instability, environmental disasters, and social and political turbulence. Amid all this, steady and decent waged work is becoming increasingly rare, inequality is widening and precarity is deepening.

These are not mere cyclical adversities, to be subdued through adaptation and innovation. They arise from the driving dynamics of a capitalist system that degrades and depletes, at increasing pace, the natural resources, social assets and political capacities that enable it to flourish. The result is an entanglement of crises.[2] Mid- to long-term social and economic planning has to anticipate a 'new normal' that is characterised by intersecting instabilities and compounded insecurities. As John Harris noted in mid-2020, 'We live ... in an age of ongoing shocks, and it is time we began to prepare ... unprecedented times demand drastic answers.'[3] Current systems for allotting the means for life are not only inadequate and unjust, they are doomed.

AHEAD OF THE CURVE

South Africa exemplifies this predicament. Economic policies have serviced the accumulation of great wealth, but at the cost of prolonging and deepening a social crisis. At least four in ten adults cannot find paid work of any kind, let alone decently paid work. Poverty remains widespread and is concentrated disproportionately among the black African majority. Massive income and wealth inequalities inherited from South Africa's colonial and apartheid past persist. With economic policies designed for growing and partially deracialising the economy – but much less for redistributing the wealth generated in it – inequalities have widened. The environmental costs of these economic choices, stretching back more than a century, continue to be borne primarily by poor communities, who are also most vulnerable to the effects of climate change.

At the same time, South Africa battles three coinciding epidemics. The overlapping HIV and tuberculosis epidemics have taken an exceptionally heavy toll, especially in low-income households and communities. Together these epidemics have killed at least 3.7 million people since 2000, most of them in what should have been the prime of their lives.[4] The COVID-19 pandemic – and the social and economic restrictions imposed to control it – has caused additional privation, ruining the livelihoods of millions of people.

Economic and social policy frameworks in South Africa continue to embody the idea that waged work is a viable and sufficiently available basis for avoiding poverty and pursuing fulfilling lives.[5] When, during the first year of the COVID-19 pandemic, the South African government introduced additional emergency grants, the initial relief package centred on expanding the Unemployment Insurance Fund, even though almost half of workers were not eligible for support from that fund.[6] This left at least six million South Africans without any direct income support during the first COVID-19 lockdown in early 2020.[7] Despite the evident scale of need, the policy reflex was still to link crisis relief to waged work. Eighteen months into the COVID-19 pandemic, with more than 40% of adults unable to find paid work, the South African finance minister's response to calls for a basic income was to fret about creating 'a cycle of dependency' and propose skills training and a 'job seeker's grant' as a way forward.[8]

Many millions of South Africans are trapped between an economic and social order that insists they sell their labour to 'earn' a chance of a dignified life, and an economy that is structured in ways that render them superfluous to its needs. There is no prospect of mass unemployment disappearing in South Africa for the foreseeable future (Chapter 2). This is not a sudden revelation. The Taylor Committee, in considering a basic income proposal in South Africa almost two decades ago, noted that 'in developing countries, where stable full-time waged formal sector labour was never the norm, it is increasingly unlikely that it will become the norm'.[9] Two decades on, that statement seems indisputable.

Strategies that tether livelihoods and the realisation of social rights to job-creating economic growth are glaringly insufficient in such conditions. South Africa offers no reasonable basis for expecting that job creation can provide a viable foundation for wide-ranging livelihood security and social inclusion. Treating waged work as the fount of security and well-being also undermines the broader pursuit of social and economic justice – by filtering those demands through a quixotic quest for 'full employment'.[10] More, better-paid and socially useful jobs are necessary, but that aspiration does not encompass and should not substitute for building a just society. Much more realistic is a framework which recognises that waged work is one of several components of social citizenship and inclusion.

CONFLICTING VIEWS ABOUT A UNIVERSAL BASIC INCOME

In the global context of ongoing economic instability and increasing inequality and insecurity, the option of a UBI is attracting widening interest and support, including in South Africa (Chapter 1). Much of this support, particularly on the Left, reflects an awareness that epochal changes are under way and that they demand new economic and social arrangements. In modest, but potentially important ways, a UBI is relevant to each of the main dimensions of crisis (economic, ecological, social and political). But the mainstreaming of the UBI idea is not an entirely 'innocent' and straightforward phenomenon: it speaks also to other underlying trends, including the reshaping of social policy in the shadow of financialised capitalism during the past thirty years and the fading authority of neoliberal capitalism (Chapter 6). Profoundly different ideas therefore circulate about the definition, design and functions of a UBI, and how it would relate to other elements of social and economic restructuring.

Left and progressive proponents support a basic income that is universal, forms part of an extensive and redistributive social provisioning system, and functions in support of systemic changes that are aimed at creating a more viable, just and egalitarian society. Those on the Right, especially the libertarian Right, see it as an opportunity to further limit the remit of the state and to expand the authority of the market by replacing – and commodifying – other forms of social provisioning and protection with a single cash payment. Other variants of a basic income find support elsewhere on the ideological spectrum. They range from forms of emergency income support that are targeted at those 'most in need', to cash grants that support people's (re)integration into the labour market. This conceptual slipperiness has enabled a potentially radical intervention to become a staple of mainstream debate.

The UBI considered in this text is defined as a regular (monthly) income that is paid unconditionally to all individuals without means-testing or work requirement. It supplements existing forms of income support (such as the child support grant, old-age pension and disability grants in South Africa) and other forms of social provisioning for low-income earners (such as free healthcare and school education; subsidised energy, transport and housing, and so on) (Chapter 1). And it functions as part of overhauled social and economic policies that are geared to reduce poverty and inequality, thus improving people's capabilities and well-being. The payment is universal: everyone benefits. It therefore satisfies the criterion of fairness. Anyone who chooses to work is rewarded in addition to the payment. Those who earn higher incomes contribute comparatively more to the financing of the UBI, but a large share of the funding is drawn not from individuals but from the circuitries in which profit is generated and appropriated in capitalist economies.

A great deal of evidence supports the expectation that a UBI can contribute substantively to improving people's livelihoods and life prospects (Chapter 3). Data from basic income pilot projects and from analogous cash transfer schemes indicate that, even if set at a low amount, a UBI would improve the financial, health and education status of low-income households, and reduce poverty.[11]

If linked to other transformative efforts, a UBI can promote and support forward-looking, adaptive change. It can function as a safety net for communities hard-hit by the effects of global warming and can provide multifaceted support as countries embark on a just transition to a low-carbon economic model. The extent of those effects would be shaped by the size of the payment and the availability of other forms of social wage provisioning. Increased income for the poorest deciles can also boost aggregate demand for basic goods and services, since low-income recipients are likely to spend rather than save income.[12]

Since it is neither conditional (in the manner of a job guarantee, for instance), targeted (like South Africa's social grants), nor means-tested, a UBI as defined here would be less complicated and less costly to administer, and it would achieve more complete coverage than standard income support schemes. Core logistical requirements are a centralised database (updated with birth and death registration, and immigration and emigration data) and a disbursement facility (electronic transfers to individual savings accounts). By drastically reducing administrative mediation, a UBI also offers fewer opportunities for patronage and corruption – pitfalls which blight the state in South Africa and elsewhere. The entanglement of the ruling ANC (and state officials) with profit-seeking ventures invites corruption, wastage and governance failure, as is evident at local[13] and national government levels in South Africa,[14] including in 'spending irregularities' during the COVID-19 pandemic.[15] A UBI could sidestep such hazards.

LIBERATING POTENTIALS

A UBI holds deeper, transformative promise as well (Chapter 3). By strengthening workers' abilities to quit a job without falling into distress or to turn down work that is exploitative or dangerous, a UBI could empower (especially low-wage) workers individually and collectively. The ability to decline waged work can help reset the balance of power between workers and employers, which would benefit workplace organising and other efforts to improve labour practices at the low-income end of the labour market. Those sorts of effects speak to the distinctiveness of a UBI. Not merely an adjustment or expansion of the existing social welfare order, it can be a qualitatively different intervention that breaks with the waged work-centric model of the old order, its paternalist frame and its patriarchal slant. It would present people with the opportunity to sidestep, at least temporarily, a fate where, as André Gorz put it, we are forever 'prepared to make any and every concession, to suffer humiliation or subjugation, to face competition and betrayal to get or keep a job, since "those who lose their jobs lose everything"'.[16]

This liberating effect can extend wider. If large enough, the payment would provide people with income security that enables them to devote their energies and time to purposes other than waged work – for example care and other socially productive work; community projects such as food gardens and repair and recycling work; cultural production; volunteer work; and studying or acquiring new skills. Those kinds of activities are especially relevant for building sustainable and viable local communities and economies. Gorz referred to them as 'socially determined' work: activities that allow one 'to feel useful to society in a general sense, rather than in a particular way subject to particular relationships, and thus to exist as a fully social individual'.[17]

A UBI also challenges the reflex to equate well-being and progress with metrics of economic output. If large enough, a UBI undercuts the power of capital by enabling people to sidestep, at least temporarily and partially, the need to 'earn' basic security by selling their labour on unfair terms. That undermines capital's power to decree the terms and conditions on which it uses low-skill labour. The demand for such a payment flows from the insistence that

> everyone has a right to a decent life whether or not they have a job, that human dignity does not depend on paid employment, that perpetual growth is not the way to prosperity, and that everyone should benefit from shared wealth and our shared planet.[18]

In such ways, a UBI that challenges the status of paid work as the decisive basis for social citizenship and entitlement serves as more than a means for individual 'enablement': it could, in Erik Olin Wright's view, 'underwrite social and institutional changes' and help shift power relations and hierarchies.[19] For Lindsey Macdonald, it also 'holds the promise of establishing the material basis needed to make freedom a lived reality'.[20] A UBI on its own would not achieve those objectives, but it could support a broad suite of efforts to achieve them. Introducing and defending a UBI require political and economic conditions that are potentially transformative. Those conditions create space to shift relations of power in ways that open the possibility for further advances towards egalitarian goals. This perspective breaks with the 'reform-versus-revolution' binary of the late-nineteenth and twentieth centuries, and resembles what Gorz referred to as 'non-reformist reforms'.[21]

A common criticism is that a UBI would encourage people to withdraw from the labour market on a scale that disrupts economies (Chapter 4). In the context of extremely high unemployment, concerns about a disincentive effect among low-skilled workers are misdirected. Even in general, basic income projects and cash transfer schemes offer scant basis for such unease.[22] Might a basic income, if too small, end up subsidising low-wage employers, thereby undermining minimum wage demands and weakening worker organisations?[23] Again, the worry seems less pertinent to a highly distressed setting such as South Africa, where hyper-unemployment already pushes the reservation wage far below a survival-level income.

Another concern on the Left is that a basic income, by fusing social welfare principles with neoliberal logic, would lubricate individuals' deeper integration into the market as consumers. It is an odd objection, which tends not to surface in the context of waged work (which, of course, is remunerated with cash). It also ignores the reality that certain essential goods and services are currently not accessible outside the market (for example, food, toiletries, clothing, telecommunications), even though some, conceivably, could be converted into public goods in the future.

A more troubling possibility is that a UBI could be used as a lever for removing existing entitlements. In the Indian context, for example, Jean Drèze has warned of 'a real danger of a UBI becoming a Trojan horse for dismantling hard-won entitlements of the underprivileged'.[24] That concern dwindles when directed at a UBI that supplements other forms of social provisioning. However, there remains a danger that a basic income could be traded off against other entitlements if fiscal conditions deteriorate. Which brings us to the most common objection to the UBI demand: that it is unaffordable.

WIDER IMPLICATIONS

A basic income scheme would be expensive; how expensive would depend on the amount of the payment, how eligibility is defined, whether and how the payment is phased in and ramped up, and how it links with existing forms of income and other social support. Blanket claims about (un)affordability are unjustified and erroneous. Detailed costing estimates for different scenarios are being developed in South Africa and elsewhere. Their fiscal feasibility depends on the financing options, a host of which are available (Chapter 5) and many of which are desirable irrespective of whether a UBI is introduced.

The fiscal choices draw into focus the linked need for supportive macroeconomic policy changes (Chapter 6). Macroeconomic policy has to facilitate industrial, labour and social policies that create more and better jobs, equitably build capabilities, are ecologically sustainable, redistribute incomes, and foster both social and productive capacities (especially in low-income communities). Fiscal and monetary policies have to simultaneously privilege societal needs and enable a shift towards a low-carbon economic model.[25] The latitude for such innovation is considerably greater than is acknowledged in orthodox economic circles.[26]

This underscores the need to approach a UBI not as a stand-alone, technocratic intervention or tool, but as an element of a broader, long-term project of transformation and emancipation. Its impact and fate will depend on how it synchronises with other economic, social and political strategies, which forces drive those strategies, and whether those forces are capable of defending the desired changes. Even when achieved, a UBI will remain a contested and politically unstable intervention. Jurgen de Wispelaere and Leticia Morales are correct to warn of a danger that

> the interaction between basic income and residual layers of traditional welfare programmes implies continuous competition over tight budgets and scarce organisational resources … gradually converting the existing scheme from the ground up into something that only formally resembles what the enacting coalition set out to achieve.[27]

Yet this social and political context tends to be overlooked in much of the current debate about a basic income. There is growing mainstream recognition of the need for some form of emergency income support as a cushion against destitution. But the size, design and financing of such a payment will be a matter of intense dispute and struggle. A generous UBI, financed along the lines discussed in Chapter 5 for example, requires fiscal and other changes that encroach on capital's ability to commandeer the bulk of the surplus it appropriates from human labour (paid and unpaid) and nature. There is more at stake than the technical design of a social policy tool.

If detached from mobilised social support and without strong institutional backing, a UBI will be vulnerable to distortion or ruin (Chapter 6). Policy interventions do not automatically or indefinitely do the bidding of their creators. Separated from a strong political and social movement of change, a UBI runs the risk of backfiring, of being captured and repurposed in ways that sustain exploitation, precarity and inequality. The process of achieving a UBI therefore is at least as important as the achievement itself. That awareness is frequently absent from the UBI debate, which tends to orbit around justifications for and critiques of a UBI. Kathi Weeks makes the crucial point that

> we would judge the success or failure of a movement for basic income not only in terms of whether the policy is implemented, but also in terms of the collective power, organizational forms, critical consciousness, and new demands that the process of demanding it manages to generate.[28]

A key variable is the state: whether and how it can be transformed from functioning as facilitator of private accumulation to creating the conditions, fostering the capabilities and furnishing the means for a just and sustainable society. Achieving and defending a UBI will require an active state that is accountable to progressive social forces and that privileges the needs and entitlements of ordinary people. Turning the state in that direction presents a massive challenge in a country like South Africa, where powerful sections of the state (notably the National

Treasury and the Reserve Bank) remain steeped in neoliberal ideology and tend to equate the fortunes of financialised capitalism with societal well-being. Nevertheless, South Africa's Constitution mandates a shift towards a state that resets the relationship between the economy and society.

HEARTS AND MINDS

There is both a manifest need and potential for a model of income distribution that does not hinge on exchanging labour for wages or on qualifying for conditional 'charity'. James Ferguson has suggested that the South African social grant system will gradually evolve into a de facto form of universal, citizenship-based entitlement, a kind of UBI 'through the back door'.[29] During the COVID-19 pandemic, a growing alliance of grassroots and non-governmental organisations, trade unions and research bodies in South Africa demanded that the state steadily graduate the newly introduced emergency grants into a full-fledged *universal* basic income scheme.[30] The urgency of those demands was highlighted when rioting and looting erupted in July 2021.

While the need for an intervention like a UBI may seem increasingly self-evident, a generalised desire for a UBI cannot be assumed. The BIG campaign in the early 2000s did not ignite popular enthusiasm, nor did it defuse conservative reticence. In Jeremy Seekings' view, 'basic income activism in South Africa has remained a largely intellectual project sustained by a small network of individuals without strong organisational or popular bases'.[31] This may be changing. Recent surveys and opinion polls suggest a majority of South Africans now support a basic income.[32] That stance could solidify as the COVID-19 pandemic and its effects drag on.

Yet, even as opportunities for waged work diminish, its intrinsic value continues to be glorified. In addition to being portrayed as the core legitimate source of income for able-bodied adults, waged work is seen to bestow virtue, earn respect, nourish pride and assign legitimacy. Invested with moral, psychological, social and political currency, its allure endures.[33] Merit, social status and entitlement continue to be tied to waged work, and politicians persist in framing reality and policies in those terms. Thus, 'job creation' still operates as a radiant substitute for the task of creating a just society.[34] In reality, pervasive and relatively secure access to decent work was realised only partially in a few industrialised countries, and those conditions survived for about two generations in the mid-twentieth century. In South Africa's case, that idyllic arrangement was available only to white workers. And yet a kind of 'melancholia' lingers, a hankering after illusory pasts that traps inventiveness inside the boundaries of contemporary capitalism. This yearning also legitimises policies that are oblivious to the dynamics shaping the nature and availability of waged work today.

A UBI destabilises cherished beliefs about the role and status of waged work in human life. How a UBI is framed and promoted is therefore vitally important – not only to build durable social and political support, but because the eventual form and function of such an intervention will be constantly contested.[35] A *universal* basic income will attract fulsome resistance from both capital and the state. Achieving and defending it will require social and political forces that are strong enough to prevail against that opposition. And *that* will require reshaping the 'common sense' people use when defining and weighing the claims they have on the common wealth, on one another and on the state.

The stigma attached to unemployment – and to non-waged income – has to be challenged, along with notions that paid work is the only authentic form of productive activity, the only legitimate way to contribute to society, and the only rightful basis for entitlement and reciprocity. As Kathi Weeks has emphasised, the arguments and tactics used to marshal support for a UBI will be important in their own right:

> A demand is not just a thing, but something that must be explained, justified, argued for and debated. The practice of demanding is itself productive of critical awareness and new political desires.[36]

It will be important to pursue social and economic policy reforms 'that change people's relationship with work: including the value we attach to work, the time we devote to it, and how work frames our judgements of other people'.[37] That means valuing and validating other forms of work (volunteering, care and other forms of social reproductive labour) and other forms of contributing to the public good – both rhetorically and practically. The gendered constructions of 'work' (which devalue care work and other social reproductive labour) are obvious candidates for change. So, too, the impulse among many men to extol waged work not only as a source of recognition and status, but as an opportunity to recuperate domineering forms of masculinity. If the social and administrative category of 'the unemployed' is made more porous and less damning, the association of waged work with authority, the stigma attached to unemployment and the disparagement of non-waged work will weaken.

* * *

The push for a fully fledged UBI recognises that tectonic shifts are underway and that they demand actions that go far beyond attempts at recuperation and repair, or short-sighted notions of 'building back better'. There are risks, unanswered questions and major challenges attached to a UBI. But as a formative intervention, the likely benefits of a UBI are, on balance, so urgent, numerous and potentially far-reaching that it should form part of a drive to create a viable and just society.

NOTES

INTRODUCTION

1   The book uses the terms 'waged work' and 'paid work' interchangeably to refer to work a person performs in exchange for a wage or salary.

2   ILO, *World Employment and Social Outlook: Trends 2018* (Geneva: International Labour Organization, 2018).

3   M. Hyde, et al., 'Trends in Work and Employment in Rapidly Developing Countries', in *Handbook of Disability, Work and Health,* Handbook Series in Occupational Health Sciences, Vol. 1, eds. U. Bültmann and J. Siegrist (Cham: Springer, 2020), 33–52.

4   ILO, *World Employment and Social Outlook: Trends 2020* (Geneva: International Labour Organization, 2020).

5   Hyde, et al., 'Trends in Work'; G. Standing, *The Precariat: The New Dangerous Class* (London: Bloomsbury, 2011); A. Ross, *Nice Work if You Can Get it: Life and Labor in Precarious Times* (New York: NYU Press, 2009).

6   ILO, *Trends 2018.*

7   If China is included, real wage growth in Asia and the Pacific has averaged at about 4% since 2000. ILO, *Trends 2020.* See also ILO, *Global Wage Report 2020–21: Wages and Minimum Wages in the Time of COVID-19* (Geneva: International Labour Organization, 2021), https://www.ilo.org/wcmsp5/groups/public/---dgreports/---dcomm/---publ/documents/publication/wcms_762534.pdf.

8   The ILO estimates that '90 per cent of women who lost their jobs in 2020 exited the labour force, which suggests that their working lives are likely to be disrupted over an extended period'. ILO, *World Employment and Social Outlook: Trends 2021* (Geneva: International Labour Organization, 2021), 14.

9   ILO, *Trends 2021.*

10   C. Lakner, et al., 'Updated Estimates of the Impact of COVID-19 on Global Poverty: Looking Back at 2020 and the Outlook for 2021', *World Bank Blogs*, 11 January 2021, https://blogs.worldbank.org/opendata/updated-estimates-impact-covid-19-global-poverty-looking-back-2020-and-outlook-2021.

11   ILO, *Trends 2020.*

12 The World Bank defines 'extreme' poverty as living on less than US$1.90 per person per day and 'moderate' poverty as living on less than US$3.20 (in purchasing parity terms). See ILO, *Trends 2021*.

13 Stats SA, *Quarterly Labour Force Survey QLFS Q2: 2021* (Pretoria: Statistics South Africa, 2021), http://www.statssa.gov.za/publications/P0211/Presentation%20QLFS%20Q2_2021.pdf.

14 Stats SA, *Poverty Trends in South Africa: An Examination of Absolute Poverty between 2006 and 2015* (Pretoria: Statistics South Africa, 2017).

15 J. Patel, 'Economic Insecurity Persists for South Africans', *Afrobarometer Dispatch*, No. 478, 22 September 2021, https://afrobarometer.org/sites/default/files/publications/Dispatches/ad478-economic_insecurity_persists_for_south_africans-afrobarometer_dispatch-18sept21.pdf.

16 J. Seekings and N. Nattrass, *Class, Race and Inequality in South Africa* (New Haven, CT: Yale University Press, 2005).

17 D. Harvey, *Seventeen Contradictions and the End of Capitalism* (New York: Oxford University Press, 2014), 110.

18 G. Palma and J.E. Stiglitz, 'Do Nations Just Get the Inequality They Deserve? The "Palma Ratio" Re-examined', in *Inequality and Growth: Patterns and Policy*, eds. K. Basu and J.E. Stiglitz (London: Palgrave Macmillan, 2016), 35–97; IMF, 'Still Sluggish Global Growth', *World Economic Outlook*, July 2019, https://www.imf.org/en/Publications/WEO/Issues/2019/07/18/WEOupdateJuly2019.

19 United Nations, *World Social Report 2020: Inequality in a Rapidly Changing World* (New York: United Nations Department of Economic and Social Affairs, 2020), https://www.un.org/development/desa/dspd/wp-content/uploads/sites/22/2020/01/World-Social-Report-2020-FullReport.pdf.

20 G. Zucman, 'Global Wealth Inequality', *Annual Review of Economics* 11, no. 1 (2019), 111.

21 N. Fraser and R. Jaeggi, *Capitalism: A Conversation in Critical Theory* (Cambridge: Polity, 2018).

22 N. Fraser, 'Climates of Capital: For a Trans-Environmental Eco-Socialism', *New Left Review* 17 (2021): 94–127.

23 J.B. Foster, 'The Financialization of Capitalism', *Monthly Review* 58, no. 11 (2007): 2.

24 Social citizenship entails people's rights or entitlements to economic and social welfare that offers the prospect of building dignified lives. But as Franco Barchiesi reminds us, the preferred routes to social citizenship are controversial and contested. Most state policies tend to tie welfare and security to waged work, while many social justice movements increasingly demand forms of provisioning that are delinked from employment and occur as entitlements or rights. In the latter case, social citizenship is pursued also through the redistribution of resources, often the provision of subsidised or free basic services and goods that are provided outside the market (and therefore are 'decommodified'). F. Barchiesi, 'South African Debates on the Basic Income Grant: Wage Labour and the Post-Apartheid Social Policy', *Journal of Southern African Studies* 33, no. 3 (2007): 563.

25 B. Raine, 'Renewed Labour', *N+1* 33 (2019): 33–46, https://nplusonemag.com/issue-33/politics/renewed-labour/; N. Klein, *This Changes Everything: Capitalism Versus the Climate* (London: Penguin Books, 2015).

26 P. van Parijs and Y. Vanderborght, *Basic Income: A Radical Proposal for a Free Society and a Sane Economy* (Cambridge, MA: Cambridge University Press, 2017); E.O. Wright, *Redesigning Distribution: Basic Income and Stakeholder Grants as Alternative Cornerstones for a More Egalitarian Capitalism* (London: Verso Books, 2003); M. Murray and C. Pateman, eds., *Basic Income* (London: Palgrave Macmillan, 2012); P. van Parijs, 'Basic Income: A Simple and Powerful Idea for the Twenty-First Century', *Politics and Society* 32, no. 1 (2004): 7–39.

27 See, for example, P. Mason, *Postcapitalism: A Guide to Our Future* (London: Farrar, Straus and Giroux, 2015); N. Srnicek and A. Williams, *Inventing the Future: Post-Capitalism and a World without Work* (London: Verso Books, 2015); G. Standing, *Basic Income: And How We Can Make it Happen* (London: Pelican Books, 2017); C. Murray, *In Our Hands: A Plan to Replace the Welfare State* (Washington, DC: AEI Press, 2006).

28 J. Ferguson, *Give a Man a Fish: Reflections on the New Politics of Distribution* (Durham, NC: Duke University Press, 2015).

29 Ferguson, *Give a Man a Fish*.

30 F. Bastagli, et al., *Cash Transfers: What Does the Evidence Say? A Rigorous Review of Programme Impact and of the Role of Design and Implementation Features* (London: Overseas Development Institute, 2016); I. Woolard and M. Leibbrandt, *The Evolution of Unconditional Cash Transfers in South Africa* (Cape Town: Southern Africa Labour and Development Research Unit, University of Cape Town, 2010).

CHAPTER 1   BEHIND THE IDEA OF A UNIVERSAL BASIC INCOME

1   R. Atkins and G. Tetlow, 'Switzerland Votes against State-Provided Basic Income', *Financial Times*, 5 June 2016, https://www.ft.com/content/002af908-2b16-11e6-a18d-a96ab29e3c95; M. Timms, 'The Case for and against Unconditional Basic Income in Switzerland', *EuropeanCEO*, 10 January 2014, https://www.europeanceo.com/finance/the-case-for-and-against-unconditional-basic-income-in-switzerland/.

2   A. Arnold, 'The Anti-Poverty Experiment', *Nature* 557 (2018): 626–628; C. Haarmann, et al., *Basic Income Grant Pilot Project Assessment Report* (Windhoek: Basic Income Grant Coalition, 2009).

3   S. Davala, et al., *Basic Income: A Transformative Policy for India* (Delhi: Bloomsbury, 2015).

4   Anon., 'Results of Finland's Basic Income Experiment: Small Employment Effects, Better Perceived Economic Security and Mental Wellbeing', *Kela News Archive*, Helsinki, 6 May 2020, https://www.kela.fi/web/en/news-archive/-/asset_publisher/lN08GY2nIrZo/content/results-of-the-basic-income-experiment-small-employment-effects-better-perceived-economic-security-and-mental-wellbeing; DIW Berlin, *Basic Income Pilot Project: How Does a Basic Income Change Our Society? We Want to Know* (Berlin: DIW Berlin, 2020), https://www.diw.de/en/diw_01.c.796681.en/projects/basic_income_pilot_project.html; K. McFarland, 'Existing and Upcoming BI-Related Experiments', Basic Income Earth Network, 15 October 2017, https://basicincome.org/news/2017/10/overview-of-current-basic-income-related-experiments-october-2017/.

5   A. Kassam, 'Ontario Plans to Launch Universal Basic Income Trial Run This Summer', *The Guardian*, 24 April 2017, https://www.theguardian.com/world/2017/apr/24/canada-basic-income-trial-ontario-summer?CMP=Share_iOSApp_Other.

6   A. Bastani, *Fully Automated Luxury Communism* (London: Verso Books, 2020); P. Frase, *Four Futures* (London: Verso Books, 2016); F. Barchiesi, 'Schooling Bodies to Hard Work: The South African State's Policy Discourse and its Moral Constructions of Welfare', *Journal of Contemporary African Studies* 34, no. 2 (2016): 221–235; N. Srnicek and A. Williams, *Inventing the Future: Post-Capitalism and a World without Work* (London: Verso Books, 2015); P. Mason, *Postcapitalism: A Guide to Our Future* (London: Farrar, Straus and Giroux, 2015).

7   G. Standing, *Basic Income: And How We Can Make it Happen* (London: Pelican Books, 2017); P. van Parijs, 'Basic Income: A Simple and Powerful Idea for the Twenty-First Century', *Politics and Society* 32, no. 1 (2004): 7–39; E.O. Wright, *Redesigning Distribution: Basic Income and Stakeholder Grants as Alternative Cornerstones for a More Egalitarian Capitalism* (London: Verso Books, 2003).

8   A. Yang, *The Freedom Dividend, Defined*, US Presidential Campaign Material, 2020, https://2020.yang2020.com/what-is-freedom-dividend-faq/; R. Bregman, *Utopia for Realists: How We Can Build the Ideal World* (New York: Little, Brown and Company, 2017).

9   C. Murray, *In Our Hands: A Plan to Replace the Welfare State* (Washington, DC: AEI Press, 2006).

10   T. Paine, *Agrarian Justice*, 1796 [digital edition 1999], http://piketty.pse.ens.fr/files/Paine1795.pdf.

11   C. Fourier, *La fausse industrie morcelée, répugnante, mensongère, et l'antidote, l'industrie naturelle, combinée, attrayante, véridique, donnant quadruple produit* (Paris: Bossange, 1835–1836).

12   J.S. Mill, *Principles of Political Economy*, Project Gutenberg, 2009 [1848], https://eet.pixel-online.org/files/etranslation/original/Mill,%20Principles%20of%20Political%20Economy.pdf.

13   Mill, *Principles*, 195.

14   D. Zamora and A. Jäger, 'Historicizing Basic Income: Response to David Zeglen', *Lateral* 8, no. 1 (2019), https://csalateral.org/forum/universal-basic-income/historicizing-basic-income-zamora-jager/.

15   B. Russell, *Roads to Freedom: Socialism, Anarchism and Syndicalism* (London: Routledge, 1993 [1918]).

16   H. Long, 'The Share Our Wealth Society', *Social Welfare History Project*, 2021 [1934]. http://socialwelfare.library.vcu.edu/eras/great-depression/long-huey/.

17   M. Friedman, *Capitalism and Freedom* (Chicago, IL: University of Chicago Press, 1962).

18   S. Santens, 'How to Reform Welfare and Taxes to Provide Every American Citizen with a Basic Income', *Medium*, 5 June 2017. https://medium.com/economicsecproj/how-to-reform-welfare-and-taxes-to-provide-every-american-citizen-with-a-basic-income-bc67d3f4c2b8.

19   R.J. Lampman, *Nixon's Family Assistance Plan* (Madison, WI: Institute for Research on Poverty, University of Wisconsin, 1969), https://www.irp.wisc.edu/publications/dps/pdfs/dp5769.pdf.

20   H. Beach, 'Feminist Theory, Gender Inequity, and Basic Income: An Interview with Almaz Zelleke', *Basic Income Today*, 16 May 2019, https://basicincometoday.com/feminist-theory-gender-inequity-and-basic-income/.

21 L. Neyfakh, 'Should the Government Pay You to Be Alive?', *The Boston Globe*, 9 February 2014, http://www.bostonglobe.com/ideas/2014/02/09/should-government-pay-you-alive/aaLVJsUAc5pKh0iYTFrXpI/story.html.

22 P. van Parijs, 'Why Surfers Should Be Fed: The Liberal Case for an Unconditional Basic Income', *Philosophy and Public Affairs* 20, no. 2 (1991): 101–131.

23 Mbulelo Musi, spokesman for the Social Development Ministry, cited in H. Matisonn and J. Seekings, 'Welfare in Wonderland? The Politics of Basic Income Grant in South Africa, 1996–2002', paper presented to the 9th International Congress of the Basic Income European Network, Geneva, 12–14 September 2002, https://basicincome.org/bien/pdf/2002MatisonnSeekings.pdf.

24 Murray, *In Our Hands*; C. Murray, 'A Guaranteed Income for Every American', American Enterprise Institute, 3 June 2016, https://www.aei.org/articles/a-guaranteed-income-for-every-american/.

25 E. Guo, 'Universal Basic Income Is Here – It Just Looks Different from What You Expected', *MIT Technology Review*, 7 May 2021, https://www.technologyreview.com/2021/05/07/1024674/ubi-guaranteed-income-pandemic/.

26 For example, Bastani, *Fully Automated*; Frase, *Four Futures*; Srnicek and Williams, *Inventing the Future*; Barchiesi, 'Schooling Bodies'; Mason, *Postcapitalism*.

27 'Post-work' refers to scenarios where paid work becomes steadily less available and on deteriorating terms, with increasing numbers of people having long periods of not working at all.

28 M. Ford, *The Rise of the Robots* (New York: Basic Books, 2015).

29 Such as Standing, *Basic Income*; P. van Parijs, 'A Simple and Powerful Idea for the 21st Century', in *Redesigning Distribution: Basic Income and Stakeholder Grants as Alternative Cornerstones for a More Egalitarian Capitalism*, ed. E.O. Wright (London: Verso Books, 2003), 7–38; Wright, *Redesigning Distribution*; E.O. Wright, 'Basic Income, Stakeholder Grants, and Class Analysis', *Politics and Society* 32, no. 1 (2004): 79–87.

30 Wright, 'Basic Income, Stakeholder Grants'.

31 Van Parijs, 'Basic Income'; Wright, *Redesigning Distribution*.

32 M. Ravallion, 'Guaranteed Employment or Guaranteed Income?', *World Development* 115, no. C (2019): 209–221.

33 D. Tondani, 'Universal Basic Income and Negative Income Tax: Two Different Ways of Thinking Redistribution', *The Journal of Socio-Economics* 38, no. 2 (2009): 246–255.

34 P. van Parijs, 'The Universal Basic Income: Why Utopian Thinking Matters, and How Sociologists Can Contribute to it', *Politics and Society* 41, no. 2 (2013): 171–182; K. Weeks, 'A Feminist Case for Basic Income: An Interview with Kathi Weeks', *Critical Legal Thinking*, 22 August 2016, https://criticallegalthinking.com/2016/08/22/feminist-case-basic-income-interview-kathi-weeks/; K. Weeks, 'Feminism and the Refusal of Work: An Interview with Kathi Weeks', *Political Critique*, 28 August 2017, http://politicalcritique.org/world/2017/souvlis-weeks-feminism-marxism-work-interview.

35 S. Davies, 'Basic Income, Labour and the Idea of Post-Capitalism', *Economic Affairs* 37, no. 3 (2017): 442–458; I. Gough, 'Universal Basic Services: A Theoretical and Moral Framework', *The Political Quarterly* 90, no. 3 (2019): 534–542.

36 M. Lawhon and T. McCreary, 'Beyond Jobs vs Environment: On the Potential of a Universal Basic Income to Reconfigure Environmental Politics', *Antipode* 52, no. 2 (2020): 458.

37   G. Allègre, *How Can a Basic Income Be Defended?* OFCE Briefing Paper 7 (Paris: L'Observatoire français des conjonctures économiques, 2014), https://spire. sciencespo.fr/hdl:/2441/25qafebie49csbsal9hbmifkr5/resources/2014-allegre-howcanabasicincomebriefing7.pdf.

38   That amount, CHF 2 500, was a little higher than the CHF 2 200 income poverty line in Switzerland at the time.

39   Stats SA, *National Poverty Lines 2021*, Statistical Release P0310.1 (Pretoria: Statistics South Africa, 2021), http://www.statssa.gov.za/publications/P03101/ P031012021.pdf.

40   T. Piketty, *Capital in the Twenty-First Century* (Cambridge, MA: Harvard University Press, 2013).

41   S. Fadaee and S. Schindler, 'The Occupy Movement and the Politics of Vulnerability', *Globalizations* 11, no. 6 (2014): 777–791.

42   Bastani, *Fully Automated*; Srnicek and Williams, *Inventing the Future*; Mason, *Postcapitalism*.

43   C.B. Frey and M.A. Osborne, 'The Future of Employment: How Susceptible Are Jobs to Computerization?', *Technological Forecasting and Social Change* 114 (2017): 254–280.

44   S. McBride, et al., *After '08: Social Policy and the Global Financial Crisis* (Vancouver: University of British Columbia Press, 2015).

45   N. Fraser, 'Legitimation Crisis? On the Political Contradictions of Financialized Capitalism', *Critical Historical Studies* 2, no. 2 (2015): 157–189; D. Harvey, *A Brief History of Neoliberalism* (Oxford: Oxford University Press, 2005); A. Saad-Filho and D. Johnston, *Neoliberalism: A Critical Reader* (London: Pluto Press, 2005).

46   N. Gilbert, *The Transformation of the Welfare State* (Oxford: Oxford University Press, 2002), 4.

47   F. Barchiesi, 'South African Debates on the Basic Income Grant: Wage Labour and the Post-Apartheid Social Policy', *Journal of Southern African Studies* 33, no. 3 (2007), 563.

48   A. Fischer, *Poverty as Ideology: Rescuing Social Justice from Global Development Agendas* (London: Zed Books, 2018); B. Fine, 'The Continuing Enigmas of Social Policy', in *Towards Universal Health Care in Emerging Economies: Social Policy in a Development Context*, ed. I. Yi (London: Palgrave Macmillan, 2017), 29–59; T. Mkandawire, 'Transformative Social Policy and Innovation in Developing Countries', *European Journal for Development Research* 19, no. 1 (2007): 13–29.

49   In the response to the HIV pandemic, for example, it became customary in the 2010s to promote cash transfers (especially conditional ones) as a way to enable girls and young women to avoid acquiring HIV infection, with greater economic autonomy assumed to increase women's control over their sexual lives. The evidence of an effect on HIV incidence is far from conclusive; see, for example, A. Pettifor, et al., 'The Effect of a Conditional Cash Transfer on HIV Incidence in Young Women in Rural South Africa (HPTN 068): A Phase 3, Randomised Controlled Trial', *Lancet Global Health* 4, no. 12 (2016): e978–e988.

50   F. Bastagli, *From Social Safety Net to Social Policy? The Role of Conditional Cash Transfers in Welfare State Development in Latin America*, Working Paper 60 (Brasilia: International Policy Centre for Inclusive Growth, 2009). Lena Lavinas has developed a critical analysis of the intellectual 'genealogy' of conditional cash

transfers. She traces it to the emergence of the concept of 'human capital' (and its links to the work of Chicago School economist Gary Becker) and to shifts towards targeted welfare spending (influenced by the rise of behavioural economics). Lavinas pinpoints the *Subsidio Único Familiar*, introduced in Augusto Pinochet's Chile in August 1981, as one of the pioneering conditional safety net interventions. L. Lavinas, '21st Century Welfare', *New Left Review* 84 (2013): 5–40.

51   L. Lavinas, *The Takeover of Social Policy by Financialization: The Brazilian Paradox* (New York: Palgrave MacMillan, 2017).

52   Fischer, *Poverty as Ideology*.

53   Iran, for example, introduced a national cash transfer programme in 2011 while phasing out state subsidies that had held down the prices of bread, water, heating, electricity and fuel. See also S. Samuel, 'Finland Gave People Free Money. It Didn't Help Them Get Jobs – but Does That Matter?', *Vox*, 9 February 2019, https://www.vox.com/future-perfect/2019/2/9/18217566/finland-basic-income.

54   N. Fraser, 'Can Society Be Commodities All the Way Down? Post-Polanyian Reflections on Capitalist Crisis', *Economy and Society* 43, no. 4 (2014): 542.

55   Lavinas, *Takeover of Social Policy*.

56   E. Torkelson, 'Collateral Damages: Cash Transfer and Debt Transfer in South Africa', *World Development* 126 (2020): 104711, https://doi.org/10.1016/j.worlddev.2019.104711.

57   World Bank, *Global Financial Development Report 2014: Financial Inclusion* (Washington, DC: World Bank, 2014), https://openknowledge.worldbank.org/bitstream/handle/10986/16238/9780821399859.pdf?sequence=4&isAllowed=y.

58   L. Gronbach, *Social Cash Transfer Payment Systems in Sub-Saharan Africa*, Working Paper 452 (Cape Town: Centre for Social Science Research, University of Cape Town, 2020).

59   S. Ashman, 'South Africa: An Economy of Extremes', in *The Essential Guide to Critical Development Studies*, eds. H. Veltmeyer and P. Bowles (Abingdon: Routledge, 2021), 171–178.

60   Torkelson, 'Collateral Damages', 1.

61   J. Clarke, 'Basic Income: Progressive Cloak and Neoliberal Dagger', *Socialist Bullet*, 4 April 2018, https://socialistproject.ca/2018/04/basic-income-progressive-cloak-and-neoliberal-dagger/.

62   Samuel, 'Finland'.

63   DIW Berlin, *Basic Income*.

64   McFarland, 'Existing and Upcoming'.

65   Kassam, 'Ontario Plans'.

66   Davala, et al., *Basic Income*.

67   Haarmann, et al., *Basic Income Grant*.

68   F. Grisolia, et al., *Busibi UCT: Preliminary Analysis on Some Key Outcomes* (Antwerp: University of Antwerp, 2021), https://drive.google.com/file/d/14pAIIOxzDsQJ3UGbDzSlGa9wXT2GQnnO/view.

69   The Stockton experiment paid a US\$500 monthly stipend to 125 residents with incomes at or below the median income line in the city (US\$46 000), without conditions, for two years. Within a year, full-time employment had increased among the recipients (from 28% to 40%) and their mental health had improved. S. West, et al., *Preliminary Analysis: SEED's First Year* (Stockton,

USA: Stockton Economic Empowerment Demonstration, 2021), https://static1. squarespace.com/static/6039d612b17d055cac14070f/t/603ef1194c474b329 f33c329/1614737690661/SEED_Preliminary+Analysis-SEEDs+First+Year_ Final+Report_Individual+Pages+-2.pdf.

70 J. Bedayn, 'Universal Basic Income? California Moves to Be First State to Fund Pilot Projects', *Cal Matters*, 21 July 2021, https://calmatters.org/ california-divide/2021/07/universal-basic-income-california/.

71 Arnold, 'Anti-Poverty Experiment'.

72 X. Vidal-Folch and M.V. Gomez, 'Spain's Guaranteed Minimum Income Scheme Will Come with €5.5 Billion Price Tag', *El Pais*, 19 April 2020, https:// english.elpais.com/economy_and_business/2020-04-19/spains-guaranteed-minimum-income-scheme-will-come-with-55bn-price-tag.html.

73 T.B. Hamilton, 'The Netherlands' Upcoming Money-for-Nothing Experiment', *The Atlantic*, 21 June 2016, https://www.theatlantic.com/business/archive/2016/06/ netherlands-utrecht-universal-basic-income-experiment/487883/.

74 S. Sodha, 'Is Finland's Basic Universal Income a Solution to Automation, Fewer Jobs and Lower Wages?', *The Guardian*, 19 February 2017, https://www. theguardian.com/society/2017/feb/19/basic-income-finland-low-wages-fewer-jobs?CMP=Share_iOSApp_Other.

75 DIW Berlin, *Basic Income*.

76 T.G. Ash and A. Zimmermann, 'In Crisis, Europeans Support Radical Positions', *Eupinions Brief*, 6 May 2020, https://eupinions.eu/de/text/in-crisis-europeans-support-radical-positions.

77 Belgium, Czechia, France, Germany, Greece, Hungary, Italy, the Netherlands, Poland, Portugal, Romania, Spain, Sweden and the United Kingdom.

78 D. Bartha, et al., *What Is the European Dream? Survey on European Dreams for the Future of Europe* (Brussels: Foundation for European Progressive Studies, 2020), https://www.feps-europe.eu/attachments/publications/ed_web.pdf.

79 J. Adriaans, et al., 'In Germany, Younger, Better Educated Persons, and Lower Income Groups Are More Likely to Be in Favor of Unconditional Basic Income', *DIW Berlin*, 10 April 2019, https://www.diw.de/en/diw_01.c.618858.en/ nachrichten/in_germany_younger_better...onditional_basic_income.html.

80 H. Gilberstadt, *More Americans Oppose than Favor the Government Providing a Universal Basic Income for All Adult Citizens* (Washington, DC: Pew Research Center, 2020), https://www.pewresearch.org/fact-tank/2020/08/19/more-americans-oppose-than-favor-the-government-providing-a-universal-basic-income-for-all-adult-citizens/.

81 E. Freeland, *What Do Americans Think about Universal Basic Income?* (Los Angeles: USC Schaeffer Center, University of Southern California, 2019), https://healthpolicy. usc.edu/evidence-base/what-do-americans-think-about-universal-basic-income/.

82 J. Horowitz, 'How 39 Million Europeans Kept Their Jobs after the Work Dried Up', *CNN Business*, 6 May 2020, https://edition.cnn.com/2020/05/06/economy/europe-part-time-work/index.html.

83 In constant 2014 US dollars. D. Calnitsky, '"More Normal than Welfare": The Mincome Experiment, Stigma, and Community Experience', *Canadian Review of Sociology* 53, no. 1 (2006): 26–71.

84 E.L. Forget, 'The Town with No Poverty: The Health Effects of a Canadian Guaranteed Annual Income Field Experiment', *Canadian Public Policy* 37, no. 3 (2011): 283–305.

85   K. Widerquist and M.W. Howard, eds., *Alaska's Permanent Fund Dividend: Examining its Suitability as a Model* (New York: Palgrave Macmillan, 2012).

86   S. Goldsmith, 'The Economic and Social Impacts of the Permanent Fund Dividend on Alaska', in *Alaska's Permanent Fund Dividend: Examining its Suitability as a Model*, eds. K. Widerquist and M.W. Howard (New York: Palgrave Macmillan, 2012), 83–106.

87   D. Jones and I. Marinescu, *The Labor Market Impacts of Universal and Permanent Cash Transfers: Evidence from the Alaska Permanent Fund*, Working Paper 24312 (Washington, DC: National Bureau of Economic Research, 2020), https://www.nber.org/system/files/working_papers/w24312/w24312.pdf.

88   M. Bruenig, 'A Specter Is Haunting Alaska – the Specter of Communism', *Demos*, 5 January 2014, https://prospect.org/power/specter-haunting-alaska-the-specter-communism/.

89   H. Yoshikawa, et al., 'The Effects of Poverty on the Mental, Emotional, and Behavioral Health of Children and Youth: Implications for Prevention', *American Psychology* 67, no. 4 (2012): 272–284.

90   Haarmann, et al., *Basic Income Grant*, 14–15.

91   Davala, et al., *Basic Income*.

92   Davala, et al., *Basic Income*.

93   R. Jhabvala, 'Basic Income Can Transform Women's Lives', *OpenDemocracy*, 19 September 2019, https://www.opendemocracy.net/en/beyond-trafficking-and-slavery/basic-income-can-transform-womens-lives/.

94   Arnold, 'Anti-Poverty Experiment'.

95   J. Ferguson and T.M. Li, *Beyond the 'Proper Job': Political-Economic Analysis after the Century of Labouring Man*, Working Paper 51 (Bellville: Institute for Poverty, Land and Agrarian Studies, 2018).

CHAPTER 2   THE CRISIS OF WAGED WORK

1   'Underemployment' refers to forms of employment that are low in productivity, irregular or part-time, and that make only partial use of a person's skills or training. In developing countries, very large proportions of working-age adults are 'underemployed' – especially in Africa and Asia, where many adults work irregularly on family farms, contributing little to output. In other sectors, many ostensibly employed workers – up to 20% in some developing countries – perform paid work for only part of the work week and for very low wages. J-H. Chang, *Economics: The User's Guide* (London: Pelican Books, 2014), 370–371.

2   J. Breman, 'A Bogus Concept', *New Left Review* 84 (2013): 131.

3   ILO, *World Employment and Social Outlook: Trends 2020* (Geneva: International Labour Organization, 2020).

4   Generally, statisticians count as 'unemployed' persons of working age who are not in employment, did not seek employment during a specified recent period and are available to take up employment if offered a job. The unemployment rate is the number of unemployed persons as a percentage of the total number of persons in the labour force.

5   ILO, *Trends 2020*, 12.

6   ILO, *Trends 2020*.

7   ILO, *Global Wage Report 2020–21: Wages and Minimum Wages in the Time of COVID-19* (Geneva: International Labour Organization, 2021), https://www.ilo.org/wcmsp5/groups/public/---dgreports/---dcomm/---publ/documents/publication/wcms_762534.pdf.

8   Breman, 'Bogus Concept'.

9   ILO, *Trends 2020*, 20.

10   ILO nomenclature separates 'developing' and 'emerging' economies; this text combines the two categories and refers to them collectively as 'developing' economies or countries.

11   ILO, *Trends 2020*.

12   ILO, *Global Wage Report 2014/2015: Wages and Income Inequality* (Geneva: International Labour Organization, 2014), 4.

13   ILO, *Trends 2020*; N. Benjamin, et al., *Informal Economy and the World Bank*, Policy Research Working Paper 6888 (Washington, DC: World Bank, 2014), www-wds.worldbank.org/external/default/WDSContentServer/WDSP/IB/2014/05/22/000158349_20140522153248/Rendered/PDF/WPS6888.pdf; D. Kucera and T. Xenogiani, 'Persisting Informal Employment: What Explains it?' in *Is Informal Normal?: Towards More and Better Jobs in Developing Countries*, eds. P. Jutting and J.R. de Laiglesia (Paris: OECD Publishing, 2009), 63–88, https://doi.org/10.1787/9789264059245-5-en.

14   ILO, *Trends 2020*, 20. Real wage trends were likely to be distorted by the impact of the COVID-19 pandemic. Since job losses have been heaviest among lower-paid workers, mean wages for 2020 and possibly also 2021 were expected to rise, since the remaining low-paid workers would constitute a smaller share of the wage-earning workforce (ILO, *Global Wage Report 2020–21*).

15   ILO, *Trends 2020*, 20.

16   ILO, *World Employment and Social Outlook: Trends 2021* (Geneva: International Labour Organization, 2021).

17   ILO, *Trends 2021*.

18   ILO, *World Employment and Social Outlook: Trends 2018* (Geneva: International Labour Organization, 2018), 8.

19   ILO, *Trends 2020*, 67.

20   Trapp's analysis shows a decrease in the labour share of income in *all* regions between 1990 and 2011, except for South Asia (based on data for only Bhutan, India and Sri Lanka), where it increased slightly. K. Trapp, *Measuring the Labour Income Share of Developing Countries: Learning from Social Accounting Matrices*, WIDER Working Paper 2015/041 (Helsinki: World Institute for Development Economics Research, 2015), https://www.wider.unu.edu/sites/default/files/wp2015-041.pdf.

21   L. Karabarbounis and B. Neiman, *The Global Decline of the Labor Share*, National Bureau of Economic Research Working Paper 19136 (Washington, DC: National Bureau of Economic Research, 2013).

22   These findings are supported by an earlier analysis. Using a dataset from 1960 to 1997, Anne Harrison split her sample of over 100 countries (from different income categories) into two groups. Her data showed that, in the group of poorer countries, labour's share in national income fell on average by 0.1% per year from 1960 to 1993, with the drop accelerating after 1993, to an average decline of 0.3% per year. In the richer sub-group, the labour share grew by 0.2% per year prior to 1993, after which it fell by 0.4% per year. A. Harrison, *Has Globalisation Eroded*

Labor's Share? Some Cross-Country Evidence (Washington, DC: National Bureau of Economic Research, 2005), https://mpra.ub.uni-muenchen.de/39649/1/MPRA_paper_39649.pdf.

23   ILO, *The Global Labour Income Share and Distribution: Key Findings* (Geneva: International Labour Organization, 2019), 1, https://www.ilo.org/wcmsp5/groups/public/---dgreports/---stat/documents/publication/wcms_712232.pdf.

24   ILO, *Global Labour Income Share*, 2.

25   B. Kunkel, *Utopia or Bust: A Guide to the Present Crisis* (London: Verso Books, 2014); D. Harvey, *The Enigma of Capital – and the Crisis of Capitalism* (London: Profile Books, 2010); R. Brenner, *The Economics of Global Turbulence: The Advanced Capitalist Economies from Long Boom to Long Downturn, 1945–2005* (London: Verso Books, 2006).

26   ILO, *Wages, Productivity and Labour Share in China* (Bangkok: ILO Regional Office for Asia and the Pacific, 2016), 1.

27   ILO, *Global Wage Report 2020–21*.

28   T. Piketty, *Capital in the Twenty-First Century* (Cambridge, MA: Harvard University Press, 2013).

29   Brenner, *Economics of Global Turbulence*.

30   Brenner, *Economics of Global Turbulence*, 4–6.

31   Brenner, *Economics of Global Turbulence*, 7.

32   C. Calhoun and G. Derluguian, *Business as Usual: The Roots of the Global Financial Meltdown* (New York: New York University Press, 2011); J.B. Foster, 'The Financialization of Capitalism', *Monthly Review* 58, no. 11 (2007): 1–12; Brenner, *Economics of Global Turbulence*.

33   R. Hilferding, *Finance Capital: A Study of the Latest Phase of Capitalist Development* (London: Routledge and Kegan Paul, 1981).

34   Harvey, *Enigma of Capital*.

35   N. Fraser and R. Jaeggi, *Capitalism: A Conversation in Critical Theory* (Cambridge: Polity, 2018); W. Streeck, *Buying Time: The Delayed Crisis of Democratic Capitalism* (London: Verso Books, 2013); G. Epstein, 'Introduction: Financialization and the World Economy', in *Financialization and the World Economy*, ed. G. Epstein (Cheltenham: Edward Elgar, 2005), 3–16.

36   J. Crotty, *The Effects of Increased Product Market Competition and Changes in Financial Markets on the Performance of Nonfinancial Corporations in the Neoliberal Era*, PERI Working Paper 44 (Amherst, MA: Political Economy Research Institute, 2003), 3.

37   Calhoun and Derluguian, *Business as Usual*; Harvey, *Enigma of Capital*. There are some exceptions to this trend, notably in parts of South America and East Asia (including China). But in much of the industrialised world, the former Soviet Union and its satellites, Africa, South Asia, the Caribbean and Central America, workers have been fighting rearguard actions to protect or extend their rights and entitlements.

38   Those crises have included the Latin American sovereign debt crisis (1982), a series of savings and loans crashes in the United States (1980s), the stock market collapse (1987), the junk bond crash (1989), the Mexican financial crisis (1994), the Asian Crisis (1997), the dotcom crash (2000), the global financial crisis (2008) and the COVID-19 crisis (2020).

39 J.B. Foster, et al., 'The Contagion of Capital: Financialized Capitalism, COVID-19 and the Great Divide', *Monthly Review* 72, no. 8 (2021), https://monthlyreview.org/2021/01/01/the-contagion-of-capital, 11.

40 Y. Varoufakis, 'The Universal Right to Capital Income', *Project Syndicate*, 31 October 2016, https://www.project-syndicate.org/commentary/basic-income-funded-by-capital-income-by-yanis-varoufakis-2016-10?barrier=accesspaylog.

41 N. Fraser, 'Climates of Capital: For a Trans-Environmental Eco-Socialism', *New Left Review* 17 (2021): 94–127; D. Harvey, *Seventeen Contradictions and the End of Capitalism* (New York: Oxford University Press, 2014); W. Streeck, 'How Will Capitalism End?', *New Left Review* 87 (2014): 35–64; Kunkel, *Utopia or Bust*.

42 J.W. Moore, *Capitalism in the Web of Life: Ecology and the Accumulation of Capital* (London: Verso Books, 2015); N. Klein, *This Changes Everything: Capitalism Versus the Climate* (London: Penguin Books, 2015); J.B. Foster, *Ecology against Capitalism* (New York: Monthly Review Press, 2002).

43 IPCC, *Global Warming of 1.5°C. Special Report* (Geneva: World Meteorological Organization, 2018), https://www.ipcc.ch/sr15/; D. Wallace-Stevens, *The Uninhabitable Earth: Life after Warming* (New York: Penguin Random House, 2016).

44 SARS, or severe acute respiratory syndrome, and MERS, or Middle East respiratory syndrome.

45 Klein, *This Changes Everything*.

46 Fraser and Jaeggi, *Capitalism*.

47 Harvey, *Seventeen Contradictions*; C.B. Frey and M.A. Osborne, 'The Future of Employment: How Susceptible Are Jobs to Computerization?', *Technological Forecasting and Social Change* 114 (2017): 254–280. In David Harvey's prognosis: 'If the current burst of innovation points in any direction at all, it is towards decreasing employment opportunities for labour and the increasing significance of rents extracted from intellectual property rights for capital' (Harvey, *Seventeen Contradictions*, xii).

48 P. Frase, *Four Futures* (London: Verso Books, 2016).

49 M. Davis, *Planet of Slums* (London: Verso Books, 2006).

50 Frey and Osborne, 'Future of Employment'. Their model predicts that most workers in the transportation and logistics sectors, along with most office and administrative support workers, and workers active in production, are at risk. Jobs in construction, journalism, hospitals and pharmacies are also on the endangered list.

51 E. Brynjolfsson and A. McAfee, *The Second Machine Age* (New York: W.W. Norton, 2016); G.A. Pratt, 'Is a Cambrian Explosion Coming for Robotics?', *Journal of Economic Perspectives* 29, no. 3 (2015): 51–60.

52 R. Solow, 'We'd Better Watch Out', *New York Times Book Review*, 12 July 1987, p. 36, http://www.standupeconomist.com/pdf/misc/solow-computer-productivity.pdf.

53 D. Henwood, 'The Robots Are Not Coming for All of Our Jobs', *Jacobin*, 23 February 2020, https://www.jacobinmag.com/2020/02/robots-jobs-united-states-gdp-wages-productivity-growth-economy.

54 A. Benanav, *Automation and the Future of Work* (London: Verso Books, 2020).

55 An example is the microwork phenomenon, which Phil Jones has documented. Much as the seemingly weightless 'clouds' of data are in fact lodged in vast,

air-conditioned industrial sheds, the artificial intelligence revolution relies heavily on microtasks which poorly paid piecemeal workers perform. Spread around the world, especially in developing countries, these workers 'bid' for fragmented computer-based tasks on terms that are unilaterally set by subcontractors, with payment typically very low and frequently withheld on arbitrary grounds. P. Jones, *Work without the Worker: Labour in the Age of Platform Capitalism* (London: Verso Books, 2021).

56 N. Srnicek and A. Williams, *Inventing the Future: Post-Capitalism and a World without Work* (London: Verso Books, 2015); Frase, *Four Futures*; F. Barchiesi, 'Liberation of, Through or from Work? Postcolonial Africa and the Problem with "Job Creation" in the Global Crisis', *Interface* 4, no. 2 (2012): 230–253; E.O. Wright, *Redesigning Distribution: Basic Income and Stakeholder Grants as Alternative Cornerstones for a More Egalitarian Capitalism* (London: Verso Books, 2003).

57 F. Barchiesi, *Precarious Liberation: Workers, the State and Contested Social Citizenship in Post-Apartheid South Africa* (Pietermaritzburg: UKZN Press, 2011); H. Marais, *South Africa Pushed to the Limit: The Political Economy of Change* (London: Zed Books, 2011).

58 World Bank, *Employment to Population Ratio, 15+, Total (%) (Modeled ILO Estimate) – Middle Income, South Africa* (Washington, DC: World Bank, 2021), https://data. worldbank.org/indicator/SL.EMP.TOTL.SP.ZS?locations=XP-ZA&name_desc=false.

59 Stats SA, *Quarterly Labour Force Survey QLFS Q2: 2021* (Pretoria: Statistics South Africa, 2021), 7–8, http://www.statssa.gov.za/publications/P0211/Presentation%20 QLFS%20Q2_2021.pdf. The official statistical agency, Statistics South Africa, calculates two unemployment levels. In the 'official definition', an unemployed person is one who is completely without work, currently available to work, and taking active steps to find work. An 'expanded definition' of unemployment excludes the requirement to have sought work. The definition of 'employment' is liberal. It includes persons who were engaged in market production activities in the week prior to being surveyed (even if only for one hour) plus those who were temporarily absent from their activities. Market production employment refers to working for a wage, salary, commission or payment in kind; managing any kind of business, of whatever size; or assisting, without being paid, in a business run by another household member.

60 Government of South Africa, *National Development Plan: Our Future, Make it Work* (Pretoria: Government of South Africa, 2012), 64, https://www.gov.za/sites/ default/files/gcis_document/201409/ndp-2030-our-future-make-it-workr.pdf.

61 J. Seekings and N. Nattrass, *Class, Race and Inequality in South Africa* (New Haven, CT: Yale University Press, 2005).

62 Stats SA, *Labour Market Dynamics in South Africa, 2019* (Pretoria: Statistics South Africa, 2019), 84.

63 World Bank, *Employment to Population Ratio* (Washington DC: World Bank, 2021).

64 Stats SA, *Quarterly Labour Force Survey QLFS Q2: 2020* (Pretoria: Statistics South Africa, 2020), 1.

65 D. Casale and D. Shepherd, *The Gendered Effects of the COVID-19 Crisis and Ongoing Lockdown in South Africa: Evidence from NIDS-CRAM Waves 1–5*, National Income Dynamics Study – Coronavirus Rapid Mobile Survey,

Wave 5, Working Paper No. 3, 2021, 6, https://cramsurvey.org/wp-content/uploads/2021/07/3.-Casale-D.-_-Shepherd-D.-2021-The-gendered-effects-of-the-Covid-19-crisis-and-ongoing-lockdown-in-South-Africa-Evidence-from-NIDS-CRAM-Waves-1-%E2%80%93-5..pdf; D. Casale and D. Posel, *Gender and the Early Effects of the COVID-19 Crisis in the Paid and Unpaid Economies in South Africa*, National Income Dynamics Study – Coronavirus Rapid Mobile Survey, Wave 1, Working Paper No. 4, 2020, https://cramsurvey.org/wp-content/uploads/2020/07/Casale-Gender-the-early-effects-of-the-COVID-19-crisis-in-the-paid-unpaid-economies-in-South-Africa.pdf.

66   R. Jain, et al., *The Labor Market and Poverty Impacts of COVID-19 in South Africa*, SALDRU Working Paper 264 (Cape Town: Southern Africa Labour and Development Research Unit, University of Cape Town, 2020), http://www.opensaldru.uct.ac.za/bitstream/handle/11090/980/2020_264_Saldruwp.pdf?sequence=1.

67   Measured by GDP, Egypt and Nigeria had larger economies in 2020, according to the World Bank, *World Development Indicators* (Washington DC: World Bank, 2021), https://databank.worldbank.org/reports.aspx?source=2&series=NY.GDP.MKTP.KD.ZG&country=MIC,ZAF#.

68   K. Lilenstein, et al., *In-Work Poverty in South Africa: The Impact of Income Sharing in the Presence of High Unemployment*, Working Paper 193 (Cape Town: Southern Africa Labour and Development Research Unit, University of Cape Town, 2016), http://opensaldru.uct.ac.za/bitstream/handle/11090/852/2016_193_Saldruwp.pdf?sequence=1.

69   J. Ferguson, *Give a Man a Fish: Reflections on the New Politics of Distribution* (Durham, NC: Duke University Press, 2015).

70   Stats SA, *Poverty Trends in South Africa: An Examination of Absolute Poverty between 2006 and 2015* (Pretoria: Statistics South Africa, 2017); M. Leibbrandt, et al., 'Describing and Decomposing Post-Apartheid Income Inequality in South Africa', *Development Southern Africa* 29, no. 1 (2012): 19–34.

71   E. Webster and D. Francis, 'The Paradox of Inequality in South Africa: A Challenge from the Workplace', *Transformation* 101 (2019): 11–35.

72   Stats SA, *Men, Women and Children: Findings of the Living Conditions Survey, 2014/2015* (Pretoria: Statistics South Africa, 2018), http://www.statssa.gov.za/publications/Report-03-10-02%20/Report-03-10-02%202015.pdf; Stats SA, *Poverty Trends*.

73   Government of South Africa, *National Development Plan*, 34.

74   Stats SA, *Men, Women and Children*, 13. The upper-bound poverty line, set at R992 for 2015, is the income threshold at which individuals have just enough income to purchase basic food and non-food needs. The lower-bound poverty line is considered a marker for distress. Individuals at or below that level, which was set at R647 for 2015, do not have enough resources to purchase food and essential non-food items; they have to sacrifice food in order to afford basic non-food items (Stats SA, *Poverty Trends*). Calibrated against the consumer price index, the lower-bound poverty line rose to R890 and the upper-bound poverty line to R1 335 for 2021. Stats SA, *National Poverty Lines 2021*, Statistical Release P0310.1 (Pretoria: Statistics South Africa, 2021), 13, http://www.statssa.gov.za/publications/P03101/P031012021.pdf.

75   Stats SA, *Poverty Trends*.

76 Bureau for Food and Agricultural Policy, *BFAP Food Inflation Brief – March 2021* (Die Wilgers: Bureau for Food and Agricultural Policy, 2021), 1, https://www.bfap.co.za/wp-content/uploads/2021/04/Food-Inflation_April-2021.pdf.

77 Stats SA, *General Household Survey 2018*, Statistical Release P0318 (Pretoria: Statistics South Africa, 2019).

78 Stats SA, *Results from Wave 2 Survey on the Impact of the COVID-19 Pandemic on Employment and Income in South Africa, May 2020*, Report 00-08-03 (Pretoria: Statistics South Africa, 2020), 6, http://www.statssa.gov.za/publications/Report-00-80-03/Report-00-80-03May2020.pdf.

79 Stats SA, *General Household Survey 2018*.

80 World Bank, *South Africa Overview* (Washington, DC: World Bank, 2018), https://www.worldbank.org/en/country/southafrica/overview.

81 UNDP, *Human Development Report 2020: The Next Frontier: Human Development and the Anthropocene* (New York: United Nations Development Programme, 2020), http://hdr.undp.org/sites/default/files/hdr2020.pdf.

82 A. Chatterjee, et al., *Extreme inequalities: The Distribution of Household Wealth in South Africa*, Southern Africa – Towards Inclusive Economic Development (SA-TIED) Research Brief 2020/45, 2020, https://sa-tied.wider.unu.edu/sites/default/files/SA-TIED-RB2020-11-extreme-inequalities_0.pdf; A. Orthofer, *Wealth Inequality in South Africa: Evidence from Survey and Tax Data*, REDI3X3 Working Paper 15, June 2016, http://www.redi3x3.org/sites/default/files/Orthofer%202016%20REDI3x3%20Working%20Paper%2015%20-%20Wealth%20inequality.pdf.

83 Chatterjee, et al., *Extreme inequalities*, 1–2. For income, the South African Gini coefficient is about 0.7, but for wealth it is between 0.9 and 0.95. Both these values are higher than in any other major economy for which such data exist (World Bank, *South Africa Overview*).

84 'Millionaires' were defined as individuals with net assets of US$1 million or more, excluding their primary residence. New World Wealth, *SA Wealth Report 2020: The Wealthiest Cities and Towns in South Africa* (Johannesburg: New World Wealth, 2020), https://cms.cnbcafrica.com/wp-content/uploads/2020/04/South-Africa-2020-1.pdf.

85 Stats SA, *General Household Survey 2018*.

86 Stats SA, *General Household Survey 2018*.

87 M. Rogan and J. Reynolds, *The Working Poor in South Africa, 1997–2012*, ISER Working Paper 2015/4 (Grahamstown: Institute of Social and Economic Research, Rhodes University, 2015), 15. Does this trend apply to both formal and informal sector workers? The inclusion of a question on the formality of employment from 2010 onward in the General Household Surveys carried out by Statistics South Africa provides a limited dataset that points in a surprising direction. The informal sector accounts for about one-fifth of the total workforce in South Africa. Informal sector workers were much more likely to be poor: their headcount poverty rate was 46% in 2010 and decreased to 41% in 2012. Over the same period, the poverty rate for formal workers stayed steady at 17%. So the risk of poverty decreased significantly between 2010 and 2012 for informal workers but there was no change for formal sector workers (Rogan and Reynolds, *Working Poor*, 15).

88 Stats SA, *National Poverty Lines 2021*.

89 Rogan and Reynolds, *Working Poor*.

90   The reservation wage is the lowest wage for which workers are willing to accept a particular kind of job.

91   Webster and Francis, 'Paradox of Inequality'.

92   M. Wittenberg, 'Wages and Wage Inequality in South Africa, 1994–2011: Part 2 – Inequality Measurement and Trends', *South African Journal of Economics* 85, no. 2 (2017): 298–318.

93   Leibbrandt, et al., 'Describing and Decomposing', 26.

94   World Bank, *World Development Indicators*.

95   S. Mohamed, 'The Political Economy of Accumulation in South Africa: Resource Extraction, Financialization, and Capital Flight as Barriers to Investment and Employment Growth', PhD diss., University of Massachusetts Amherst, 2019, https://scholarworks.umass.edu/dissertations_2/1533; V. Padayachee, *Beyond a Treasury View of the World: Reflections from Theory and History on Heterodox Economic Policy Options for South Africa*, Working Paper 2 (Johannesburg: Southern Centre for Inequality Studies, University of the Witwatersrand, 2018); R. McKenzie and S. Mohamed, 'The Political Economy of South Africa and its Interaction with Processes of Financialisation', in *Studies in Financial Systems No. 15: The South African Financial System*, ed. S. Mohamed (Financialisation, Economy, Society and Sustainable Development (FESSUD), SOAS University of London, 2017), 11–25, https://eprints.kingston.ac.uk/id/eprint/37224/1/McKenzie-R-37224.pdf; S. Ashman, et al., 'The Crisis in South Africa: Neoliberalism, Financialization and Uneven and Combined Development', *Socialist Register* 47 (2011): 174–195; B. Fine and Z. Rustomjee, *The Political Economy of South Africa: From Mineral-Energy Complex to Industrialization* (London: Hurst & Co., 1996).

96   S. Mohamed, 'Financialization of the South African Economy', *Development* 59, no. 1–2 (2016): 137–142; Mohamed, 'Political Economy of Accumulation'; Ashman, et al., 'Crisis in South Africa'.

97   Mohamed, 'Political Economy of Accumulation'; V. Padayachee and R. van Niekerk, *Shadow of Liberation: Contestation and Compromise in the Economic and Social Policy of the African National Congress, 1943–1996* (Johannesburg: Wits University Press, 2019).

98   Fine and Rustomjee, *Political Economy of South Africa*.

99   S. Newman, et al., *A New Growth Path for South African Industrialisation: An Input-Output Analysis* (Pretoria: Industrial Policy Research Support Project, Department of Trade and Industry, South Africa, 2010).

100   Mohamed, 'Political Economy of Accumulation'; Padayachee and Van Niekerk, *Shadow of Liberation*; Marais, *South Africa*.

101   Mohamed, 'Political Economy of Accumulation'.

102   McKenzie and Mohamed, 'Political Economy of South Africa'.

103   Mohamed, 'Political Economy of Accumulation'.

104   McKenzie and Mohamed, 'Political Economy of South Africa'.

105   A great deal of that wealth generation is delinked from productive economic activities, a trend South Africa shares with many other economies. This was reflected, for example, in the 18% rise in the share value of the forty largest companies trading on the Johannesburg Stock Exchange in 2020, despite a contracting economy, soaring unemployment and debt, and a deepening social crisis. S. Gunnion, 'Business of the Bourse: SA Equities Outperform Global Indices', *Daily*

Maverick, 19 February 2021, https://www.dailymaverick.co.za/article/2021-02-18-business-of-the-bourse-sa-equities-outperform-global-indices/.

106 E. Webster and R. Omar, 'Work Restructuring in Post-Apartheid South Africa', *Work and Occupations* 30, no. 2 (2003): 195.

107 Webster and Francis, 'Paradox of Inequality'; N. Pons-Vignon and W. Anseeuw, 'Great Expectations: Working Conditions in South Africa since the End of Apartheid', *Journal of Southern African Studies* 35, no. 4 (2009): 883–899; S. Buhlungu and E. Webster, 'Work Restructuring and the Future of Labour in South Africa', in *The State of the Nation: South Africa 2005*–2006, eds. S. Buhlungu, J. Daniel, R. Southall and J. Lutchman (Cape Town: HSRC Press, 2006), 248–269.

108 A. Bezuidenhout and M. Tshoaedi, *Labour beyond Cosatu: Mapping the Rupture in South Africa's Labour Landscape* (Johannesburg: Wits University Press, 2017).

109 Trade union density (the percentage of workers who belong to a trade union) was 28.1% in 2016, down from over 30% in 2010. ILO, *Statistics on Union Membership*, ILOSTAT (Geneva: International Labour Organization, 2021), https://www.ilo.org/shinyapps/bulkexplorer44/?lang=en&segment=indicator&id =ILR_TUMT_NOC_RT_A.

110 Pons-Vignon and Anseeuw, 'Great Expectations'; B. Kenny and E. Webster, 'Eroding the Core: Flexibility and the Resegmentation of the South African Labour Market', *Critical Sociology* 24, no. 3 (1998): 216–243.

111 M. Di Paola and N. Pons-Vignon, 'Labour Market Restructuring in South Africa: Low Wages, High Insecurity', *Review of African Political Economy* 40, no. 138 (2013): 628–638; E. Webster and S. Buhlungu, 'Between Marginalization and Revitalization? The State of Trade Unionism in South Africa', *Review of African Political Economy* 31, no. 100 (2004): 229–245.

112 N. Spaull, et al. *NIDS-CRAM Synthesis Report Wave 1: Overview and Findings (National Income Dynamics Study – Coronavirus Rapid Mobile Survey)*, 3, https:// cramsurvey.org/wp-content/uploads/2020/07/Spaull-et-al.-NIDS-CRAM-Wave-1-Synthesis-Report-Overview-and-Findings-1.pdf.

113 Stats SA, *Facts You Might Not Know about Social Grants* (Pretoria: Statistics South Africa, 2016), http://www.statssa.gov.za/?p=7756; B. Leubolt, *Social Policies and Redistribution in South Africa*, Global Labour University Working Paper 25 (Geneva: International Labour Organization, 2014).

114 K. Button, et al., *South Africa's Hybrid Care Regime: The Changing and Contested Roles of Individuals, Families and the State in South Africa*, Working Paper 404 (Cape Town: Centre for Social Science Research, University of Cape Town, 2017); I. Woolard and M. Leibbrandt, *The Evolution of Unconditional Cash Transfers in South Africa* (Cape Town: Southern Africa Labour and Development Research Unit, University of Cape Town, 2010); F. Lund, *Changing Social Policy: The Child Support Grant in South Africa* (Cape Town: HSRC Press, 2008).

115 T. Mkandawire, 'Transformative Social Policy and Innovation in Developing Countries', *European Journal for Development Research* 19, no. 1 (2007): 13–29.

116 T. Mkandawire, *Social Policy in a Development Context*, Social Policy and Development Programme Paper No. 7 (Geneva: United Nations Research Institute for Social Development, June 2001), 19, https://www.files.ethz.ch/isn/102709/7.pdf.

117 S. Plagerson, et al., 'Social Policy in South Africa: Navigating the Route to Social Development', *World Development* 113 (2019): 1–9; F. Barchiesi, 'South African

Debates on the Basic Income Grant: Wage Labour and the Post-Apartheid Social Policy', *Journal of Southern African Studies* 33, no. 3 (2007): 561–575.

118 Many definitions of the social wage are in circulation. In the South African context, the term generally refers to public social spending that accrues to lower-income individuals or households. J. May, 'Poverty, Social Policy and the Social Wage', paper presented at the conference 'The Politics of Socio-Economic Rights in South Africa: 10 Years after Apartheid', Oslo, 8–9 June 2004, https://sarpn.org/documents/d0000880.old/P996-May_Poverty-SocialPolicy-Wage_200405.pdf.

119 Leubolt, *Social Policies*.

120 South African Government, *Old Age Pension*, Information Sheet (Pretoria: South African Government, 2021), https://www.gov.za/services/social-benefits-retirement-and-old-age/old-age-pension.

121 A. Case and A. Deaton, 'Large Cash Transfers to the Elderly in South Africa', *The Economic Journal* 108, no. 450 (1998): 1330–1361.

122 South African Government, *Child Support Grant*, Information Sheet (Pretoria: South African Government, 2021), https://www.gov.za/services/child-care-social-benefits/child-support-grant.

123 Stats SA, *National Poverty Lines 2021*.

124 Pietermaritzburg Economic Justice and Dignity Group, *Household Affordability Index, January 2021* (Pietermaritzburg: Pietermaritzburg Economic Justice and Dignity Group, 2021), https://pmbejd.org.za/wp-content/uploads/2021/01/January-2021-Household-Affordability-Index-PMBEJD_27012021.pdf.

125 Parliamentary Budget Office, *Social Grant Performance as at End March 20/21* (Cape Town: Parliament of the Republic of South Africa, 2021), https://www.parliament.gov.za/storage/app/media/PBO/National_Development_Plan_Analysis/2021/june/03-06-2021/May_2021_Social_Grant_fact_sheet.pdf.

126 South African Government, *Foster Child Grant*, Information Sheet (Pretoria: South African Government, 2021), https://www.gov.za/services/child-care-social-benefits/foster-child-grant.

127 H. Bhorat and A. Cassim, 'South Africa's Welfare Success Story II: Poverty-Reducing Social Grants', *Africa in Focus* (Brookings), 27 January 2014, https://www.brookings.edu/blog/africa-in-focus/2014/01/27/south-africas-welfare-success-story-ii-poverty-reducing-social-grants/.

128 A. Cooper, et al., 'The Relationship between Social Welfare Policy and Multidimensional Well-Being: An Analysis Using the South African Child Support Grant', *Transformation: Critical Perspectives on Southern Africa* 102 (2020): 73–94.

129 Barchiesi, 'South African Debates'.

130 Parliamentary Budget Office, *Social Grant Performance*: 2. Beneficiaries can receive more than one social grant; in early 2021, approximately 2.1 million people were receiving two grants.

131 Stats SA, *Labour Market Dynamics*.

132 Stats SA, *Poverty Trends*; Stats SA, *Facts You Might Not Know*; Leubolt, *Social Policies*.

133 Rogan and Reynolds, *Working Poor*.

134 Stats SA, *General Household Survey 2018*.

135 Stats SA, *General Household Survey 2019*, Statistical Release P0318 (Pretoria: Statistics South Africa, 2020), http://www.statssa.gov.za/publications/P0318/P03182018.pdf.

136 G. Wright, et al., 'Social Assistance and Dignity: South African Women's Experiences of the Child Support Grant', *Development Southern Africa* 32, no. 4 (2015): 443–457.

137 C. Webb and N. Vally, 'South Africa Has Raised Social Grants: Why This Shouldn't Be a Stop-Gap Measure', *The Conversation*, 7 May 2020, https://theconversation.com/south-africa-has-raised-social-grants-why-this-shouldnt-be-a-stop-gap-measure-138023; E. Senona, et al., *Social Protection in a Time of Covid: Lessons for Basic Income Support* (Mowbray: Black Sash, 2021), https://www.blacksash.org.za/images/0541_BS_-_Social_Protection_in_a_Time_of_Covid_Final_-_Web.pdf.

CHAPTER 3 THE ATTRACTIONS OF A UNIVERSAL BASIC INCOME

1   S. Terkel, *Working: People Talk about What They Do All Day and What They Feel about What They Do* (New York: Ballantine Books, 1972), i.

2   J. Hagen-Zanker, et al., *Understanding the Impact of Cash Transfers: The Evidence* (London: Overseas Development Institute, 2016), https://www.calpnetwork.org/wp-content/uploads/2020/09/10748.pdf.

3   World Bank, *The State of Social Safety Nets 2018: Report Overview* (Washington, DC: World Bank, 2018), 60. The calculation was based on monetary data from 79 countries in different regions. The absolute poverty line used by the World Bank is US$1.90 per person per day in purchasing power parity terms.

4   C. Meth, *What Is Pro-Poor Growth? What Are Some of the Things that Hinder its Achievement in South Africa?* Research Report (Johannesburg: OXFAM-GB, 2007).

5   Stats SA, *Income and Expenditure of Households 2010/2011*, Statistical Release P0100 (Pretoria: Statistics South Africa, 2012).

6   T. Satumba, et al., 'The Impact of Social Grants on Poverty Reduction in South Africa', *Journal of Economics* 8, no. 1 (2017), 42.

7   D. Posel, *Inter-household Transfers in South Africa: Prevalence, Patterns and Poverty*, Working Paper 180, NIDS Discussion Paper 2016/7 (Cape Town: Southern Africa Labour and Development Research Unit, University of Cape Town, 2016), 17, https://www.opensaldru.uct.ac.za/bitstream/handle/11090/838/2016_180_Saldruwp.pdf?sequence=1.

8   A. du Toit and D. Neves, 'The Government of Poverty and the Arts of Survival: Mobile and Recombinant Strategies at the Margins of the South African Economy', *The Journal of Peasant Studies* 41, no. 5 (2014): 833–853.

9   Institute for Economic Justice, *The Case for Extending the COVID-19 Special Grants*, COVID-19 Fact Sheet No. 5 (Johannesburg: Institute for Economic Justice, 2020), 4, https://iej.org.za/wp-content/uploads/2020/10/IEJ-COVID-19-factsheet-5---SRD-FINAL.pdf.

10   S. Granlund and T. Hochfeld, '"That Child Support Grant Gives Me Powers" – Exploring Social and Relational Aspects of Cash Transfers in South Africa in Times of Livelihood Change', *The Journal of Development Studies* 56, no. 6 (2020): 1241.

11   L. Lavinas, '21st Century Welfare', *New Left Review* 84 (2013): 32.

12   S. Soares, et al., 'Os impactos do benefício do programa Bolsa Família sobre a desigualdade e a pobreza', in *Bolsa Família 2003–2010: avanços e desafios*, eds. J. Abrahão de Castro and L. Modesto (Brasília: Instituto de Pesquisa Econômica

Aplicada, 2010), 25–52 [cited in A. Fischer, *Poverty as Ideology: Rescuing Social Justice from Global Development Agendas* (London: Zed Books, 2018), 235].

13   World Bank, *Unemployment, Total (% of Total Labor Force) (Modeled ILO Estimate) – South Africa, Brazil* (Washington, DC: World Bank, 2021), https://data.worldbank. org/indicator/SL.UEM.TOTL.ZS?locations=ZA-BR&name_desc=false.

14   Stats SA, *Quarterly Labour Force Survey QLFS Q2: 2021* (Pretoria: Statistics South Africa, 2021), http://www.statssa.gov.za/publications/P0211/Presentation%20 QLFS%20Q2_2021.pdf.

15   H. Bhorat and A. Cassim, 'South Africa's Welfare Success Story II: Poverty-Reducing Social Grants', *Africa in Focus* (Brookings), 27 January 2014, https:// www.brookings.edu/blog/africa-in-focus/2014/01/27/south-africas-welfare-success-story-ii-poverty-reducing-social-grants/.

16   H. Reed and S. Lansley, *Universal Basic Income: An Idea Whose Time Has Come?* (London: Compass, 2016), http://www.compassonline.org.uk/wp-content/ uploads/2016/05/UniversalBasicIncomeByCompass-Spreads.pdf.

17   Bhorat and Kohler, *Social Assistance*, 9; Institute for Economic Justice, *Designing a Basic Income Guarantee: Targeting, Universality and Other Considerations*, Social Protection Series Policy Brief No. 3 (Johannesburg: Institute for Economic Justice, 2021), https://www.iej.org.za/wp-content/uploads/2021/10/IEJ-policy-brief-UBIG-3_2.pdf.

18   T. Mkandawire, *Targeting and Universalism in Poverty Reduction* (Geneva: UNRISD, 2005), https://www.unrisd.org/en/library/publications/targeting-and-universalism-in-135.

19   Lavinas, '21st Century Welfare'; C.L. Kerstenetzky, 'Redistribution and Development? The Political Economy of the Bolsa Família Program', *Dados* 52, no. 1 (2009): 53–83. The social relief of distress grant introduced in South Africa during the COVID-19 pandemic encountered these and additional problems, according to an Auditor-General report. It found that the administrating structure had been using outdated, limited databases, which allowed for several thousand fraudulent claims of the grant. Tightened verification processes then led to month-long delays and rejection rates as high as 33%. See L. Daniel, 'Covid R350 Grants: Millions Rejected, but Only 10 People Are Dealing with All the Appeals', *Business Insider*, 10 December 2020, https://www.businessinsider.co.za/one-in-every-three-covid-19-sassa-grant-applications-rejected-here-are-the-reasons-why-2020-12; E. Senona, et al., *Social Protection in a Time of Covid: Lessons for Basic Income Support* (Mowbray: Black Sash, 2021), https://www.blacksash.org.za/ images/0541_BS_-_Social_Protection_in_a_Time_of_Covid_Final_-_Web.pdf.

20   S. Kidd and D. Athias, *Hit and Miss: An Assessment of Targeting Effectiveness in Social Protection* (London: Development Pathways, 2020), ii, https://www. developmentpathways.co.uk/wp-content/uploads/2019/03/Hit-and-miss-long-report-.pdf. The schemes studied were in 25 low- and middle-income countries in Asia, Africa and the Americas.

21   It is sometimes claimed that community-based targeting is more accurate, since communities are more likely to know who needs and qualifies for support. But Kidd and Athias's analysis of community-based targeting schemes in Ethiopia and Rwanda found them to have limited effectiveness, with exclusion errors of

80% and more. Even when community-based targeting is combined with a proxy means-testing approach (as in Kenya's Hunger Safety Net Programme), the exclusion error was 70% (Kidd and Athias, *Hit and Miss*, 23).

22 J. Ferguson, 'Formalities of Poverty: Thinking about Social Assistance in Neoliberal South Africa', *African Studies Review* 50, no. 2 (2007): 71–86.

23 F. Ellis, '"We Are All Poor Here": Economic Difference, Social Divisiveness, and Targeting Cash Transfers in Sub-Saharan Africa', paper prepared for the Conference on Social Protection for the Poorest in Africa: Learning from Experience, Uganda, 8–10 September 2008.

24 Ellis, '"We Are All Poor Here"', 9.

25 R. Walker, *The Shame of Poverty* (Oxford: Oxford University Press, 2014).

26 Mkandawire, *Targeting and Universalism*.

27 M. Ravallion, *Guaranteed Employment or Guaranteed Income?* CGD Working Paper 482 (Washington, DC: Center for Global Development, 2018), 22, https://www.cgdev.org/publication/guaranteed-employment-or-guaranteed-income.

28 A. Sen, *Development as Freedom* (Oxford: Oxford University Press, 1999).

29 Kerstenetzky, 'Redistribution and Development?'

30 A combination of four earlier income transfer schemes (including the *Bolsa Escola*), this means-tested scheme focused on improving schooling, nutrition and health. *Bolsa Familia* targeted the poorest 20% of households and paid them a stipend on condition that children achieved school attendance of 85% or more and had regular medical check-ups. E. Skoufias, *Progresa and its Impact on the Human Capital and Welfare of Households in Rural Mexico: A Synthesis of the Results of an Evaluation by IFPRI*, Research Report 139 (Washington, DC: International Food Policy Research Institute, 2005), https://core.ac.uk/download/pdf/6289672.pdf.

31 E. Huber and J.D. Stephens, *Democracy and the Left: Social Policy and Inequality in Latin America* (Chicago, IL: University of Chicago Press, 2012); W. Korpi and J. Palme, 'The Paradox of Redistribution and Strategies of Equality: Welfare State Institutions, Inequality and Poverty in the Western Countries', *American Sociological Review* 63, no. 5 (1998): 661–687. For a refinement of Korpi and Palme's proposition, see O. Jacques and A. Noel, 'The Case for Welfare State Universalism, or the Lasting Relevance of the Paradox of Redistribution', *The Journal of European Social Policy* 28, no. 1 (2018): 70–85.

32 Lavinas, '21st Century Welfare'.

33 D.K. Evans and A. Popova, 'Cash Transfers and Temptation Goods', *Economic Development and Cultural Change* 65, no. 2 (2017): 189–221.

34 Bhorat and Kohler, *Social Assistance*.

35 A. Zelleke, 'Real-World Lessons', contribution to GTI forum 'Universal Basic Income: Has the Time Come?' Great Transition Initiative, November 2020, https://greattransition.org/gti-forum/basic-income-zelleke.

36 F. Pega, et al., 'Unconditional Cash Transfers for Reducing Poverty and Vulnerabilities: Effect on Use of Health Services and Health Outcomes in Low- and Middle-Income Countries', *Cochrane Database of Systematic Reviews* 11, no. 11 (2017): CD011135; F. Bastagli, et al., *Cash Transfers: What Does the Evidence Say? A Rigorous Review of Programme Impact and of the Role of Design and Implementation Features* (London: Overseas Development Institute, 2016);

Stats SA, *Social Grants: In-Depth Analysis of the General Household Survey Data 2003–2007*, GHS series Vol. 1, Statistical Release P0318.1 (Pretoria: Statistics South Africa, 2009); J.M. Aguero, et al., *The Impact of Unconditional Cash Transfers on Nutrition: The South African Child Support Grant*, Working Paper 8 (Cape Town: Southern Africa Labour and Development Research Unit, University of Cape Town, 2006); Case et al., 'The Reach and Impact of Child Support Grants: Evidence from KwaZulu-Natal', *Development Southern Africa* 22, no. 4 (2005): 467–482.

37   S. Baird, et al., 'Income Shocks and Adolescent Mental Health', *Journal of Human Resources* 48, no. 2 (2013): 370–403.

38   E. Moore and J. Seekings, 'Consequences of Social Protection on Intergenerational Relationships in South Africa: Introduction', *Critical Social Policy* 39, no. 4 (2019): 513–524; G. Wright, et al., 'Social Assistance and Dignity: South African Women's Experiences of the Child Support Grant', *Development Southern Africa* 32, no. 4 (2015): 443–457; W. Zembe-Mkabile, et al., 'The Experience of Cash Transfers in Alleviating Childhood Poverty in South Africa: Mothers' Experiences of the Child Support Grant', *Global Public Health* 10, no. 7 (2015): 834–851.

39   Pega, et al., 'Unconditional Cash Transfers'; M. Lagarde, et al., 'The Impact of Conditional Cash Transfers on Health Outcomes and Use of Health Services in Low- and Middle-Income Countries', *Cochrane Database of Systematic Reviews* 4 (2009), doi: 10.1002/14651858.CD008137.

40   Lagarde, et al., 'Impact of Conditional Cash Transfers'.

41   Fischer, *Poverty as Ideology*; B. Fine, *The Continuing Enigmas of Social Policy*, Working Paper 2014-10 (Geneva: United Nations Research Institute for Social Development, 2014), https://www.unrisd.org/80256B3C005BCCF9/%28httpAuxP ages%29/30B153EE73F52ABFC1257D0200420A61/$file/Fine.pdf.

42   Fischer, *Poverty as Ideology*, 234.

43   O.P. Ottersen, et al., 'The Political Origins of Health Inequity: Prospects for Change', *Lancet* 383, no. 9917 (2014): 630–667; H. Coovadia, et al., 'The Health and Health System of South Africa: Historical Roots of Current Public Health Challenges', *Lancet* 374, no. 9692 (2009): 817–834.

44   Fischer, *Poverty as Ideology*.

45   Department for International Development, *Cash Transfers*, Evidence Paper of the Policy Division of DFID (London: Department for International Development, 2011).

46   D. Sánchez-Ancochea and L. Mattei, 'Bolsa Família, Poverty and Inequality: Political and Economic Effects in the Short and Long Run', *Global Social Policy* 11, no. 2/3 (2011): 313.

47   Fischer, *Poverty as Ideology*.

48   M. Nikiforos, et al., *Modeling the Macroeconomic Effects of a Universal Basic Income* (Washington, DC: Roosevelt Institute, 2017), https://rooseveltinstitute. org/wp-content/uploads/2020/07/RI-Macroeconomic-Effects-of-UBI-201708.pdf.

49   Even in a deficit-financed policy, the increase in government's liabilities is offset to some degree by the increase in aggregate demand. The model assumed that the payment would not reduce household labour participation (a very reasonable assumption for such a small payment).

50   M. Blyth and E. Lonergan, 'Print Less but Transfer More: Why Central Banks Should Give More Money Directly to the People', *Foreign Affairs*, September/October 2014, https://www.foreignaffairs.com/articles/united-states/2014-08-11/print-less-transfer-more.

51   M. Williams, 'Women in Rural South Africa: A Post-Wage Existence and the Role of the State', *Equality, Diversity and Inclusion* 37, no. 4 (2018): 392–410.

52   J.K. Gibson-Graham, 'Building Community Economies: Women and the Economies of Place', in *Women and the Politics of Place*, eds. W. Harcourt and A. Escobar (Bloomfield, CT: Kumarian Press, 2005), 130–157.

53   Bastagli, et al., *Cash Transfers*.

54   Williams, 'Women in Rural South Africa'.

55   UNFCCC, *Paris Agreement* (New York: United Nations Framework Convention on Climate Change, 2015), 2, https://unfccc.int/sites/default/files/english_paris_agreement.pdf.

56   J. Cock, 'The "Green Economy": A Just and Sustainable Development Path or a "Wolf in Sheep's Clothing"?' *Global Labour Journal* 5, no. 1 (2014): 23–44.

57   A. Eisenberg, 'Just Transitions', *Southern California Law Review* 92, no. 101 (2019): 282.

58   D. Stevis and R. Felli, 'Green Transitions, Just Transitions? Broadening and Deepening Justice', *Kurswechsel* 3 (2016): 35–45.

59   P. Bond, *The Politics of Environmental Justice* (Durban: UKZN Press, 2011), 2.

60   Cock, 'The "Green Economy"'; C. Farrel, 'Just Transition: Lessons Learned from the Environmental Justice Movement', *Duke Forum for Law and Social Change* 4 (2012): 35–45.

61   R. Warner, 'Ecological Modernization Theory: Towards a Critical Ecopolitics of Change', *Environmental Politics* 19, no. 4 (2010): 553.

62   M. Bookchin, *Social Ecology and Communalism* (Oakland, CA: AK Press, 2007).

63   Eisenberg, 'Just Transitions'; Climate Justice Alliance, *Just Transition Principles* (Washington, DC: Climate Justice Alliance, 2018), https://climatejusticealliance.org/wp-content/uploads/2018/06/CJA_JustTransition_Principles_final_hi-rez.pdf; N. Healy and J. Barry, 'Politicizing Energy Justice and Energy System Transitions: Fossil Fuel Divestment and a "Just Transition"', *Energy Policy* 108 (2017): 451–459.

64   Stevis and Felli, 'Green Transitions'.

65   Cock, 'The "Green Economy"'.

66   W. Cao, et al., 'The Effect of Environmental Regulation on Employment in Resource-Based Areas of China: An Empirical Research Based on the Mediating Effect Model', *International Journal of Environmental Research and Public Health* 14, no. 12 (2017): 1598; R. Golombek and A. Raknerud, 'Do Environmental Standards Harm Manufacturing Employment?', *The Scandinavian Journal of Economics* 99, no. 1 (1997): 29–44.

67   J. Horbach and K. Rennings, 'Environmental Innovation and Employment Dynamics in Different Technology Fields – an Analysis Based on the German Community Innovation Survey 2009', *Journal of Cleaner Production* 57 (2013): 158–165.

68   UNFCCC, *Paris Agreement*. The concept of a just transition originated within the labour movement, and is often traced to the American labour and environmental activist Tony Mazzochi, who emphasised the need to go beyond zero-sum scenarios that pitted environmental demands as threats to workers' interests and livelihoods.

69   R. Pollin and B. Callaci, 'A Just Transition for U.S. Fossil Fuel Industry Workers', *The American Prospect*, July 2016, https://prospect.org/environment/just-transition-u.s.-fossil-fuel-industry-workers/.

70   G. Piggot, et al., *Realizing a Just and Equitable Transition away from Fossil Fuels*, Discussion Brief (Stockholm: Stockholm Environment Institute, 2019), https://cdn.sei.org/wp-content/uploads/2019/01/realizing-a-just-and-equitable-transition-away-from-fossil-fuels.pdf.

71   Stevis and Felli, 'Green Transitions', 38.

72   Cock, 'The "Green Economy"'; V. Satgar, 'The Climate Crisis and Systemic Alternatives', in *The Climate Crisis: South African and Global Democratic Eco-Socialist Alternatives*, ed. V. Satgar (Johannesburg: Wits University Press, 2018), 1–28; D. Hallowes and V. Munnik, *Down to Zero: The Politics of Just Transition – The GroundWork Report 2019* (Pietermaritzburg: GroundWork, 2019), https://www.groundwork.org.za/reports/gW_Report_2019.pdf; Union of Concerned Scientists, *Each Country's Share of CO_2 Emissions*, 12 August 2020, https://www.ucsusa.org/resources/each-countrys-share-co2-emissions.

73   Cock, 'The "Green Economy"', 29–30.

74   Particularly those at the heart of the minerals-energy complex.

75   This reliance was reaffirmed at the Conference of the Parties 26th meeting in November 2021, when South Africa sided with China and India to dilute the final agreement's wording from 'phasing out unabated coal and fossil fuel subsidies' to 'phasing down unabated coal and inefficient fossil-fuel subsidies'. This was despite South Africa having secured US$8.5 billion in grants to finance the early mothballing of coal plants, introduce cleaner energy alternatives and support coal-reliant areas. N. Kumleben, 'South Africa's Coal Deal Is a New Model for Climate Change', *Foreign Policy*, 12 November 2021, https://foreignpolicy.com/2021/11/12/coal-climate-south-africa-cop26-agreement/.

76   M. Williams, 'Energy, Labour and Democracy in South Africa', in *The Climate Crisis: South African and Global Democratic Eco-Socialist Alternatives*, ed. V. Satgar (Johannesburg: Wits University Press, 2018), 240.

77   Hallowes and Munnik, *Down to Zero*, 116.

78   Hallowes and Munnik, *Down to Zero*.

79   Minerals Council South Africa, *Facts and Figures 2019* (Johannesburg: Minerals Council South Africa, 2019), 23, https://www.mineralscouncil.org.za/downloads/send/18-current/1250-facts-and-figures-2019.

80   Eskom, *Integrated Report, 31 March 2017* (Sandton: Eskom, 2017), 8, https://www.eskom.co.za/wp-content/uploads/2021/02/Eskom_integrated_report_2017.pdf.

81   Sasol, *Investing in Our People: Human Capital Management* (Johannesburg: Sasol, 2018), 41, https://www.sasol.com/sites/default/files/content/files/SASOL_Investing%20in%20our%20People%20Brochure.pdf.

82   According to the South African Chamber of Mines, the average monthly salary for a coal miner in 2019 was R25 600 (slightly more than the average R23 200 monthly salary earned by workers in gold mining) (Minerals Council South Africa, *Facts and Figures 2019*, 12).

83 Almost 80% of workers in South Africa's mining sector were members of a trade union in 2017, as were 64% of workers in the utilities sector, making them the sectors with the highest rates of unionisation. In both sectors, union membership levels had risen in the previous five years. See Stats SA, *Labour Market Dynamics in South Africa, 2017* (Pretoria: Statistics South Africa, 2017).

84 M. Cruywagen, et al., *Estimating the Cost of a Just Transition in South Africa's Coal Sector: Protecting Workers, Stimulating Regional Development and Accelerating a Low-Carbon Transition* (Stellenbosch: Centre for Complex Systems in Transition, Stellenbosch University, 2019), https://www.tips.org.za/images/Estimating_the_cost_of_a_just_transition_in_South_Africas_coal_sector.pdf.

85 That would involve a phased end to the use of coal for electricity generation, to coal exports, to the use of industrial and metallurgical coal, and to Sasol's coal-to-liquid fuel industry.

86 The costing includes compensation for five years (for the wage differential between coal mining jobs and renewables jobs), retraining, relocation (for workers originally from other provinces) and rehabilitation and other support to local communities and economies.

87 Cruywagen, et al., *Estimating the Cost*, 8.

88 That includes R1.6 billion in direct subsidies through the basic fuel price and a further R6.5 billion due to exemptions from the Carbon Tax Act 15 of 2019, under which Sasol pays no carbon tax on more than 90% of its emissions. See A. Pant, et al., *Understanding the Role of Subsidies in South Africa's Coal-Based Liquid Fuel Sector* (Winnipeg: International Institute for Sustainable Development, 2020), 4–5. https://www.iisd.org/system/files/2020-10/subsidies-south-africa-coal-liquid-fuel.pdf.

89 Similarly, a phased shift away from coal-based to renewable electricity generation also seems to be feasible and affordable. Coal supplies to Eskom accounted for about 38 000 coal miner jobs in 2017, a little under half of the total workforce in that industry. All else being equal, entirely phasing out Eskom-tied coal mining jobs over twenty years would require new employment and/or livelihood support for 1 200 to 1 300 workers per year.

90 M. Lawhon and T. McCreary, 'Beyond Jobs vs Environment: On the Potential of a Universal Basic Income to Reconfigure Environmental Politics', *Antipode* 52, no. 2 (2020): 452–474.

91 Cock, 'The "Green Economy"'.

92 A. Yang, *The Freedom Dividend, Defined*, US Presidential Campaign Material, 2020, https://2020.yang2020.com/what-is-freedom-dividend-faq/; N. Srnicek and A. Williams, *Inventing the Future: Post-Capitalism and a World without Work* (London: Verso Books, 2015); P. Mason, *Postcapitalism: A Guide to Our Future* (London: Farrar, Straus and Giroux, 2015).

93 D. Henwood, 'The Robots Are Not Coming for All of Our Jobs', *Jacobin*, 23 February 2020, https://www.jacobinmag.com/2020/02/robots-jobs-united-states-gdp-wages-productivity-growth-economy; D. Baker, 'The Job-Killing Robot Myth', *The Los Angeles Times*, 6 May 2015, https://www.latimes.com/opinion/op-ed/la-oe-baker-robots-20150507-story.html; D.H. Autor, 'Why Are There Still So Many Jobs? The History and Future of Workplace Automation', *Journal of Economic Perspectives* 29, no. 3 (2015): 3–30.

94   S.N. Houseman, *Understanding the Decline of U.S. Manufacturing Employment*, Working Paper 18-287 (Kalamazoo, MI: W.E. Upjohn Institute for Employment Research, 2018).

95   P. Frase, *Four Futures* (London: Verso Books, 2016).

96   P. van Parijs, 'Basic Income: A Simple and Powerful Idea for the Twenty-First Century', *Politics and Society* 32, no. 1 (2004): 7–39; E.O. Wright, *Redesigning Distribution: Basic Income and Stakeholder Grants as Alternative Cornerstones for a More Egalitarian Capitalism* (London: Verso Books, 2003); Srnicek and Williams, *Inventing the Future*; B. Raine, 'Renewed Labour', *N+1* 33 (2019): 33–46, https://nplusonemag.com/issue-33/politics/renewed-labour/.

97   G. Standing, *The Precariat: The New Dangerous Class* (London: Bloomsbury, 2011).

98   M. Kalecki, 'Political Aspects of Full Employment', *Political Quarterly* 14, no. 4 (1943): 322–331, https://delong.typepad.com/kalecki43.pdf.

99   Wright, *Redesigning Distribution*, 79.

100 P. van Parijs, 'A Simple and Powerful Idea for the 21st Century', in *Redesigning Distribution: Basic Income and Stakeholder Grants as Alternative Cornerstones for a More Egalitarian Capitalism*, ed. E.O. Wright (London: Verso Books, 2003), 10.

101 A. Battistoni, 'Jobs Guarantee or Universal Basic Income? Why Not Both?', *In These Times*, July 2018, http://inthesetimes.com/features/universal-basic-income-federal-jobs-guarantee-climate-change-inequality.html.

102 E.O. Wright, 'Basic Income, Stakeholder Grants, and Class Analysis', *Politics and Society* 32, no. 1 (2004): 84.

103 Y. Varoufakis, 'Why the Universal Basic Income Is a Necessity', lecture to Gottlieb Duttweiler Institute, 30 April 2017, https://www.youtube.com/watch?v=22eQ9iLBfY4.

104 D. Zamora, 'The Case against a Basic Income', *Jacobin*, December 2017, https://www.jacobinmag.com/2017/12/universal-basic-income-inequality-work; J. Clarke, 'Basic Income: Progressive Cloak and Neoliberal Dagger', *Socialist Bullet*, 4 April 2018, https://socialistproject.ca/2018/04/basic-income-progressive-cloak-and-neoliberal-dagger/.

105 H. Hester, 'Care under Capitalism: The Crisis of "Women's Work"', *Progressive Review* 24, no. 4 (2018): 344.

106 N. Fraser, 'Behind Marx's Hidden Abode', *New Left Review* 86 (2014): 61.

107 Fraser, 'Behind Marx's Hidden Abode'; K. Weeks, *The Problem with Work: Feminism, Marxism, Antiwork Politics, and Postwork Imaginaries* (Durham, NC: Duke University Press, 2011).

108 J. Cock, 'The Climate Crisis and a "Just Transition" in South Africa: An Eco-Feminist-Socialist Perspective', in *The Climate Crisis: South African and Global Democratic Eco-Socialist Alternatives*, ed. V. Satgar (Johannesburg: Wits University Press, 2018), 212.

109 N. Fraser, 'Contradictions of Capital and Care', *New Left Review* 100 (2016): 99–117; Weeks, *Problem with Work*.

110 K. Weeks, 'A Feminist Case for Basic Income: An Interview with Kathi Weeks', *Critical Legal Thinking*, 22 August 2016, https://criticallegalthinking.com/2016/08/22/feminist-case-basic-income-interview-kathi-weeks/.

111 C. Pateman, 'Democratizing Citizenship: Some Advantages of a Basic Income', *Politics and Society* 32, no. 1 (2004): 89–105.

112 A. Withorn, 'Women and Basic Income in the US: Is One Man's Ceiling Another Woman's Floor?', *Journal of Progressive Human Services* 4, no. 1 (1990): 32.

113 J.U. Bidadanure, 'The Political Theory of Universal Basic Income', *Annual Review of Political Science* 22 (2019): 481–501.

114 Cock, 'Climate Crisis'; M. Flatø, et al., 'Women, Weather, and Woes: The Triangular Dynamics of Female-Headed Households, Economic Vulnerability, and Climate Variability in South Africa', *World Development* 90 (2017): 41–62.

115 Pateman, 'Democratizing Citizenship'.

116 S. Birnbaum, *Basic Income Reconsidered* (New York: Palgrave Macmillan, 2012). A household-based basic income would hide the ways in which marriage, the labour market and gender relations determine women's social citizenship (since women would 'disappear' within the unit of the family or household).

117 K. Weeks, 'Feminist Politics and a Case for Basic Income. Debate: Could a Basic Income Play a Role in the Fight against Unfree Labour?', *OpenDemocracy*, 18 September 2019, https://www.opendemocracy.net/en/beyond-trafficking-and-slavery/feminist-politics-and-case-basic-income/.

118 A.S. Orloff, 'Why Basic Income Does Not Promote Gender Equality', in *Basic Income: An Anthology of Contemporary Research*, eds. K. Widerquist, J.A. Noguera, Y. Vanderborght and J. de Wispelaere (Chichester: Blackwell Publishing, 2013), 149–152; A. Gheaus, 'Basic Income, Gender Justice and the Costs of Gender-Symmetrical Lifestyles', *Basic Income Studies* 3, no. 3 (2008): 1–8.

119 T. Fitzpatrick, 'A Basic Income for Feminists?', in *Basic Income: An Anthology of Contemporary Research*, eds. K. Widerquist, J.A. Noguera, Y. Vanderborght and J. de Wispelaere (Chichester: Blackwell Publishing, 2013), 163–172.

120 Weeks, *Problem with Work*, 124.

121 Wright, et al., 'Social Assistance and Dignity'; L. Patel and T. Hochfeld, 'It Buys Food but Does it Change Gender Relations? Child Support Grants in Soweto, South Africa', *Gender and Development* 19, no. 2 (2011): 229–240.

122 Granlund and Hochfeld, '"That Child Support Grant Gives Me Powers"'.

123 Patel and Hochfeld, 'It Buys Food'; M. Scarlato and G. d'Agostino, 'Cash Transfers, Labor Supply, and Gender Inequality: Evidence from South Africa', *Feminist Economics* 25, no. 4 (2019): 159–184.

124 S. Federici, *Revolution at Point Zero: Housework, Reproduction, and Feminism* (Oakland, CA: PM Press, 2012).

125 L. Macdonald, 'We Are All Housewives: Universal Basic Income as Wages for Housework', *Lateral* 7, no. 2 (2018), https://csalateral.org/issue/7-2/basic-income-housewives-wages-housework-macdonald/.

126 Macdonald, 'We Are All Housewives', 11.

127 H. Marais, *Buckling: The Impact of AIDS in South Africa* (Pretoria: Centre for the Study of AIDS, 2005).

128 Weeks, 'A Feminist Case'.

129 In South Africa, black African women, especially those who are unemployed or 'own account workers', are by far the most likely to do volunteer work. Stats SA, *Volunteer Activities Survey, 2010* (Pretoria: Statistics South Africa, 2011).

130 I. Robeyns, 'Hush Money or Emancipation Fee? A Gender Analysis of Basic Income', in *Basic Income on the Agenda: Policy Objectives and Political Chances*, eds. R. van der Veen and L. Groot (Amsterdam: Amsterdam University Press, 2000), 121–136.

131 Williams, 'Women in Rural South Africa'.

132 S. Hassim, 'Social Justice, Care and Developmental Welfare in South Africa: A Capabilities Perspective', *Social Dynamics* 34, no. 2 (2008): 104–118.

133 K. Marx, and F. Engels, *The Communist Manifesto*, ed. F.L. Bender (New York: W.W. Norton, 1988 [1848]).

134 R. Nixon, 'Transcript of the President's Labor Day Address', *New York Times*, 7 September 1971, https://www.nytimes.com/1971/09/07/archives/transcript-of-the-presidents-labor-day-address.html.

135 F. Barchiesi, 'The Debate on the Basic Income Grant in South Africa: Social Citizenship, Wage Labour and the Reconstruction of Working-Class Politics', paper presented at the Harold Wolpe Memorial Trust's 10th Anniversary Colloquium, 'Engaging Silences and Unresolved Issues in the Political Economy of South Africa', Cape Town, 21–23 September 2006, p. 3.

136 K. Vonnegut, *Player Piano* (New York: Simon and Schuster, 1952).

137 B. Herbig, et al., 'Health in the Long-Term Unemployed', *Deutsches Ärzteblatt International* 110, no. 23/24 (2013): 413–419; K.I. Paul and K. Moser, 'Unemployment Impairs Mental Health: Meta-Analyses', *Journal of Vocational Behavior* 74, no. 3 (2009): 264–282.

138 J.E. Brand, 'The Far-Reaching Impact of Job Loss and Unemployment', *Annual Review of Sociology* 41 (2015): 359–375; F. McKee-Ryan, et al., 'Psychological and Physical Well-Being during Unemployment: A Meta-Analytic Study', *Journal of Applied Psychology* 90, no. 1 (2005): 53–76.

139 M. Jahoda, *Employment and Unemployment: A Social-Psychological Analysis* (Cambridge: Cambridge University Press, 1982).

140 D. Fryer and R. Fagan, 'Towards a Critical Community Psychological Perspective on Unemployment and Mental Health', *American Journal of Community Psychology* 32, no. 1/2 (2003): 89–96.

141 A.E. Clark and A.J. Oswald, 'Unhappiness and Unemployment', *The Economic Journal* 104 (1994): 648–659.

142 N. Carlos, et al., 'Modelling Suicide and Unemployment: A Longitudinal Analysis Covering 63 Countries, 2000–11', *The Lancet Psychiatry* 2, no. 3 (2015): 239–245.

143 Y.H. Noh, 'Does Unemployment Increase Suicide Rates? The OECD Panel Evidence', *Journal of Economic Psychology* 30, no. 4 (2009): 575–582; T.A. Blakely, et al., 'Unemployment and Suicide: Evidence for a Causal Association?', *Journal of Epidemiology and Community Health* 57, no. 8 (2003): 594–600. 'Linked' or 'associated' because the causality is not clearly established. Studies in New Zealand, for example, found that being unemployed was associated with a two- to threefold increased relative risk of death by suicide, compared with being employed. However, at least half of this association might have been attributable to confounding factors such as mental illness. See Blakely, et al., 'Unemployment and Suicide'.

144 S. Rueda, et al., 'Association of Returning to Work with Better Health in Working-Aged Adults: A Systematic Review', *American Journal of Public Health* 102, no. 3 (2012): 541–556.

145 C. Estlund, 'Three Big Ideas for a Future of Less Work and a Three-Dimensional Alternative', *Law and Contemporary Problems* 82, no. 3 (2019): 6.

146 Frase, *Four Futures*.

147 P.T. Martikainen and T. Valkonen, 'Excess Mortality of Unemployed Men and Women during a Period of Rapidly Increasing Unemployment', *Lancet* 348, no. 9032 (1996): 909–912.

148 J. Cylus, et al., 'Do Generous Unemployment Benefit Programs Reduce Suicide Rates? A State Fixed-Effect Analysis Covering 1968–2008', *American Journal of Epidemiology* 189, no. 1 (2014): 45–52.

149 C. Hetschko, et al., 'Changing Identity: Retiring from Unemployment', *The Economic Journal* 124, no. 575 (2014): 149–166.

150 D. Sage, 'Work and Social Norms: Why We Need to Challenge the Centrality of Employment in Society', *LSE Blog*, 16 July 2018, https://blogs.lse.ac.uk/politicsandpolicy/work-and-social-norms-why-we-need-to-challenge-the-centrality-of-employment-in-our-society/; D. Sage, 'Unemployment, Wellbeing and the Power of the Work Ethic: Implications for Social Policy', *Critical Social Policy* 39, no. 2 (2019): 205–228.

151 K.L.A. Roex and J.J. Rozer, 'The Social Norm to Work and the Well-Being of the Short- and Long-Term Unemployed', *Social Indicators Research* 139 (2018): 1037–1064.

152 M. Strandh, et al., 'Unemployment, Gender and Mental Health: The Role of the Gender Regime', *Sociology of Health and Illness* 35, no. 5 (2013): 649–665.

153 R. Morrell, et al., 'Hegemonic Masculinity/Masculinities in South Africa: Culture, Power, and Gender Politics', *Men and Masculinities* 15, no. 1 (2012): 11–30; L. Walker, 'Men Behaving Differently: South African Men since 1994', *Culture, Health and Sexuality* 7, no. 3 (2005): 225–238; L. Richter and R. Morrell, eds., *Baba: Men and Fatherhood in South Africa* (Cape Town: HSRC Press, 2006).

154 As the writer George Orwell noted: 'Beggars do not work, it is said, but, then, what is work? A navvy works by swinging a pick. An accountant works by adding up figures. A beggar works by standing out of doors in all weathers and getting varicose veins, chronic bronchitis, etc.' G. Orwell, *Down and out in Paris and London* (London: Penguin Books, 1989), 206.

155 ILO, *Safety and Health at the Heart of the Future of Work: Building on 100 Years of Experience* (Geneva: International Labour Organization, 2019), https://www.ilo.org/wcmsp5/groups/public/---dgreports/---dcomm/documents/publication/wcms_686645.pdf.

156 P. Hämäläinen, et al., *Global Estimates of Occupational Accidents and Work-Related Illnesses, 2017* (Helsinki: Ministry of Social Affairs and Health, Finland), 2017, http://www.icohweb.org/site/images/news/pdf/Report%20Global%20Estimates%20of%20Occupational%20Accidents%20and%20Work-related%20Illnesses%202017%20rev1.pdf.

157 T. Chandola and N. Zhang, 'Re-employment, Job Quality, Health and Allostatic Load Biomarkers: Prospective Evidence from the UK Household Longitudinal Study', *International Journal of Epidemiology* 47, no. 1 (2018): 47–57.

158 Terkel, *Working*, xiii.

159 L. Boltanski and E. Chiapello, *The New Spirit of Capitalism* (London: Verso Books, 2005); M. Bunting, *Willing Slaves: How the Overwork Culture Is Ruling Our Lives* (London: Harper Perennial, 2005).

160 F. Barchiesi, 'Liberation of, Through or from Work? Postcolonial Africa and the Problem with "Job Creation" in the Global Crisis', *Interface* 4, no. 2 (2012): 236.

161 This harks back to origins of the word 'job', which in fourteenth-century English referred to a lump or piece of some object which people carried around with them. See R. Sennett, *The Corrosion of Character: The Personal Consequences of Work in the New Capitalism* (New York: W.W. Norton, 1998).

162 Srnicek and Williams, 2015; F. Barchiesi, *Precarious Liberation: Workers, the State and Contested Social Citizenships in Post-Apartheid South Africa* (Pietermaritzburg: UKZN Press, 2011); Wright, *Redesigning Distribution*; Wright, 'Basic Income, Stakeholder Grants'.

163 K. Weeks, 'Feminism and the Refusal of Work: An Interview with Kathi Weeks', *Political Critique*, 28 August 2017, http://politicalcritique.org/world/2017/souvlis-weeks-feminism-marxism-work-interview/.

164 A. Bastani, *Fully Automated Luxury Communism* (London: Verso Books, 2020).

165 Srnicek and Williams, *Inventing the Future*.

166 Mason, *Postcapitalism*.

167 A Marxist in more ways than one (he was the son-in-law of Karl Marx), Lafargue founded the first French socialist party and authored numerous texts, the most famous of which was *The Right to Be Lazy*. In it, he lamented that: 'Instead of taking advantage of periods of crisis, for a general distribution of their products and a universal holiday, the laborers, perishing with hunger, go and beat their heads against the doors of the workshops'. See P. Lafargue, *The Right to be Lazy*, trans. C. Kerr (London: Charles Kerr and Company, 1883 [online version 2000]), https://www.marxists.org/archive/lafargue/1883/lazy/index.htm, Chapter 2, para 15.

168 B. Russell, B. *Roads to Freedom: Socialism, Anarchism and Syndicalism* (London: Routledge, 1918, 1993 edition); A. Gorz, *Reclaiming Work: Beyond the Wage-based Society* (Cambridge: Polity Press, 1999).

169 Bastani, *Fully Automated*.

170 Frase, *Four Futures*.

171 Mason, *Postcapitalism*.

172 Weeks, 'Feminism and the Refusal of Work'.

173 Weeks, 'Feminism and the Refusal of Work'.

174 Van Parijs, 'Simple and Powerful'.

175 A. Gorz, *Paths to Paradise* (London: Pluto Books, 1985), 54.

176 Gorz, *Paths to Paradise*, 40.

177 A. Little, *The Political Thought of Andre Gorz* (New York: Routledge, 1996).

CHAPTER 4   TESTING THE ARGUMENTS AGAINST

1 Former Minister of Social Development, Zola Skweyiya, supported the introduction of a universal income grant, but was unable to win over enough of his colleagues in government and the ANC to that position. See, for example, L. Ensor, 'Skweyiya Calls for Basic Income Grant for Poor', *Business Day*, 10 November 2006.

2 J. Seekings and H. Matisonn, *The Continuing Politics of Basic Income in South Africa*, Working Paper 286 (Cape Town: Centre for Social Science Research, University of Cape Town, 2010).

3 S. Liebenberg, 'Universal Access to Social Security Rights: Can a Basic Income Grant Meet the Challenge?', *ESR Review* 3, no. 2 (2002), 9–10. The poverty gap refers to the total income shortfall of households living below the poverty line. A narrowing poverty gap means more households have edged closer to, or above, the poverty line.

4   W. Gumede, *Thabo Mbeki and the Battle for the Soul of the ANC* (Cape Town: Zebra Press, 2005).

5   Department of Social Development, *Transforming the Present – Protecting the Future: Report of the Committee of Inquiry into a Comprehensive System of Social Security for South Africa* (Pretoria: Government Printer, 2002), 15.

6   Cosatu, 'Submission on Comprehensive Social Security', submitted to the Taylor Task Team on Social Security (Johannesburg: Congress of South African Trade Unions, 2000), para 3.2

7   The Committee speculated, for example, that the grant might empower recipients 'to take the risks needed to break out of the poverty cycle. Rather than serving as a disincentive to engage in higher return activities [the grant] could encourage risk-taking and self-reliance. Such an income could thus become a springboard for development' (Department of Social Development, *Transforming the Present*, 61).

8   J. Ferguson, 'Formalities of Poverty: Thinking about Social Assistance in Neoliberal South Africa', *African Studies Review* 50, no. 2 (2007): 71–86.

9   Cited in C. Meth, 'Ideology and Social Policy: "Handouts" and the Spectre of "Dependency"', *Transformation* 56 (2004): 2.

10   Meth, 'Ideology and Social Policy', 22.

11   P. le Roux, 'Financing a Universal Income Grant in South Africa', *Social Dynamics* 28, no. 2 (2003), 115.

12   S. van der Berg, 'The BIG Grant: Comments on the Report of the Committee of Inquiry into a Comprehensive System of Social Security for South Africa', *Viewpoint*, July (Johannesburg: South Africa Foundation, 2002); H. Bhorat, 'A Universal Income Grant Scheme for South Africa: An Empirical Assessment', paper presented at the 9th International Congress of the Basic Income European Network, Geneva, 12–14 September 2002.

13   A. McCord, *An Overview of the Performance and Potential of Public Works Programmes in South Africa*, CSSR Working Paper 49 (Cape Town: Centre for Social Science Research, University of Cape Town, 2003), 18.

14   Le Roux, 'Financing a Universal Income Grant', 99.

15   According to Franco Barchiesi, publication of the Taylor Committee's report was delayed by almost four months to allow the Department of Finance to raise its objections ahead of final publication. F. Barchiesi, 'South African Debates on the Basic Income Grant: Wage Labour and the Post-Apartheid Social Policy', *Journal of Southern African Studies* 33, no. 3 (2007): 561–575.

16   The ANC's 2002 National Policy Conference supported the Taylor Committee's vision of a comprehensive social protection framework, but avoided any specific mention of a BIG. ANC, 'Draft Resolutions of the National Policy Conference', *Umrabulo* 17 (2002), http://www.anc.org.za/ancdocs/pubs/umrabulo/umrabulo17/index.html.

17   Ministry of Finance, *2004 Budget Speech*, Cape Town, 18 February 2004, https://www.gov.za/2004-budget-speech.

18   Quoted in G. Hart, 'Beyond Neoliberalism? Post-Apartheid Developments in Historical and Comparative Perspective', in *The Development Decade? Economic and Social Change in South Africa: 1994–2004*, ed. V. Padayachee (Cape Town: HSRC Press, 2006), 26.

19   Anon, 'Didiza Cautious about Basic Income Grant', *Business Day*, 14 August 2002.

20   N. Coleman, 'Current Debates around BIG: The Political and Socio-Economic Context', in *A Basic Income Grant for South Africa*, eds. G. Standing and M. Samson (Cape Town: UCT Press, 2003), 122.

21   T. Mbeki, *State of the Nation Address to the Joint Sitting of the Houses of Parliament*, Cape Town, 8 February 2003.

22   ANC, *ANC 52nd National Conference 2007 Resolutions* (Johannesburg: African National Congress, 2007), 13–14, https://www.anc1912.org.za/resolutions-2/.

23   D. Everatt, 'The Undeserving Poor: Poverty and the Politics of Service Delivery in the Poorest Nodes of South Africa', *Politikon* 35, no. 3 (2008): 303.

24   A. Musgrave and K. Brown, 'Social Welfare System Revisited', *Business Day*, 21 October 2008.

25   Cosatu, *A Growth Path towards Full Employment*, Framework Document (Johannesburg: Congress of South African Trade Unions, 2010).

26   In India, for example, less than 5% of the adult population file tax returns and less than 2% pay taxes. M. Ghatak, 'Universal Basic Income: The Case for UBI in Developed Versus Developing Countries', presentation at London School of Economics, 24 November 2017, http://personal.lse.ac.uk/ghatak/UBI-Slides_LSE-SAC_Nov24_2017.pdf.

27   W.A. Jackson, 'Basic Income and the Right to Work: A Keynesian Approach', *Journal of Post-Keynesian Economics* 21, no. 4 (1999), 24–25.

28   S. Santens, 'Wouldn't Unconditional Basic Income Just Cause Massive Inflation?', *Medium*, 22 November 2014, https://medium.com/basic-income/wouldnt-unconditional-basic-income-just-cause-massive-inflation-fe71d69f15e7.

29   N. Irwin, 'Quantitative Easing Is Ending. Here's What it Did, in Charts', *The New York Times*, 29 October 2014, https://www.nytimes.com/2014/10/30/upshot/quantitative-easing-is-about-to-end-heres-what-it-did-in-seven-charts.html.

30   S. Handa, et al., 'Myth-Busting? Confronting Six Common Perceptions about Unconditional Cash Transfers as a Poverty Reduction Strategy in Africa', *The World Bank Research Observer* 33, no. 2 (2018): 259–298.

31   D. Egger, et al., *General Equilibrium Effects of Cash Transfers: Experimental Evidence from Kenya*, Working Paper 26600 (Washington, DC: National Bureau of Economic Research, 2019), https://www.nber.org/papers/w26600.

32   J. Cunha, et al., 'The Price Effects of Cash Versus In-kind Transfers', *The Review of Economic Studies* 86, no. 1 (2019): 240–281.

33   J. Peck, *Workfare States* (New York: Guilford Press, 2001).

34   Transcripts of the meeting of the Taylor Committee of Inquiry, 6 October 2000, p. 17, cited in F. Barchiesi, 'The Debate on the Basic Income Grant in South Africa: Social Citizenship, Wage Labour and the Reconstruction of Working-Class Politics', paper presented at the Harold Wolpe Memorial Trust's 10th Anniversary Colloquium, 'Engaging Silences and Unresolved Issues in the Political Economy of South Africa', Cape Town, 21–23 September 2006, p. 14.

35   S. Davala, et al., *Basic Income: A Transformative Policy for India* (Delhi: Bloomsbury, 2015); E.L. Forget, 'The Town with No Poverty: The Health Effects of a Canadian Guaranteed Annual Income Field Experiment', *Canadian Public Policy* 37, no. 3 (2011): 283–305; C. Haarmann, et al., *Basic Income Grant Pilot Project Assessment Report* (Windhoek: Basic Income Grant Coalition, 2009), http://www.bignam.org/Publications/BIG_Assessment_report_08b.pdf.

36   M. Noble and P. Ntshongwana, *No Sign of a Dependency Culture in South Africa*, HSRC Policy Brief, March 2008, http://www.hsrc.ac.za/uploads/pageContent/1090/No%20sign%20of%20a%20dependency%20culture%20in%20SA.pdf.

37   R. Gilbert, et al., *Would a Basic Income Guarantee Reduce the Motivation to Work? An Analysis of Labor Responses in 16 Trial Programs* (California: Loyola Marymount University, 2018).

38   A. Banerjee, et al., 'Debunking the Stereotype of the Lazy Welfare Recipient: Evidence from Cash Transfer Programmes', *The World Bank Research Observer* 32, no. 2 (2017): 155–184; M.L. Alzúa, et al., 'Welfare Programmes and Labor Supply in Developing Countries: Experimental Evidence from Latin America', *Journal of Population Economics* 26, no. 4 (2013): 1255–1284.

39   E. Prifti, et al., 'Casual Pathways of the Productive Impacts of Cash Transfers: Experimental Evidence from Lesotho', *World Development* 115 (2019): 258–268.

40   D. Jones and I. Marinescu, *The Labor Market Impacts of Universal and Permanent Cash Transfers: Evidence from the Alaska Permanent Fund*, Working Paper 24312 (Washington, DC: National Bureau of Economic Research, 2020), https://www.nber.org/system/files/working_papers/w24312/w24312.pdf.

41   E. Skoufias and V. di Maro, 'Conditional Cash Transfers, Adult Work Incentives, and Poverty', *The Journal of Development Studies* 44, no. 7 (2008), 946.

42   Honduras, Indonesia, Morocco, Mexico, Nicaragua and the Philippines.

43   Banerjee, et al., 'Debunking the Stereotype'.

44   Skoufias and Di Maro, 'Conditional Cash Transfers'.

45   R. Maurizio and G. Vázquez, 'Argentina: efectos del programa Asignación Universal por Hijo en el comportamiento laboral de los adultos', *Revista CEPAL* 113 (2014): 121–144; A. Mideros and C. O'Donoghue, 'The Effect of Unconditional Cash Transfers on Adult Labour Supply: A Unitary Discrete Choice Model for the Case of Ecuador', *Basic Income Studies* 10, no. 2 (2015): 225–255.

46   A. Barrientos and M. Nino-Zarazua, *Effects of Non-Contributory Social Transfers in Developing Countries: A Compendium* (Geneva: International Labour Organization, 2010).

47   A. Mideros, et al., *Estimation of Rates of Return on Social Protection: Making the Case for Non-Contributory Social Transfers in Cambodia*, MERIT Working Papers 2013-063 (Maastricht: United Nations University, Maastricht Economic and Social Research Institute on Innovation and Technology, 2013).

48   M. Foguel and R. de Barros, 'The Effects of Conditional Cash Transfer Programmes on Adult Labour Supply: An Empirical Analysis Using a Time-Series-Cross-Section Sample of Brazilian Municipalities', *Estudos Econômicos* 40, no. 2 (2010): 259–293.

49   D.A. Vera-Cossio, 'Dependence or Constraints? Cash Transfers and Labor Supply', *Economic Development and Cultural Change* (2021), https//doi.org/10.1086/714010.

50   E. Fisher, et al., 'The Livelihood Impacts of Cash Transfers in Sub-Saharan Africa: Beneficiary Perspectives from Six Countries', *World Development* 99 (2017): 299–319.

51   Handa, et al., 'Myth-Busting?', 277.

52   E. Braunstein and S. Seguino, 'The Impact of Economic Policy and Structural Change on Gender Employment Inequality in Latin America 1990-2010', *Review of Keynesian Economics* 6, no. 3 (2018): 307–332.

53 Stats SA, *Social Grants: In-Depth Analysis of the General Household Survey Data 2003–2007*, GHS series Vol. 1, Statistical Release P0318.1 (Pretoria: Statistics South Africa, 2009), 31.

54 M. Leibbrandt, et al., *The Influence of Social Transfers on Labour Supply: A South African and International Review*, Working Paper 112 (Cape Town: Southern Africa Labour and Development Research Unit, University of Cape Town, 2013), http://www.opensaldru.uct.ac.za/bitstream/handle/11090/670/2013_112.pdf?sequence=1.

55 D. Posel, et al., 'Labour Migration and Households: A Reconsideration of the Effects of the Social Pension on Labour Supply in South Africa', *Economic Modelling* 23 (2006): 836–853.

56 Leibbrandt, et al., *Influence of Social Transfers*.

57 M.B. Sawicky, 'Foul Shot', *The Baffler*, 7 March 2018.

58 Quoted in J. Jowitt, 'Strivers v. Shirkers: The Language of the Welfare Debate', *The Guardian*, 8 January 2013, https://www.theguardian.com/politics/2013/jan/08/strivers-shirkers-language-welfare.

59 E. Granter, *Critical Social Theory and the End of Work* (New York: Routledge, 2009), 182.

60 It seems fitting that the discipline of economics initially emerged out of moral philosophy, which in turn, as David Graeber reminds us, originally evolved as a branch of theology. D. Graeber, *Bullshit Jobs: A Theory* (New York: Simon & Schuster, 2018).

61 G. Standing, *How Cash Transfers Boost Work and Economic Security*, Working Paper No. 58 (New York: Department of Economic and Social Affairs, United Nations, April 2008), 25.

62 J. Ferguson, *Give a Man a Fish: Reflections on the New Politics of Distribution* (Durham, NC: Duke University Press, 2015), 233.

63 J. Seekings, 'Basic Income Activism in South Africa, 1997–2019', in *Political Activism and Basic Income Guarantee: Exploring the Basic Income Guarantee*, eds. R. Caputo and L. Liu (London: Palgrave Macmillan, 2020), 617.

64 Seekings, 'Basic Income Activism'.

65 H.J. Dawson and E. Fouksman, 'Labour, Laziness and Distribution: Work Imaginaries among the South African Unemployed', *Africa* 90, no. 2 (2020): 229–251.

66 M. Kelly, 'Regulating the Reproduction and Mothering of Poor Women: The Controlling Image of the Welfare Mother in Television News Coverage of Welfare Reform', *Journal of Poverty* 14, no. 1 (2010): 76–96; L. Gordon, *Pitied but Not Entitled: Single Mothers and the History of Welfare 1890–1935* (New York: Free Press, 1994).

67 Seekings, 'Basic Income Activism', 599.

68 Dawson and Fouksman, 'Labour, Laziness and Distribution'.

69 C. Jeske, 'Why Work? Do We Understand What Motivates Work-Related Decisions in South Africa?', *Journal of Southern African Studies* 44, no. 1 (2018): 27–42.

70 Dawson and Fouksman, 'Labour, Laziness and Distribution'.

71 Barchiesi, 'Debate on the Basic Income Grant', 3.

72 Everatt, 'Undeserving Poor'.

73 Dawson and Fouksman, 'Labour, Laziness and Distribution'.

74   C. Meth, *The (Lame) Duck Unchained Tries to Count the Poor*, Working Paper No. 49 (Durban: School of Development Studies, University of KwaZulu-Natal, 2008), 27.

75   T. Hochfeld and S. Plagerson, 'Dignity and Stigma among South African Female Cash Transfer Recipients', *IDS Bulletin* 42, no. 6 (2011): 53–59.

76   Seekings and Matisonn, *Continuing Politics*; Dawson and Fouksman, 'Labour, Laziness and Distribution'.

77   Anon, 'Economic Crisis Will Not Derail State Plans', *The Independent*, 3 June 2009.

78   O. Molatlhwa, 'JZ: If I Were a Dictator', *Times Live*, 25 March 2015, https://www.timeslive.co.za/thetimes/2015/03/25/jz-if-i-were-a-dictator.

79   Anon, 'People Must Help Themselves', *Business Day*, 17 March 2008.

80   Presidency of South Africa, *Government's Programme of Action: 2005 (Social Cluster)* (Pretoria: Government of South Africa, 2005), https://www.gov.za/about-government/social-cluster-2.

81   Government of South Africa, *RDP White Paper* (Pretoria: Government of South Africa, 1994), para 2.3.

82   J. Ferguson, 'Declaration of Dependence: Labour, Personhood, and Welfare in Southern Africa', *Journal of the Royal Anthropological Institute* 19, no. 2 (2013): 223.

83   E. Hull and D. James, 'Introduction: Popular Economies in South Africa', *Africa* 82, no. 1 (2012): 1–19.

84   M. Hunter, 'The Changing Political Economy of Sex in South Africa: The Significance of Unemployment and Inequalities to the Scale of the AIDS Pandemic', *Social Science and Medicine* 64, no. 3 (2007): 689–700.

85   Ferguson, 'Declaration of Dependence', 228.

86   Hochfeld and Plagerson, 'Dignity and Stigma'.

87   A. Sen, *Development as Freedom* (Oxford: Oxford University Press, 1999).

88   Ferguson, *Give a Man a Fish*, 138.

89   Ferguson, *Give a Man a Fish*.

90   A. du Toit and D. Neves, *Trading on a Grant: Integrating Formal and Informal Social Protection in Post-Apartheid Migrant Networks*, Working Paper 3 (Cape Town: Programme for Land and Agrarian Studies (PLAAS), University of the Western Cape, 2009).

91   Ferguson, *Give a Man a Fish*, 97.

92   Hunter, 'Changing Political Economy'.

93   D. Posel and M. Rogan, 'Women, Income and Poverty: Gendered Access to Resources in Post-Apartheid South Africa', *Agenda* 81, no. 23 (2009): 25–34.

94   J. Pauli and R. van Dijk, 'Marriage as an End or the End of Marriage? Change and Continuity in Southern African Marriages', *Anthropology Southern Africa* 39, no. 4 (2016): 257–266.

95   R. Morrell, et al., 'Hegemonic Masculinity/Masculinities in South Africa: Culture, Power, and Gender Politics', *Men and Masculinities* 15, no. 1 (2012): 11–30; M. Seedat, et al., 'Violence and Injuries in South Africa: Prioritising an Agenda for Prevention', *The Lancet* 374, no. 9694 (2009): 1011–1022.

96   Z.K. Mokoene and G. Khunou, 'Parental Absence: Intergenerational Tensions and Contestations of Social Grants in South Africa', *Critical Social Policy* 39, no. 4 (2019): 525–540; G. Wright, et al., 'Social Assistance and Dignity: South African Women's Experiences of the Child Support Grant', *Development Southern Africa* 32, no. 4 (2015): 443–457.

97 Ferguson, 'Declaration of Dependence', 232.

98 Ferguson, *Give a Man a Fish*, 163.

99 P. van Parijs, 'Why Surfers Should Be Fed: The Liberal Case for an Unconditional Basic Income', *Philosophy and Public Affairs* 20, no. 2 (1991): 101–131.

100 J. Rawls, *Justice as Fairness: A Restatement* (Cambridge, MA: Harvard University Press, 2001).

101 Van Parijs, 'Why Surfers Should Be Fed'; P. van Parijs, *Real Freedom for All: What (if Anything) Can Justify Capitalism?* (Oxford: Oxford University Press, 1998).

102 H. Arendt, *The Human Condition* (Chicago, IL: University of Chicago Press, 1958).

103 Carole Pateman has highlighted this blind spot in the 'free-rider' debate, which rarely takes in the more prevalent reality of men, in or out of jobs, free-riding on women's domestic and other unpaid care work. She sees a basic income as one way to help counteract such forms of gendered free-riding. C. Pateman, 'Democratizing Citizenship: Some Advantages of a Basic Income', *Politics and Society* 32, no. 1 (2004): 89–105.

104 J.U. Bidadanure, 'The Political Theory of Universal Basic Income', *Annual Review of Political Science* 22 (2019): 489. It is reasonable to ask: in which, if any, circumstances would a principle of reciprocity *not* apply? Does a person have to make some kind of contribution in order to qualify for any form of social benefit or provisioning? Answering 'yes' invites absurd scenarios – surely no one would impose a requirement of reciprocity on an infant, for example. But what about a child: would it have to fulfil this requirement in order to be entitled to various forms of provisioning? And if so, from what age, and on what basis? At the very least, greater clarity is needed about what 'reciprocity' refers to when invoked in debates about a basic income.

105 A. Gorz, 'On the Difference between Society and Community, and Why Basic Income Cannot by Itself Confer Full Membership of Either', in *Arguing for Basic Income*, ed. P. van Parijs (London: Verso, 1992), 184.

106 A. Gorz, *The Immaterial: Knowledge, Value and Capital* (London: Seagull Books, 2010), 28.

107 A. Gorz, *Paths to Paradise* (London: Pluto Books, 1985), 54.

108 Arendt, *Human Condition*.

109 I. Jansson, 'Occupation and Basic Income through the Lens of Arendt's *Vita Activa*', *Journal of Occupational Science* 27, no. 1 (2020): 125–137.

110 A.B. Atkinson, 'The Case for a Participation Income', *Political Quarterly* 67, no. 1 (1996): 67–70; A.B. Atkinson, *Inequality: What Can Be Done?* (Cambridge, MA: Harvard University Press, 2015).

111 Pateman, 'Democratizing Citizenship', 102.

112 A. Gourevitch and L. Stanczyk, 'The Basic Income Illusion', *Catalyst: A Critical Journal of Theory and Strategy* 1, no. 4 (2018): 151–177.

113 Gourevitch and Stanczyk, 'The Basic Income Illusion', 154.

114 L. Boltanski and E. Chiapello, *The New Spirit of Capitalism* (London: Verso Books, 2005).

115 B.W. Sculos, 'Changing Lives and Minds: Progress, Strategy, and Universal Basic Income', *New Political Science* 41, no. 2 (2019): 234–247.

116 A.C. Dinerstein, 'The Dream of Dignified Work: On Good and Bad Utopias', *Development and Change* 45, no. 5 (2014): 1037–1058.

117 M. Williams, 'Women in Rural South Africa: A Post-Wage Existence and the Role of the State', *Equality, Diversity and Inclusion* 37, no. 4 (2018): 392–410.

118 Pietermaritzburg Economic Justice and Dignity Group, *Household Affordability Index, January 2021* (Pietermaritzburg: Pietermaritzburg Economic Justice and Dignity Group, 2021). https://pmbejd.org.za/wp-content/uploads/2021/01/January-2021-Household-Affordability-Index-PMBEJD_27012021.pdf.

119 The total cost of typical monthly household expenses which households living on low incomes say they reasonably expect amounted to R7 624 in July 2019 (Pietermaritzburg Economic Justice and Dignity Group, *Household Affordability Index*).

120 A. Yang, *The Freedom Dividend, Defined*, US Presidential Campaign Material, 2020, https://2020.yang2020.com/what-is-freedom-dividend-faq/.

121 A. Stern, *Raising the Floor: How a Universal Basic Income Can Renew Our Economy and Rebuild the American Dream* (New York: Public Affairs Books, 2016).

122 S. Ashman, 'South Africa: An Economy of Extremes', in *The Essential Guide to Critical Development Studies*, eds. H. Veltmeyer and P. Bowles (Abingdon: Routledge, 2021): 171–178.

123 L. Gronbach, *Social Cash Transfer Payment Systems in Sub-Saharan Africa*, Working Paper 452 (Cape Town: Centre for Social Science Research, University of Cape Town, 2020); E. Torkelson, 'Collateral Damages: Cash Transfer and Debt Transfer in South Africa', *World Development* 126 (2020): 104711, https://doi.org/10.1016/j.worlddev.2019.104711.

124 N. Fraser, 'Can Society Be Commodities All the Way Down? Post-Polanyian Reflections on Capitalist Crisis', *Economy and Society* 43, no. 4 (2014): 541–558.

125 Torkelson, 'Collateral Damages', 9.

126 Torkelson, 'Collateral Damages'; E. Torkelson, 'Sophia's Choice: Debt, Social Welfare, and Racial Finance Capitalism', *Environment and Planning D: Society and Space* 39, no. 1 (2021): 67–84.

127 Ashman, 'South Africa', 174–175.

128 Torkelson, 'Sophia's Choice', 15.

129 Ferguson, *Give a Man a Fish*.

130 Williams, 'Women in Rural South Africa'.

131 Gibson-Graham, 'Building Community Economies', 130–157.

132 M. Lawhon and T. McCreary, 'Beyond Jobs vs Environment: On the Potential of a Universal Basic Income to Reconfigure Environmental Politics', *Antipode* 52, no. 2 (2020), 466.

133 In the United States, Martin Luther King famously called for an economic bill of rights that 'would also guarantee an income for all who are not able to work', quoted in J. Nichols, 'A $2,000 Check Is a Good Start, but Struggling Americans Need $2,000 Every Month', *The Nation*, 18 January 2021. https://www.thenation.com/article/economy/mlk-covid-biden-plan/. A guaranteed income proposal also appeared in the Black Panther Party's ten-point manifesto in October 1966. See S. Myers-Lipton, *Ending Extreme Inequality: An Economic Bill of Rights to Eliminate Poverty* (London: Routledge, 2015).

134 P.R. Tcherneva, 'Evaluating the Economic and Environmental Viability of Basic Income and Job Guarantees', in *Environment and Employment: A Reconciliation*, ed. P. Lawn (London: Routledge, 2009): 184–205.

135 Tcherneva, 'Evaluating the Economic', 184.

136 M. Paul, et al., *The Federal Job Guarantee: A Policy to Achieve Permanent Full Employment* (Washington, DC: Center on Budget and Policy Priorities, 2018), https://www.cbpp.org/sites/default/files/atoms/files/3-9-18fe.pdf.

137 E. Noguchi, 'The Cost-Efficiency of a Guaranteed Jobs Program: Really? A Response to Harvey', *Basic Income Studies* 7, no. 2 (2012): 52–65.

138 P.R. Tcherneva, *What Are the Relative Macroeconomic Merits and Environmental Impacts of Direct Job Creation and Basic Income Guarantees?* Working Paper 517 (New York: Levy Economics Institute of Bard College, 2007), http://www.levyinstitute.org/pubs/wp_517.pdf.

139 C. Estlund, 'Three Big Ideas for a Future of Less Work and a Three-Dimensional Alternative', *Law and Contemporary Problems* 82, no. 3 (2019): 1–43.

140 M. Ravallion, 'Guaranteed Employment or Guaranteed Income?', *World Development* 115, no. C (2019): 209–221.

141 Sculos, 'Changing Lives and Minds'.

142 Jackson, 'Basic Income'.

143 A. Godin, *Guaranteed Green Jobs: Sustainable Full Employment*, Working Paper 722 (New York: Levy Economics Institute of Bard College, 2012), http://www.levyinstitute.org/pubs/wp_722.pdf.

144 W. Mitchell and T. Fazi, *Reclaiming the State: A Progressive Vision of Sovereignty for a Post-Neoliberal World* (London: Pluto Press, 2017), 230–231.

145 Tcherneva, 'Evaluating the Economic'.

146 M. Bruenig, 'Just What Is a Job Guarantee?', *Jacobin*, 13 May 2018, https://www.jacobinmag.com/2018/05/full-employment-job-guarantee-bernie-bruenig; M. Bruenig, 'Some Notes on Federal Job Guarantee Proposals', People's Policy Project, 22 March 2018, https://www.peoplespolicyproject.org/2018/03/22/some-notes-on-federal-job-guarantee-proposals/.

147 Ravallion, 'Guaranteed Employment', 210.

148 Bruenig, 'Just What Is a Job Guarantee?'

149 B. Sanders, *Jobs and an Economy for All*, 2020, https://berniesanders.com/issues/jobs-for-all/.

150 Hart, 'Beyond Neoliberalism?', 26.

151 S. Hassim, *Gender, Welfare and the Developmental State in South Africa* (Geneva: UNRISD, 2005), 13, https://sarpn.org/documents/d0001335/P1593-UNRISD_Hassim_May2005.pdf.

152 Tcherneva, *Relative Macroeconomic Merits*.

153 P.R. Tcherneva, 'The Job Guarantee: Delivering the Benefits that Basic Income Only Promises – A Response to Guy Standing', *Basic Income Studies* 7, no. 2 (2012): 66–87.

154 Ravallion, 'Guaranteed Employment'.

155 P.R. Tcherneva, *The Job Guarantee: Design, Jobs and Implementation*, Working Paper 902 (New York: Levy Economics Institute of Bard College, 2018), http://www.levyinstitute.org/pubs/wp_902.pdf.

156 Ravallion, 'Guaranteed Employment'.

157 R. Murgai, et al., 'Is Workfare Cost-Effective against Poverty in a Poor Labor-Surplus Economy?', *World Bank Economic Review* 30, no. 3 (2016), 434.

158 P. Dutta, et al., *Right to Work? Assessing India's Employment Guarantee Scheme in Bihar* (Washington, DC: World Bank, 2014), xxv.

159 C. Imbert and J. Papp, 'Labor Market Effects of Social Programs: Evidence from India's Employment Guarantee', *American Economic Journal: Applied Economics* 7, no. 2 (2015): 233–263.

160 Ravallion, 'Guaranteed Employment', 218.

161 A. McCord, 'The Social Protection Function of Short-Term Public Works Programmes in the Context of Chronic Poverty', in *Social Protection for the Poor and Poorest*, eds. A. Barrientos and D. Hulme (London: Palgrave Macmillan, 2008): 160–180.

162 C. van der Westhuizen, 'Setting the Scene: Public Works Employment from the RDP to the NDP', in *Who Cares? South Africa's Expanded Public Works Programme in the Social Sector and its Impact on Women*, eds. P. Parenzee and D. Budlender (Johannesburg: Heinrich Boll Foundation, Southern Africa, 2016), 11–34, https://za.boell.org/sites/default/files/hb_final_ebook_1.pdf.

163 V. Ranchod and N. Finn, *Estimating the Effects of South Africa's Youth Employment Tax Incentive – An Update*, SALDRU Working Paper 152 (Cape Town: Southern Africa Labour and Development Research Unit, University of Cape Town, 2015).

164 C. Meth, *Employer of Last Resort? South Africa's Expanded Public Works Programme (EPWP)*, Working Paper 58 (Cape Town: SALDRU, 2011), https://www.opensaldru.uct.ac.za/bitstream/handle/11090/59/2011_58.pdf?sequence=1.

165 Estlund, 'Three Big Ideas'.

166 P.R. Tcherneva, 'Universal Assurances in the Public Interest: Evaluating the Economic Viability of Basic Income and Job Guarantees', *International Journal of Environment, Workplace, and Employment* 2, no. 1 (2006): 69–88; Tcherneva, *Relative Macroeconomic Merits*.

167 A. Adelzadeh, et al., *COVID-19 and South Africa's Future Economic Outlook* (California: Applied Development Research Solutions, 2021).

168 Atkinson, 'The Case for a Participation Income'.

169 A. Painter and C. Thoung, *Creative Citizen, Creative State: The Principled and Pragmatic Case for a Universal Basic Income* (London: RSA, 2015), https://www.thersa.org/globalassets/reports/rsa_basic_income_20151216.pdf.

170 Similar to the Organisation Workshop, developed in Brazil and implemented in Latin America and Africa. R. Carmen and M. Sobrado, *A Future for the Excluded* (London: Zed Books, 2000).

171 C. Kagan, 'Universal Basic Income: Is it the Only Cornerstone of a Just Society?' *Steady State Manchester*, 15 March 2017, https://steadystatemanchester.net/2017/03/15/universal-basic-income-is-it-the-only-cornerstone-of-a-just-society/, p. 10.

CHAPTER 5   FINANCING A UNIVERSAL BASIC INCOME

1   R. Greenstein, *Commentary: Universal Basic Income May Sound Attractive but, if it Occurred, Would Likelier Increase Poverty than Reduce it* (Washington, DC: Center on Budget and Policy Priorities, 2019), 1, https://www.cbpp.org/sites/default/files/atoms/files/5-31-16bud.pdf.

2   Greenstein, *Commentary*, 1.

3   J. Wiederspan, et al., 'Expanding the Discourse on Antipoverty Policy: Reconsidering a Negative Income Tax', *Journal of Poverty* 19, no. 2 (2015), 219.

4   D. Tondani, 'Universal Basic Income and Negative Income Tax: Two Different Ways of Thinking Redistribution', *The Journal of Socio-Economics* 38, no. 2 (2009): 246–255.

5   UBI Works, *Recovering UBI Funding Options – 8 Ways to Pay for the Recovery UBI*, September 2020, https://docs.google.com/spreadsheets/d/1hujEV1pDz1_1GeqH dcwhkbPNgPdsFfpVKBCd7r2ReGU/edit#gid=1348990911. It proposes a combi-nation of financing options, including: (i) a land-value tax of 2.91% on the value of land (potential revenue of Can$130 billion); (ii) reducing federal corporate sub-sidies, removing tax loopholes and raising the carbon tax revenue to Can$75 (Can$ 43 billion); (iii) taxes on environmental degradation and use of commons (Can$27 billion); and (iv) a financial transactions tax (Can$7 billion), among other options.

6   P. Peaudry, *How Quantitative Easing Works. Speech Summary*, Bank of Canada, Ottawa, 10 December 2020, https://www.bankofcanada.ca/2020/12/how-quantitative-easing-works/.

7   S. Lansley, *Meeting the Economic and Livelihood Crisis: From a Recovery Basic Income to a Permanent Income Floor* (London: Compass, 2020), https://www.compassonline.org.uk/wp-content/uploads/2020/04/BasicIncomeFloor_SL_FINAL.pdf.

8   Lansley, *Economic and Livelihood Crisis*, 10–11.

9   Stats SA, *National Poverty Lines 2020*, Statistical Release P0310.1 (Pretoria: Statistics South Africa, 2020), http://www.statssa.gov.za/publications/P03101/P031012020.pdf. Unless otherwise indicated, these values are for 2020, the most recent year for which the relevant estimates were available.

10   National Treasury, *Budget Review 2020* (Pretoria: National Treasury, Republic of South Africa, 2020), 56.

11   Stats SA, *Mid-year Population Estimates 2019*, Statistical Release P0302 (Pretoria: Statistics South Africa, 2019), v & 10.

12   Indeed, a South African court in June 2020 ordered the government to include asylum seekers and special permit holders among people eligible to receive the COVID-19 social relief of distress grant. E. Ellis, 'Special Permit Holders and Asylum Seekers in SA Must Get Covid-19 Grant, Court Orders', *Daily Maverick*, 19 June 2020, https://www.dailymaverick.co.za/article/2020-06-19-refugees-and-asylum-seekers-in-sa-must-get-covid-19-grant-court-orders/ (paywall).

13   M. Lawhon and T. McCreary, 'Beyond Jobs vs Environment: On the Potential of a Universal Basic Income to Reconfigure Environmental Politics', *Antipode* 52, no. 2 (2020): 452–474.

14   S. Santens, 'How to Reform Welfare and Taxes to Provide Every American Citizen with a Basic Income', *Medium*, 5 June 2017, https://medium.com/economicsecproj/how-to-reform-welfare-and-taxes-to-provide-every-american-citizen-with-a-basic-income-bc67d3f4c2b8.

15   Including the #UBIGNOW campaign, Black Sash, Code Red, Pay the Grants, the COVID-19 People's Coalition, the Institute for Economic Justice, the Studies in Poverty and Inequality Institute, the Alternative Information and Development Centre, the Community Constituency of the National Economic, Development and Labour Council (NEDLAC), the Assembly of the Unemployed, the Budget

Justice Coalition, the Rural Women's Assembly, the Inyanda Land Movement, and the Cooperative and Policy Alternatives Centre.

16   C. Ramaphosa, *Nelson Mandela Memorial Lecture*, 18 July 2021, https://www. youtube.com/watch?v=AMVmGRf3O0c. Earlier in 2021, President Ramaphosa had tweeted a similar remark; the tweet was reportedly removed within a few hours. C. Hallink, 'South Africa's Time for a Basic Income Grant Has Come – but the ANC Is Still Apprehensive and Non-Committal', *Daily Maverick*, 2 February 2021, https://www.dailymaverick.co.za/article/2021-02-02-south-africas-time-for-a-basic-income-grant-has-come-but-the-anc-is-still- apprehensive-and-non-committal/.

17   R. Davis, 'BIG Is Best: Civil Society Campaign Highlights Urgency of Basic Income Grant after Recent Looting', *Daily Maverick*, 19 July 2021, https://www.dailymaverick.co.za/article/2021-07-19-big-is-best-civil-society-campaign-highlights-urgency-of-basic-income-grant-after-recent-looting/.

18   African National Congress Social Transformation Committee, *Basic Income Grants, Social Relief and Food Security* (Johannesburg: African National Congress, 2020); Institute for Economic Justice, *Introducing a Universal Basic Income Guarantee for South Africa: Towards Income Security for All*, Social Protection Series Policy Brief No. 1 (Johannesburg: Institute for Economic Justice, 2021).

19   Institute for Economic Justice, *Introducing a Universal Basic Income Guarantee*. Using 2019 data, the department estimated that paying a basic income to everyone aged 18–59 years would cost about R197 billion annually (calculated against the 2019 food poverty line of R560 per month), R285 billion (if set at the lower-bound poverty line) and R422 billion (at the upper-bound poverty line) (Institute for Economic Justice, *Introducing a Universal Basic Income Guarantee*, 5–6).

20   South African Government, *Green Paper on Comprehensive Social Security and Retirement Reform*, Government Gazette No. 45006, Vol. 674 (Gazetted 18 August 2021), 2021, https://www.gov.za/sites/default/files/gcis_document/202108/45006gon741.pdf.

21   South African Government, *Green Paper*, 57.

22   South African Government, *Green Paper*, 57.

23   South African Government, *Green Paper*.

24   M. Toyana, 'Minister Lindiwe Zulu Withdraws Social Security Green Paper after Public Backlash', *Daily Maverick*, 1 September 2021, https://www.dailymaverick.co.za/article/2021-09-01-minister-zulu-withdraws-social-security-green-paper-after-public-backlash/. The National Treasury went on to champion a highly restrictive 'family poverty grant', supposedly modelled on Brazil's *Bolsa Familia*, Mexico's *Prospera* and the Philippine's *Pantawid Pamilyang Pilipino* programmes. Institute for Economic Justice, *Designing a Basic Income Guarantee: Targeting, Universality and Other Considerations*, Social Protection Series Policy Brief No. 3 (Johannesburg: Institute for Economic Justice, 2021), https://www.iej.org.za/wp-content/uploads/2021/10/IEJ-policy-brief-UBIG-3_2.pdf. As outlined in a leaked draft of a government antipoverty strategy, the envisaged family grant would go to families with a monthly per capita income below the food poverty line (R624 per month in 2021). It would be paid at first to one million households and would then increase gradually until all eligible households were covered. Other cash transfers would gradually be consolidated with the family grant. L. Human, 'High Noon: Civil Society Coalition and National Treasury Heading for

Showdown over Crucial Income Grant', *Daily Maverick*, 29 October 2021, https://www.dailymaverick.co.za/article/2021-10-29-high-noon-civil-society-coalition-and-national-treasury-heading-for-showdown-over-crucial-income-grant/. Spirited reactions from civil society organisations and criticism from authors of the research saw the South African government back away from the family grant proposal, though perhaps only temporarily. H. Bassier and J. Budlender, 'Proposed Family Poverty Grant Is Excellent in Theory – but There Are Problems with its Implementation', *Daily Maverick*, 8 November 2021, https://www.dailymaverick.co.za/article/2021-11-08-proposed-family-poverty-grant-is-excellent-in-theory-but-there-are-problems-with-its-implementation/.

25   Expert Panel on Basic Income Support, *Final Report* (Pretoria: Department of Social Development, December 2021), https://www.dsd.gov.za/index.php/documents?task=download.send&id=356&catid=58&m=0.

26   Senona, et al., *Social Protection*.

27   Institute for Economic Justice, *Introducing a Universal Basic Income Guarantee*.

28   G. Bridgman, et al., *Hunger in South Africa during 2020: Results from Wave 2 of NIDS-CRAM* (Stellenbosch: National Income Dynamics Study, University of Stellenbosch, 2020), https://cramsurvey.org/wp-content/uploads/2020/09/3.-Bridgman-G.-Van-der-Berg-S.-_-Patel-L.-2020-Hunger-in-South-Africa-during-2020-Results-from-Wave-2-of-NIDS-CRAM.pdf.

29   Institute for Economic Justice, *Introducing a Universal Basic Income Guarantee*.

30   Institute for Economic Justice, *Introducing a Universal Basic Income Guarantee*.

31   Institute for Economic Justice, *Introducing a Universal Basic Income Guarantee*, 18.

32   National Treasury, *Budget Review 2020*, iv–v.

33   In these scenarios, the bottom income quintiles would target the beneficiaries, while the top quintiles would bear the overall cost of the new payments, directly and indirectly. The payments would be as fiscally neutral as possible, with funding occurring mainly through a range of tax measures (a land tax, wealth tax, financial transaction tax, income tax, export duties, and so on). The bottom two quintiles would receive the payment with no changes to their income and wealth tax liabilities. Individuals in the third quintile who receive the payment would return an equivalent amount via adjusted income and wealth tax liabilities. People in the top two quintiles receiving the payment would return more than the equivalent amount via income and wealth tax adjustments.

34   The Expert Panel convened by the Department of Social Development in 2021 made a similar projection. It also found that income inequality, as measured by the Gini coefficient, would improve significantly, from 0.65 to 0.55. Expert Panel on Basic Income Support, *Final Report*, 173.

35   Applied Development Research Solutions, 'Fiscally Neutral Basic Income Grant Scenarios: Economic and Development Impacts', *The Bridge* no. 7 (May 2021); A. Adelzadeh, 'Preliminary Modelling Results of a Basic Income Grant in South Africa', presentation to #UBIG Workshop, 29 January 2021.

36   Senona, et al., *Social Protection*.

37   Even the payment process, which relied in part on a malfunctioning national post office service (even though many applicants had provided banking details), was shambolic, with many recipients camping out overnight in front of post office

branches in the hope of making it to the front of the queue before the cash ran out (Senona, et al., *Social Protection*).

38   P. le Roux, 'Financing a Universal Income Grant in South Africa', *Social Dynamics* 28, no. 2 (2003): 98–121.

39   J. Seekings and H. Matisonn, *The Continuing Politics of Basic Income in South Africa*, Working Paper 286 (Cape Town: Centre for Social Science Research, University of Cape Town, 2010), 24.

40   Le Roux, 'Financing a Universal Income Grant', 105.

41   BIG Financing Reference Group, *Breaking the Poverty Trap: Financing a Basic Income Grant in South Africa* (Cape Town: BIG Financing Reference Group, 2004), 24.

42   Institute for Economic Justice, *Financing Options for a Universal Basic Income in South Africa*, Social Protection Series Policy Brief No. 2 (Johannesburg: Institute for Economic Justice, 2021), https://www.iej.org.za/wp-content/uploads/2021/08/IEJ-policy-brief-UBIG-july2021_3.pdf.

43   Detailed descriptions of each financing source are available (Institute for Economic Justice, *Financing Options*).

44   Fiscal policy in South Africa currently does not favour ring-fencing specific tax revenues for specific sectors or purposes. There is no insurmountable reason why this policy cannot be suspended in the case of a social security tax or a carbon tax.

45   K. Widerquist and M. Howard, eds., *Alaska's Permanent Fund Dividend: Examining its Suitability as a Model* (New York: Palgrave Macmillan, 2012).

46   Y. Varoufakis, 'The Universal Right to Capital Income', *Project Syndicate*, 31 October 2016, https://www.project-syndicate.org/commentary/basic-income-funded-by-capital-income-by-yanis-varoufakis-2016-10?barrier=accesspaylog.

47   G. Palma, 'Homogeneous Middles vs. Heterogeneous Tails, and the End of the "Inverted-U": The Share of the Rich Is What it's All About', *Development and Change* 42, no. 1 (2011): 87–153.

48   This would assume a 30% evasion rate and 20% stock value depreciation.

49   This would be levied on the buying/selling of foreign currency for domestic currency, and it would be collected at point of settlement. South Africa does not yet have such a tax (Institute for Economic Justice, *Financing Options*).

50   Davis Tax Committee, *Report on Feasibility of a Wealth Tax in South Africa* (Johannesburg: Davis Tax Committee, 2018), http://www.sataxguide.co.za/wp-content/uploads/2018/05/20180329-Final-DTC-Wealth-Tax-Report-To-Minister.pdf.

51   For example, between 1995 and 2015, the South African government allocated R477 billion (in 2015/16 rands) to support industrial development initiatives, mainly in manufacturing. About 60% of that support went to multinational corporations in the capital-intensive automotive sector. Formal employment levels in the manufacturing sector overall shrank by more than 20% during that period as companies used at least some of the support to shift to capital-intensive production, largely at the expense of low- and semi-skilled jobs. The 1.43 million people employed in the manufacturing sector in 1994 decreased to 1.1 million in 2014; in the automotive sector, employment numbers fell to levels last seen in 1970. Parliamentary Budget Office, *The Costs and Outcomes of Industrial Development Initiatives 1994/95–2014/15* (Cape Town: Parliament of the Republic of South Africa, 2016).

52   Institute for Economic Justice, *Financing Options*.

53   Davis Tax Committee, *Feasibility of a Wealth Tax*.

54   Corporate taxes do not address that reality. They essentially remunerate the state (very partially, in most instances) for the infrastructure and services it provides (including education, security, healthcare, transport, research and development, and more), all of which establish the conditions in which companies operate.

55   Varoufakis, 'Universal Right'.

56   M. Bruenig, 'Social Wealth Fund for America', People's Policy Project, 2019, https://www.peoplespolicyproject.org/projects/social-wealth-fund/.

57   Anon, 'JSE Markets' Weekly Statistics', *Market Statistics, JSE*, 28 August 2018.

58   Bruenig, 'Social Wealth Fund'.

59   Economic rent can be defined as the difference between the 'reward' a company or other economic actor appropriates and their contribution to creating that additional value. This can occur 'due to the ownership of a scarce asset, the creation of monopolistic conditions that enable rising returns in a specific sector … or policy decisions that assign certain legal rights'. M. Mazzucato, et al., *Theorising and Mapping Modern Economic Rents*, UCL Institute for Innovation and Public Purpose, Working Paper Series (IIPP WP 2020-13), 2020, 3, https://www.ucl.ac.uk/bartlett/public-purpose/wp2020-13.

60   Mazzucato, et al., *Theorising and Mapping*.

61   Institute for Economic Justice, *Financing Options*.

62   The tax which James Tobin proposed in 1972 was intended to penalise short-term currency speculation; it later came to be understood as a tax on any short-term financial transactions. It is not a particularly 'modern' intervention: the 'stamp duty', which dates to 1694 in England, is a kind of tax on financial transactions.

63   J. Bivens and H. Blair, *A Financial Transaction Tax Would Help Ensure Wall Street Works for Main Street* (Washington, DC: Economic Policy Institute, 2016), https://files.epi.org/pdf/110651.pdf.

64   Bivens and Blair, *Financial Transaction Tax*.

65   Bivens and Blair, *Financial Transaction Tax*. As to the tax rate, legislation introduced in the US Senate in 2015 proposed a rate of 0.5% for all stock transactions, for example. A similar rate is levied in the United Kingdom (by way of a stamp duty), though the large number of exemptions reduces the funds raised (only about 20% of stock trading is taxable). There, it raised 0.3%–0.5% of GDP from 2000–2008, though Robert Pollin and colleagues have calculated that fewer exemptions would increase this to 0.7% of GDP. They have also proposed a sliding scale for bonds, futures, options and other derivative instruments. For bonds, the rate could be 0.01% for every year to maturity (i.e. 0.1% for a 10-year bond). The impact of the tax would be greatest on short-term speculation, which accounts for a majority of financial market activity. If set too low, however, an FTT would neither raise large amounts of revenue, nor discourage excessive speculative trading. R. Pollin, et al., 'The Revenue Potential of a Financial Transaction Tax for U.S. Financial Markets', *International Review of Applied Economics* 32, no. 6 (2018): 772–806.

66   D. Baker, 'The Economics and Politics of Financial Transactions Taxes and Wealth Taxes', *Counterpunch*, 14 October 2019, https://www.counterpunch.org/2019/10/14/the-economics-and-politics-of-financial-transactions-taxes-and-wealth-taxes/.

67   BNY Mellon, *Financial Transaction Taxes: A Global Perspective* (New York: BNY Mellon, 2019), https://www.bnymellon.com/content/dam/bnymellon/documents/pdf/emea/ftt-globalperspective-brochure-03-2018.pdf.

68   Pollin, et al., 'Revenue Potential', 783.

69   Varoufakis, 'Universal Right'.

70   In the United States, the value of stock market trading was about 1.2 times larger than productive investments in the 1970s; it has been at least 22 times greater since the late 1990s. There has been no associated increase in the share of productive investments relative to GDP or to the rate of GDP growth (Pollin, et al., 'Revenue Potential'). Instead, the 500 largest companies on Standard & Poor's 500 stock index spent approximately US\$8.3 trillion since 2000 buying their own stock to hoist the price – over half their profits and equal to almost 20% of total business investment, as Doug Henwood has detailed. D. Henwood, 'The GameStop Bubble Is a Lesson in the Absurdity and Uselessness of the Stock Market', *Jacobin*, 21 January 2021, https://www.jacobinmag.com/2021/01/gamestop-stock-market-reddit.

71   Discussed in greater detail in the 'What kind of macroeconomic strategy is needed?' section of Chapter 6.

72   L.E. Burman, et al., 'Financial Transaction Taxes in Theory and Practice', *National Tax Journal* 69, no. 1 (2016): 171–216.

73   A. Pekanov and M. Schratzenstaller, *A Global Financial Transaction Tax: Theory, Practice and Potential Revenues*, Working Paper 582 (Vienna: Austrian Institute of Economic Research, 2019), https://www.wifo.ac.at/jart/prj3/wifo/resources/person_dokument/person_dokument.jart?publikationsid=61805&mime_type=application/pdf.

74   Pollin, et al., 'Revenue Potential'.

75   Bivens and Blair, *Financial Transaction Tax*, 7.

76   According to Bivens and Blair, 'current elasticity estimates are based on FTTs that are not particularly well designed to discourage arbitrage among asset classes or among national trading exchanges' (*Financial Transaction Tax*, 3).

77   Pollin, et al., 'Revenue Potential.

78   Burman, et al., 'Financial Transaction Taxes'.

79   Pollin, et al., 'Revenue Potential'.

80   Greenstein, *Commentary*.

81   S. Carattini, 'How to Win Public Support for a Global Carbon Tax', *Nature* 565, no. 7739 (2019): 289–291.

82   A carbon tax would need to be accompanied by mechanisms that protect low-income households against possible electricity and other price increases.

83   South African Government, *President Cyril Ramaphosa Signs 2019 Carbon Tax Act into Law*, 2019, https://www.gov.za/speeches/publication-2019-carbon-tax-act-26-may-2019-0000.

84   High-Level Commission on Carbon Prices, *Report of the High-Level Commission on Carbon Prices* (Washington, DC: World Bank, 2017), https://www.carbonpricingleadership.org/report-of-the-highlevel-commission-on-carbon-prices/.

85   South African Revenue Service, *Carbon Tax*, 2020, https://www.sars.gov.za/ClientSegments/Customs-Excise/Excise/Environmental-Levy-Products/Pages/Carbon-Tax.aspx.

86   Carattini, 'How to Win Public Support', 290.

87   J. van Heerden, et al., 'The Economic and Environmental Effects of a Carbon Tax in South Africa: A Dynamic CGE Modelling Approach', *South African Journal of Economic Management Science* 19, no. 5 (2016): 714–732.

88   Since the supply of land is fixed, a land tax also would not affect economic efficiency.

89 Davis Tax Committee, *Feasibility of a Wealth Tax.*

90 A. Coleman and A. Grimes, 'Fiscal, Distributional and Efficiency Impacts of Land and Property Taxes', *New Zealand Economic Papers* 44, no. 2 (2010), 43.

91 M. Kalkuhl, et al., 'Can Land Taxes Foster Sustainable Development? An Assessment of Fiscal, Distributional and Implementation Issues', *Land Use Policy* 78 (2018): 338–352.

92 Davis Tax Committee, *Feasibility of a Wealth Tax.*

93 Davis Tax Committee, *Feasibility of a Wealth Tax.*

94 Kalkuhl, et al., 2018. In addition to municipal property rates, immovable property in South Africa is potentially also taxed through a capital gains tax (in reality a tax on deferred income), and a transfer duty or VAT payable by the purchaser of immovable property.

CHAPTER 6   THE POLITICS AND ECONOMICS OF A UNIVERSAL BASIC INCOME

1 T. Mkandawire, *Social Policy in a Development Context*, Social Policy and Development Programme Paper No. 7 (Geneva: United Nations Research Institute for Social Development, June 2001), 28, https://www.files.ethz.ch/isn/102709/7.pdf.

2 D. Zamora, 'The Case against a Basic Income', *Jacobin*, December 2017, https://www.jacobinmag.com/2017/12/universal-basic-income-inequality-work; P. Sloman, 'Universal Basic Income in British Politics, 1918–2018: From a "Vagabond's Wage" to a Global Debate', *Journal of Social Policy* 47, no. 3 (2018): 625–642.

3 D. Zamora and A. Jäger, 'Historicizing Basic Income: Response to David Zeglen', *Lateral* 8, no. 1 (2019), https://csalateral.org/forum/universal-basic-income/historicizing-basic-income-zamora-jager/.

4 Zamora and Jäger, 'Historicizing Basic Income'; A. Gourevitch and L. Stanczyk, 'The Basic Income Illusion', *Catalyst: A Critical Journal of Theory and Strategy* 1, no. 4 (2018): 151–177.

5 Zamora and Jäger, 'Historicizing Basic Income'.

6 This surplus is produced principally by appropriating value from the exploited labour of workers and from the 'gifts' of social reproductive labour (which capital does not remunerate) and 'cheap nature'.

7 The concept of a 'surplus' seems relevant in another respect, too. Following Marx, we can think of 'surplus populations' as those workers who are without regular access to paid work and who, for significant stretches of time, are superfluous to capital's demand for labour, yet are intrinsic to capitalist production. In South Africa, vast numbers of people fit this description. Surplus to the requirements of capital, these populations do not group around any unifying (class) identity. A UBI might offer a focal point for their collective claims-staking, as rights-bearing members of society. K. Marx, *Capital, Volume 1* (London: Penguin, 1990 [1867]).

8 This also underpins a key principle of the neoliberal era: that the responsibility for building a livelihood and the risk of failing to do so rest fundamentally with individuals; they are not to be shared or socialised across society through various systems of redistribution. That principle, of course, does not apply to the capitalist class. Its risks and failures are socialised, through cutting jobs, abandoning debt through bankruptcy, or laying claim to state bailouts funded from the public fiscus.

9   L. Omarjee, 'Basic Income Grant for SA Not "Radical" but Necessary, Says ex Goldman Sachs CEO', *News24*, 4 October 2021, https://www.news24.com/fin24/economy/basic-income-grant-for-sa-not-radical-but-necessary-says-ex-goldman-sachs-ceo-20211004.

10   R. Greenstein, *Commentary: Universal Basic Income May Sound Attractive but, if it Occurred, Would Likelier Increase Poverty than Reduce it* (Washington, DC: Center on Budget and Policy Priorities, 2019), https://www.cbpp.org/sites/default/files/atoms/files/5-31-16bud.pdf.

11   R. McKenzie and S. Mohamed, 'The Political Economy of South Africa and its Interaction with Processes of Financialisation', in *Studies in Financial Systems No. 15: The South African Financial System*, ed. S. Mohamed (Financialisation, Economy, Society and Sustainable Development (FESSUD), SOAS University of London, 2017), 11–25, https://eprints.kingston.ac.uk/id/eprint/37224/1/McKenzie-R-37224.pdf; F. Barchiesi, 'Liberation of, Through or from Work? Postcolonial Africa and the Problem with "Job Creation" in the Global Crisis', *Interface* 4, no. 2 (2012): 230–253; H. Marais, *South Africa Pushed to the Limit: The Political Economy of Change* (London: Zed Books, 2011).

12   H. Marais, 'Swept Along: The Left in Post-Apartheid South Africa', in *New Leaders, New Dawns? South Africa and Zimbabwe under Cyril Ramaphosa and Emmerson Mnangagwa*, eds. B. Rutherford, C. Brown and D. Moore (Montreal: McGill-Queen's University Press, in press): 138–178.

13   S. Mohamed, 'The Political Economy of Accumulation in South Africa: Resource Extraction, Financialization, and Capital Flight as Barriers to Investment and Employment Growth', PhD diss., University of Massachusetts Amherst, 2019, https://scholarworks.umass.edu/dissertations_2/1533; V. Padayachee and R. van Niekerk, *Shadow of Liberation: Contestation and Compromise in the Economic and Social Policy of the African National Congress, 1943–1996* (Johannesburg: Wits University Press, 2019); Marais, *South Africa*.

14   A less dramatic breakthrough occurred in Uganda, as well. There, the government agreed to introduce a social pension despite strong resistance from its finance ministry, which eventually yielded to a transnational coalition that brought together international donors, other government departments and civil society organisations. The coalition succeeded in presenting the pension proposal both as a necessary welfare intervention and as a pragmatic step to temper social and political disquiet. The achievement should not be oversold, though. The pension payment is very small, reaches a tiny proportion of Uganda's poor, and appears to have been used as part of a clientelist strategy to shore up political power. But it is a reminder that political dynamics ultimately determine the scope for social policy shifts. S. Hickey and B. Bukenya, 'The Politics of Promoting Social Cash Transfers in Uganda: The Potential and Pitfalls of "Thinking and Working Politically"', *Development Policy Review* 39, no. S1 (2021): 1–20, https://doi.org/10.1111/dpr.12474.

15   L. Lawson, *Side Effects: The Story of AIDS in South Africa* (Cape Town: Double Storey Books, 2008).

16   Department for International Development, *Social Transfers and Chronic Poverty: Emerging Evidence and the Challenge Ahead* (London: Department for International Development, 2005), http://epri.org.za/wp-content/uploads/2016/07/DFID2005Social TransfersAndChronicPoverty.pdf; World Bank, *Managing Risk, Promoting*

Growth: Developing Systems for Social Protection in Africa: World Bank's Africa Social Protection Strategy 2012–2022 (Washington, DC: World Bank, 2010).

17 United Nations, *Transforming Our World: The 2030 Agenda for Sustainable Development*, Resolution adopted by the General Assembly on 25 September 2015, A/RES/70/1 (New York: United Nations, 2015), https://www.un.org/ga/search/view_doc.asp?symbol=A/RES/70/1&Lang=E.

18 J. Hanlon, et al., *Just Give Money to the Poor* (Sterling, VA: Kumarian Books, 2010).

19 S. Hickey and J. Seekings, 'Who Should Get What, How and Why? DFID and the Transnational Politics of Social Cash Transfers in Sub-Saharan Africa', in *The Politics of Social Protection in Eastern and Southern Africa*, eds. S. Hickey, T. Lavers, M. Nino-Zarazua and J. Seekings (Oxford: Oxford University Press, 2020): 249–275.

20 Marais, *South Africa*.

21 S. Friedman and S. Mottiar, 'Seeking the High Ground: The Treatment Action Campaign and the Politics of Morality', in *Voices of Protest: Social Movements in Post-Apartheid South Africa*, eds. R. Ballard, A. Habib and I. Valodia (Pietermaritzburg: UKZN Press, 2006): 23–44.

22 J. Seekings and H. Matisonn, *The Continuing Politics of Basic Income in South Africa*, Working Paper 286 (Cape Town: Centre for Social Science Research, University of Cape Town, 2010), 18.

23 K. Alexander and N. Bohler-Muller, *UJ-HSRC COVID-19 Democracy Survey: Summary National Results, Round 2* (Johannesburg: Centre for Social Change, University of Johannesburg, October 2020), 7, http://www.hsrc.ac.za/uploads/pageContent/12241/Coronavirus%20Impact%20Survey%20Round%202%20summary%20national%20results.pdf.

24 Human Sciences Research Council, *South African Social Attitudes Survey (SASAS) 2016* (Cape Town: HSRC Press, 2016), cited in C. Pienaar, et al. The Big Question: COVID-19 and Policy Support for a Basic Income Grant. Policy Brief (Cape Town: Human Sciences Research Council, March 2021), 9. The level of support was similar to that found in Belgium, Hungary, Israel, the Russian Federation and Slovenia in the European Social Survey Round 8. European Social Survey, *The Past, Present and Future of European Welfare Attitudes: Topline Results from Round 8 of the European Social Survey* (London: European Social Survey, 2018), https://www.europeansocialsurvey.org/docs/findings/ESS8_toplines_issue_8_welfare.pdf.

25 M. Moosa and J. Patel, *South Africans Support Social Grants, but Say Work at Any Wage Beats Unemployment*, Afrobarometer Dispatch 364 (Johannesburg: Institute for Justice and Reconciliation, 2020), 2–6.

26 M. Leibbrandt, et al., *Employment and Inequality Outcomes in South Africa* (Cape Town: Southern Africa Labour and Development Research Unit and School of Economics, University of Cape Town, 2015).

27 S. Friedman, 'The People Can Vote – but Not Decide?', *Democracy Development Program blog*, 16 August 2021, https://ddp.org.za/blog/2021/08/16/the-people-can-vote-but-not-decide/.

28 S. Skiti, 'Godongwana Hints a Plan to Invest in Employment for "Young Black Kids"', *Sunday Times*, 8 August 2021, https://www.timeslive.co.za/sunday-times/

news/2021-08-08-godongwana-hints-at-plan-to-invest-in-employment-for-young-black-kids/ (paywall).

29   As outlined in Department for Women, Youth and Persons with Disabilities, *National Youth Policy 2020–2030* (Pretoria: Department for Women, Youth and Persons with Disabilities, 2021), https://www.gov.za/sites/default/files/gcis_document/202103/nationalyouthpolicy.pdf.

30   S. Hall, 'The Problem of Ideology: Marxism without Guarantees', in *Stuart Hall: Critical Dialogues in Cultural Studies*, eds. D. Morley and K-H. Chen (London: Routledge, 1996): 26–46.

31   K. Weeks, 'A Feminist Case for Basic Income: An Interview with Kathi Weeks', *Critical Legal Thinking*, 22 August 2016, https://criticallegalthinking.com/2016/08/22/feminist-case-basic-income-interview-kathi-weeks/.

32   G. Labica, *Robespierre – une politique de la philosophie* (Paris: Presses Universitaires de France, 1990), 54–55.

33   This framing is not far removed from the principle that underpins taxation: at its core, tax systems assume that society generates a surplus of wealth, in excess of what significant sections of society can reasonably consider necessary for a dignified and fulfilling life. D. Zeglen, 'Basic Income as Ideology from Below', *Lateral* 7.2 (2018), https://csalateral.org/forum/universal-basic-income/basic-income-ideology-from-below-zeglen/.

34   It is in harmony, for example, with the 1955 Freedom Charter and its neglected precursor, the African National Congress' 1943 African Claims document (Padayachee and Van Niekerk, *Shadow of Liberation*).

35   Y. Varoufakis, 'Why the Universal Basic Income Is a Necessity', lecture to Gottlieb Duttweiler Institute, 30 April 2017, https://www.youtube.com/watch?v=22eQ9iLBfY4.

36   J. Ferguson, *Give a Man a Fish: Reflections on the New Politics of Distribution* (Durham, NC: Duke University Press, 2015), 178.

37   Presenting a UBI as a kind of reparation also holds appeal, though it can be problematic. If the UBI demand is framed in the context of colonial (and, in South Africa, apartheid) history as a form of redress, it becomes difficult to assign the claim to everybody. A small but significant proportion of South Africa's population historically has seized much more than any 'rightful share' – and it continues to do so. Presenting a UBI as a mechanism for retroactive redistribution raises questions about its universality. Income tax policy can be used to tax back the payment from non-poor recipients – but that would involve withdrawing an ostensible 'reparation' from historically disadvantaged citizens who are now better off.

38   D. Gibson, et al., 'The State of Our Environment: Safeguarding the Foundation for Development', in *State of the Nation: South Africa 2008*, eds. P. Kagwanja and K. Kondlo (Cape Town: HSRC Press, 2008): 178–200; J. Cock, 'Connecting the Red, Brown and Green: The Environmental Justice Movement in South Africa', in *Voices of Protest: Social Movements in Post-Apartheid South Africa*, eds. R. Ballard, A. Habib and I. Valodia (Pietermaritzburg: UKZN Press, 2006): 203–224.

39   For some critics, this puts the cart before the horse. They argue that a generous UBI is impossible unless control of the surplus is wrested from capital, which implies that a subsistence-level UBI is unattainable under capitalism. In David Zeglen's ('Basic Income as Ideology') summary, 'capitalism's ability to dominate

the organization of the surplus negates movements towards egalitarianism based on wealth redistributions like the basic income'.

40 Government of South Africa, *The Constitution of South Africa, Chapter 2: Bill of Rights* (Pretoria: Government of South Africa, 1996).

41 South African Human Rights Commission, *Basic Income Grant Policy Brief* (Johannesburg: South African Human Rights Commission, 2018), 10, https://www.sahrc.org.za/home/21/files/A%20Policy%20Brief%20on%20a%20Basic%20Income%20Grant%202017-2018.pdf.

42 Institute for Economic Justice, *Introducing a Universal Basic Income Guarantee for South Africa: Towards Income Security for All*, Social Protection Series Policy Brief No. 1 (Johannesburg: Institute for Economic Justice, 2021).

43 South African Human Rights Commission, *Basic Income Grant Policy Brief*.

44 B. Fine, 'Can South Africa Be a Developmental State?', in *Constructing a Democratic Developmental State in South Africa: Potentials and Challenges*, ed. O. Edigheji (Cape Town: HSRC Press, 2010), 169–182; W. Freund, 'South Africa as a Developmental State', *Africanus* 37, no. 2 (2007): 170–175; W. Freund, 'Post-Apartheid South Africa under ANC Rule: A Response to John S Saul on South Africa', *Transformation* 89 (2015): 50–75.

45 C. Johnson, *MITI and the Japanese Miracle: The Growth of Industrial Policy, 1925–1975* (Stanford, CA: Stanford University Press, 1982).

46 Mkandawire, *Social Policy*; M. Woo-Cuming, ed., *The Developmental State* (New York: Cornell University Press, 1999); P. Evans, *Embedded Autonomy: States and Industrial Transformation* (Princeton, NJ: Princeton University Press, 1995).

47 Evans, *Embedded Autonomy*.

48 Evans, *Embedded Autonomy*; Mkandawire, *Social Policy*. A range of other factors and conditions were also relevant: the geopolitical context, the diminished political power of landed elites which made possible agrarian reforms (G. Hart, *Disabling Globalization: Places of Power in Post-Apartheid South Africa* (Pietermaritzburg: UKZN Press, 2002)), a capacity to repress labour (T. Mkandawire, 'Transformative Social Policy and Innovation in Developing Countries', *European Journal for Development Research* 19, no. 1 (2007): 13–29), limited penetration of national economies by multinational, especially financial, capital (P. Evans, *In Search of the 21st Century Developmental State* (Berkeley, CA: University of California Press, 2007)), and a strong emphasis on basic education, especially in the applied sciences (Freund, 'South Africa as a Developmental State').

49 The 2012 National Development Plan, for example, was described as an instrument for creating a 'capable and developmental state able to intervene to correct our historical inequities', according to the foreword (written by Finance Minister Trevor Manuel). See Government of South Africa, *National Development Plan: Our Future, Make it Work* (Pretoria: Government of South Africa, 2012), 1, https://www.gov.za/sites/default/files/gcis_document/201409/ndp-2030-our-future-make-it-workr.pdf.

50 Evans, *In Search*, 24.

51 C. Olver, *How to Steal a City: The Battle for Nelson Mandela Bay* (Johannesburg: Jonathan Ball, 2017); R. Southall, 'Democracy at Risk? Politics and Governance under the ANC', *The ANNALS of the American Academy of Political and Social Science* 652 (2014): 48–69; R. Southall, 'The Coming Crisis of Zuma's ANC: The Party State Confronts Fiscal Crisis', *Review of African Political Economy* 43, no. 147 (2016): 73–88.

52 K. von Holdt, 'Nationalism, Bureaucracy and the Developmental State: The South African Case', *South African Review of Sociology* 41, no. 1 (2014): 4–27.

53 P. Evans, 'The Capability Enhancing Developmental State: Concepts and National Trajectories', in *The South Korean Development Experience: Beyond Aid*, ed. E. Kim (London: Palgrave, 2010), 83–110.

54 P. Evans and P. Heller, 'Human Development, State Transformation and the Politics of the Developmental State', in *The Oxford Handbook of Transformations of the State*, eds. S. Leibfried, E. Huber, M. Lange, J.D. Levy and J.D. Stephens (Oxford: Oxford University Press, 2013): 691–713.

55 Evans, 'The Capability Enhancing Developmental State', 90.

56 Evans and Heller, 'Human Development'.

57 Evans, 'The Capability Enhancing Developmental State'.

58 Evans and Heller, 'Human Development', 10.

59 V. Padayachee, 'Can Progressive Macroeconomic Policy Address Growth and Employment while Reducing Inequality in South Africa?', *The Economic and Labour Relations Review* 30, no. 1 (2019): 3.

60 A. Saad-Filho, *For a Just and Democratic Development Approach to Macro-Economic Policy to Advance the Deep Just Transition*, Policy Brief (Johannesburg: Emancipatory Futures Studies Inter- and Transdisciplinary Project, 2020); J.M. Fournier, *The Positive Effect of Public Investment on Potential Growth*, OECD Economics Department Working Paper 1347 (Paris: OECD Publishing, 2016), https://www.oecd-ilibrary.org/economics/the-positive-effect-of-public-investment-on-potential-growth_15e400d4-en?crawler=true. This would include renewable electricity generation and overhauling transmission lines, retrofitting building stock, subsidising building insulation, public transport and more.

61 Padayachee, 'Progressive Macroeconomic Policy', 4.

62 Padayachee and Van Niekerk, *Shadow of Liberation*; Marais, *South Africa*.

63 In South Africa's case, long-term investment capital tends to be sourced from retained earnings or the securities markets, not from banks and other financial institutions. The latter specialise in extending short-term credit, home mortgages and vehicle lease arrangements. S. Mohamed, 'The State of the South African Economy', in *New South Africa Review 1. 2010: Development or Decline?* eds. J. Daniel, P. Naidoo, D. Pillay and R. Southall (Johannesburg: Wits University Press, 2010), 39–64.

64 Mohamed, 'Political Economy of Accumulation'; McKenzie and Mohamed, 'Political Economy of South Africa'; S. Ansari, 'The Neo-Liberal Incentive Structure and the Absence of the Developmental State in Post-Apartheid South Africa', *African Affairs* 116, no. 463 (2017): 206–232.

65 Padayachee, 'Progressive Macroeconomic Policy'; Mohamed, 'Political Economy of Accumulation'. Minor adjustments have been made, for example in the 2006 Accelerated and Shared Growth Initiative (AsgiSA), the 2011 New Growth Path Framework and the 2012 National Development Plan, but none has shifted the key principles and trajectory of macroeconomic policy. S. Mohamed, 'Financialization of the South African Economy', *Development* 59, no. 1–2 (2016): 137–142.

66 G. Isaacs and A. Kaltenbrunner, 'Financialization and Liberalization: South Africa's New Forms of External Vulnerability', *Competition and Change* 22, no. 4 (2018): 437–463.

67 Isaacs and Kaltenbrunner, 'Financialization and Liberalization', 445 & 446.

68 G. Epstein, 'Introduction: Financialization and the World Economy', in *Financialization and the World Economy*, ed. G. Epstein (Cheltenham: Edward Elgar, 2005), 3–16; J. Crotty, *The Effects of Increased Product Market Competition and Changes in Financial Markets on the Performance of Nonfinancial Corporations in the Neoliberal Era*, PERI Working Paper 44 (Amherst, MA: Political Economy Research Institute, 2003).

69 Mohamed, 'Political Economy of Accumulation', 203.

70 K. Hart and V. Padayachee, 'A History of South African Capitalism in National and Global Perspective', *Transformation: Critical Perspectives on Southern Africa* 81/82 (2013): 55–85.

71 Isaacs and Kaltenbrunner, 'Financialization and Liberalization', 457.

72 S. Ashman, et al., 'The Crisis in South Africa: Neoliberalism, Financialization and Uneven and Combined Development', *Socialist Register* 47 (2011): 174–195; Mohamed, 'Financialization'; Isaacs and Kaltenbrunner, 'Financialization and Liberalization'.

73 Isaacs and Kaltenbrunner, 'Financialization and Liberalization'.

74 Mohamed, 'Political Economy of Accumulation'; Marais, *South Africa*.

75 I. Alami, 'Capital Accumulation and Capital Controls in South Africa: A Class Perspective', *Review of African Political Economy* 45, no. 156 (2017): 223–249; Hart and Padayachee, 'History of South African Capitalism'.

76 Padayachee and Van Niekerk, *Shadow of Liberation*; S. Ashman and B. Fine, 'Neo-Liberalism, Varieties of Capitalism, and the Shifting Contours of South Africa's Financial System', *Transformation: Critical Perspectives on Southern Africa* 81/82 (2013): 144–178.

77 Freund, 'South Africa as a Developmental State'; Freund, 'Post-Apartheid South Africa'.

78 Freund, 'Post-Apartheid South Africa', 64–65.

79 Ansari, 'Neo-Liberal Incentive Structure'.

80 Among other activities, the Forum sells a range of 'memberships' that grant subscribers access to ministers and key policymakers, along with opportunities to 'give input' into policymaking discussions.

81 Ansari, 'Neo-Liberal Incentive Structure'; Alami, 'Capital Accumulation'.

82 Padayachee and Van Niekerk, *Shadow of Liberation*. In mid-2021, for example, opposition from the National Treasury led to the Department of Social Development withdrawing a set of gazetted recommendations for the creation of a social security fund that would be financed through the tax system.

83 M. Swilling, 'Can Economic Policy Escape State Capture?', *New Agenda: South African Journal of Social and Economic Policy* 72 (2019): 24–27.

84 Padayachee, 'Progressive Macroeconomic Policy', 11.

85 Macro-Economic Research Group, *Making Democracy Work: A Framework for Macroeconomic Policy in South Africa* (Bellville: Centre for Development Studies, University of the Western Cape, 1993).

86 Padayachee and Van Niekerk, *Shadow of Liberation*; V. Padayachee and J. Sender, 'Vella Pillay: Revolutionary Activism and Economic Policy Analysis', *Journal of Southern African Studies* 44, no. 1 (2018): 149–165; W. Freund, 'Swimming against the Tide: The Macro-Economic Research Group in the South African Transition 1991–94', *Review of African Political Economy* 40, no. 138 (2013): 519–536.

87   Macro-Economic Research Group, *Making Democracy Work*.

88   Saad-Filho, *Just and Democratic Development Approach*, 12.

89   Saad-Filho, *Just and Democratic Development Approach*, 12.

90   J. Williamson, 'What Washington Means by Policy Reform', in *Latin American Adjustment: How Much Has Happened?* ed. J. Williamson (Washington, DC: Institute for International Economics, 1990), 7–20.

91   J. Williamson, 'What Should the World Bank Think about the Washington Consensus?', *The World Bank Research Observer* 15, no. 2 (2000): 251–264.

92   S. Mohamed, 'Let's Listen to Heterodox Economists for a Change', *New Frame*, 25 February 2021, https://www.newframe.com/lets-listen-to-heterodox-economists-for-a-change/; Padayachee, 'Progressive Macroeconomic Policy'; V. Padayachee, 'Beyond the Fiscal Cliff? Some Questions for Reflection', *New Agenda* 70 (2018): 34–37.

93   A. Pekanov, *The New View on Fiscal Policy and its Implications for the European Monetary Union*, Working Paper 562 (Vienna: Austrian Institute of Economic Research, 2018), https://www.wifo.ac.at/jart/prj3/wifo/resources/person_dokument/person_dokument.jart?publikationsid=61037&mime_type=application/pdf; J. Furman, *The New View of Fiscal Policy and its Application*, VoxEU and CEPR, 2 November 2016, https://voxeu.org/article/new-view-fiscal-policy-and-its-application.

94   J.G. Gravelle and D.J. Marples, *Fiscal Policy and Recovery from the COVID-19 Recession*, Congressional Research Service Report R46460 (Washington, DC: Congressional Research Service, 2021), https://crsreports.congress.gov/product/pdf/R/R46460; S. Gechert, et al., 'Long-Term Effects of Fiscal Stimulus and Austerity in Europe', *Oxford Bulletin of Economics and Statistics* 81, no. 3 (2018): 647–666; O.J. Blanchard and D. Leigh, 'Effects of Fiscal Policy in Deep Recessions: Simple and Hopefully Credible Empirical Evidence', *American Economic Review: Papers & Proceedings* 103, no. 3 (2013): 117–120.

95   V. Gaspar, et al., *Macroeconomic Management When Policy Space Is Constrained: A Comprehensive, Consistent and Coordinated Approach to Economic Policy*, IMF Staff Discussion Note SDN/16/09 (Washington, DC: International Monetary Fund, 2016), https://www.imf.org/external/pubs/ft/sdn/2016/sdn1609.pdf.

96   M. Sachs, 'South Africa's Budget and the Absence of Social Solidarity', *New Frame*, 22 February 2021, https://www.newframe.com/sas-budget-and-the-absence-of-social-solidarity/.

97   M. Mbeki, et al., 'South Africa's Fiscal Cliff Barometer', *New Agenda* 70 (2018): 29–33.

98   Padayachee, 'Beyond the Fiscal Cliff?'

99   IMF, *World Economic Outlook Database*, January 2021, https://www.imf.org/en/Countries/ZAF.

100   US Congressional Budget Office, *Federal Debt: A Primer* (Washington, DC: United States Congress, March 2020), https://www.cbo.gov/publication/56309; US Congressional Budget Office, *The 2020 Long-Term Outlook* (Washington, DC: United States Congress, September 2020), https://www.cbo.gov/system/files/2020-09/56516-LTBO.pdf.

101   T. Herndon, et al., 'Does High Public Debt Consistently Stifle Economic Growth? A Critique of Reinhart and Rogoff', *Cambridge Journal of Economics* 38, no. 2 (2014): 257–279.

102 S. Kelton, *The Deficit Myth: Modern Monetary Theory and the Birth of the People's Economy* (New York: Public Affairs, 2020); Y. Nersisyan and L.R. Wray, 'Modern Money Theory and the Facts of Experience', *Cambridge Journal of Economics* 40, no. 5 (2016): 1297–1316.

103 Padayachee, 'Beyond the Fiscal Cliff?', 36.

104 Saad-Filho, *Just and Democratic Development Approach*; A. Amsden, 'Bringing Production Back in', *World Development* 25, no. 4 (1997): 469–480.

105 P. Carmody, 'Between Globalization and (Post) Apartheid: The Political Economy of Restructuring in South Africa', *Journal of Southern African Studies* 28, no. 2 (2002): 255–275.

106 I. Grabel, *When Things Don't Fall Apart: Global Financial Governance and Developmental Finance in an Age of Productive Incoherence* (Amherst, MA: MIT Press, 2018).

107 Several 'developing' economies have applied substantive controls on capital flows since the 2008 global financial crisis, and a number of hybrid national and regional financial institutions have been created (e.g. in Brazil and some Asian countries). This creates a more 'complex, decentralized, multi-tiered, pluripolar global financial system' and 'widens policy space for development', according to Grabel (quoted in C.J. Polychroniou, 'Global Financial Governance Ten Years after the Crisis: An Interview with Ilene Grabel', *Global Policy Journal*, 4 June 2020, Opinion blogpost, p. 4, https://www.globalpolicyjournal.com/blog/04/06/2018/global-financial-governance-ten-years-after-crisis-interview-ilene-grabel).

108 In Polychroniou, 'Global Financial Governance', para 10.

109 Padayachee, 'Progressive Macroeconomic Policy'.

110 Padayachee, 'Progressive Macroeconomic Policy'; Saad-Filho, *Just and Democratic Development Approach*. Other mechanisms proposed by Saad-Filho include 'restrictions on foreign currency bank accounts and currency transfers … restrictions on foreign payments for "technical assistance" between connected firms; controls on foreign borrowing [and] multiple exchange rates determined by the priority of the investment' (*Just and Democratic Development Approach*, 16).

111 Padayachee, 'Progressive Macroeconomic Policy'; Padayachee and Van Niekerk, *Shadow of Liberation*.

112 Former South African finance minister, Pravin Gordhan, provided an insightful and less rigid interpretation of that mandate in a 2010 letter. B. Turok, 'Pravin Clarified the Reserve Bank's Mandate Years Ago', *New Agenda: South African Journal of Social and Economic Policy* 74 (2019): 13–15.

113 J. Rossouw, et al., 'Inflation Targeting in Context of "Nationalisation" Debate', *New Agenda* 72 (2019): 19–22. In 2017, the ANC resolved to nationalise the Reserve Bank, a decision which seemed to stem from intra-party political manoeuvrings rather than economic policy ambitions. A related motion was tabled in Parliament the following year, but was withdrawn without debate (Rossouw, et al., 'Inflation Targeting').

114 Padayachee, 'Progressive Macroeconomic Policy'.

115 Swilling, 'Can Economic Policy Escape State Capture?', 25.

CONCLUSION

1   P. Daszak, et al., *IPBES Workshop on Biodiversity and Pandemics: Workshop Report* (Bonn: Intergovernmental Science-Policy Platform on Biodiversity and Ecosystem Services (IPBES), 2020), https://www.ipbes.net/sites/default/files/2020-12/IPBES%20Workshop%20on%20Biodiversity%20and%20Pandemics%20Report_0.pdf.
2   N. Fraser, 'Climates of Capital: For a Trans-Environmental Eco-Socialism', *New Left Review* 17 (2021): 94–127.
3   J. Harris, 'Why Universal Basic Income Could Help Us Fight the Next Wave of Economic Shocks', *The Guardian*, 3 May 2020, https://www.theguardian.com/commentisfree/2020/may/03/universal-basic-income-coronavirus-shocks.
4   There were an estimated 3.4 million AIDS-related deaths in South Africa from 2000–2019, and approximately one million TB deaths in the same period (about two-thirds of which had HIV infection as an underlying cause). See https://aidsinfo.unaids.org for official estimates of annual AIDS mortality in South Africa. TB death estimates are based on data from M. Loveday, et al., 'Figures of the Dead: A Decade of Tuberculosis Mortality Registrations in South Africa', *South African Medical Journal* 109, no. 10 (2019): 728–732.
5   J. Ferguson and T.M. Li, *Beyond the 'Proper Job': Political-Economic Analysis after the Century of Labouring Man*, Working Paper 51 (Bellville: Institute for Poverty, Land and Agrarian Studies, 2018).
6   C. Webb and N. Vally, 'South Africa Has Raised Social Grants: Why This Shouldn't Be a Stop-Gap Measure', *The Conversation*, 7 May 2020, https://theconversation.com/south-africa-has-raised-social-grants-why-this-shouldnt-be-a-stop-gap-measure-138023.
7   J. Seekings, 'Basic Income Activism in South Africa, 1997–2019', in *Political Activism and Basic Income Guarantee: Exploring the Basic Income Guarantee*, eds. R. Caputo and L. Liu (London: Palgrave Macmillan, 2020): 253–272; Institute for Economic Justice, *Introducing a Universal Basic Income Guarantee for South Africa: Towards Income Security for All*, Social Protection Series Policy Brief No. 1 (Johannesburg: Institute for Economic Justice, 2021).
8   J. Cronje, 'Godongwana Warns against "Cycle of Dependency" for Youth in Basic Income Debate', *News24*, 8 August 2021, https://www.news24.com/fin24/economy/godongwana-warns-against-cycle-of-dependency-for-youth-in-basic-income-debate-report-20210808.
9   Department of Social Development, *Transforming the Present – Protecting the Future: Report of the Committee of Inquiry into a Comprehensive System of Social Security for South Africa* (Pretoria: Government Printer, 2002), 38.
10 F. Barchiesi, *Precarious Liberation: Workers, the State and Contested Social Citizenships in Post-Apartheid South Africa* (Pietermaritzburg: UKZN Press, 2011).
11 G. Standing, *Basic Income: And How We Can Make it Happen* (London: Pelican Books, 2017); P. van Parijs and Y. Vanderborght, *Basic Income: A Radical Proposal for a Free Society and a Sane Economy* (Cambridge, MA: Cambridge University Press, 2017); F. Bastagli, et al., *Cash Transfers: What Does the Evidence Say? A Rigorous Review of Programme Impact and of the Role of Design and Implementation Features*

(London: Overseas Development Institute, 2016); S. Davala, et al., *Basic Income: A Transformative Policy for India* (Delhi: Bloomsbury, 2015); C. Haarmann, et al., *Basic Income Grant Pilot Project Assessment Report* (Windhoek: Basic Income Grant Coalition, 2009), http://www.bignam.org/Publications/BIG_Assessment_report_08b.pdf.

12   A. Lowrey, *Give People Money* (London: W.H. Allen, 2018); M. Blyth and E. Lonergan, 'Print Less but Transfer More: Why Central Banks Should Give More Money Directly to the People', *Foreign Affairs*, September/October 2014, https://www.foreignaffairs.com/articles/united-states/2014-08-11/print-less-transfer-more.

13   M. Ndletyana, *Anatomy of the ANC in Power: Insights from Port Elizabeth, 1990–2019* (Cape Town: HSRC Press, 2020); C. Olver, *How to Steal a City: The Battle for Nelson Mandela Bay* (Johannesburg: Jonathan Ball, 2017).

14   T. Lodge, 'Neo-Patrimonial Politics in the ANC', *African Affairs* 113, No. 450 (2014): 1–23.

15   M. Heywood, 'Gauteng Department of Education Spent R431-Million in Three Months on Unnecessary "Deep Cleaning" and "Decontamination" of Schools', *Daily Maverick*, 26 January 2021, https://www.dailymaverick.co.za/article/2021-01-26-gauteng-department-of-education-spent-r431-million-in-three-months-on-unnecessary-deep-cleaning-and-decontamination-of-schools/; Transparency International, 'In South Africa, COVID-19 Has Exposed Greed and Spurred Long-Needed Action against Corruption', *Corruption Watch*, 4 September 2020, https://www.transparency.org/en/blog/in-south-africa-covid-19-has-exposed-greed-and-spurred-long-needed-action-against-corruption.

16   A. Gorz, *Reclaiming Work: Beyond the Wage-Based Society* (Cambridge: Polity Press, 1999), 56.

17   A. Gorz, *Paths to Paradise* (London: Pluto Books, 1985), 54.

18   A. Battistoni, 'Jobs Guarantee or Universal Basic Income? Why Not Both?', *In These Times*, July 2018, http://inthesetimes.com/features/universal-basic-income-federal-jobs-guarantee-climate-change-inequality.html.

19   E.O. Wright, 'Basic Income as a Socialist Project', paper presented at the annual US-BIG Congress, Madison, WI, University of Wisconsin, 4–6 March 2005, p. 6, https://www.ssc.wisc.edu/~wright/Basic%20Income%20as%20a%20Socialist%20Project.pdf.

20   L. Macdonald, 'We Are All Housewives: Universal Basic Income as Wages for Housework', *Lateral* 7, no. 2 (2018), https://csalateral.org/issue/7-2/basic-income-housewives-wages-housework-macdonald/.

21   A. Gorz, *Strategy for Labor: A Radical Proposal* (Boston: Beacon Press, 1967).

22   D. Jones and I. Marinescu, *The Labor Market Impacts of Universal and Permanent Cash Transfers: Evidence from the Alaska Permanent Fund*, Working Paper 24312 (Washington, DC: National Bureau of Economic Research, 2020), https://www.nber.org/system/files/working_papers/w24312/w24312.pdf; A. Banerjee, et al., 'Debunking the Stereotype of the Lazy Welfare Recipient: Evidence from Cash Transfer Programmes', *The World Bank Research Observer* 32, no. 2 (2017): 155–184; Standing, *Basic Income*; E. Skoufias and V. di Maro, 'Conditional Cash Transfers, Adult Work Incentives, and Poverty', *The Journal of Development Studies* 44, no. 7 (2008): 935–960.

23 D. Zamora, 'The Case against a Basic Income', *Jacobin*, December 2017, https://www.jacobinmag.com/2017/12/universal-basic-income-inequality-work; J. Clarke, 'Basic Income: Progressive Cloak and Neoliberal Dagger', *Socialist Bullet*, 4 April 2018, https://socialistproject.ca/2018/04/basic-income-progressive-cloak-and-neoliberal-dagger/.

24 J. Drèze, 'Universal Basic Income for India Suddenly Trendy. Look Out', *NDTV blog*, 16 January 2017, p. 2, https://www.ndtv.com/opinion/decoding-universal-basic-income-for-india-1649293.

25 A. Saad-Filho, *For a Just and Democratic Development Approach to Macro-Economic Policy to Advance the Deep Just Transition*, Policy Brief (Johannesburg: Emancipatory Futures Studies Inter- and Transdisciplinary Project, 2020); J.M. Fournier, *The Positive Effect of Public Investment on Potential Growth*, OECD Economics Department Working Paper 1347 (Paris: OECD Publishing, 2016), https://www.oecd-ilibrary.org/economics/the-positive-effect-of-public-investment-on-potential-growth_15e400d4-en?crawler=true.

26 S. Mohamed, 'Let's Listen to Heterodox Economists for a Change', *New Frame*, 25 February 2021, https://www.newframe.com/lets-listen-to-heterodox-economists-for-a-change/; V. Padayachee, *Beyond a Treasury View of the World: Reflections from Theory and History on Heterodox Economic Policy Options for South Africa*, Working Paper 2 (Johannesburg: Southern Centre for Inequality Studies, University of the Witwatersrand, 2018); V. Padayachee, 'Beyond the Fiscal Cliff? Some Questions for Reflection', *New Agenda* 70 (2018): 34–37; V. Padayachee, 'Can Progressive Macroeconomic Policy Address Growth and Employment while Reducing Inequality in South Africa?', *The Economic and Labour Relations Review* 30, no. 1 (2019): 3–21; I. Grabel, *When Things Don't Fall Apart: Global Financial Governance and Developmental Finance in an Age of Productive Incoherence* (Amherst, MA: MIT Press, 2018); J. Furman, *The New View of Fiscal Policy and its Application*, VoxEU and CEPR, 2 November 2016, https://voxeu.org/article/new-view-fiscal-policy-and-its-application.

27 J. de Wispelaere and L. Morales, 'The Stability of Basic Income: A Constitutional Solution for a Political Problem?', *Journal of Public Policy* 36, no. 4 (2016): 521–545.

28 K. Weeks, 'A Feminist Case for Basic Income: An Interview with Kathi Weeks', *Critical Legal Thinking*, 22 August 2016, https://criticallegalthinking.com/2016/08/22/feminist-case-basic-income-interview-kathi-weeks/.

29 J. Ferguson, *Give a Man a Fish: Reflections on the New Politics of Distribution* (Durham, NC: Duke University Press, 2015), 205.

30 #UBIGNOW, *#UBIGNOW Policy Approach and Proposals* (Johannesburg: Climate Justice Charter Movement, February 2021), https://www.safsc.org.za/wp-content/uploads/2021/02/UBIG_Policy-Approach-and-Proposals_FEB2021.pdf; Institute for Economic Justice, *Financing Options for a Universal Basic Income in South Africa*, Social Protection Series Policy Brief No. 2 (Johannesburg: Institute for Economic Justice, 2021), https://www.iej.org.za/wp-content/uploads/2021/08/IEJ-policy-brief-UBIG-july2021_3.pdf; E. Senona, et al., *Social Protection in a Time of Covid: Lessons for Basic Income Support* (Mowbray: Black Sash, 2021), https://www.blacksash.org.za/images/0541_BS_-_Social_Protection_in_a_Time_of_Covid_Final_-_Web.pdf.

31 Seekings, 'Basic Income Activism', 253.

32 M. Moosa and J. Patel, *South Africans Support Social Grants, but Say Work at Any Wage Beats Unemployment*, Afrobarometer Dispatch 364 (Johannesburg: Institute for Justice and Reconciliation, 2020), https://afrobarometer.org/sites/default/files/publications/Dépêches/ab_r7_dispatchno364_south_africans_support_social_grants_but_want_jobs.pdf; K. Alexander and N. Bohler-Muller, *UJ-HSRC COVID-19 Democracy Survey: Summary National Results, Round 2 (3 July–8 Sept)* (Johannesburg: University of Johannesburg, October 2020), http://www.hsrc.ac.za/uploads/pageContent/12241/Coronavirus%20Impact%20Survey%20Round%202%20summary%20national%20results.pdf.

33 C. Estlund, 'Three Big Ideas for a Future of Less Work and a Three-Dimensional Alternative', *Law and Contemporary Problems* 82, no. 3 (2019): 1–43.

34 F. Barchiesi, 'Liberation of, Through or from Work? Postcolonial Africa and the Problem with "Job Creation" in the Global Crisis', *Interface* 4, no. 2 (2012): 230–253.

35 D. Calnitsky, 'Basic Income and the Pitfalls of Randomization', *Contexts* 18, no. 1 (2019): 22–29.

36 Weeks, 'A Feminist Case'.

37 D. Sage, 'Work and Social Norms: Why We Need to Challenge the Centrality of Employment in Society', *LSE Blog*, 16 July 2018, https://blogs.lse.ac.uk/politicsandpolicy/work-and-social-norms-why-we-need-to-challenge-the-centrality-of-employment-in-our-society/.

BIBLIOGRAPHY

Adelzadeh, A. 'Preliminary Modelling Results of a Basic Income Grant in South Africa'. Presentation to #UBIG Workshop, 29 January 2021.

Adelzadeh, A., S. Malumisa and J. Benecke. *COVID-19 and South Africa's Future Economic Outlook*. California: Applied Development Research Solutions, 2021.

Adriaans, J., S. Liebig and J. Schupp. 'In Germany, Younger, Better Educated Persons, and Lower Income Groups Are More Likely to Be in Favor of Unconditional Basic Income'. *DIW Berlin*, 10 April 2019. https://www.diw.de/en/diw_01.c.618858.en/nachrichten/in_germany_younger_better...onditional_basic_income.html.

African National Congress Social Transformation Committee. *Basic Income Grants, Social Relief and Food Security*. Johannesburg: African National Congress, 2020.

Afrobarometer. *Are Democratic Citizens Emerging in Africa? Evidence from the Afrobarometer*. Afrobarometer Briefing Paper 70. Pretoria: Institute for Democracy in South Africa, 2009.

Aguero, J.M., M.R. Carter and I. Woolard. *The Impact of Unconditional Cash Transfers on Nutrition: The South African Child Support Grant*. Working Paper 8. Cape Town: Southern Africa Labour and Development Research Unit, University of Cape Town, 2006.

Alami, I. 'Capital Accumulation and Capital Controls in South Africa: A Class Perspective'. *Review of African Political Economy* 45, no. 156 (2017): 223–249.

Alexander, K. and N. Bohler-Muller. *UJ-HSRC COVID-19 Democracy Survey: Summary National Results, Round 2*. Johannesburg: Centre for Social Change, University of Johannesburg, August 2020. http://www.hsrc.ac.za/uploads/pageContent/12241/Coronavirus%20Impact%20Survey%20Round%202%20summary%20national%20results.pdf.

Allègre, G. *How Can a Basic Income Be Defended?* OFCE Briefing Paper 7. Paris: L'Observatoire français des conjonctures économiques (OFCE), 2014. https://spire.sciencespo.fr/hdl:/2441/25qafebie49csbsal9hbmifkr5/resources/2014-allegre-howcanabasicincomebriefing7.pdf.

Alzúa, M.L., G. Cruces and L. Ripani. 'Welfare Programmes and Labor Supply in Developing Countries: Experimental Evidence from Latin America'. *Journal of Population Economics* 26, no. 4 (2013): 1255–1284.

Amsden, A. 'Bringing Production Back in'. *World Development* 25, no. 4 (1997): 469–480.

ANC (African National Congress). 'Draft Resolutions of the National Policy Conference'. *Umrabulo* 17 (2002). http://www.anc.org.za/ancdocs/pubs/umrabulo/umrabulo17/index.html.

ANC. *ANC 52nd National Conference 2007 Resolutions*. Johannesburg: African National Congress, 2007. https://www.anc1912.org.za/resolutions-2/.

Anon. 'Didiza Cautious about Basic Income Grant'. *Business Day*, 14 August 2002.

Anon. 'People Must Help Themselves'. *Business Day*, 17 March 2008.

Anon. 'Economic Crisis Will Not Derail State Plans'. *The Independent*, 3 June 2009.

Anon. 'JSE Markets' Weekly Statistics'. *Market Statistics, JSE*, 28 August 2018.

Anon. 'Results of Finland's Basic Income Experiment: Small Employment Effects, Better Perceived Economic Security and Mental Wellbeing'. *Kela News Archive*, Helsinki, 6 May 2020. https://www.kela.fi/web/en/news-archive/-/asset_publisher/lN08GY2nIrZo/content/results-of-the-basic-income-experiment-small-employment-effects-better-perceived-economic-security-and-mental-wellbeing.

Ansari, S. 2017. 'The Neo-Liberal Incentive Structure and the Absence of the Developmental State in Post-Apartheid South Africa'. *African Affairs* 116, no. 463 (2017): 206–232.

Applied Development Research Solutions. 'Fiscally Neutral Basic Income Grant Scenarios: Economic and Development Impacts'. *The Bridge* no. 7 (May 2021).

Arendt, H. *The Human Condition*. Chicago, IL: University of Chicago Press, 1958.

Arnold, A. 'The Anti-Poverty Experiment'. *Nature* 557 (2018): 626–628.

Ash, T.G. and A. Zimmermann. 'In Crisis, Europeans Support Radical Positions'. *Eupinions Brief*, 6 May 2020. https://eupinions.eu/de/text/in-crisis-europeans-support-radical-positions.

Ashman, S. 'South Africa: An Economy of Extremes'. In *The Essential Guide to Critical Development Studies*, edited by H. Veltmeyer and P. Bowles, 171–178. Abingdon: Routledge, 2021.

Ashman, S. and B. Fine. 'Neo-Liberalism, Varieties of Capitalism, and the Shifting Contours of South Africa's Financial System'. *Transformation: Critical Perspectives on Southern Africa* 81/82 (2013): 144–178.

Ashman, S., B. Fine and S. Newman. 'The Crisis in South Africa: Neoliberalism, Financialization and Uneven and Combined Development'. *Socialist Register* 47 (2011): 174–195.

Atkins, R. and G. Tetlow. 'Switzerland Votes against State-Provided Basic Income'. *Financial Times*, 5 June 2016. https://www.ft.com/content/002af908-2b16-11e6-a18d-a96ab29e3c95.

Atkinson, A.B. 'The Case for a Participation Income'. *Political Quarterly* 67, no. 1 (1996): 67–70.

Atkinson, A.B. *Inequality: What Can Be Done?* Cambridge, MA: Harvard University Press, 2015.

Autor, D.H. 'Why Are There Still So Many Jobs? The History and Future of Workplace Automation'. *Journal of Economic Perspectives* 29, no. 3 (2015): 3–30.

Baird, S., J. de Hoop and B. Özler. 'Income Shocks and Adolescent Mental Health'. *Journal of Human Resources* 48, no. 2 (2013): 370–403.

Baker, D. 'The Job-Killing Robot Myth'. *The Los Angeles Times*, 6 May 2015. https://www.latimes.com/opinion/op-ed/la-oe-baker-robots-20150507-story.html.

Baker, D. 'The Economics and Politics of Financial Transactions Taxes and Wealth Taxes'. *Counterpunch*, 14 October 2019. https://www.counterpunch.org/2019/10/14/the-economics-and-politics-of-financial-transactions-taxes-and-wealth-taxes/.

Banerjee, A., R. Hanna, G. Kreindler and B.A. Olken. 'Debunking the Stereotype of the Lazy Welfare Recipient: Evidence from Cash Transfer Programmes'. *The World Bank Research Observer* 32, no. 2 (2017): 155–184.

Barchiesi, F. 'The Debate on the Basic Income Grant in South Africa: Social Citizenship, Wage Labour and the Reconstruction of Working-Class Politics'. Paper presented at the Harold Wolpe Memorial Trust's 10th Anniversary Colloquium, 'Engaging Silences and Unresolved Issues in the Political Economy of South Africa', Cape Town, 21–23 September 2006.

Barchiesi, F. 'South African Debates on the Basic Income Grant: Wage Labour and the Post-Apartheid Social Policy'. *Journal of Southern African Studies* 33, no. 3 (2007): 561–575.

Barchiesi, F. *Precarious Liberation: Workers, the State and Contested Social Citizenships in Post-Apartheid South Africa*. Pietermaritzburg: UKZN Press, 2011.

Barchiesi, F. 'Liberation of, Through or from Work? Postcolonial Africa and the Problem with "Job Creation" in the Global Crisis'. *Interface* 4, no. 2 (2012): 230–253.

Barchiesi, F. 'Schooling Bodies to Hard Work: The South African State's Policy Discourse and its Moral Constructions of Welfare'. *Journal of Contemporary African Studies* 34, no. 2 (2016): 221–235.

Barrientos, A. and M. Nino-Zarazua. *Effects of Non-Contributory Social Transfers in Developing Countries: A Compendium*. Geneva: International Labour Organization, 2010.

Bartha, D., T. Boros, M. Freitas, G. Laki and M. Stringer. *What Is the European Dream? Survey on European Dreams for the Future of Europe*. Brussels: Foundation for European Progressive Studies, 2020. https://www.feps-europe.eu/attachments/publications/ed_web.pdf.

Bassier, H. and J. Budlender. 'Proposed Family Poverty Grant Is Excellent in Theory – but There Are Problems with its Implementation'. *Daily Maverick*, 8 November 2021. https://www.dailymaverick.co.za/article/2021-11-08-proposed-family-poverty-grant-is-excellent-in-theory-but-there-are-problems-with-its-implementation/.

Bastagli, F. *From Social Safety Net to Social Policy? The Role of Conditional Cash Transfers in Welfare State Development in Latin America*. Working Paper 60. Brasilia: International Policy Centre for Inclusive Growth, 2009.

Bastagli, F., J. Hagen-Zanker, L. Harman, V. Barca, G. Sturge and T. Schmidt. *Cash Transfers: What Does the Evidence Say? A Rigorous Review of Programme Impact and of the Role of Design and Implementation Features*. London: Overseas Development Institute, 2016.

Bastani, A. *Fully Automated Luxury Communism*. London: Verso Books, 2020.

Battistoni, A. 'Jobs Guarantee or Universal Basic Income? Why Not Both?' *In These Times*, July 2018. http://inthesetimes.com/features/universal-basic-income-federal-jobs-guarantee-climate-change-inequality.html.

Beach, H. 'Feminist Theory, Gender Inequity, and Basic Income: An Interview with Almaz Zelleke'. *Basic Income Today*, 16 May 2019. https://basicincometoday.com/feminist-theory-gender-inequity-and-basic-income/.

Bedayn, J. 'Universal Basic Income? California Moves to Be First State to Fund Pilot Projects'. *Cal Matters*, 21 July 2021. https://calmatters.org/california-divide/2021/07/universal-basic-income-california/.

Benanav, A. *Automation and the Future of Work*. London: Verso Books, 2020.

Benjamin, N., K. Beegle, F. Recanatini and M. Santini. *Informal Economy and the World Bank*. Policy Research Working Paper 6888. Washington, DC: World Bank, 2014. www-wds.worldbank.org/external/default/WDSContentServer/WDSP/IB/2014/05/22/000158349_20140522153248/Rendered/PDF/WPS6888.pdf.

Bezuidenhout, A. and M. Tshoaedi. *Labour beyond Cosatu: Mapping the Rupture in South Africa's Labour Landscape*. Johannesburg: Wits University Press, 2017.

Bhorat, H. 'A Universal Income Grant Scheme for South Africa: An Empirical Assessment'. Paper presented at the 9th International Congress of the Basic Income European Network, Geneva, 12–14 September 2002.

Bhorat, H. and A. Cassim. 'South Africa's Welfare Success Story II: Poverty-Reducing Social Grants'. *Africa in Focus* (Brookings), 27 January 2014. https://www.brookings.edu/blog/africa-in-focus/2014/01/27/south-africas-welfare-success-story-ii-poverty-reducing-social-grants/.

Bhorat, H. and T. Kohler. *Social Assistance during South Africa's National Lockdown: Examining the COVID-19 Grant, Changes to the Child Support Grant, and Post-October Policy Options*. Working Paper 202009. Cape Town: Development Policy Research Unit, University of Cape Town, 2020. http://www.dpru.uct.ac.za/sites/default/files/image_tool/images/36/Publications/Working_Papers/DPRU%20WP%20202009.pdf.

Bidadanure, J.U. 'The Political Theory of Universal Basic Income'. *Annual Review of Political Science* 22 (2019): 481–501.

BIG Financing Reference Group. *Breaking the Poverty Trap: Financing a Basic Income Grant in South Africa*. Cape Town: BIG Financing Reference Group, 2004.

Birnbaum, S. *Basic Income Reconsidered*. New York: Palgrave Macmillan, 2012.

Bivens, J. and H. Blair. *A Financial Transaction Tax Would Help Ensure Wall Street Works for Main Street*. Washington, DC: Economic Policy Institute, 2016. https://files.epi.org/pdf/110651.pdf.

Blakely, T.A., S.C. Collings and J. Atkinson. 'Unemployment and Suicide: Evidence for a Causal Association?' *Journal of Epidemiology and Community Health* 57, no. 8 (2003): 594–600.

Blanchard, O.J. and D. Leigh. 'Effects of Fiscal Policy in Deep Recessions: Simple and Hopefully Credible Empirical Evidence'. *American Economic Review: Papers and Proceedings* 103, no. 3 (2013): 117–120.

Blyth, M. and E. Lonergan. 'Print Less but Transfer More: Why Central Banks Should Give More Money Directly to the People'. *Foreign Affairs*, September/October 2014. https://www.foreignaffairs.com/articles/united-states/2014-08-11/print-less-transfer-more.

BNY Mellon. *Financial Transaction Taxes: A Global Perspective*. New York: BNY Mellon, 2019. https://www.bnymellon.com/content/dam/bnymellon/documents/pdf/emea/ftt-globalperspective-brochure-03-2018.pdf.

Boltanski, L. and E. Chiapello. *The New Spirit of Capitalism*. London: Verso Books, 2005.

Bond, P. *The Politics of Environmental Justice*. Durban: UKZN Press, 2011.

Bookchin, M. *Social Ecology and Communalism*. Oakland, CA: AK Press, 2007.

Brand, J.E. 'The Far-Reaching Impact of Job Loss and Unemployment'. *Annual Review of Sociology* 41 (2015): 359–375.

Braunstein, E. and S. Seguino. 'The Impact of Economic Policy and Structural Change on Gender Employment Inequality in Latin America 1990–2010'. *Review of Keynesian Economics* 6, no. 3 (2018): 307–332.

Bregman, R. *Utopia for Realists: How We Can Build the Ideal World*. New York: Little, Brown and Company, 2017.

Breman, J. 'A Bogus Concept'. *New Left Review* 84 (2013): 130–138.

Brenner, R. *The Economics of Global Turbulence: The Advanced Capitalist Economies from Long Boom to Long Downturn, 1945–2005*. London: Verso Books, 2006.

Bridgman, G., S. van der Berg and L. Patel. *Hunger in South Africa during 2020: Results from Wave 2 of NIDS-CRAM*. Stellenbosch: National Income Dynamics Study, University of Stellenbosch, 2020. https://cramsurvey.org/wp-content/uploads/2020/09/3.-Bridgman-G.-Van-der-Berg-S.-_-Patel-L.-2020-Hunger-in-South-Africa-during-2020-Results-from-Wave-2-of-NIDS-CRAM.pdf.

Bruenig, M. 'A Specter Is Haunting Alaska – the Specter of Communism'. *Demos*, 5 January 2014. https://prospect.org/power/specter-haunting-alaska-the-specter-communism/.

Bruenig, M. 'Just What Is a Job Guarantee?' *Jacobin*, 13 May 2018. https://www.jacobinmag.com/2018/05/full-employment-job-guarantee-bernie-bruenig.

Bruenig, M. 'Some Notes on Federal Job Guarantee Proposals'. People's Policy Project, 22 March 2018. https://www.peoplespolicyproject.org/2018/03/22/some-notes-on-federal-job-guarantee-proposals/.

Bruenig, M. 'Social Wealth Fund for America'. People's Policy Project, 2019. https://www.peoplespolicyproject.org/projects/social-wealth-fund/.

Brynjolfsson, E. and A. McAfee. *The Second Machine Age*. New York: W.W. Norton, 2016.

Buhlungu, S. and E. Webster. 'Work Restructuring and the Future of Labour in South Africa'. In *The State of the Nation: South Africa 2005–2006*, edited by S. Buhlungu, J. Daniel, R. Southall and J. Lutchman, 248–269. Cape Town: HSRC Press, 2006.

Bunting, M. *Willing Slaves: How the Overwork Culture Is Ruling Our Lives*. London: Harper Perennial, 2005.

Bureau for Food and Agricultural Policy. *BFAP Food Inflation Brief – March 2021*. Die Wilgers: Bureau for Food and Agricultural Policy, 2021. https://www.bfap.co.za/wp-content/uploads/2021/04/Food-Inflation_April-2021.pdf.

Burman, L.E., W.G. Gale, S. Gault, B. Kim, J. Nunns and S. Rosenthal. 'Financial Transaction Taxes in Theory and Practice'. *National Tax Journal* 69, no. 1 (2016): 171–216.

Button, K., E. Moore and J. Seekings. *South Africa's Hybrid Care Regime: The Changing and Contested Roles of Individuals, Families and the State in South Africa*. Working Paper 404. Cape Town: Centre for Social Science Research, University of Cape Town, 2017.

Calhoun, C. and G. Derluguian. *Business as Usual: The Roots of the Global Financial Meltdown*. New York: New York University Press, 2011.

Calnitsky, D. '"More Normal than Welfare": The Mincome Experiment, Stigma, and Community Experience'. *Canadian Review of Sociology* 53, no. 1 (2006): 26–71.

Calnitsky, D. 'Basic Income and the Pitfalls of Randomization'. *Contexts* 18, no. 1 (2019): 22–29.

Cao, W., H. Wang and H. Ying. 'The Effect of Environmental Regulation on Employment in Resource-Based Areas of China: An Empirical Research Based on the Mediating Effect Model'. *International Journal of Environmental Research and Public Health* 14, no. 12 (2017): 1598.

Carattini, S. 'How to Win Public Support for a Global Carbon Tax'. *Nature* 565, no. 7739 (2019): 289–291.

Carlos, N., I. Warnke, E. Seifritz and W. Kawohl. 'Modelling Suicide and Unemployment: A Longitudinal Analysis Covering 63 Countries, 2000–11'. *The Lancet Psychiatry* 2, no. 3 (2015): 239–245.

Carmen, R. and M. Sobrado. *A Future for the Excluded.* London: Zed Books, 2000.

Carmody, P. 'Between Globalization and (Post) Apartheid: The Political Economy of Restructuring in South Africa'. *Journal of Southern African Studies* 28, no. 2 (2002): 255–275.

Casale, D. and D. Posel. *Gender and the Early Effects of the COVID-19 Crisis in the Paid and Unpaid Economies in South Africa.* National Income Dynamics Study – Coronavirus Rapid Mobile Survey, Wave 1, Working Paper No. 4, 2020. https://cramsurvey.org/wp-content/uploads/2020/07/Casale-Gender-the-early-effects-of-the-COVID-19-crisis-in-the-paid-unpaid-economies-in-South-Africa.pdf.

Casale, D. and D. Shepherd. *The Gendered Effects of the COVID-19 Crisis and Ongoing Lockdown in South Africa: Evidence from NIDS-CRAM Waves 1–5.* National Income Dynamics Study – Coronavirus Rapid Mobile Survey, Wave 5, Working Paper No. 3, 2021. https://cramsurvey.org/wp-content/uploads/2021/07/3.-Casale-D.-_-Shepherd-D.-2021-The-gendered-effects-of-the-Covid-19-crisis-and-ongoing-lockdown-in-South-Africa-Evidence-from-NIDS-CRAM-Waves-1-%E2%80%93-5..pdf.

Case, A. and A. Deaton. 'Large Cash Transfers to the Elderly in South Africa'. *The Economic Journal* 108, no. 450 (1998): 1330–1361.

Case, A., V. Hosegood and F. Lund. 'The Reach and Impact of Child Support Grants: Evidence from KwaZulu-Natal'. *Development Southern Africa* 22, no. 4 (2005): 467–482.

Chandola, T. and N. Zhang. 'Re-employment, Job Quality, Health and Allostatic Load Biomarkers: Prospective Evidence from the UK Household Longitudinal Study'. *International Journal of Epidemiology* 47, no. 1 (2018): 47–57.

Chang, J-H. *Economics: The User's Guide.* London: Pelican Books, 2014.

Chatterjee, A., L. Czajka and A. Gethin. *Extreme inequalities: The Distribution of Household Wealth in South Africa.* Southern Africa – Towards Inclusive Economic Development (SA-TIED) Research Brief 2020/45, 2020. https://sa-tied.wider.unu.edu/sites/default/files/SA-TIED-RB2020-11-extreme-inequalities_0.pdf.

Clark, A.E. and A.J. Oswald. 'Unhappiness and Unemployment'. *The Economic Journal* 104 (1994): 648–659.

Clarke, J. 'Basic Income: Progressive Cloak and Neoliberal Dagger'. *Socialist Bullet,* 4 April 2018. https://socialistproject.ca/2018/04/basic-income-progressive-cloak-and-neoliberal-dagger/.

Climate Justice Alliance. *Just Transition Principles*. Washington, DC: Climate Justice Alliance, 2018. https://climatejusticealliance.org/wp-content/uploads/2018/06/CJA_JustTransition_Principles_final_hi-rez.pdf.

Cock, J. 'Connecting the Red, Brown and Green: The Environmental Justice Movement in South Africa'. In *Voices of Protest: Social Movements in Post-Apartheid South Africa*, edited by R. Ballard, A. Habib and I. Valodia, 203–224. Pietermaritzburg: UKZN Press, 2006.

Cock, J. 'The "Green Economy": A Just and Sustainable Development Path or a "Wolf in Sheep's Clothing"?' *Global Labour Journal* 5, no. 1 (2014): 23–44.

Cock, J. 'The Climate Crisis and a "Just Transition" in South Africa: An Eco-Feminist-Socialist Perspective'. In *The Climate Crisis: South African and Global Democratic Eco-Socialist Alternatives*, edited by V. Satgar, 201–230. Johannesburg: Wits University Press, 2018.

Coleman, A. and A. Grimes. 'Fiscal, Distributional and Efficiency Impacts of Land and Property Taxes'. *New Zealand Economic Papers* 44, no. 2 (2010): 179–199.

Coleman, N. 'Current Debates around BIG: The Political and Socio-Economic Context'. In *A Basic Income Grant for South Africa*, edited by G. Standing and M. Samson, 120–142. Cape Town: UCT Press, 2003.

Cooper, A., Z. Mokomane and A.W. Fadiji. 'The Relationship between Social Welfare Policy and Multidimensional Well-Being: An Analysis Using the South African Child Support Grant'. *Transformation: Critical Perspectives on Southern Africa* 102 (2020): 73–94.

Coovadia, H., R. Jewkes, P. Barron, D. Sanders and D. McIntyre. 'The Health and Health System of South Africa: Historical Roots of Current Public Health Challenges'. *Lancet* 374, no. 9692 (2009): 817–834.

Cosatu (Congress of South African Trade Unions). 'Submission on Comprehensive Social Security'. Submitted to the Taylor Task Team on Social Security. Johannesburg: Congress of South African Trade Unions, 2000.

Cosatu. *A Growth Path towards Full Employment*. Framework Document. Johannesburg: Congress of South African Trade Unions, 2010.

Cronje, J. 'Godongwana Warns against "Cycle of Dependency" for Youth in Basic Income Debate'. *News24*, 8 August 2021. https://www.news24.com/fin24/economy/godongwana-warns-against-cycle-of-dependency-for-youth-in-basic-income-debate-report-20210808.

Crotty, J. *The Effects of Increased Product Market Competition and Changes in Financial Markets on the Performance of Nonfinancial Corporations in the Neoliberal Era*. PERI Working Paper 44. Amherst, MA: Political Economy Research Institute, 2003.

Cruywagen, M., M. Davies and M. Swilling. *Estimating the Cost of a Just Transition in South Africa's Coal Sector: Protecting Workers, Stimulating Regional Development and Accelerating a Low-Carbon Transition*. Stellenbosch: Centre for Complex Systems in Transition, Stellenbosch University, 2019. https://www.tips.org.za/images/report_Estimating_the_cost_of_a_just_transition_in_South_Africas_coal_sector.pdf.

Cunha, J., G. de Giorgi and S. Jayachandran. 'The Price Effects of Cash Versus in-Kind Transfers'. *The Review of Economic Studies* 86, no. 1 (2019): 240–281.

Cylus, J., M.M. Glymour and M. Avendano. 'Do Generous Unemployment Benefit Programs Reduce Suicide Rates? A State Fixed-Effect Analysis Covering 1968–2008'. *American Journal of Epidemiology* 189, no. 1 (2014): 45–52.

Daniel, L. 'Covid R350 Grants: Millions Rejected, but Only 10 People Are Dealing with All the Appeals'. *Business Insider*, 10 December 2020. https://www.businessinsider.co.za/one-in-every-three-covid-19-sassa-grant-applications-rejected-here-are-the-reasons-why-2020-12.

Daszak, P., J. Amuasi, C.G. das Neves, D. Hayman, T. Kuiken, B. Roche, C. Zambrana-Torrelio, et al. *IPBES Workshop on Biodiversity and Pandemics: Workshop Report.* Bonn: Intergovernmental Science-Policy Platform on Biodiversity and Ecosystem Services (IPBES), 2020. https://www.ipbes.net/sites/default/files/2020-12/IPBES%20Workshop%20on%20Biodiversity%20and%20Pandemics%20Report_0.pdf.

Davala, S., R. Jhabvala, G. Standing and S.K. Mehta. *Basic Income: A Transformative Policy for India.* Delhi: Bloomsbury, 2015.

Davies, S. 'Basic Income, Labour and the Idea of Post-Capitalism'. *Economic Affairs* 37, no. 3 (2017): 442–458.

Davis, M. *Planet of Slums.* London: Verso Books, 2006.

Davis, R. 'BIG Is Best: Civil Society Campaign Highlights Urgency of Basic Income Grant after Recent Looting'. *Daily Maverick*, 19 July 2021. https://www.dailymaverick.co.za/article/2021-07-19-big-is-best-civil-society-campaign-highlights-urgency-of-basic-income-grant-after-recent-looting/.

Davis Tax Committee. *Report on Feasibility of a Wealth Tax in South Africa.* Johannesburg: Davis Tax Committee, 2018. http://www.sataxguide.co.za/wp-content/uploads/2018/05/20180329-Final-DTC-Wealth-Tax-Report-To-Minister.pdf.

Dawson, H.J. and E. Fouksman. 'Labour, Laziness and Distribution: Work Imaginaries among the South African Unemployed'. *Africa* 90, no. 2 (2020): 229–251.

Department for International Development. *Social Transfers and Chronic Poverty: Emerging Evidence and the Challenge Ahead.* London: Department for International Development, 2005. http://epri.org.za/wp-content/uploads/2016/07/DFID2005Social TransfersAndChronicPoverty.pdf.

Department for International Development. *Cash Transfers.* Evidence Paper of the Policy Division of DFID. London: Department for International Development, 2011.

Department for Women, Youth and Persons with Disabilities. *National Youth Policy 2020–2030.* Pretoria: Department for Women, Youth and Persons with Disabilities, 2021. https://www.gov.za/sites/default/files/gcis_document/202103/nationalyouthpolicy.pdf.

Department of Social Development. *Transforming the Present – Protecting the Future: Report of the Committee of Inquiry into a Comprehensive System of Social Security for South Africa.* Pretoria: Government Printer, 2002.

De Wispelaere, J. and L. Morales. 'The Stability of Basic Income: A Constitutional Solution for a Political Problem?' *Journal of Public Policy* 36, no. 4 (2016): 521–545.

Dinerstein, A.C. 'The Dream of Dignified Work: On Good and Bad Utopias'. *Development and Change* 45, no. 5 (2014): 1037–1058.

Di Paola, M. and N. Pons-Vignon. 'Labour Market Restructuring in South Africa: Low Wages, High Insecurity'. *Review of African Political Economy* 40, no. 138 (2013): 628–638.

DIW Berlin. *Basic Income Pilot Project: How Does a Basic Income Change Our Society? We Want to Know.* Berlin: DIW Berlin, 2020. https://www.diw.de/en/diw_01.c.796681.en/projects/basic_income_pilot_project.html.

Drèze, J. 'Universal Basic Income for India Suddenly Trendy. Look Out'. *NDTV blog*, 16 January 2017. https://www.ndtv.com/opinion/decoding-universal-basic-income-for-india-1649293.

Du Toit, A. and D. Neves. *Trading on a Grant: Integrating Formal and Informal Social Protection in Post-Apartheid Migrant Networks.* Working Paper 3. Cape Town: Programme for Land and Agrarian Studies (PLAAS), University of the Western Cape, 2009.

Du Toit, A. and D. Neves. 'The Government of Poverty and the Arts of Survival: Mobile and Recombinant Strategies at the Margins of the South African Economy'. *The Journal of Peasant Studies* 41, no. 5 (2014): 833–853.

Dutta, P., R. Murgai, M. Ravallion and D. van de Walle. *Right to Work? Assessing India's Employment Guarantee Scheme in Bihar.* Washington, DC: World Bank, 2014.

Egger, D., J. Haushofer, E. Miguel, P. Niehaus and M.W. Walker. *General Equilibrium Effects of Cash Transfers: Experimental Evidence from Kenya.* Working Paper 26600. Washington, DC: National Bureau of Economic Research, 2019. https://www.nber.org/papers/w26600.

Eisenberg, A. 'Just Transitions'. *Southern California Law Review* 92, no. 101 (2019): 273–330.

Ellis, E. 'Special Permit Holders and Asylum Seekers in SA Must Get Covid-19 Grant, Court Orders'. *Daily Maverick*, 19 June 2020. https://www.dailymaverick.co.za/article/2020-06-19-refugees-and-asylum-seekers-in-sa-must-get-covid-19-grant-court-orders/ (paywall).

Ellis, F. '"We Are All Poor Here": Economic Difference, Social Divisiveness, and Targeting Cash Transfers in Sub-Saharan Africa'. Paper prepared for the Conference on Social Protection for the Poorest in Africa: Learning from Experience, Uganda, 8–10 September 2008.

Ensor, L. 'Skweyiya Calls for Basic Income Grant for Poor'. *Business Day*, 10 November 2006.

Epstein, G. 'Introduction: Financialization and the World Economy'. In *Financialization and the World Economy*, edited by G. Epstein, 3–16. Cheltenham: Edward Elgar, 2005.

Eskom. *Integrated Report, 31 March 2017.* Sandton: Eskom, 2017. https://www.eskom.co.za/wp-content/uploads/2021/02/Eskom_integrated_report_2017.pdf.

Estlund, C. 'Three Big Ideas for a Future of Less Work and a Three-Dimensional Alternative'. *Law and Contemporary Problems* 82, no. 3 (2019): 1–43.

European Social Survey. *The Past, Present and Future of European Welfare Attitudes: Topline Results from Round 8 of the European Social Survey.* London: European Social Survey, 2018. https://www.europeansocialsurvey.org/docs/findings/ESS8_toplines_issue_8_welfare.pdf.

Evans, D.K. and A. Popova. 'Cash Transfers and Temptation Goods'. *Economic Development and Cultural Change* 65, no. 2 (2017): 189–221.

Evans, P. *Embedded Autonomy: States and Industrial Transformation.* Princeton, NJ: Princeton University Press, 1995.

Evans, P. *In Search of the 21st Century Developmental State.* Berkeley, CA: University of California Press, 2007.

Evans, P. 'The Capability Enhancing Developmental State: Concepts and National Trajectories'. In *The South Korean Development Experience: Beyond Aid*, edited by E. Kim, 83–110. London: Palgrave, 2010.

Evans, P. and P. Heller. 'Human Development, State Transformation and the Politics of the Developmental State'. In *The Oxford Handbook of Transformations of the State*, edited by S. Leibfried, E. Huber, M. Lange, J.D. Levy and J.D. Stephens, 691–713. Oxford: Oxford University Press, 2013.

Everatt, D. 'The Undeserving Poor: Poverty and the Politics of Service Delivery in the Poorest Nodes of South Africa'. *Politikon* 35, no. 3 (2008): 293–319.

Expert Panel on Basic Income Support. *Executive Summary*. Pretoria: Department of Social Development, December 2021. https://www.dsd.gov.za/index.php/documents?task=download.send&id=357&catid=58&m=0

Expert Panel on Basic Income Support. *Final Report*. Pretoria: Department of Social Development, December 2021. https://www.dsd.gov.za/index.php/documents?task=download.send&id=356&catid=58&m=0.

Fadaee, S. and S. Schindler. 'The Occupy Movement and the Politics of Vulnerability'. *Globalizations* 11, no. 6 (2014): 777–791.

Farrel, C. 'Just Transition: Lessons Learned from the Environmental Justice Movement'. *Duke Forum for Law and Social Change* 4 (2012): 35–45.

Federici, S. *Revolution at Point Zero: Housework, Reproduction, and Feminism*. Oakland, CA: PM Press, 2012.

Ferguson, J. 'Formalities of Poverty: Thinking about Social Assistance in Neoliberal South Africa'. *African Studies Review* 50, no. 2 (2007): 71–86.

Ferguson, J. 'Declaration of Dependence: Labour, Personhood, and Welfare in Southern Africa'. *Journal of the Royal Anthropological Institute* 19, no. 2 (2013): 223–242.

Ferguson, J. *Give a Man a Fish: Reflections on the New Politics of Distribution*. Durham, NC: Duke University Press, 2015.

Ferguson, J. and T.M. Li. *Beyond the 'Proper Job': Political-Economic Analysis after the Century of Labouring Man*. Working Paper 51. Bellville: Institute for Poverty, Land and Agrarian Studies, 2018.

Fine, B. 'Can South Africa Be a Developmental State?' In *Constructing a Democratic Developmental State in South Africa: Potentials and Challenges*, edited by O. Edigheji, 169–182. Cape Town: HSRC Press, 2010.

Fine, B. *The Continuing Enigmas of Social Policy*. Working Paper 2014-10. Geneva: United Nations Research Institute for Social Development, 2014. https://www.unrisd.org/80256B3C005BCCF9/%28httpAuxPages%29/30B153EE73F52ABFC12 57D0200420A61/$file/Fine.pdf.

Fine, B. 'The Continuing Enigmas of Social Policy'. In *Towards Universal Health Care in Emerging Economies: Social Policy in a Development Context*, edited by I. Yi, 29–59. London: Palgrave Macmillan, 2017.

Fine, B. and Z. Rustomjee. *The Political Economy of South Africa: From Mineral-Energy Complex to Industrialization*. London: Hurst and Co., 1996.

Fischer, A. *Poverty as Ideology: Rescuing Social Justice from Global Development Agendas*. London: Zed Books, 2018.

Fisher, E., R. Attah, V. Barca, C. O'Brien, S. Brook, J. Holland, A. Kardan, S. Pavanello and P. Pozarny. 'The Livelihood Impacts of Cash Transfers in Sub-Saharan Africa:

Beneficiary Perspectives from Six Countries'. *World Development* 99 (2017): 299–319.

Fitzpatrick, T. 'A Basic Income for Feminists?' In *Basic Income: An Anthology of Contemporary Research*, edited by K. Widerquist, J.A. Noguera, Y. Vanderborght and J. de Wispelaere, 163–172. Chichester: Blackwell Publishing, 2013.

Flatø, M., R. Muttarak and A. Pelser. 'Women, Weather, and Woes: The Triangular Dynamics of Female-Headed Households, Economic Vulnerability, and Climate Variability in South Africa'. *World Development* 90 (2017): 41–62.

Foguel, M. and R.de Barros. 'The Effects of Conditional Cash Transfer Programmes on Adult Labour Supply: An Empirical Analysis Using a Time-Series-Cross-Section Sample of Brazilian Municipalities'. *Estudos Econômicos* 40, no. 2 (2010): 259–293.

Ford, M. *The Rise of the Robots*. New York: Basic Books, 2015.

Forget, E.L. 'The Town with No Poverty: The Health Effects of a Canadian Guaranteed Annual Income Field Experiment'. *Canadian Public Policy* 37, no. 3 (2011): 283–305.

Foster, J.B. *Ecology against Capitalism*. New York: Monthly Review Press, 2002.

Foster, J.B. 'The Financialization of Capitalism'. *Monthly Review* 58, no. 11 (2007): 1–12.

Foster, J.B., R.J. Jonna and B. Clark. 'The Contagion of Capital: Financialized Capitalism, COVID-19 and the Great Divide'. *Monthly Review* 72, no. 8 (2021). https://monthlyreview.org/2021/01/01/the-contagion-of-capital/.

Fourier, C. *La fausse industrie morcelée, répugnante, mensongère, et l'antidote, l'industrie naturelle, combinée, attrayante, véridique, donnant quadruple produit.* Paris: Bossange, 1835–1836.

Fournier, J.M. *The Positive Effect of Public Investment on Potential Growth.* OECD Economics Department Working Paper 1347. Paris: OECD Publishing, 2016. https://www.oecd-ilibrary.org/economics/the-positive-effect-of-public-investment-on-potential-growth_15e400d4-en?crawler=true.

Frase, P. *Four Futures*. London: Verso Books, 2016.

Fraser, N. 'Behind Marx's Hidden Abode'. *New Left Review* 86 (2014): 55–72.

Fraser, N. 'Can Society Be Commodities All the Way Down? Post-Polanyian Reflections on Capitalist Crisis'. *Economy and Society* 43, no. 4 (2014): 541–558.

Fraser, N. 'Legitimation Crisis? On the Political Contradictions of Financialized Capitalism'. *Critical Historical Studies* 2, no. 2 (2015): 157–189.

Fraser, N. 'Contradictions of Capital and Care'. *New Left Review* 100 (2016): 99–117.

Fraser, N. 'Climates of Capital: For a Trans-Environmental Eco-Socialism'. *New Left Review* 17 (2021): 94–127.

Fraser, N. and R. Jaeggi. *Capitalism: A Conversation in Critical Theory.* Cambridge: Polity, 2018.

Freeland, E. *What Do Americans Think about Universal Basic Income?* Los Angeles: USC Schaeffer Center, University of Southern California, 2019. https://healthpolicy.usc.edu/evidence-base/what-do-americans-think-about-universal-basic-income/.

Freund, W. 'South Africa as a Developmental State'. *Africanus* 37, no. 2 (2007): 170–175.

Freund, W. 'Swimming against the Tide: The Macro-Economic Research Group in the South African Transition 1991–94'. *Review of African Political Economy* 40, no. 138 (2013): 519–536.

Freund, W. 'Post-Apartheid South Africa under ANC Rule: A Response to John S Saul on South Africa'. *Transformation* 89 (2015): 50–75.

Frey, C.B. and M.A. Osborne. 'The Future of Employment: How Susceptible Are Jobs to Computerization?' *Technological Forecasting and Social Change* 114 (2017): 254–280.

Friedman, M. *Capitalism and Freedom*. Chicago, IL: University of Chicago Press, 1962.

Friedman, S. 'The People Can Vote – but Not Decide?' *Democracy Development Program* blog, 16 August 2021. https://ddp.org.za/blog/2021/08/16/the-people-can-vote-but-not-decide/.

Friedman, S. and S. Mottiar. 'Seeking the High Ground: The Treatment Action Campaign and the Politics of Morality'. In *Voices of Protest: Social Movements in Post-Apartheid South Africa*, edited by R. Ballard, A. Habib and I. Valodia, 23–44. Pietermaritzburg: UKZN Press, 2006.

Fryer, D. and R. Fagan. 'Towards a Critical Community Psychological Perspective on Unemployment and Mental Health'. *American Journal of Community Psychology* 32, no. 1/2 (2003): 89–96.

Furman, J. *The New View of Fiscal Policy and its Application*. VoxEU and CEPR, 2 November 2016. https://voxeu.org/article/new-view-fiscal-policy-and-its-application.

Gaspar, V., M. Obstfeld and R. Sahay. *Macroeconomic Management When Policy Space Is Constrained: A Comprehensive, Consistent and Coordinated Approach to Economic Policy*. IMF Staff Discussion Note SDN/16/09. Washington, DC: International Monetary Fund, 2016. https://www.imf.org/external/pubs/ft/sdn/2016/sdn1609.pdf.

Gechert, S., G. Horn and C. Paetz. 'Long-Term Effects of Fiscal Stimulus and Austerity in Europe'. *Oxford Bulletin of Economics and Statistics* 81, no. 3 (2018): 647–666.

Ghatak, M. 'Universal Basic Income: The Case for UBI in Developed Versus Developing Countries'. Presentation at London School of Economics, 24 November 2017. http://personal.lse.ac.uk/ghatak/UBI-Slides_LSE-SAC_Nov24_2017.pdf.

Gheaus, A. 'Basic Income, Gender Justice and the Costs of Gender-Symmetrical Lifestyles'. *Basic Income Studies* 3, no. 3 (2008): 1–8.

Gibson, D., A. Ismail, D. Kilian and M. Matshikiza. 'The State of Our Environment: Safeguarding the Foundation for Development'. In *State of the Nation: South Africa 2008*, edited by P. Kagwanja and K. Kondlo, 178–200. Cape Town: HSRC Press, 2008.

Gibson-Graham, J.K. 'Building Community Economies: Women and the Economies of Place'. In *Women and the Politics of Place*, edited by W. Harcourt and A. Escobar, 130–157. Bloomfield, CT: Kumarian Press, 2005.

Gilberstadt, H. *More Americans Oppose than Favor the Government Providing a Universal Basic Income for All Adult Citizens*. Washington, DC: Pew Research Center, 2020. https://www.pewresearch.org/fact-tank/2020/08/19/more-americans-oppose-than-favor-the-government-providing-a-universal-basic-income-for-all-adult-citizens/.

Gilbert, N. *The Transformation of the Welfare State*. Oxford: Oxford University Press, 2002.

Gilbert, R., N.A. Murphy and A. Stepka. *Would a Basic Income Guarantee Reduce the Motivation to Work? An Analysis of Labor Responses in 16 Trial Programs*. California: Loyola Marymount University, 2018.

Godin, A. *Guaranteed Green Jobs: Sustainable Full Employment*. Working Paper 722. New York: Levy Economics Institute of Bard College, 2012. http://www.levyinstitute.org/pubs/wp_722.pdf.

Goldin, I. and M. Mariathasan. *The Butterfly Defect: How Globalization Creates Systemic Risks, and What to Do about it*. Princeton, NJ: Princeton University Press, 2014.

Goldsmith, S. 'The Economic and Social Impacts of the Permanent Fund Dividend on Alaska'. In *Alaska's Permanent Fund Dividend: Examining its Suitability as a Model*, edited by K. Widerquist and M.W. Howard, 83–106. New York: Palgrave Macmillan, 2012.

Golombek, R. and A. Raknerud. 'Do Environmental Standards Harm Manufacturing Employment?' *The Scandinavian Journal of Economics* 99, no. 1 (1997): 29–44.

Gordon, L. *Pitied but Not Entitled: Single Mothers and the History of Welfare 1890–1935*. New York: Free Press, 1994.

Gorz, A. *Strategy for Labor: A Radical Proposal*. Boston: Beacon Press, 1967.

Gorz, A. *Paths to Paradise*. London: Pluto Books, 1985.

Gorz, A. 'On the Difference between Society and Community, and Why Basic Income Cannot by Itself Confer Full Membership of Either'. In *Arguing for Basic Income*, edited by P. van Parijs, 178–184. London: Verso, 1992.

Gorz, A. *Reclaiming Work: Beyond the Wage-Based Society*. Cambridge: Polity Press, 1999.

Gorz, A. *The Immaterial: Knowledge, Value and Capital*. London: Seagull Books, 2010.

Gough, I. 'Universal Basic Services: A Theoretical and Moral Framework'. *The Political Quarterly* 90, no. 3 (2019): 534–542.

Gourevitch, A. and L. Stanczyk. 'The Basic Income Illusion'. *Catalyst: A Critical Journal of Theory and Strategy* 1, no. 4 (2018): 151–177.

Government of South Africa. *RDP White Paper*. Pretoria: Government of South Africa, 1994.

Government of South Africa. *The Constitution of South Africa. Chapter 2: Bill of Rights*. Pretoria: Government of South Africa, 1996.

Government of South Africa. *National Development Plan: Our Future, Make it Work*. Pretoria: Government of South Africa, 2012. https://www.gov.za/sites/default/files/gcis_document/201409/ndp-2030-our-future-make-it-workr.pdf.

Grabel, I. *When Things Don't Fall Apart: Global Financial Governance and Developmental Finance in an Age of Productive Incoherence*. Amherst, MA: MIT Press, 2018.

Graeber, D. *Bullshit Jobs: A Theory*. New York: Simon and Schuster, 2018.

Granlund, S. and T. Hochfeld. '"That Child Support Grant Gives Me Powers" – Exploring Social and Relational Aspects of Cash Transfers in South Africa in Times of Livelihood Change'. *The Journal of Development Studies* 56, no. 6 (2020): 1230–1244.

Granter, E. *Critical Social Theory and the End of Work*. New York: Routledge, 2009.

Gravelle, J.G. and D.J. Marples. *Fiscal Policy and Recovery from the COVID-19 Recession*. Congressional Research Service Report R46460. Washington, DC: Congressional Research Service, 2021. https://crsreports.congress.gov/product/pdf/R/R46460.

Greenstein, R. *Commentary: Universal Basic Income May Sound Attractive but, if it Occurred, Would Likelier Increase Poverty than Reduce it*. Washington, DC: Center on Budget and Policy Priorities, 2019. https://www.cbpp.org/sites/default/files/atoms/files/5-31-16bud.pdf.

Grisolia, F., N. Holvoet and S. Dewachter. *Busibi UCT: Preliminary Analysis on Some Key Outcomes*. Antwerp: University of Antwerp, 2021. https://drive.google.com/file/d/14pAIIOxzDsQJ3UGbDzSlGa9wXT2GQnnO/view.

Gronbach, L. *Social Cash Transfer Payment Systems in Sub-Saharan Africa*. Working Paper 452. Cape Town: Centre for Social Science Research, University of Cape Town, 2020.

Gumede, W. *Thabo Mbeki and the Battle for the Soul of the ANC*. Cape Town: Zebra Press, 2005.

Gunnion, S. 'Business of the Bourse: SA Equities Outperform Global Indices'. *Daily Maverick*, 19 February 2021. https://www.dailymaverick.co.za/article/2021-02-18-business-of-the-bourse-sa-equities-outperform-global-indices/.

Guo, E. 'Universal Basic Income Is Here – it Just Looks Different from What You Expected'. *MIT Technology Review*, 7 May 2021. https://www.technologyreview.com/2021/05/07/1024674/ubi-guaranteed-income-pandemic/.

Haarmann, C., D. Haarmann, H. Jauch, H. Shindondola-Mote, N. Nattrass, I. van Niekerk and M. Samson. *Basic Income Grant Pilot Project Assessment Report*. Windhoek: Basic Income Grant Coalition, 2009. http://www.bignam.org/Publications/BIG_Assessment_report_08b.pdf.

Hagen-Zanker, J., F. Bastagli, L. Harman, V. Barca, G. Sturge and T. Schmidt. *Understanding the Impact of Cash Transfers: The Evidence*. London: Overseas Development Institute, 2016. https://www.calpnetwork.org/wp-content/uploads/2020/09/10748.pdf.

Hall, S. 'The Problem of Ideology: Marxism without Guarantees'. In *Stuart Hall: Critical Dialogues in Cultural Studies*, edited by D. Morley and K-H. Chen, 25–46. London: Routledge, 1996.

Hallink, C. 'South Africa's Time for a Basic Income Grant Has Come – but the ANC Is Still Apprehensive and Non-Committal'. *Daily Maverick*, 2 February 2021. https://www.dailymaverick.co.za/article/2021-02-02-south-africas-time-for-a-basic-income-grant-has-come-but-the-anc-is-still-apprehensive-and-non-committal/.

Hallowes, D. and V. Munnik. *Down to Zero: The Politics of Just Transition – The GroundWork Report 2019*. Pietermaritzburg: GroundWork, 2019. https://www.groundwork.org.za/reports/gW_Report_2019.pdf.

Hämäläinen, P., J. Takala and T.B. Kiat. *Global Estimates of Occupational Accidents and Work-Related Illnesses, 2017*. Helsinki: Ministry of Social Affairs and Health (Finland), 2017. http://www.icohweb.org/site/images/news/pdf/Report%20Global%20Estimates%20of%20Occupational%20Accidents%20and%20Work-related%20Illnesses%202017%20rev1.pdf.

Hamilton, T.B. 'The Netherlands' Upcoming Money-for-Nothing Experiment'. *The Atlantic*, 21 June 2016. https://www.theatlantic.com/business/archive/2016/06/netherlands-utrecht-universal-basic-income-experiment/487883/.

Handa, S., S. Daidone, A. Peterman, B. Davis, A. Pereira, T. Palermo and J. Yablonski. 'Myth-Busting? Confronting Six Common Perceptions about Unconditional Cash Transfers as a Poverty Reduction Strategy in Africa'. *The World Bank Research Observer* 33, no. 2 (2018): 259–298.

Hanlon, J., A. Barrientos and D. Hulme. *Just Give Money to the Poor*. Sterling, VA: Kumarian Books, 2010.

Harris, J. 'Why Universal Basic Income Could Help Us Fight the Next Wave of Economic Shocks'. *The Guardian*, 3 May 2020. https://www.theguardian.com/commentisfree/2020/may/03/universal-basic-income-coronavirus-shocks.

Harrison, A. *Has Globalisation Eroded Labor's Share? Some Cross-Country Evidence*. Washington, DC: National Bureau of Economic Research, 2005. https://mpra.ub.uni-muenchen.de/39649/1/MPRA_paper_39649.pdf.

Hart, G. *Disabling Globalization: Places of Power in Post-Apartheid South Africa*. Pietermaritzburg: UKZN Press, 2002.

Hart, G. 'Beyond Neoliberalism? Post-Apartheid Developments in Historical and Comparative Perspective'. In *The Development Decade? Economic and Social Change in South Africa: 1994–2004*, edited by V. Padayachee, 13–32. Cape Town: HSRC Press, 2006.

Hart, K. and V. Padayachee. 'A History of South African Capitalism in National and Global Perspective'. *Transformation: Critical Perspectives on Southern Africa* 81/82 (2013): 55–85.

Harvey, D. *A Brief History of Neoliberalism*. Oxford: Oxford University Press, 2005.

Harvey, D. *The Enigma of Capital – and the Crisis of Capitalism*. London: Profile Books, 2010.

Harvey, D. *Seventeen Contradictions and the End of Capitalism*. New York: Oxford University Press, 2014.

Hassim, S. *Gender, Welfare and the Developmental State in South Africa*. Geneva: UNRISD, 2005. https://sarpn.org/documents/d0001335/index.php.

Hassim, S. 'Social Justice, Care and Developmental Welfare in South Africa: A Capabilities Perspective'. *Social Dynamics* 34, no. 2 (2008): 104–118.

Healy, N. and J. Barry. 'Politicizing Energy Justice and Energy System Transitions: Fossil Fuel Divestment and a "Just Transition"'. *Energy Policy* 108 (2017): 451–459.

Henwood, D. 'The Robots Are Not Coming for All of Our Jobs'. *Jacobin*, 23 February 2020. https://www.jacobinmag.com/2020/02/robots-jobs-united-states-gdp-wages-productivity-growth-economy.

Henwood, D. 'The GameStop Bubble Is a Lesson in the Absurdity and Uselessness of the Stock Market'. *Jacobin*, 21 January 2021. https://www.jacobinmag.com/2021/01/gamestop-stock-market-reddit.

Herbig, B., N. Dragano and P. Angerer. 'Health in the Long-Term Unemployed'. *Deutsches Ärzteblatt International* 110, no. 23/24 (2013): 413–419.

Herndon, T., M. Ash and R. Pollin. 'Does High Public Debt Consistently Stifle Economic Growth? A Critique of Reinhart and Rogoff'. *Cambridge Journal of Economics* 38, no. 2 (2014): 257–279.

Hester, H. 'Care under Capitalism: The Crisis of "Women's Work"'. *Progressive Review* 24, no. 4 (2018): 343–352.

Hetschko, C., A. Knabe and R. Schöb. 'Changing Identity: Retiring from Unemployment'. *The Economic Journal* 124, no. 575 (2014): 149–166.

Heywood, M. 'Gauteng Department of Education Spent R431-Million in Three Months on Unnecessary "Deep Cleaning" and "Decontamination" of Schools'. *Daily Maverick*, 26 January 2021. https://www.dailymaverick.co.za/article/2021-01-26-gauteng-department-of-education-spent-r431-million-in-three-months-on-unnecessary-deep-cleaning-and-decontamination-of-schools/.

Hickey, S. and B. Bukenya. 'The Politics of Promoting Social Cash Transfers in Uganda: The Potential and Pitfalls of "Thinking and Working Politically"'. *Development Policy Review* 39, no. S1 (2021): 1–20. https://doi.org/10.1111/dpr.12474.

Hickey, S. and J. Seekings. 'Who Should Get What, How and Why? DFID and the Transnational Politics of Social Cash Transfers in Sub-Saharan Africa'. In *The Politics of Social Protection in Eastern and Southern Africa*, edited by S. Hickey, T. Lavers, M. Nino-Zarazua and J. Seekings, 249–275. Oxford: Oxford University Press, 2020.

High-Level Commission on Carbon Prices. *Report of the High-Level Commission on Carbon Prices*. Washington, DC: World Bank, 2017. https://www.carbonpricingleadership.org/report-of-the-highlevel-commission-on-carbon-prices/.

Hilferding, R. *Finance Capital: A Study of the Latest Phase of Capitalist Development*. London: Routledge and Kegan Paul, 1981.

Hochfeld, T. and S. Plagerson. 'Dignity and Stigma among South African Female Cash Transfer Recipients'. *IDS Bulletin* 42, no. 6 (2011): 53–59.

Horbach, J. and K. Rennings. 'Environmental Innovation and Employment Dynamics in Different Technology Fields – an Analysis Based on the German Community Innovation Survey 2009'. *Journal of Cleaner Production* 57 (2013): 158–165.

Horowitz, J. 'How 39 Million Europeans Kept Their Jobs after the Work Dried Up'. *CNN Business*, 6 May 2020. https://edition.cnn.com/2020/05/06/economy/europe-part-time-work/index.html.

Houseman, S.N. *Understanding the Decline of U.S. Manufacturing Employment*. Working Paper 18-287. Kalamazoo, MI: W.E. Upjohn Institute for Employment Research, 2018.

Huber, E. and J.D. Stephens. *Democracy and the Left: Social Policy and Inequality in Latin America*. Chicago, IL: University of Chicago Press, 2012.

Hull, E. and D. James. 'Introduction: Popular Economies in South Africa'. *Africa* 82, no. 1 (2012): 1–19.

Human, L. 'High Noon: Civil Society Coalition and National Treasury Heading for Showdown over Crucial Income Grant'. *Daily Maverick*, 29 October 2021. https://www.dailymaverick.co.za/article/2021-10-29-high-noon-civil-society-coalition-and-national-treasury-heading-for-showdown-over-crucial-income-grant/.

Human Sciences Research Council. *South African Social Attitudes Survey (SASAS) 2016*. Cape Town: HSRC Press, 2016.

Hunter, M. 'The Changing Political Economy of Sex in South Africa: The Significance of Unemployment and Inequalities to the Scale of the AIDS Pandemic'. *Social Science and Medicine* 64, no. 3 (2007): 689–700.

Hyde, M., S. George and V. Kumar. 'Trends in Work and Employment in Rapidly Developing Countries'. In *Handbook of Disability, Work and Health*. Handbook Series in Occupational Health Sciences, Vol. 1, edited by U. Bültmann and J. Siegrist, 33–52. Cham: Springer, 2020.

ILO (International Labour Organization). *Report of the Director-General: Decent Work*. International Labour Conference, 87th Session. Geneva: International Labour Organization, 1999.

ILO. *Global Wage Report 2014/2015: Wages and Income Inequality*. Geneva: International Labour Organization, 2014.

ILO. *Women and Men in the Informal Economy: A Statistical Picture*. Geneva: International Labour Organization, 2018.

ILO. *World Employment and Social Outlook: Trends 2018*. Geneva: International Labour Organization, 2018.

ILO. *The Global Labour Income Share and Distribution: Key Findings*. Geneva: International Labour Organization, 2019. https://www.ilo.org/wcmsp5/groups/public/---dgreports/---stat/documents/publication/wcms_712232.pdf.

ILO. *Safety and Health at the Heart of the Future of Work: Building on 100 Years of Experience*. Geneva: International Labour Organization, 2019. https://www.ilo. org/wcmsp5/groups/public/---dgreports/---dcomm/documents/publication/ wcms_686645.pdf.

ILO. *World Employment and Social Outlook: Trends 2020*. Geneva: International Labour Organization, 2020.

ILO. *Global Wage Report 2020–21: Wages and Minimum Wages in the Time of COVID-19*. Geneva: International Labour Organization, 2021. https://www.ilo.org/wcmsp5/groups/ public/---dgreports/---dcomm/---publ/documents/publication/wcms_762534.pdf.

ILO. *Statistics on Union Membership*. ILOSTAT. Geneva: International Labour Organization, 2021. https://www.ilo.org/shinyapps/bulkexplorer44/?lang=en&seg ment=indicator&id=ILR_TUMT_NOC_RT_A.

ILO. *World Employment and Social Outlook: Trends 2021*. Geneva: International Labour Organization, 2021.

ILO. *World Employment and Social Outlook: Trends 2022*. Geneva: International Labour Organization, 2022.

Imbert, C. and J. Papp. 'Labor Market Effects of Social Programs: Evidence from India's Employment Guarantee'. *American Economic Journal: Applied Economics* 7, no. 2 (2015): 233–263.

IMF (International Monetary Fund). 'Still Sluggish Global Growth'. *World Economic Outlook*, July 2019. https://www.imf.org/en/Publications/WEO/Issues/2019/07/18/ WEOupdateJuly2019.

IMF. *World Economic Outlook Database*. January 2021. https://www.imf.org/en/ Countries/ZAF.

Institute for Economic Justice. *The Case for Extending the COVID-19 Special Grants*. COVID-19 Fact Sheet No. 5. Johannesburg: Institute for Economic Justice, 2020. https://iej.org.za/wp-content/uploads/2020/10/IEJ-COVID-19-factsheet-5---SRD-FINAL.pdf.

Institute for Economic Justice. *Introducing a Universal Basic Income Guarantee for South Africa: Towards Income Security for All*. Social Protection Series Policy Brief No. 1. Johannesburg: Institute for Economic Justice, 2021. https://www.iej.org.za/ wp-content/uploads/2021/03/IEJ-policy-brief-UBIG_2.pdf.

Institute for Economic Justice. *Financing Options for a Universal Basic Income in South Africa*. Social Protection Series Policy Brief No. 2. Johannesburg: Institute for Economic Justice, 2021. https://www.iej.org.za/wp-content/uploads/2021/08/IEJ-policy-brief-UBIG-july2021_3.pdf.

Institute for Economic Justice. *Designing a Basic Income Guarantee: Targeting, Universality and Other Considerations*. Social Protection Series Policy Brief No. 3. Johannesburg: Institute for Economic Justice, 2021. https://www.iej.org.za/ wp-content/uploads/2021/10/IEJ-policy-brief-UBIG-3_2.pdf.

IPCC (Intergovernmental Panel on Climate Change). *Global Warming of 1.5°C: Special Report*. Geneva: World Meteorological Organization, 2018. https://www.ipcc.ch/sr15/.

Irwin, N. 'Quantitative Easing Is Ending. Here's What it Did, in Charts'. *The New York Times*, 29 October 2014. https://www.nytimes.com/2014/10/30/upshot/ quantitative-easing-is-about-to-end-heres-what-it-did-in-seven-charts.html.

Isaacs, G. and A. Kaltenbrunner. 'Financialization and Liberalization: South Africa's New Forms of External Vulnerability'. *Competition and Change* 22, no. 4 (2018): 437–463.

Jackson, W.A. 'Basic Income and the Right to Work: A Keynesian Approach'. *Journal of Post-Keynesian Economics* 21, no. 4 (1999): 639–662.

Jacques, O. and A. Noel. 'The Case for Welfare State Universalism, or the Lasting Relevance of the Paradox of Redistribution'. *The Journal of European Social Policy* 28, no. 1 (2018): 70–85.

Jahoda, M. *Employment and Unemployment: A Social-Psychological Analysis.* Cambridge: Cambridge University Press, 1982.

Jain, R., J. Budlender, R. Zizzamia and I. Bassier. *The Labor Market and Poverty Impacts of COVID-19 in South Africa.* SALDRU Working Paper 264. Cape Town: Southern Africa Labour and Development Research Unit, University of Cape Town, 2020. http://www.opensaldru.uct.ac.za/bitstream/handle/11090/980/2020_264_Saldruwp.pdf?sequence=1.

Jansson, I. 'Occupation and Basic Income through the Lens of Arendt's *Vita Activa*'. *Journal of Occupational Science* 27, no. 1 (2020): 125–137.

Jeske, C. 'Why Work? Do We Understand What Motivates Work-Related Decisions in South Africa?' *Journal of Southern African Studies* 44, no. 1 (2018): 27–42.

Jhabvala, R. 'Basic Income Can Transform Women's Lives'. *OpenDemocracy*, 19 September 2019. https://www.opendemocracy.net/en/beyond-trafficking-and-slavery/basic-income-can-transform-womens-lives/.

Johnson, C. *MITI and the Japanese Miracle: The Growth of Industrial Policy, 1925–1975.* Stanford, CA: Stanford University Press, 1982.

Jones, D. and I. Marinescu. *The Labor Market Impacts of Universal and Permanent Cash Transfers: Evidence from the Alaska Permanent Fund.* Working Paper 24312. Washington, DC: National Bureau of Economic Research, 2020. https://www.nber.org/system/files/working_papers/w24312/w24312.pdf.

Jones, P. *Work without the Worker: Labour in the Age of Platform Capitalism.* London: Verso Books, 2021.

Jowitt, J. 'Strivers v. Shirkers: The Language of the Welfare Debate'. *The Guardian*, 8 January 2013. https://www.theguardian.com/politics/2013/jan/08/strivers-shirkers-language-welfare.

Kagan, C. 'Universal Basic Income: Is it the Only Cornerstone of a Just Society?' *Steady State Manchester*, 15 March 2017. https://steadystatemanchester.net/2017/03/15/universal-basic-income-is-it-the-only-cornerstone-of-a-just-society/.

Kalecki, M. 'Political Aspects of Full Employment'. *Political Quarterly* 14, no. 4 (1943): 322–331. https://delong.typepad.com/kalecki43.pdf.

Kalkuhl, M., B.F. Milan, G. Schwerhoff, M. Jakob, M. Hahnen and F. Creutzig. 'Can Land Taxes Foster Sustainable Development? An Assessment of Fiscal, Distributional and Implementation Issues'. *Land Use Policy* 78 (2018): 338–352.

Karabarbounis, L. and B. Neiman. *The Global Decline of the Labor Share.* National Bureau of Economic Research Working Paper 19136. Washington, DC: National Bureau of Economic Research, 2013.

Kassam, A. 'Ontario Plans to Launch Universal Basic Income Trial Run This Summer'. *The Guardian*, 24 April 2017. https://www.theguardian.com/world/2017/apr/24/canada-basic-income-trial-ontario-summer?CMP=Share_iOSApp_Other.

Kelly, M. 'Regulating the Reproduction and Mothering of Poor Women: The Controlling Image of the Welfare Mother in Television News Coverage of Welfare Reform'. *Journal of Poverty* 14, no. 1 (2010): 76–96.

Kelton, S. *The Deficit Myth: Modern Monetary Theory and the Birth of the People's Economy*. New York: Public Affairs, 2020.

Kenny, B. and E. Webster. 'Eroding the Core: Flexibility and the Resegmentation of the South African Labour Market'. *Critical Sociology* 24, no. 3 (1998): 216–243.

Kerstenetzky, C.L. 'Redistribution and Development? The Political Economy of the Bolsa Família Program'. *Dados* 52, no. 1 (2009): 53–83.

Kidd, S. and D. Athias. *Hit and Miss: An Assessment of Targeting Effectiveness in Social Protection*. London: Development Pathways, 2020. https://www.developmentpathways.co.uk/wp-content/uploads/2019/03/Hit-and-miss-long-report-.pdf.

Klein, N. *This Changes Everything: Capitalism Versus the Climate*. London: Penguin Books, 2015.

Korpi, W. and J. Palme. 'The Paradox of Redistribution and Strategies of Equality: Welfare State Institutions, Inequality and Poverty in the Western Countries'. *American Sociological Review* 63, no. 5 (1998): 661–687.

Kucera, D. and T. Xenogiani. 'Persisting Informal Employment: What Explains it?' In *Is Informal Normal?: Towards More and Better Jobs in Developing Countries*, edited by P. Jutting and J.R. de Laiglesia, 89–114. Paris: OECD Publishing, 2009. https://doi.org/10.1787/9789264059245-5-en.

Kumleben, N. 'South Africa's Coal Deal Is a New Model for Climate Change'. *Foreign Policy*, 12 November 2021. https://foreignpolicy.com/2021/11/12/coal-climate-south-africa-cop26-agreement/.

Kunkel, B. *Utopia or Bust: A Guide to the Present Crisis*. London: Verso Books, 2014.

Labica, G. *Robespierre – une politique de la philosophie*. Paris: Presses Universitaires de France, 1990.

Lafargue, P. *The Right to be Lazy*. Translated by C. Kerr. London: Charles Kerr and Company, 1883 [online version 2000]. https://www.marxists.org/archive/lafargue/1883/lazy/index.htm.

Lagarde, M., A. Haines and N. Palmer. 'The Impact of Conditional Cash Transfers on Health Outcomes and Use of Health Services in Low and Middle Income Countries'. *Cochrane Database of Systematic Reviews* 4 (2009). doi: 10.1002/14651858. CD008137.

Lakner, C., N. Yonzan, D.G. Mahler, R.A. Aguilar and H. Wu. 'Updated Estimates of the Impact of COVID-19 on Global Poverty: Looking Back at 2020 and the Outlook for 2021'. *World Bank Blogs*, 11 January 2021. https://blogs.worldbank.org/opendata/updated-estimates-impact-covid-19-global-poverty-looking-back-2020-and-outlook-2021.

Lampman, R.J. *Nixon's Family Assistance Plan*. Madison, WI: Institute for Research on Poverty, University of Wisconsin, 1969. https://www.irp.wisc.edu/publications/dps/pdfs/dp5769.pdf.

Lansley, S. *Meeting the Economic and Livelihood Crisis: From a Recovery Basic Income to a Permanent Income Floor*. London: Compass, 2020. https://www.compassonline.org.uk/wp-content/uploads/2020/04/BasicIncomeFloor_SL_FINAL.pdf.

Lavinas, L. '21st Century Welfare'. *New Left Review* 84 (2013): 5–40.

Lavinas, L. *The Takeover of Social Policy by Financialization: The Brazilian Paradox.* New York: Palgrave MacMillan, 2017.

Lawhon, M. and T. McCreary. 'Beyond Jobs vs Environment: On the Potential of a Universal Basic Income to Reconfigure Environmental Politics'. *Antipode* 52, no. 2 (2020): 452–474.

Lawson, L. *Side Effects: The Story of AIDS in South Africa.* Cape Town: Double Storey Books, 2008.

Leibbrandt, M., A. Finn and I. Woolard. 'Describing and Decomposing Post-Apartheid Income Inequality in South Africa'. *Development Southern Africa* 29, no. 1 (2012): 19–34.

Leibbrandt, M., K. Lelenstein, C. Shenker and I. Woolard. *The Influence of Social Transfers on Labour Supply: A South African and International Review.* Working Paper 112. Cape Town: Southern Africa Labour and Development Research Unit, University of Cape Town, 2013. http://www.opensaldru.uct.ac.za/bitstream/handle/11090/670/2013_112.pdf?sequence=1.

Leibbrandt, M., I. Woolard, H. McEwen and C. Koep. *Employment and Inequality Outcomes in South Africa.* Cape Town: Southern Africa Labour and Development Research Unit and School of Economics, University of Cape Town, 2015.

Le Roux, P. 'Financing a Universal Income Grant in South Africa'. *Social Dynamics* 28, no. 2 (2003): 98–121.

Leubolt, B. *Social Policies and Redistribution in South Africa.* Global Labour University Working Paper 25. Geneva: International Labour Organization, 2014.

Liebenberg, S. 'Universal Access to Social Security Rights: Can a Basic Income Grant Meet the Challenge?' *ESR Review* 3, no. 2 (2002).

Lilenstein, K., I. Woolard and M. Leibbrandt. *In-Work Poverty in South Africa: The Impact of Income Sharing in the Presence of High Unemployment.* Working Paper 193. Cape Town: Southern Africa Labour and Development Research Unit, University of Cape Town, 2016.

Lindeberg, R. 'Robots Are Now Everywhere, Except in the Productivity Statistics'. *Bloomberg*, 10 April 2018. https://www.bloombergquint.com/global-economics/robots-are-now-everywhere-except-in-the-productivity-statistics.

Little, A. *The Political Thought of Andre Gorz.* New York: Routledge, 1996.

Lodge, T. 'Neo-Patrimonial Politics in the ANC'. *African Affairs* 113, no. 450 (2014): 1–23.

Long, H. 'The Share Our Wealth Society'. *Social Welfare History Project*, 2021 [1934]. http://socialwelfare.library.vcu.edu/eras/great-depression/long-huey/.

Loveday, M., Y.N. Mzobe, Y. Pillay and P. Barron. 'Figures of the Dead: A Decade of Tuberculosis Mortality Registrations in South Africa'. *South African Medical Journal* 109, no. 10 (2019): 728–732.

Lowrey, A. *Give People Money.* London: W.H. Allen, 2018.

Lund, F. *Changing Social Policy: The Child Support Grant in South Africa.* Cape Town: HSRC Press, 2008.

Macdonald, L. 'We Are All Housewives: Universal Basic Income as Wages for Housework'. *Lateral* 7, no. 2 (2018). https://csalateral.org/issue/7-2/basic-income-housewives-wages-housework-macdonald/.

Macro-Economic Research Group. *Making Democracy Work: A Framework for Macroeconomic Policy in South Africa*. Bellville: Centre for Development Studies, University of the Western Cape, 1993.

Marais, H. *Buckling: The Impact of AIDS in South Africa*. Pretoria: Centre for the Study of AIDS, 2005.

Marais, H. *South Africa Pushed to the Limit: The Political Economy of Change*. London: Zed Books, 2011.

Marais, H. 'The Employment Crisis, Just Transition and the Universal Basic Income Grant'. In *The Climate Crisis: South African and Global Democratic Eco-Socialist Alternatives*, edited by V. Satgar, 70–106. Johannesburg: Wits University Press, 2018.

Marais, H. 'The Crisis of Waged Work and the Option of a Universal Basic Income Grant for South Africa'. *Globalizations* 17, no. 2 (2020): 352–379.

Marais, H. 'Swept Along: The Left in Post-Apartheid South Africa'. In *New Leaders, New Dawns? South Africa and Zimbabwe under Cyril Ramaphosa and Emmerson Mnangagwa*, edited by B. Rutherford, C. Brown and D. Moore, 138–178. Montreal: McGill-Queen's University Press, in press.

Martikainen, P.T. and T. Valkonen. 'Excess Mortality of Unemployed Men and Women during a Period of Rapidly Increasing Unemployment'. *Lancet* 348, no. 9032 (1996): 909–912.

Marx, K. *Capital, Volume 1*. London: Penguin, 1990 [1867].

Marx, K. and F. Engels. *The Communist Manifesto*. Edited by F.L. Bender. New York: W.W. Norton, 1988 [1848].

Mason, P. *Postcapitalism: A Guide to Our Future*. London: Farrar, Straus and Giroux, 2015.

Matisonn, H. and J. Seekings. 'Welfare in Wonderland? The Politics of Basic Income Grant in South Africa, 1996–2002'. Paper presented to the 9th International Congress of the Basic Income European Network, Geneva, 12–14 September 2002. https://basicincome.org/bien/pdf/2002MatisonnSeekings.pdf.

Maurizio, R. and G. Vázquez. 'Argentina: efectos del programa Asignación Universal por Hijo en el comportamiento laboral de los adultos'. *Revista CEPAL* 113 (2014): 121–144.

May, J. 'Poverty, Social Policy and the Social Wage'. Paper presented at the conference 'The Politics of Socio-Economic Rights in South Africa: 10 Years after Apartheid', Oslo, 8–9 June 2004. https://sarpn.org/documents/d0000880.old/P996-May_Poverty-SocialPolicy-Wage_200405.pdf.

Mazzucato, M., J. Ryan-Collins and G. Gouzoulis. *Theorising and Mapping Modern Economic Rents*. UCL Institute for Innovation and Public Purpose, Working Paper Series (IIPP WP 2020-13), 2020. https://www.ucl.ac.uk/bartlett/public-purpose/wp2020-13.

Mbeki, M., J. Rossouw, F. Joubert and A. Breytenbach. 'South Africa's Fiscal Cliff Barometer'. *New Agenda* 70 (2018): 29–33.

Mbeki, T. *State of the Nation Address to the Joint Sitting of the Houses of Parliament*. Cape Town, 8 February 2003.

McBride, S., R. Mahon and G.W. Boychuk. *After '08: Social Policy and the Global Financial Crisis.* Vancouver: University of British Columbia Press, 2015.

McCord, A. *An Overview of the Performance and Potential of Public Works Programmes in South Africa.* CSSR Working Paper 49. Cape Town: Centre for Social Science Research, University of Cape Town, 2003.

McCord, A. 'The Social Protection Function of Short-Term Public Works Programmes in the Context of Chronic Poverty'. In *Social Protection for the Poor and Poorest*, edited by A. Barrientos and D. Hulme, 160–180. London: Palgrave Macmillan, 2008.

McFarland, K. 'Existing and Upcoming BI-Related Experiments'. Basic Income Earth Network, 15 October 2017. https://basicincome.org/news/2017/10/overview-of-current-basic-income-related-experiments-october-2017/.

McKee-Ryan, F., Z. Song, C.R. Wanberg and A. Kinicki. 'Psychological and Physical Well-Being during Unemployment: A Meta-Analytic Study'. *Journal of Applied Psychology* 90, no. 1 (2005): 53–76.

McKenzie, R. and S. Mohamed. 'The Political Economy of South Africa and its Interaction with Processes of Financialisation'. In *Studies in Financial Systems No. 15: The South African Financial System*, edited by S. Mohamed, 11–25. Financialisation, Economy, Society and Sustainable Development (FESSUD), SOAS University of London, 2017. https://eprints.kingston.ac.uk/id/eprint/37224/1/McKenzie-R-37224.pdf.

Meth, C. 'Ideology and Social Policy: "Handouts" and the Spectre of "Dependency"'. *Transformation* 56 (2004): 1–30.

Meth, C. *What Is Pro-Poor Growth? What Are Some of the Things that Hinder its Achievement in South Africa?* Research Report. Johannesburg: OXFAM-GB, 2007.

Meth, C. *The (Lame) Duck Unchained Tries to Count the Poor.* Working Paper No. 49. Durban: School of Development Studies, University of KwaZulu-Natal, 2008.

Meth, C. *Employer of Last Resort? South Africa's Expanded Public Works Programme (EPWP).* Working Paper 58. Cape Town: SALDRU, 2011. https://www.opensaldru.uct.ac.za/bitstream/handle/11090/59/2011_58.pdf?sequence=1.

Mideros, A. and C. O'Donoghue. 'The Effect of Unconditional Cash Transfers on Adult Labour Supply: A Unitary Discrete Choice Model for the Case of Ecuador'. *Basic Income Studies* 10, no. 2 (2015): 225–255.

Mideros, A., F. Gassmann and P. Mohnen. *Estimation of Rates of Return on Social Protection: Making the Case for Non-Contributory Social Transfers in Cambodia.* MERIT Working Papers 2013-063. Maastricht: United Nations University, Maastricht Economic and Social Research Institute on Innovation and Technology, 2013.

Mill, J.S. *Principles of Political Economy.* Project Gutenberg, 2009 [1848]. https://eet.pixel-online.org/files/etranslation/original/Mill,%20Principles%20of%20Political%20Economy.pdf.

Minerals Council South Africa. *Facts and Figures 2019.* Johannesburg: Minerals Council South Africa, 2019. https://www.mineralscouncil.org.za/downloads/send/18-current/1250-facts-and-figures-2019.

Ministry of Finance. *2004 Budget Speech.* Cape Town, 18 February 2004. https://www.gov.za/2004-budget-speech.

Mitchell, W. and T. Fazi. *Reclaiming the State: A Progressive Vision of Sovereignty for a Post-Neoliberal World*. London: Pluto Press, 2017.

Mkandawire, T. *Social Policy in a Development Context*. Social Policy and Development Programme Paper No. 7. Geneva: United Nations Research Institute for Social Development, June 2001. https://www.files.ethz.ch/isn/102709/7.pdf.

Mkandawire, T. *Targeting and Universalism in Poverty Reduction*. Geneva: UNRISD, 2005. https://www.unrisd.org/en/library/publications/targeting-and-universalism-in-135.

Mkandawire, T. 'Transformative Social Policy and Innovation in Developing Countries'. *European Journal for Development Research* 19, no. 1 (2007): 13–29.

Mohamed, S. 'The State of the South African Economy'. In *New South Africa Review 1. 2010: Development or Decline?* edited by J. Daniel, P. Naidoo, D. Pillay and R. Southall, 39–64. Johannesburg: Wits University Press, 2010.

Mohamed, S. 'Financialization of the South African Economy'. *Development* 59, no. 1–2 (2016): 137–142.

Mohamed, S. 'The Political Economy of Accumulation in South Africa: Resource Extraction, Financialization, and Capital Flight as Barriers to Investment and Employment Growth'. PhD diss., University of Massachusetts Amherst, 2019. https://scholarworks.umass.edu/dissertations_2/1533.

Mohamed, S. 'Let's Listen to Heterodox Economists for a Change'. *New Frame*, 25 February 2021. https://www.newframe.com/lets-listen-to-heterodox-economists-for-a-change/.

Mokoene, Z.K. and G. Khunou. 'Parental Absence: Intergenerational Tensions and Contestations of Social Grants in South Africa'. *Critical Social Policy* 39, no. 4 (2019): 525–540.

Molatlhwa, O. 'JZ: If I Were a Dictator'. *Times Live*, 25 March 2015. https://www.timeslive.co.za/thetimes/2015/03/25/jz-if-i-were-a-dictator.

Moore, E. and J.Seekings. 'Consequences of Social Protection on Intergenerational Relationships in South Africa: Introduction'. *Critical Social Policy* 39, no. 4 (2019): 513–524.

Moore, J.W. *Capitalism in the Web of Life: Ecology and the Accumulation of Capital*. London: Verso Books, 2015.

Moosa, M. and J. Patel. *South Africans Support Social Grants, but Say Work at Any Wage Beats Unemployment*. Afrobarometer Dispatch 364. Johannesburg: Institute for Justice and Reconciliation, 2020. https://afrobarometer.org/sites/default/files/publications/Dépêches/ab_r7_dispatchno364_south_africans_support_social_grants_but_want_jobs.pdf.

Morrell, R., R. Jewkes and G. Lindegger. 'Hegemonic Masculinity/Masculinities in South Africa: Culture, Power, and Gender Politics'. *Men and Masculinities* 15, no. 1 (2012): 11–30.

Murgai, R., M. Ravallion and D. van de Walle. 'Is Workfare Cost-Effective against Poverty in a Poor Labor-Surplus Economy?' *World Bank Economic Review* 30, no. 3 (2016): 413–445.

Murray, C. *In Our Hands: A Plan to Replace the Welfare State*. Washington, DC: AEI Press, 2006.

Murray, C. 'A Guaranteed Income for Every American'. American Enterprise Institute, 3 June 2016. https://www.aei.org/articles/a-guaranteed-income-for-every-american/.

Murray, M. and C. Pateman, eds. *Basic Income*. London: Palgrave Macmillan, 2012.

Musgrave, A. asnd K. Brown. 'Social Welfare System Revisited'. *Business Day*, 21 October 2008.

Myers-Lipton, S. *Ending Extreme Inequality: An Economic Bill of Rights to Eliminate Poverty*. London: Routledge, 2015.

National Treasury. *Consolidated Government Expenditure Functions and Budget Reviews*. Pretoria: National Treasury, Republic of South Africa, 2019.

National Treasury. *Budget Review 2020*. Pretoria: National Treasury, Republic of South Africa, 2020.

Ndletyana, M. *Anatomy of the ANC in Power: Insights from Port Elizabeth, 1990–2019*. Cape Town: HSRC Press, 2020.

Nersisyan, Y. and L.R. Wray. 'Modern Money Theory and the Facts of Experience'. *Cambridge Journal of Economics* 40, no. 5 (2016): 1297–1316.

Newman, S., B. Baloyi and P. Ncube. *A New Growth Path for South African Industrialisation: An Input-Output Analysis*. Pretoria: Industrial Policy Research Support Project, Department of Trade and Industry, South Africa, 2010.

New World Wealth. *SA Wealth Report 2020: The Wealthiest Cities and Towns in South Africa*. Johannesburg: New World Wealth, 2020. https://cms.cnbcafrica.com/wp-content/uploads/2020/04/South-Africa-2020-1.pdf.

Neyfakh, L. 'Should the Government Pay You to Be Alive?' *The Boston Globe*, 9 February 2014. http://www.bostonglobe.com/ideas/2014/02/09/should-government-pay-you-alive/aaLVJsUAc5pKh0iYTFrXpI/story.html.

Nichols, J. 'A $2,000 Check Is a Good Start, but Struggling Americans Need $2,000 Every Month', *The Nation*, 18 January 2021. https://www.thenation.com/article/economy/mlk-covid-biden-plan/.

Nikiforos, M., M. Steinbaum and G. Zezza. *Modeling the Macroeconomic Effects of a Universal Basic Income*. Washington, DC: Roosevelt Institute, 2017. https://rooseveltinstitute.org/wp-content/uploads/2020/07/RI-Macroeconomic-Effects-of-UBI-201708.pdf.

Nixon, R. 'Transcript of the President's Labor Day Address', *New York Times*, 7 September 1971. https://www.nytimes.com/1971/09/07/archives/transcript-of-the-presidents-labor-day-address.html.

Noble, M. and P. Ntshongwana. *No Sign of a Dependency Culture in South Africa*. HSRC Policy Brief, March 2008. http://www.hsrc.ac.za/uploads/pageContent/1090/No%20sign%20of%20a%20dependency%20culture%20in%20SA.pdf.

Noguchi, E. 'The Cost-Efficiency of a Guaranteed Jobs Program: Really? A Response to Harvey'. *Basic Income Studies* 7, no. 2 (2012): 52–65.

Noh, Y.H. 'Does Unemployment Increase Suicide Rates? The OECD Panel Evidence'. *Journal of Economic Psychology* 30, no. 4 (2009): 575–582.

Olver, C. *How to Steal a City: The Battle for Nelson Mandela Bay*. Johannesburg: Jonathan Ball, 2017.

Omarjee, L. 'Basic Income Grant for SA Not "Radical" but Necessary, Says ex Goldman Sachs CEO'. *News24*, 4 October 2021. https://www.news24.com/fin24/economy/basic-income-grant-for-sa-not-radical-but-necessary-says-ex-goldman-sachs-ceo-20211004.

Orloff, A.S. 'Why Basic Income Does Not Promote Gender Equality'. In *Basic Income: An Anthology of Contemporary Research*, edited by K. Widerquist, J.A. Noguera, Y. Vanderborght and J. de Wispelaere, 149–152. Chichester: Blackwell Publishing, 2013.

Orthofer, A. *Wealth Inequality in South Africa: Evidence from Survey and Tax Data*. REDI3X3 Working Paper 15, June 2016. http://www.redi3x3.org/sites/default/files/ Orthofer%202016%20REDI3x3%20Working%20Paper%2015%20-%20Wealth%20 inequality.pdf.

Orwell, G. *Down and out in Paris and London*. London: Penguin Books, 1989.

Ottersen, O.P., J. Dasgupta, C. Blouin, P. Buss, V. Chongsuvivatwong, J. Frenk, S. Fukuda-Parr, et al. 'The Political Origins of Health Inequity: Prospects for Change'. *Lancet* 383, no. 9917 (2014): 630–667.

Padayachee, V. *Beyond a Treasury View of the World: Reflections from Theory and History on Heterodox Economic Policy Options for South Africa*. Working Paper 2. Johannesburg: Southern Centre for Inequality Studies, University of the Witwatersrand, 2018.

Padayachee, V. 'Beyond the Fiscal Cliff? Some Questions for Reflection'. *New Agenda* 70 (2018): 34–37.

Padayachee, V. 'Can Progressive Macroeconomic Policy Address Growth and Employment while Reducing Inequality in South Africa?' *The Economic and Labour Relations Review* 30, no. 1 (2019): 3–21.

Padayachee, V. and J. Sender. 'Vella Pillay: Revolutionary Activism and Economic Policy Analysis'. *Journal of Southern African Studies* 44, no. 1 (2018): 149–165.

Padayachee, V. and R. van Niekerk. *Shadow of Liberation: Contestation and Compromise in the Economic and Social Policy of the African National Congress, 1943–1996*. Johannesburg: Wits University Press, 2019.

Paine, T. *Agrarian Justice*. 1796 [digital edition 1999]. http://piketty.pse.ens.fr/files/ Paine1795.pdf.

Painter, A. and C. Thoung. *Creative Citizen, Creative State: The Principled and Pragmatic Case for a Universal Basic Income*. London: RSA, 2015. https://www.thersa.org/ globalassets/reports/rsa_basic_income_20151216.pdf.

Palma, G. 'Homogeneous Middles vs. Heterogeneous Tails, and the End of the "Inverted-U": The Share of the Rich Is What it's All About'. *Development and Change* 42, no. 1 (2011): 87–153.

Palma, G. and J.E. Stiglitz. 'Do Nations Just Get the Inequality They Deserve? The "Palma Ratio" Re-examined'. In *Inequality and Growth: Patterns and Policy*, edited by K. Basu and J.E. Stiglitz, 35–97. London: Palgrave Macmillan, 2016.

Pant, A., M. Mostafa and R. Bridle. *Understanding the Role of Subsidies in South Africa's Coal-Based Liquid Fuel Sector*. Winnipeg: International Institute for Sustainable Development, 2020. https://www.iisd.org/system/files/2020-10/subsidies-south-africa-coal-liquid-fuel.pdf.

Parliamentary Budget Office. *The Costs and Outcomes of Industrial Development Initiatives 1994/95–2014/15*. Cape Town: Parliament of the Republic of South Africa, 2016.

Parliamentary Budget Office. *Social Grant Performance as at End March 20/21*. Cape Town: Parliament of the Republic of South Africa, 2021. https://www.parliament. gov.za/storage/app/media/PBO/National_Development_Plan_Analysis/2021/ june/03-06-2021/May_2021_Social_Grant_fact_sheet.pdf.

Patel, J. 'Economic Insecurity Persists for South Africans'. *Afrobarometer Dispatch*, No. 478, 22 September 2021. https://afrobarometer.org/sites/default/files/publications/Dispatches/ad478-economic_insecurity_persists_for_south_africans-afrobarometer_dispatch-18sept21.pdf.

Patel, L. and T. Hochfeld. 'It Buys Food but Does it Change Gender Relations? Child Support Grants in Soweto, South Africa'. *Gender and Development* 19, no. 2 (2011): 229–240.

Patel, L., T. Knijn and F. van Wel. 'Child Support Grants in South Africa: A Pathway to Women's Empowerment and Child Well-Being'. *Journal of Social Policy* 44, no. 2 (2015): 377–397.

Pateman, C. 'Democratizing Citizenship: Some Advantages of a Basic Income'. *Politics and Society* 32, no. 1 (2004): 89–105.

Paul, K.I. and K. Moser. 'Unemployment Impairs Mental Health: Meta-Analyses'. *Journal of Vocational Behavior* 74, no. 3 (2009): 264–282.

Paul, M., W. Darity and D. Hamilton. *The Federal Job Guarantee: A Policy to Achieve Permanent Full Employment*. Washington, DC: Center on Budget and Policy Priorities, 2018. https://www.cbpp.org/sites/default/files/atoms/files/3-9-18fe.pdf.

Pauli, J. and R. van Dijk. 'Marriage as an End or the End of Marriage? Change and Continuity in Southern African Marriages'. *Anthropology Southern Africa* 39, no. 4 (2016): 257–266.

Peaudry, P. *How Quantitative Easing Works. Speech Summary*. Bank of Canada, Ottawa, 10 December 2020. https://www.bankofcanada.ca/2020/12/how-quantitative-easing-works/.

Peck, J. *Workfare States*. New York: Guilford Press, 2001.

Pega, F., S.Y. Liu, S. Walter, R. Pabayo, R. Saith and S.K. Lhachimi. 'Unconditional Cash Transfers for Reducing Poverty and Vulnerabilities: Effect on Use of Health Services and Health Outcomes in Low- and Middle-Income Countries'. *Cochrane Database of Systematic Reviews* 11, no. 11 (2017): CD011135.

Pekanov, A. *The New View on Fiscal Policy and its Implications for the European Monetary Union*. Working Paper 562. Vienna: Austrian Institute of Economic Research, 2018. https://www.wifo.ac.at/jart/prj3/wifo/resources/person_dokument/person_dokument.jart?publikationsid=61037&mime_type=application/pdf.

Pekanov, A. and M. Schratzenstaller. *A Global Financial Transaction Tax: Theory, Practice and Potential Revenues*. Working Paper 582. Vienna: Austrian Institute of Economic Research, 2019. https://www.wifo.ac.at/jart/prj3/wifo/resources/person_dokument/person_dokument.jart?publikationsid=61805&mime_type=application/pdf.

Pettifor, A., C. MacPhail, J.P. Hughes, A. Selin, M.S. Jing Wang, F.X.Gómez-Olivé, S. Eshleman, et al. 'The Effect of a Conditional Cash Transfer on HIV Incidence in Young Women in Rural South Africa (HPTN 068): A Phase 3, Randomised Controlled Trial'. *Lancet Global Health* 4, no. 12 (2016): e978–e988.

Pienaar, C.,Y.D. Davids, B. Roberts, M. Makaoe and T. Hart. *The Big Question: COVID-19 and Policy Support for a Basic Income Grant*, Policy Brief (Cape Town: Human Sciences Research Council, March 2021). https://repository.hsrc.ac.za/bitstream/handle/20.500.11910/15936/11895.pdf?sequence=1&isAllowed=y.

Pietermaritzburg Economic Justice and Dignity Group. *Household Affordability Index, January 2021*. Pietermaritzburg: Pietermaritzburg Economic Justice and Dignity Group, 2021. https://pmbejd.org.za/wp-content/uploads/2021/01/January-2021-Household-Affordability-Index-PMBEJD_27012021.pdf.

Piggot, G., M. Boyland, A. Down and A. Raluca Torre. *Realizing a Just and Equitable Transition away from Fossil Fuels*. Discussion Brief. Stockholm: Stockholm Environment Institute, 2019. https://www.sei.org/wp-content/uploads/2019/01/realizing-a-just-and-equitable-transition-away-from-fossil-fuels.pdf.

Piketty, T. *Capital in the Twenty-First Century*. Cambridge, MA: Harvard University Press, 2013.

Plagerson, S., L. Patel, T. Hochfeld and M.S. Ulriksen. 'Social Policy in South Africa: Navigating the Route to Social Development'. *World Development* 113 (2019): 1–9.

Pollin, R. and B. Callaci. 'A Just Transition for U.S. Fossil Fuel Industry Workers'. *The American Prospect*, July 2016. https://prospect.org/environment/just-transition-u.s.-fossil-fuel-industry-workers/.

Pollin, R., J. Heintz and T. Herndon. 'The Revenue Potential of a Financial Transaction Tax for U.S. Financial Markets'. *International Review of Applied Economics* 32, no. 6 (2018): 772–806.

Polychroniou, C.J. 'Global Financial Governance Ten Years after the Crisis: An Interview with Ilene Grabel'. *Global Policy Journal*, 4 June 2018. Opinion blogpost. https://www.globalpolicyjournal.com/blog/04/06/2018/global-financial-governance-ten-years-after-crisis-interview-ilene-grabel.

Pons-Vignon, N. and W. Anseeuw. 'Great Expectations: Working Conditions in South Africa since the End of Apartheid'. *Journal of Southern African Studies* 35, no. 4 (2009): 883–899.

Posel, D. *Inter-household Transfers in South Africa: Prevalence, Patterns and Poverty*. Working Paper 180, NIDS Discussion Paper 2016/7. Cape Town: Southern Africa Labour and Development Research Unit, University of Cape Town, 2016. https://www.opensaldru.uct.ac.za/bitstream/handle/11090/838/2016_180_Saldruwp.pdf?sequence=1.

Posel, D., J.A. Fairburn and F. Lund. 'Labour Migration and Households: A Reconsideration of the Effects of the Social Pension on Labour Supply in South Africa'. *Economic Modelling* 23 (2006): 836–853.

Posel, D. and M. Rogan. 'Women, Income and Poverty: Gendered Access to Resources in Post-Apartheid South Africa'. *Agenda* 81, no. 23 (2009): 25–34.

Pratt, G.A. 'Is a Cambrian Explosion Coming for Robotics?' *Journal of Economic Perspectives* 29, no. 3 (2015): 51–60.

Presidency of South Africa. *Government's Programme of Action: 2005 (Social Cluster)*. Pretoria: Government of South Africa, 2005.

Prifti, E., S. Daidone and B. Davis. 'Casual Pathways of the Productive Impacts of Cash Transfers: Experimental Evidence from Lesotho'. *World Development* 115 (2019): 258–268.

Raine, B. 'Renewed Labour'. *N+1* 33 (2019): 33–46. https://nplusonemag.com/issue-33/politics/renewed-labour/.

Ramaphosa, C. *Nelson Mandela Memorial Lecture*. 18 July 2021. https://www.youtube.com/watch?v=AMVmGRf3O0c.

Ranchod, V. and N. Finn. *Estimating the Effects of South Africa's Youth Employment Tax Incentive – An Update.* SALDRU Working Paper 152. Cape Town: Southern Africa Labour and Development Research Unit, University of Cape Town, 2015.

Ravallion, M. *Guaranteed Employment or Guaranteed Income?* CGD Working Paper 482. Washington, DC: Center for Global Development, 2018. https://www.cgdev.org/publication/guaranteed-employment-or-guaranteed-income.

Ravallion, M. 'Guaranteed Employment or Guaranteed Income?' *World Development* 115, no. C (2019): 209–221.

Rawls, J. *Justice as Fairness: A Restatement.* Cambridge, MA: Harvard University Press, 2001.

Reed, H. and S. Lansley. *Universal Basic Income: An Idea Whose Time Has Come?* London: Compass, 2016. http://www.compassonline.org.uk/wp-content/uploads/2016/05/UniversalBasicIncomeByCompass-Spreads.pdf.

Richter, L. and R. Morrell, eds. *Baba: Men and Fatherhood in South Africa.* Cape Town: HSRC Press, 2006.

Robeyns, I. 'Hush Money or Emancipation Fee? A Gender Analysis of Basic Income'. In *Basic Income on the Agenda: Policy Objectives and Political Chances*, edited by R. van der Veen and L. Groot, 121–136. Amsterdam: Amsterdam University Press, 2000.

Roex, K.L.A. and J.J. Rozer. 'The Social Norm to Work and the Well-Being of the Short- and Long-Term Unemployed'. *Social Indicators Research* 139 (2018): 1037–1064.

Rogan, M. and J. Reynolds. *The Working Poor in South Africa, 1997–2012.* ISER Working Paper 2015/4. Grahamstown: Institute of Social and Economic Research, Rhodes University, 2015.

Ross, A. *Nice Work if You Can Get it: Life and Labor in Precarious Times.* New York: NYU Press, 2009.

Rossouw, J., L. Mondi and V. Padayachee. 'Inflation Targeting in Context of "Nationalisation" Debate'. *New Agenda* 72 (2019): 19–22.

Rueda, S., L. Chambers, M. Wilson, C. Mustard, S.B. Rourke, A. Bayoumi, J. Raboud and J. Lavis. 'Association of Returning to Work with Better Health in Working-Aged Adults: A Systematic Review'. *American Journal of Public Health* 102, no. 3 (2012): 541–556.

Russell, B. *Roads to Freedom: Socialism, Anarchism and Syndicalism.* London: Routledge, 1993 [1918].

Saad-Filho, A. *For a Just and Democratic Development Approach to Macro-Economic Policy to Advance the Deep Just Transition.* Policy Brief. Johannesburg: Emancipatory Futures Studies Inter- and Transdisciplinary Project, 2020.

Saad-Filho, A. and D. Johnston. *Neoliberalism: A Critical Reader.* London: Pluto Press, 2005.

Sachs, M. 'South Africa's Budget and the Absence of Social Solidarity'. *New Frame*, 22 February 2021. https://www.newframe.com/sas-budget-and-the-absence-of-social-solidarity/.

Sage, D. 'Work and Social Norms: Why We Need to Challenge the Centrality of Employment in Society'. *LSE Blog*, 16 July 2018. https://blogs.lse.ac.uk/politicsandpolicy/work-and-social-norms-why-we-need-to-challenge-the-centrality-of-employment-in-our-society/.

Sage, D. 'Unemployment, Wellbeing and the Power of the Work Ethic: Implications for Social Policy'. *Critical Social Policy* 39, no. 2 (2019): 205–228.

Samuel, S. 'Finland Gave People Free Money. It Didn't Help Them Get Jobs – but Does That Matter?' *Vox*, 9 February 2019. https://www.vox.com/future-perfect/2019/2/9/18217566/finland-basic-income.

Sánchez-Ancochea, D. and L. Mattei. 'Bolsa Família, Poverty and Inequality: Political and Economic Effects in the Short and Long Run'. *Global Social Policy* 11, no. 2/3 (2011): 299–318.

Sanders, B. *Jobs and an Economy for All.* 2020. https://berniesanders.com/issues/jobs-for-all/.

Santens, S. 'Wouldn't Unconditional Basic Income Just Cause Massive Inflation?' *Medium*, 22 November 2014. https://medium.com/basic-income/wouldnt-unconditional-basic-income-just-cause-massive-inflation-fe71d69f15e7.

Santens, S. 'Negative Income Tax (NIT) and Unconditional Basic Income'. *Blogpost*, 17 December 2014. https://www.scottsantens.com/negative-income-tax-nit-and-unconditional-basic-income-ubi-what-makes-them-the-same-and-what-makes-them-different.

Santens, S. 'How to Reform Welfare and Taxes to Provide Every American Citizen with a Basic Income'. *Medium*, 5 June 2017. https://medium.com/economicsecproj/how-to-reform-welfare-and-taxes-to-provide-every-american-citizen-with-a-basic-income-bc67d3f4c2b8.

Sasol. *Investing in Our People: Human Capital Management.* Johannesburg: Sasol, 2018. https://www.sasol.com/sites/default/files/content/files/SASOL_Investing%20in%20our%20People%20Brochure.pdf.

Satgar, V. 'The Climate Crisis and Systemic Alternatives'. In *The Climate Crisis: South African and Global Democratic Eco-Socialist Alternatives*, edited by V. Satgar, 1–28. Johannesburg: Wits University Press, 2018.

Satumba, T., A. Bayat and S. Mohamed. 'The Impact of Social Grants on Poverty Reduction in South Africa'. *Journal of Economics* 8, no. 1 (2017): 33–49.

Sawicky, M.B. 'Foul Shot'. *The Baffler*, 7 March 2018.

Scarlato, M. and G. d'Agostino. 'Cash Transfers, Labor Supply, and Gender Inequality: Evidence from South Africa'. *Feminist Economics* 25, no. 4 (2019): 159–184.

Sculos, B.W. 'Changing Lives and Minds: Progress, Strategy, and Universal Basic Income'. *New Political Science* 41, no. 2 (2019): 234–247.

Seedat, M., A. van Niekerk, R. Jewkes, S. Suffla and K. Ratele. 'Violence and Injuries in South Africa: Prioritising an Agenda for Prevention'. *The Lancet* 374, no. 9694 (2009): 1011–1022.

Seekings, J. 'Basic Income Activism in South Africa, 1997–2019'. In *Political Activism and Basic Income Guarantee: Exploring the Basic Income Guarantee*, edited by R. Caputo and L. Liu, 253–272. London: Palgrave Macmillan, 2020.

Seekings, J. and H. Matisonn. *The Continuing Politics of Basic Income in South Africa.* Working Paper 286. Cape Town: Centre for Social Science Research, University of Cape Town, 2010.

Seekings, J. and N. Nattrass. *Class, Race and Inequality in South Africa.* New Haven, CT: Yale University Press, 2005.

Sen, A. *Development as Freedom*. Oxford: Oxford University Press, 1999.

Sennett, R. *The Corrosion of Character: The Personal Consequences of Work in the New Capitalism*. New York: W.W. Norton, 1998.

Senona, E., E. Torkelson and W. Zembe-Mkabile. *Social Protection in a Time of Covid: Lessons for Basic Income Support*. Mowbray: Black Sash, 2021. https://www. blacksash.org.za/images/0541_BS_-_Social_Protection_in_a_Time_of_Covid_ Final_-_Web.pdf.

Skiti, S. 'Godongwana Hints a Plan to Invest in Employment for "Young Black Kids"'. *Sunday Times*, 8 August 2021. https://www.timeslive.co.za/sunday-times/ news/2021-08-08-godongwana-hints-at-plan-to-invest-in-employment-for-young-black-kids/ (paywall).

Skoufias, E. *Progresa and its Impact on the Human Capital and Welfare of Households in Rural Mexico: A Synthesis of the Results of an Evaluation by IFPRI*. Research Report 139. Washington, DC: International Food Policy Research Institute, 2005. https:// core.ac.uk/download/pdf/6289672.pdf.

Skoufias, E. and V. di Maro. 'Conditional Cash Transfers, Adult Work Incentives, and Poverty'. *The Journal of Development Studies* 44, no. 7 (2008): 935–960.

Sloman, P. 'Universal Basic Income in British Politics, 1918–2018: From a "Vagabond's Wage" to a Global Debate'. *Journal of Social Policy* 47, no. 3 (2018): 625–642.

Soares, S., P.H.G. Ferreira de Souza, R.G. Osório and F.G. Silveira. 'Os impactos do benefício do programa Bolsa Família sobre a desigualdade e a pobreza'. In *Bolsa Família 2003–2010: avanços e desafios*, edited by J. Abrahão de Castro and L. Modesto, 25–52. Brasília: Instituto de Pesquisa Econômica Aplicada, 2010 (cited in Fischer, *Poverty as Ideology*, 235).

Sodha, S. 'Is Finland's Basic Universal Income a Solution to Automation, Fewer Jobs and Lower Wages?' *The Guardian*, 19 February 2017. https://www.theguardian.com/ society/2017/feb/19/basic-income-finland-low-wages-fewer-jobs?CMP=Share_ iOSApp_Other.

Solow, R. 'We'd Better Watch Out'. *New York Times Book Review*, 12 July 1987, p. 36. http://www.standupeconomist.com/pdf/misc/solow-computer-productivity.pdf.

South African Government. *President Cyril Ramaphosa Signs 2019 Carbon Tax Act into Law*. 2019. https://www.gov.za/speeches/publication-2019-carbon-tax-act-26-may-2019-0000.

South African Government. *Child Support Grant*. Information Sheet. Pretoria: South African Government, 2021. https://www.gov.za/services/child-care-social-benefits/ child-support-grant.

South African Government. *Foster Child Grant*. Information Sheet. Pretoria: South African Government, 2021. https://www.gov.za/services/child-care-social-benefits/ foster-child-grant.

South African Government. *Old Age Pension*. Information Sheet. Pretoria: South African Government, 2021. https://www.gov.za/services/social-benefits-retirement-and-old-age/old-age-pension.

South African Government. *Green Paper on Comprehensive Social Security and Retirement Reform*. Government Gazette No. 45006, Vol. 674 (Gazetted 18 August 2021). 2021. https://www.gov.za/sites/default/files/gcis_document/202108/ 45006gon741.pdf.

South African Human Rights Commission. *Basic Income Grant Policy Brief.* Johannesburg: South African Human Rights Commission, 2018. https://www.sahrc.org.za/home/21/files/A%20Policy%20Brief%20on%20a%20Basic%20Income%20Grant%202017-2018.pdf.

South African Revenue Service. *Carbon Tax.* 2020. https://www.sars.gov.za/ClientSegments/Customs-Excise/Excise/Environmental-Levy-Products/Pages/Carbon-Tax.aspx.

South African Social Security Agency. *You and Your Grants 2020/21.* Pretoria: South African Social Security Agency, 2020. https://www.sassa.gov.za/publications/Documents/You%20and%20Your%20Grants%202020%20-%20English.pdf.

Southall, R. 'Democracy at Risk? Politics and Governance under the ANC'. *The ANNALS of the American Academy of Political and Social Science* 652 (2014): 48–69.

Southall, R. 'The Coming Crisis of Zuma's ANC: The Party State Confronts Fiscal Crisis'. *Review of African Political Economy* 43, no. 147 (2016): 73–88.

Spaull, N., C. Ardington, I. Bassier, Bhorat, H., Bridgman, G., Brophy, T., et al. *NIDS-CRAM Synthesis Report Wave 1: Overview and Findings (National Income Dynamics Study – Coronavirus Rapid Mobile Survey).* Cape Town: Datafirst, 2020. https://cramsurvey.org/wp-content/uploads/2020/07/Spaull-et-al.-NIDS-CRAM-Wave-1-Synthesis-Report-Overview-and-Findings-1.pdf.

Srnicek, N. and A. Williams. *Inventing the Future: Post-Capitalism and a World without Work.* London: Verso Books, 2015.

Standing, G. *How Cash Transfers Boost Work and Economic Security.* Working Paper No. 58. New York: Department of Economic and Social Affairs, United Nations, April 2008.

Standing, G. *The Precariat: The New Dangerous Class.* London: Bloomsbury, 2011.

Standing, G. *Basic Income: And How We Can Make it Happen.* London: Pelican Books, 2017.

Stats SA (Statistics South Africa). *Social Grants: In-Depth Analysis of the General Household Survey Data 2003–2007.* GHS series Vol. 1, Statistical Release P0318.1. Pretoria: Statistics South Africa, 2009.

Stats SA. *Volunteer Activities Survey, 2010.* Pretoria: Statistics South Africa, 2011.

Stats SA. *Income and Expenditure of Households 2010/2011.* Statistical Release P0100. Pretoria: Statistics South Africa, 2012.

Stats SA. *Facts You Might Not Know about Social Grants.* Pretoria: Statistics South Africa, 2016. http://www.statssa.gov.za/?p=7756.

Stats SA. *Labour Market Dynamics in South Africa, 2017.* Pretoria: Statistics South Africa, 2017.

Stats SA. *Poverty Trends in South Africa: An Examination of Absolute Poverty between 2006 and 2015.* Pretoria: Statistics South Africa, 2017.

Stats SA. *Men, Women and Children: Findings of the Living Conditions Survey, 2014/2015.* Pretoria: Statistics South Africa, 2018. http://www.statssa.gov.za/publications/Report-03-10-02%20/Report-03-10-02%202015.pdf.

Stats SA. *General Household Survey 2018.* Statistical Release P0318. Pretoria: Statistics South Africa, 2019.

Stats SA. *Mid-year Population Estimates 2019*, Statistical Release P0302. Pretoria: Statistics South Africa, 2019. https://www.statssa.gov.za/publications/P0302/P03022019.pdf.

Stats SA. *General Household Survey 2019.* Statistical Release P0318. Pretoria: Statistics South Africa, 2020. http://www.statssa.gov.za/publications/P0318/P03182018.pdf.

Stats SA. *National Poverty Lines 2020*. Statistical Release P0310.1. Pretoria: Statistics South Africa, 2020. http://www.statssa.gov.za/publications/P03101/P031012020.pdf.

Stats SA. *Quarterly Labour Force Survey QLFS Q2: 2020*. Pretoria: Statistics South Africa, 2020.

Stats SA. *Results from Wave 2 Survey on the Impact of the COVID-19 Pandemic on Employment and Income in South Africa, May 2020*. Report 00-08-03. Pretoria: Statistics South Africa, 2020. http://www.statssa.gov.za/publications/Report-00-80-03/Report-00-80-03May2020.pdf.

Stats SA. *National Poverty Lines 2021*. Statistical Release P0310.1. Pretoria: Statistics South Africa, 2021. http://www.statssa.gov.za/publications/P03101/P031012021.pdf.

Stats SA. *Quarterly Labour Force Survey QLFS Q2: 2021*. Pretoria: Statistics South Africa, 2021. http://www.statssa.gov.za/publications/P0211/Presentation%20QLFS%20Q2_2021.pdf.

Stern, A. *Raising the Floor: How a Universal Basic Income Can Renew Our Economy and Rebuild the American Dream*. New York: Public Affairs Books, 2016.

Stevis, D. and R. Felli. 'Green Transitions, Just Transitions? Broadening and Deepening Justice'. *Kurswechsel* 3 (2016): 35–45.

Strandh, M., A. Hammarström, K. Nilsson, M. Nordenmark and H. Russel. 'Unemployment, Gender and Mental Health: The Role of the Gender Regime'. *Sociology of Health and Illness* 35, no. 5 (2013): 649–665.

Streeck, W. *Buying Time: The Delayed Crisis of Democratic Capitalism*. London: Verso Books, 2013.

Streeck, W. 'How Will Capitalism End?' *New Left Review* 87 (2014): 35–64.

Swilling, M. 'Can Economic Policy Escape State Capture?' *New Agenda: South African Journal of Social and Economic Policy* 72 (2019): 24–27.

Tcherneva, P.R. 'Universal Assurances in the Public Interest: Evaluating the Economic Viability of Basic Income and Job Guarantees'. *International Journal of Environment, Workplace, and Employment* 2, no. 1 (2006): 69–88.

Tcherneva, P.R. *What Are the Relative Macroeconomic Merits and Environmental Impacts of Direct Job Creation and Basic Income Guarantees?* Working Paper 517. New York: Levy Economics Institute of Bard College, 2007. http://www.levyinstitute.org/pubs/wp_517.pdf.

Tcherneva, P.R. 'Evaluating the Economic and Environmental Viability of Basic Income and Job Guarantees'. In *Environment and Employment: A Reconciliation*, edited by P. Lawn, 204–225. London: Routledge, 2009.

Tcherneva, P.R. 'The Job Guarantee: Delivering the Benefits that Basic Income Only Promises – a Response to Guy Standing'. *Basic Income Studies* 7, no. 2 (2012): 66–87.

Tcherneva, P.R. *The Job Guarantee: Design, Jobs and Implementation*. Working Paper 902. New York: Levy Economics Institute of Bard College, 2018. http://www.levyinstitute.org/pubs/wp_902.pdf.

Terkel, S. *Working: People Talk about What They Do All Day and What They Feel about What They Do*. New York: Ballantine Books, 1972.

Timms, M. 'The Case for and against Unconditional Basic Income in Switzerland'. *EuropeanCEO*, 10 January 2014. https://www.europeanceo.com/finance/the-case-for-and-against-unconditional-basic-income-in-switzerland/.

Tondani, D. 'Universal Basic Income and Negative Income Tax: Two Different Ways of Thinking Redistribution'. *The Journal of Socio-Economics* 38, no. 2 (2009): 246–255.

Torkelson, E. 'Collateral Damages: Cash Transfer and Debt Transfer in South Africa'. *World Development* 126 (2020): 104711. https://doi.org/10.1016/j.worlddev.2019.104711.

Torkelson, E. 'Sophia's Choice: Debt, Social Welfare, and Racial Finance Capitalism'. *Environment and Planning D: Society and Space* 39, no. 1 (2021): 67–84.

Toyana, M. 'Minister Lindiwe Zulu Withdraws Social Security Green Paper after Public Backlash'. *Daily Maverick*, 1 September 2021. https://www.dailymaverick.co.za/article/2021-09-01-minister-zulu-withdraws-social-security-green-paper-after-public-backlash/.

Transparency International. 'In South Africa, COVID-19 Has Exposed Greed and Spurred Long-Needed Action against Corruption'. *Corruption Watch*, 4 September 2020. https://www.transparency.org/en/blog/in-south-africa-covid-19-has-exposed-greed-and-spurred-long-needed-action-against-corruption.

Trapp, K. *Measuring the Labour Income Share of Developing Countries: Learning from Social Accounting Matrices*. WIDER Working Paper 2015/041. Helsinki: World Institute for Development Economics Research, 2015. https://www.wider.unu.edu/sites/default/files/wp2015-041.pdf.

Turok, B. 'Pravin Clarified the Reserve Bank's Mandate Years Ago'. *New Agenda: South African Journal of Social and Economic Policy* 74 (2019): 13–15.

#UBIGNOW. *#UBIGNOW Policy Approach and Proposals*. Johannesburg: Climate Justice Charter Movement, February 2021. https://www.safsc.org.za/wp-content/uploads/2021/02/UBIG_Policy-Approach-and-Proposals_FEB2021.pdf.

UBI Works. *Recovering UBI Funding Options – 8 Ways to Pay for the Recovery UBI*. September 2020. https://docs.google.com/spreadsheets/d/1hujEV1pDz1_1GeqHdcwhkbPNgPdsFfpVKBCd7r2ReGU/edit#gid=1348990911.

UNDP (United Nations Development Programme). *Human Development Report 2020: The Next Frontier: Human Development and the Anthropocene*. New York: United Nations Development Programme, 2020. http://hdr.undp.org/sites/default/files/hdr2020.pdf.

UNFCCC (United Nations Framework Convention on Climate Change). *Paris Agreement*. New York: United Nations Framework Convention on Climate Change, 2015. https://unfccc.int/sites/default/files/english_paris_agreement.pdf.

Union of Concerned Scientists. *Each Country's Share of CO_2 Emissions*. 12 August 2020. https://www.ucsusa.org/resources/each-countrys-share-co2-emissions.

United Nations. *Transforming Our World: The 2030 Agenda for Sustainable Development*. Resolution adopted by the General Assembly on 25 September 2015, A/RES/70/1. New York: United Nations, 2015. https://www.un.org/ga/search/view_doc.asp?symbol=A/RES/70/1&Lang=E.

United Nations. *World Social Report 2020: Inequality in a Rapidly Changing World*. New York: United Nations Department of Economic and Social Affairs, 2020. https://www.un.org/development/desa/dspd/wp-content/uploads/sites/22/2020/01/World-Social-Report-2020-FullReport.pdf.

US Congressional Budget Office. *Federal Debt: A Primer*. Washington, DC: United States Congress, March 2020. https://www.cbo.gov/publication/56309.

US Congressional Budget Office. *The 2020 Long-Term Outlook*. Washington, DC: United States Congress, September 2020. https://www.cbo.gov/system/files/2020-09/56516-LTBO.pdf.

Van der Berg, S. 'The BIG Grant: Comments on the Report of the Committee of Inquiry into a Comprehensive System of Social Security for South Africa'. *Viewpoint*, July. Johannesburg: South Africa Foundation, 2002.

Van der Westhuizen, C. 'Setting the Scene: Public Works Employment from the RDP to the NDP'. In *Who Cares? South Africa's Expanded Public Works Programme in the Social Sector and its Impact on Women*, edited by P. Parenzee and D. Budlender, 11–34. Johannesburg: Heinrich Boll Foundation, Southern Africa, 2016. https://za.boell.org/sites/default/files/hb_final_ebook_1.pdf.

Van Heerden, J., J. Blignaut, H. Bohlmann, A. Cartwright, N. Diederichs and M. Mander. 'The Economic and Environmental Effects of a Carbon Tax in South Africa: A Dynamic CGE Modelling Approach'. *South African Journal of Economic Management Science* 19, no. 5 (2016): 714–732.

Van Parijs, P. 'Why Surfers Should Be Fed: The Liberal Case for an Unconditional Basic Income'. *Philosophy and Public Affairs* 20, no. 2 (1991): 101–131.

Van Parijs, P. *Real Freedom for All: What (if Anything) Can Justify Capitalism?* Oxford: Oxford University Press, 1998.

Van Parijs, P. 'A Simple and Powerful Idea for the 21st Century'. In *Redesigning Distribution: Basic Income and Stakeholder Grants as Alternative Cornerstones for a More Egalitarian Capitalism*, edited by E.O. Wright, 7–38. London: Verso Books, 2003.

Van Parijs, P. 'Basic Income: A Simple and Powerful Idea for the Twenty-First Century'. *Politics and Society* 32, no. 1 (2004): 7–39.

Van Parijs, P. 'The Universal Basic Income: Why Utopian Thinking Matters, and How Sociologists Can Contribute to it'. *Politics and Society* 41, no. 2 (2013): 171–182.

Van Parijs, P. and Y. Vanderborght. *Basic Income: A Radical Proposal for a Free Society and a Sane Economy*. Cambridge, MA: Cambridge University Press, 2017.

Varoufakis, Y. 'The Universal Right to Capital Income'. *Project Syndicate*, 31 October 2016. https://www.project-syndicate.org/commentary/basic-income-funded-by-capital-income-by-yanis-varoufakis-2016-10?barrier=accesspaylog.

Varoufakis, Y. 'Why the Universal Basic Income Is a Necessity'. Lecture to Gottlieb Duttweiler Institute, 30 April 2017. https://www.youtube.com/watch?v=22eQ9iLBfY4.

Vera-Cossio, D.A. 'Dependence or Constraints? Cash Transfers and Labor Supply'. *Economic Development and Cultural Change* (2021). https//doi.org/10.1086/714010.

Vidal-Folch, X. and M.V. Gomez. 'Spain's Guaranteed Minimum Income Scheme Will Come with €5.5 Billion Price Tag'. *El Pais*, 19 April 2020. https://english.elpais.com/economy_and_business/2020-04-19/spains-guaranteed-minimum-income-scheme-will-come-with-55bn-price-tag.html.

Von Holdt, K. 'Nationalism, Bureaucracy and the Developmental State: The South African Case'. *South African Review of Sociology* 41, no. 1 (2014): 4–27.

Vonnegut, K. *Player Piano*. New York: Simon and Schuster, 1952.

Walker, L. 'Men Behaving Differently: South African Men since 1994'. *Culture, Health and Sexuality* 7, no. 3 (2005): 225–238.

Walker, R. *The Shame of Poverty*. Oxford: Oxford University Press, 2014.

Wallace-Stevens, D. *The Uninhabitable Earth: Life after Warming*. New York: Penguin Random House, 2016.

Warner, R. 'Ecological Modernization Theory: Towards a Critical Ecopolitics of Change'. *Environmental Politics* 19, no. 4 (2010): 538–556.

Webb, C. and N. Vally. 'South Africa Has Raised Social Grants: Why This Shouldn't Be a Stop-Gap Measure'. *The Conversation*, 7 May 2020. https://theconversation. com/south-africa-has-raised-social-grants-why-this-shouldnt-be-a-stop-gap-measure-138023.

Webster, E. and S. Buhlungu. 'Between Marginalization and Revitalization? The State of Trade Unionism in South Africa'. *Review of African Political Economy* 31, no. 100 (2004): 229–245.

Webster, E. and D. Francis. 'The Paradox of Inequality in South Africa: A Challenge from the Workplace'. *Transformation* 101 (2019): 11–35.

Webster, E. and R. Omar. 'Work Restructuring in Post-Apartheid South Africa'. *Work and Occupations* 30, no. 2 (2003): 194–213.

Weeks, K. *The Problem with Work: Feminism, Marxism, Antiwork Politics, and Postwork Imaginaries*. Durham, NC: Duke University Press, 2011.

Weeks, K. 'A Feminist Case for Basic Income: An Interview with Kathi Weeks'. *Critical Legal Thinking*, 22 August 2016. https://criticallegalthinking.com/2016/08/22/ feminist-case-basic-income-interview-kathi-weeks/.

Weeks, K. 'Feminism and the Refusal of Work: An Interview with Kathi Weeks'. *Political Critique*, 28 August 2017. http://politicalcritique.org/world/2017/souvlis-weeks-feminism-marxism-work-interview/.

Weeks, K. 'Feminist Politics and a Case for Basic Income. Debate: Could a Basic Income Play a Role in the Fight against Unfree Labour?' *OpenDemocracy*, 18 September 2019. https://www.opendemocracy.net/en/beyond-trafficking-and-slavery/ feminist-politics-and-case-basic-income/.

West, S., S.C. Baker, S. Samra and E. Coltrera. *Preliminary Analysis: SEED's First Year*. Stockton, USA: Stockton Economic Empowerment Demonstration, 2021. https:// static1.squarespace.com/static/6039d612b17d055cac14070f/t/603ef1194c474b 329f33c329/1614737690661/SEED_Preliminary+Analysis-SEEDs+First+Year_ Final+Report_Individual+Pages+-2.pdf.

Widerquist, K. and M.W. Howard, eds. *Alaska's Permanent Fund Dividend: Examining its Suitability as a Model*. New York: Palgrave Macmillan, 2012.

Wiederspan, J., E. Rhodes and H.J. Shaefer. 'Expanding the Discourse on Antipoverty Policy: Reconsidering a Negative Income Tax'. *Journal of Poverty* 19, no. 2 (2015): 218–238.

Williams, M. 'Energy, Labour and Democracy in South Africa'. In *The Climate Crisis: South African and Global Democratic Eco-Socialist Alternatives*, edited by V. Satgar, 231–251. Johannesburg: Wits University Press, 2018.

Williams, M. 'Women in Rural South Africa: A Post-Wage Existence and the Role of the State'. *Equality, Diversity and Inclusion* 37, no. 4 (2018): 392–410.

Williamson, J. 'What Washington Means by Policy Reform'. In *Latin American Adjustment: How Much Has Happened?* edited by J. Williamson, 7–20. Washington, DC: Institute for International Economics, 1990.

Williamson, J. 'What Should the World Bank Think about the Washington Consensus?' *The World Bank Research Observer* 15, no. 2 (2000): 251–264.

Withorn, A. 'Women and Basic Income in the US: Is One Man's Ceiling Another Woman's Floor?' *Journal of Progressive Human Services* 4, no. 1 (1990): 29–43.

Wittenberg, M. 'Wages and Wage Inequality in South Africa, 1994–2011: Part 2 – Inequality Measurement and Trends'. *South African Journal of Economics* 85, no. 2 (2017): 298–318.

Woo-Cuming, M., ed. *The Developmental State*. New York: Cornell University Press, 1999.

Woolard, I. and M. Leibbrandt. *The Evolution of Unconditional Cash Transfers in South Africa*. Cape Town: Southern Africa Labour and Development Research Unit, University of Cape Town, 2010.

World Bank. *Managing Risk, Promoting Growth: Developing Systems for Social Protection in Africa: World Bank's Africa Social Protection Strategy 2012–2022*. Washington, DC: World Bank, 2010.

World Bank. *Global Financial Development Report 2014: Financial Inclusion*. Washington, DC: World Bank, 2014. https://openknowledge.worldbank.org/bitstream/handle/10986/16238/9780821399859.pdf?sequence=4&isAllowed=y.

World Bank. *South Africa Overview*. Washington, DC: World Bank, 2018. https://www.worldbank.org/en/country/southafrica/overview.

World Bank. *The State of Social Safety Nets 2018: Report Overview*. Washington, DC: World Bank, 2018. https://openknowledge.worldbank.org/bitstream/handle/10986/29115/211254.pdf?sequence=4&isAllowed=y.

World Bank. *Employment to Population Ratio, 15+, Total (%) (Modeled ILO Estimate) – Middle Income, South Africa*. Washington, DC: World Bank, 2021. https://data.worldbank.org/indicator/SL.EMP.TOTL.SP.ZS?locations=XP-ZA&name_desc=false.

World Bank. *Unemployment, Total (% of Total Labor Force) (Modeled ILO Estimate) – South Africa, Brazil*. Washington, DC: World Bank, 2021. https://data.worldbank.org/indicator/SL.UEM.TOTL.ZS?locations=ZA-BR&name_desc=false.

World Bank. *World Development Indicators*. Washington, DC: World Bank, 2021. https://databank.worldbank.org/reports.aspx?source=2&series=NY.GDP.MKTP.KD.ZG&country=MIC,ZAF#.

Wright, E.O. *Redesigning Distribution: Basic Income and Stakeholder Grants as Alternative Cornerstones for a More Egalitarian Capitalism*. London: Verso Books, 2003.

Wright, E.O. 'Basic Income, Stakeholder Grants, and Class Analysis'. *Politics and Society* 32, no. 1 (2004): 79–87.

Wright, E.O. 'Basic Income as a Socialist Project'. Paper presented at the annual US-BIG Congress, Madison, WI, University of Wisconsin, 4–6 March 2005. https://www.ssc.wisc.edu/~wright/Basic%20Income%20as%20a%20Socialist%20Project.pdf.

Wright, G., D. Neves, P. Ntshongwana and M. Noble. 'Social Assistance and Dignity: South African Women's Experiences of the Child Support Grant'. *Development Southern Africa* 32, no. 4 (2015): 443–457.

Yang, A. *The Freedom Dividend, Defined*. US Presidential Campaign Material, 2020. https://2020.yang2020.com/what-is-freedom-dividend-faq/.

Yoshikawa, H., J.L. Aber and W.R. Beardslee. 'The Effects of Poverty on the Mental, Emotional, and Behavioral Health of Children and Youth: Implications for Prevention'. *American Psychology* 67, no. 4 (2012): 272–284.

Zamora, D. 'The Case against a Basic Income'. *Jacobin*, December 2017. https://www.jacobinmag.com/2017/12/universal-basic-income-inequality-work.

Zamora, D. and A. Jäger. 'Historicizing Basic Income: Response to David Zeglen'. *Lateral* 8, no. 1 (2019). https://csalateral.org/forum/universal-basic-income/historicizing-basic-income-zamora-jager/.

Zeglen, D. 'Basic Income as Ideology from Below'. *Lateral* 7.2 (2018). https://csalateral.org/forum/universal-basic-income/basic-income-ideology-from-below-zeglen/.

Zelleke, A. 'Real-World Lessons'. Contribution to GTI forum 'Universal Basic Income: Has the Time Come?' Great Transition Initiative, November 2020. https://greattransition.org/gti-forum/basic-income-zelleke.

Zembe-Mkabile, W., R. Surender, D. Sanders, D. Jackson and T. Doherty. 'The Experience of Cash Transfers in Alleviating Childhood Poverty in South Africa: Mothers' Experiences of the Child Support Grant'. *Global Public Health* 10, no. 7 (2015): 834–851.

Zucman, G. 'Global Wealth Inequality'. *Annual Review of Economics* 11, no. 1 (2019): 109–138.

INDEX

Hein Marais delivers a theoretically powerful, impressively documented, timely and urgent case for radical redistribution and universal income to counter state-sponsored coercion into precarious, poverty-ridden and often lethal jobs as one's sole survival prospect. The book supports a basic income not as a policy fix, but as a far-reaching political and imaginative response to the collapse of a wage-centered social order and to a mounting, worldwide refusal of waged work. This is a book destined to have lasting influence.

— **Franco Barchiesi**, Ohio State University, author of
*Precarious Liberation: Workers, the State, and Contested
Social Citizenship in Post-apartheid South Africa*

If you have been searching for a way to clearly understand the concept of a universal basic income, then this is the book that you have been waiting for.

— **Awande Buthelezi**, coordinator for the #UBIGNOW Campaign
and activist with the Climate Justice Charter Movement

Grounded in a lucid analysis of the long-term prospects of waged work, Marais' book even-handedly assesses the case for a universal basic income. Clearly written and original in its approach, this is a major contribution to our understanding of the possibilities for policies to achieve more equitable levels of well-being in the contemporary political economy of South Africa and globally.

— **Peter B. Evans**, Professor Emeritus Department
of Sociology, University of California, Berkeley

This is a must-read, narrative-changing book on a universal basic income.

— **Ferial Haffajee**, Associate Editor, *Daily Maverick*

By locating the demand for a universal basic income in the context of the crisis of waged work, Marais' book is an original contribution. His discerning examination of diverse literature and practical evidence enables him to weigh the arguments for and against, and to present well-considered, creative and realistic policy proposals. It is these interconnected features that make this book unlike any other on the basic income debate. Finally, it is his proposed agenda for action that activists, movements, researchers and policy-makers must now respond to with a sense of urgency and purpose.

— **Mazibuko Jara**, Executive Director, Pathways Institute, and co-founder
of Ntinga Ntaba kaNdoda, a community-based rural movement